THE DIARY OF

SIR HYDE GOWAN

Introduction to India 1933–38, and the Diaries of
Sir Hyde Gowan, K.C.S.I, C.I.E.,V.D. , I.C.S.
including some of his Speeches and Appreciations

Sir Hyde Gowan was Governor of
The Central Provinces, India, during the years
1933 to 1938.

Introduction by James Gowan,

Edited by Timothy Gowan
© Timothy J Gowan 2013.

THE DIARY OF

SIR HYDE GOWAN

Introduction to India 1933–38, and the Diaries of
Sir Hyde Gowan, K.C.S.I, C.I.E.,V.D. , I.C.S.
including some of his Speeches and Appreciations

Sir Hyde Gowan was Governor of
The Central Provinces, India, during the years
1933 to 1938.

Introduction by James Gowan,

Edited by Timothy Gowan
© Timothy J Gowan 2013.

MEMOIRS

Cirencester

Mereo Books

1A The Wool Market Dyer Street Cirencester Gloucestershire GL7 2PR
An imprint of Memoirs Publishing www.mereobooks.com

Diary of Sir Hyde Gowan: 978-1-909874-86-2

First published in Great Britain in 2015
by Mereo Books, an imprint of Memoirs Publishing

Copyright ©2015

Timothy Gowan has asserted his right under the Copyright Designs and Patents
A CIP catalogue record for this book is available from the British Library.

The address for Memoirs Publishing Group Limited can be found at www.memoirspublishing.com

The Memoirs Publishing Group Ltd Reg. No. 7834348

The Memoirs Publishing Group supports both The Forest Stewardship Council® (FSC®) and the
PEFC® leading international forest-certification organisations. Our books carrying both the FSC
label and the PEFC® and are printed on FSC®-certified paper. FSC® is the only
forest-certification scheme supported by the leading environmental organisations including
Greenpeace. Our paper procurement policy can be found at
www.memoirspublishing.com/environment

Typeset in 11/16pt Bembo
by Wiltshire Associates Publisher Services Ltd. Printed and bound in Great Britain by
Printondemand-Worldwide, Peterborough PE2 6XD

CONTENTS

CHAPTER 1

DIARY OF
SIR HYDE GOWAN

1. The Clan Gowan

This is the title which my father, James, gave to his scholarly work in two volumes documenting both male and female lines of my relations. There are over 3000 names in the book which includes many biographical references. The name Gowan is a corruption of an Irish word meaning Armourer or Smith. Such people had skills which kept them at the top of the pecking order and near to the clan chief.

My father claimed that the clan is descended from Milesius of Spain who married the daughter of a Pharaoh circa 3,500 BC. Their descendants called MacGowan settled in Ireland and our branch moved to Leinster, (dropping the Mac) and perhaps 50 generations after Milesius, Jonathan Gowan (born 1668) was a very prosperous landowner, settled at Mount Nebo near Dublin and became loyal to the British Crown and converted to Protestantism. Ireland was for many years difficult to govern and there were a series of insurrections particularly the Wexford revolt of 1798, when Mount Nebo was burnt, so in about 1800, Philip Gowan (born 1779) moved to London and founded a firm called "Gowan and Marx" an import/export company specialising in trade with The United States and Canada.

Philip had a large house in Dulwich called Woodlawn. Other members of the clan at about this time emigrated to the USA and Canada and many of them prospered particularly Sir James Gowan, who was a Senator of Canada.

A family tree is shown on Page 4, which attempts to explain the relationship of my Grandfather Sir Hyde Gowan to the Hyde family. The 3rd Earl of Clarendon was Edward Hyde, Governor of New York and New Jersey between 1701 and 1708. Elizabeth Wall, Mary Ray and Elizabeth Bowie (married names) give a link to Sarah Clementina Bowie who married Philip Gowan's eldest son George in 1838. George must have been sent to The USA on business by his father and snapped up a prestigious bride. They had several children, and his third son was named Bowie Campbell and was Sir Hyde's father.

In his early years Bowie was a Royal Navy Officer, but resigned his commission and trained and qualified as an engineer; he decided to visit his cousins in the United States and met Leila Davidson, whom he married. Leila was also a descendant of Edward Hyde through the Ray family. Leila was the daughter of Admiral Hunter Davidson, who in his early career had been First Lieutenant on board the Merrimac in the celebrated battle with the Monitor near Hampton Roads Va. on March 9th 1862, during the American Civil War. These were the first ironclad battle-ships ever constructed. Admiral Davidson claimed to have invented the Torpedo and certainly did some very early experiments with underwater weapons. Leila, Hyde's mother had many stories about the sacking of Richmond during the war, and how she and her brother (Hunter) ran around the house with wet blankets chasing sparks and smothering fires before they eventually obtained a Governor's pass to leave the city ahead of the invading Northern army. It is noteworthy that Bowie's children had both an American mother and grandmother.

After his marriage, Bowie went to Australia where he was engaged for several years in a pioneering survey for the railways and his first son, Hyde, was born on 4th July 1878 in Sydney New South Wales. The family left Australia soon after but the fact that he was born there gave the Australian press the excuse to call Sir Hyde one of their own. On returning to England Bowie decided on a third new career and trained as a medical doctor and bought a practice in Stanmore, Middlesex, then a village in the country outside London. He invented a procedure for Rickets called "The Gowan Operation" but the business failed and he retired to Marnhull in Dorset naming his house "Arlington" after Leila's home in Maryland.

Bowie and Leila had three children, Hyde, George, and Cecil Hunter. George was a mining engineer, who died in 1936, while Cecil Hunter was a successful Naval Officer and retired with the rank of Commodore.

Hyde was sent to school at Elstree and on to Rugby School where during his last year in the sixth form he was in the Rugby fifteen, the running eight, and the Cricket eleven. He won the senior Classical Scholarship, to New College, Oxford and later the Senior Open Scholarship. While at New College, Oxford, he met his future wife Edna Brown daughter of James Brown, a Lancashire Mill owner who later founded the Amalgamated Cotton Trust. Edna, my Grandmother was a woman of much charm and character and early fighter for women's rights. At Oxford she was a student at Lady Margaret Hall and was one of the first women to take the full examination in the tripos of "English Language and Literature". Before her time, women had been considered too delicate to stand the rigours of the full examination paper as given to the men and had only been allowed to take a shorter and easier exam. However, Edna insisted on taking the full paper in which she gained a First Class Honours Degree, which was actually better than the degree which Hyde attained. (He got a 2:1 in "Greats").

James was told a story about their courtship, involving a punt on the river with ladies in one punt and the gentlemen in another – showing off their skill – and ending up with Hyde breaking his punt pole and falling in the river. James when telling this story implies that Hyde's rescue from the accident was dramatic, claiming that his future, even his very existence was, at that moment, uncertain!

Hyde and Edna had three children, all boys, James Hyde Bowie (JHBG), born in Nagpur in 1907, Christopher d'Olier, born in UK in 1909 and Antony Campbell, born in UK in 1918. James had four children, Timothy James (TJG) the Editor of these diaries born 1937, with three sisters born after World War II. These are Olivia Helen (Yates), born 1946, Carol Margaret, born 1947 and Nicola Frances, born 1950.

Gowan Geneology since 17th Century

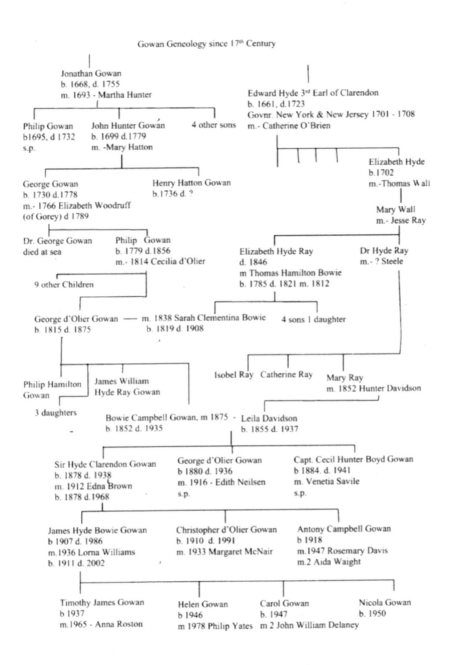

2.Sir Hyde's Career

Hyde left Oxford in 1902 and entered the Indian Civil Service, starting work as an Under-Secretary to the Government of the Central Provinces. Hyde's entire career was in this province and he was one of the few people to be promoted to Governor in the province in which he had served his time. Normally, the Governor was appointed from outside the province. Sir Hyde (as he became on appointment) succeeded Sir Montague Butler (Monty in the diaries) who is reported as a man of stern character and strict discipline. Sir Montague's son, Mr R.A.Butler (known as Rab) became Lord Butler of Saffron Walden and was parliamentary Under-Secretary to Sir Samuel Hoare, Secretary of State for India, and was one of the formulators of the Government of India Act 1935 and piloted it through the House of Commons. When Sir Hyde was appointed it was intimated to him that a slight relaxation of Monty's strict regime would be in order.

Sir Hyde's appointments:

Under Secretary to the Government of the Central Provinces	1904 – 08
Under Secretary to the Govt. of India, Commerce & Industry Dept.	1908
Settlement Officer, Hoshangabad District	1913
Financial Secretary to the Government of the C.P.	1918 – 21
Lt-Col Nagpur Rifles	1920 –25
Police Department	1923
Financial Secretary to the Government of the C.P.	1925 – 26

Chief Secretary to the Government of the C.P.	1927 – 32
Member of the Executive Council	1932 – 33
Governor of the Central Provinces and Berar	1933 – 38
Obit	1.4.1938

From the many praises which Sir Hyde received on his retirement we can honestly say that his was a job well done and that his efforts for India were worthwhile and, at the time, well received.

8. Appreciations on Appointment

Beside formal letters of appointment from the Government, Sir Hyde received a heartening letter from Pandit Joshini of Hoshangabad. This is in Nagri script on and illuminated page with coloured hand-printed borders I have the original in my files. A translation is on the next page.

Respected Sir,

By the very kindness of Almighty God not only we but the whole population of the C.P. have been fortunate to get this auspicious opportunity which like Chakor we had been looking for a long time for Sir Hyde Gowan to adorn the Governorship of the province. Now this desire is now fulfilled and our hearts are beating fast with joy. And in this happiness we have ventured to submit a message of our good wishes in a few lines below:-

In order to have the happiness of seeing you, dear friend, we are most uneasy, give us comfort by coming to us: May

Brahma, Vishnu, Mahadeo with their wives Saraswati, Laxmi and Parvati respectively, with the Wheel, Tumba and Trident in the respective hands, riding on Bullock, Swan and Garur protect your family.

You are grave as ocean and intelligent. May God make you the Lord for you look after the poor. May Vishnu and Jagdash bestow favours on you and may you live long and prosperous.

My blessing is this:-

May prosperity be with your family, relations and children, this is our first prayer on waking up.

You give us happiness, drive off our troubles, you are real appreciator.

May you, Lady Gowan and Master Gowan remain always happy.

Your well-wisher,

Rameshwar (Pdt., Jotishi)

Hoshangabad.

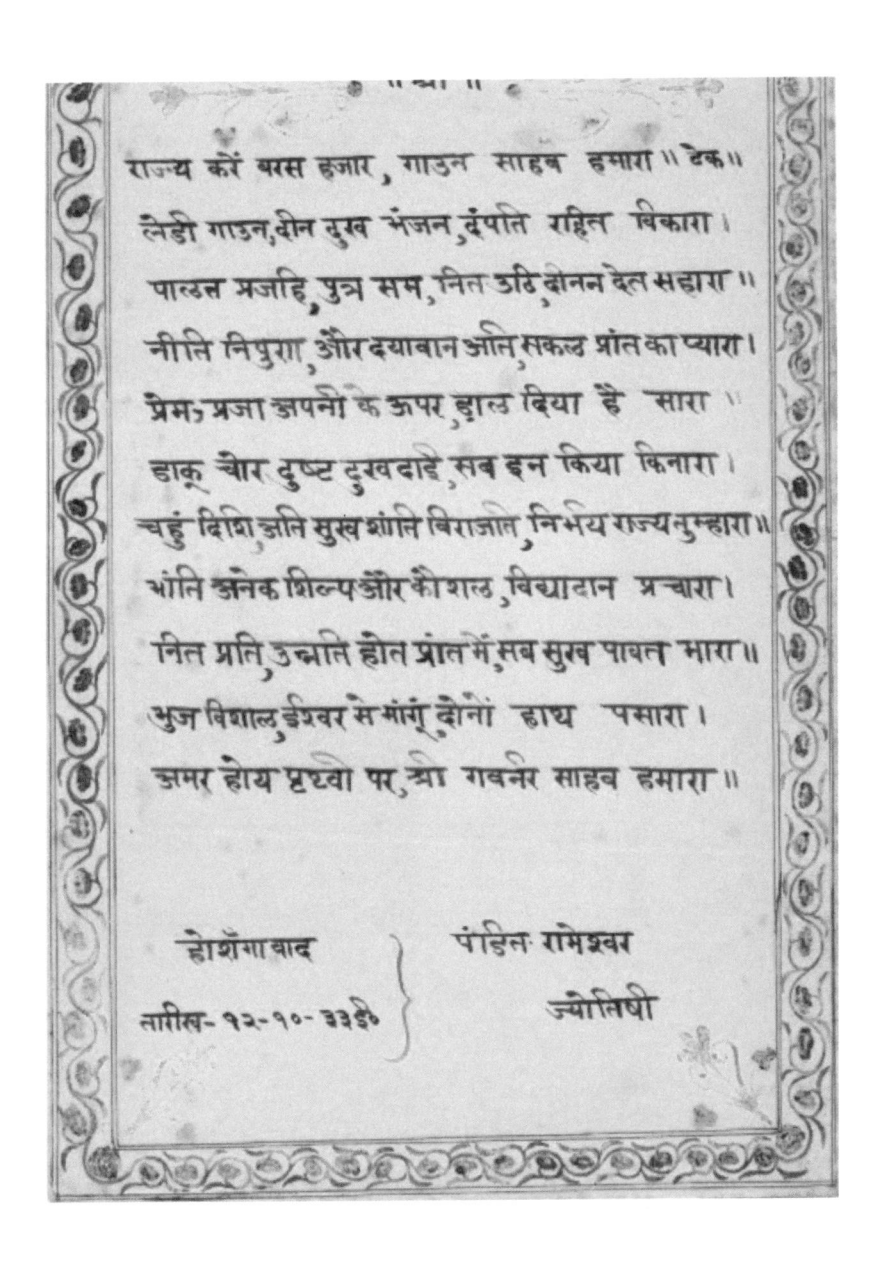

॥ श्री ॥

राज्य करें बरस हजार, गाउन साहब हमारा ॥ टेक ॥

लेड़ी गाउन, दीन सुख भंजन, दंपति रहित विकारा ।

पालत प्रजहि, पुत्र सम, नित उठि दोनन देत सहारा ॥

नीति निपुराण, और दयाबान अति सकल प्रांत का प्यारा ।

प्रेम, प्रजा अपनी के ऊपर डाल दिया है सारा ॥

डाकू चोर दुष्ट दुखदाई, सब इन किया किनारा ।

चहुं दिशि अति सुख शांति विराजत निर्भय राज्य तुम्हारा ॥

भांति अनेक शिल्प और कौशल, विद्यादान प्रचारा ।

नित प्रति उन्नति होत प्रांत में, सब सुख पावत भारा ॥

भुज विशाल ईश्वर से मांगूं दोनों हाथ पसारा ।

अमर होय पृथ्वी पर, या गवनर साहब हमारा ॥

होशंगाबाद
तारीख- १२-१०-३३ ई.

पंडित रामेश्वर
ज्योतिषी

The following also appeared in the Pienneer, Lucknow:

APPRECIATIONS OF THE ADMINISTRATION OF SIR HYDE GOWAN THE C. P. GOVERNOR

On its merits the appointment of Mr. Hyde Gowan to succeed Sir Montagu Butler as Governor of the Central Provinces will be widely welcomed. Mr. Gowan has had exceptional opportunities of understanding the conditions in the province and he has made himself personally popular. A man of resource as well as energy and with a flexible mind he may be expected to make a success of his office. His preferment will naturally recall the most interesting, if also the most trying, episode in his career. Mr. Gowan was Deputy Commissioner of Nagpur ten years ago when the Flag satyagraha agitation was in full swing. The issue had shifted from Jubbulpore to Nagpur and the Congressmen were determined to disobey the interdict on carrying the National Flag through the Civil Lines. As usual in questions of the kind the violation of executive orders became more important than the marching of bannerbearing hordes through any particular locality. The struggle caused interest all over India and volunteers poured in from every part of the country to defy a ban which the Administration would enforce and the Congress leaders had decided should be resisted. Thanks to the intervention of the Patel brothers the dispute ended abruptly, but it was fortunate that while it continued the contending parties were represented by Mr. Gowan and Seth Jamnalal Bajaj respectively. If the Deputy Commissioner was firm in handling the situation his courtesy never failed him and while the equally commendable attitude of Seth Jamnalal Bajaj prevented the rise of subsidiary quarrels or the diversion of the exuberance of the civil resisters along dangerous paths, it was not a little due to the personality of Mr. Gowan that bitterness was eschewed and goodwill consistently maintained. At this distance of time it is needless to go more fully into the origin, course or effects of the occurrence. But it is worth mention that the district officer called upon to deal with critical developments came out with enhanced credit. The experience was, no doubt, something of an education to Mr. Gowan and in subsequent years he has made a good name for himself. It may, therefore, be held that Mr. Gowan with his intimate knowledge of men and matters relating to the Central Provinces is eminently capable of avoiding dangers by tact and forbearance as well as of meeting difficult situations with sternness when occasion demands.

[The Pieneer (Lucknow), 8th May 1933.]

The viceroy also welcomed Sir Hyde in a very nice handwritten letter dated 3.5.33 marked "Private":

Dear Mr Gowan   Viceregal Lodge
                                 Simla

This is just a line to tell you that His Majesty has approved yr. appointment in succession to Sir M. Butler as Governor of the Central Provinces, and I write to express the hope that you will be able to accept the appointment, & to, in anticipation, congratulate you on securing the post. I am quite sure that the affairs of the Province will be admirably guided under yr. care.

I have heard nothing about future arrangements with regard especially to yr. leave which I understand you to want, but will let you know as to this as soon as I possibly can. Hoping we shall meet soon

Yrs. sincerely
Willingdon

Obituary from The Times

Saturday April 2nd 1938

SIR HYDE GOWAN
GOVERNORSHIP OF THE CENTRAL PROVINCES

Sir Hyde Gowan, K.C.S.1., C.I.E., whose five years' term as Governor of the Central Provinces was substantially shortened on grounds of impaired health, died at a London hospital yesterday at the age of 59. Last week he arrived in a serious condition at Tilbury with Lady Gowan in the *Rajputana* from Bombay. There will be profound regret among his many friends and admirers in the Province which he governed for four-and-a-half years and far beyond its borders that cherished hopes of his recovery of health were not to be fulfilled and that he was not destined to enjoy a well-earned retirement.

Hyde Clarendon Gowan was one of a number of able men Australia has provided for the Indian Services. He was born at Sydney, N.S.W., on July 4th, 1878, the son of the late Dr. Bowie Campbell Gowan. At Rugby he was Senior Classical Scholar and at New College, Oxford, Senior Open Scholar. He entered the Indian Civil Service and went to the Central Provinces at the close of 1902. Except for a few months in 1908, when he was officiating Under-Secretary to the Government of India in the Commerce and Industry Department, the whole of his service was in the Central Provinces, where he had good experience in both settlement and revenue district work. He was Under-Secretary to the Government there from 1904 to 1908, and was Financial Secretary from 1918 to 1921, and again in 1925-26. A man of athletic tastes, he was a keen volunteer, and from 1920 to 1925 was lieutenant-colonel commanding the Nagpur Rifles, Indian Auxiliary Force. For this service he was given the V.D.

Gowan was Chief Secretary to Government from March 1927, and had the advantage of the guidance of so successful an administrator as Sir Montagu Butler. He served on two occasions as temporary Member of the Governor's Executive Council, and was confirmed in the appointment in the summer of 1932. When a year later Sir Montagu Butler resigned from his second term of Governorship to become Lieutenant-Governor of the Isle of Man, Gowan was selected as his successor. The choice gave much satisfaction, for he was generally liked both by Indians and his British colleagues. His dignified bearing and firmness of purpose were combined with a natural courtesy, and in times of stress and strain he was upheld by a serenity of mind which never deserted him. Now and again he gave eloquent expression to the clear-cut convictions on public matters by which he was guided. In Lady Gowan – Edna Brown, of Mere Oaks, Wigan – whom he married in 1905, he had a helpmeet who did specially valuable service in the cause of women's education. A year ago Gowan was one of the Governors called upon to guide the Provinces from the old dyarchical to the new system of Ministerial responsibility. In the C.P. as in five other Provinces the leaders of the Congress Party, successful at the polls, made acceptance of office conditional on receiving certain assurances from the Governors which were held by higher authority to be inconsistent with obligations laid upon them by the Government of India Act, 1935. Gowan kept in step with his fellow Governors and in close touch with the Viceroy, and made his own contribution to the ending of the impasse last July by the Congress withdrawal, stage by stage, of the condition which had been laid down. Only a month ago Dr. Khare the Premier, paid testimony to the happy relations between the Governor and his Ministers, and said that if on rare occasions there had been a conflict of opinion, the impressions left thereby were never of a rankling character.

These relations were of shorter duration than had been expected. In the ordinary course Sir Hyde would have been in charge until next September, but early in this year it was announced that as he had expressed a desire, for domestic reasons, to be relieved in the spring, the King had accepted his resignation as from May 27th. Unhappily the Governor's illness took a sudden turn for the worse a month ago, and he relinquished charge and travelled to Bombay, where he was admitted to hospital. He was much cheered by a telegraphic message of good wishes from Lord Linlithgow, the Viceroy, referring to "outstanding service to his Province and India", and to "the most friendly and cordial relationships" existing between them. Indeed, the Viceroy's appreciation of his services was so strong, that it is understood to have been the Viceroy's intention before Sir Hyde's breakdown in health, to offer him a two year extension of the governorship. Sir Hyde voyaged to this country and reached Tilbury on March 25th, only to be admitted at once to the Masonic Hospital in London. He was a keen Freemason, and was P.S.G.E. of the Grand Lodge of England. He was made C.I.E. in 1928. C.S.I. in 1932 and K.C. on becoming Governor of the Central Provinces in 1933. He leaves three sons.

Cremation will take place privately Golders Green on Monday at 11a.m.

Telegram from The Viceroy.

000 LB NEW DELHIO 5 STE PTY 113 IMMEDIATE SIR HYDE GOWAN PASSENGER SS RAJPUTANA BOMBAY MY WIFE AND I SEND OR WARMEST GOOD WISHES TO YOU FOR YOUR JOURNEY HOME LET ME SAY HOW VERY DEEPLY I REGRET THE LOSS OF A COLLEAGUE WHO HAS RENDERED SUCH OUTSTANDING SERVICE TO HIS PROVINCE AND TO INDIA AND HOW MUCH I FEEL THIS PREMATURE SEVERANCE OF THE MOST CORDIAL AND FRIENDLY RELATIONSHIP WHICH HAS EXISTED BETWEEN US EVER SINCE I FIRST ASSUMED OFFICE. YOU CARRY WITH YOU IN YOUR RETIREMENT THE BEST WISHES AND THE SYMPATHY OF YOUR OWN PROVINCE AND ALL OF US WHO HAVE HAD THE PLEASURE OF WORKING WITH YOU.

= VICEROY

And from The King:

To Lady Gowan

The Queen and I have heard with great regret of the death of your husband whose distinguished services to India will be long remembered. We send our deepest sympathy to you and your family.

George R.I.

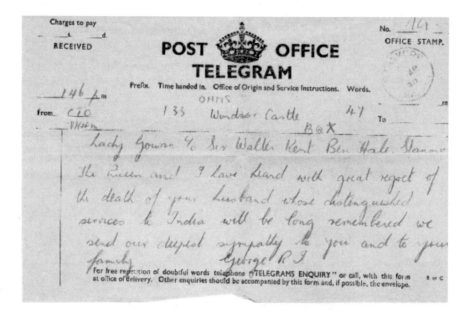

CHAPTER 2

"ULTA PULTA DESH"

Introduction to India

This Introduction "Ulta Pulta Desh" was written by Sir Hyde's son, James in 1976 and substantially revised by his grandson Timothy, in 2013. This was written to attempt to give an insight into the Indian mind at the time Sir Hyde was writing his diary, so that the politics and events in India at that time may be better understood.

1. A flavour of India, *Ulta Pulta Desh!*

At the time Sir Hyde started writing his diary in 1933, having recently been appointed as Governor of the Central Provinces, the culture of India and the thought processes of the Indian population were, even after a considerable period of colonial rule, difficult for the European mind to understand. During the war, when James, my father, served in India between 1941-44 an American serviceman summed it up in a deep Southern accent "It's mysteereious", and even a Scot whom he met who had lived all his life in various parts of India and should have known the country well, summed it up: "Laddie" he said "If I had seven lives and lived them all in India, I might just begin to start to think that I knew something about the place".

For instance, as late as 1976, a note was published in the Indian Express from Nagpur which was the Provincial capital during Sir Hyde's Governorship. (Nagpur means "House of the Snake"). Quote:"Urban Development Minister Rafiq Zakari told Legislative Council today during question hour that municipalities still permitting the practice of carrying night soil on head will not get any share of entertainment tax."!

So in reading the diaries we have to understand the Victorian upbringing of my grandfather – born 1878, and we have to realise that the Indians with whom he had to deal were also living in two cultures, their own caste system which had lasted for centuries, and an imposed European monarchical model. Sir Hyde, having lived all his working life in India, partly understood the problem but it infuriated him. Nothing worked quite the way he would have liked and he coined the term "Ulta pulta desh" meaning "Upside-down-country" or possibly "Arsi-tarsi-land". So one must read the diaries with this in mind.

Sir Hyde, having by 1933, already completed thirty-one years in the country, largely in the "mofusil" or jungle countryside far from the seats of the mighty in Delhi, knew probably as much about India and the Indians as any European, yet he never lost his sense of wonder and sense of fair play. Since he has recorded in his diaries his more intimate thoughts in dealing with the Indians in both official and private capacities, these thoughts should at least be of interest to anyone attempting to get to grips with the inner workings of the pre-war Indian mind and the issues at the time in the Indian sub-continent.

The object of this introduction is to give a background or flavour of Indian thinking before the Second World War that may possibly provide some criteria against which historical events can be judged. All events turn up as "history" at some time, but all history needs interpretation against a background before these events make sense. Too often, unfortunately, historians try to judge the events and the actions of one age against the morals and criteria of another, the results being usually misleading.

Reading through the diaries, one is able to get an all too brief glimpse of the background to the trouble which every Indian Prime Minister from Nehru through Mrs Indira Gandhi and to the present day has had to deal with. The British left behind them a potential democracy, but only potential; they sowed the seeds and nothing more, because democracy is foreign to the Indian nature. Power, Politics and Nepotism, not to mention Corruption, are ingrained in their blood and thinking through centuries, indeed millennia, and it takes more than a few years of Colonial rule, however benevolent, and democratic to leach them out. We, in the United Kingdom on the other hand have a history of a thousand years of democracy, going back to the Saxon "moots" that William the Conqueror found on his arrival and which developed via Magna Carta into our present parliament. We have had our ups and downs, civil wars, republican sentiment, monarchy redefined but have always preferred some kind of democracy. That is up to the present day, but it is probable that democracy needs longer than 1,000 years to be considered a hardy perennial plant. The early 20th Century showed how easily dictatorship can arise. In contrast the Indian has had two thousand years of autocratic rule, and autocracy in that form always means looking after your own interest. Each person must look after his own affairs. This defines the attitude of the Indian; the appreciation of autocratic rule and that it applies to both the ruler and the ruled.

2. The Rulers and the Ruled

During the latter years of British rule, (mid-20th Century) there was always an umpire or referee who was either the Governor of the Province or the Senior District Commissioner or the Editor of the National or Local Newspaper who did their best to make sure that the rules of democracy were being obeyed. They did not interfere with the actual laws passed, unless those laws were manifestly unjust; if the ruling party wanted to pass bad laws that was their own affair, but only when such parties started breaking the rules of fair play, by passing laws, good or bad, by trickery, by trying to get away with scandalous malpractice or by disobeying what the Act had laid down as the basic ground rules, did the Raj intervene. In this connection one notices Sir Hyde's insistence on, and use of the words, "sportsman" and "sportsmanship", a tradition in which he, both at Rugby and at Oxford, had been studiously brought up, but a tradition which was, of course, completely foreign to the Indian mentality, however much he tried to inculcate it in them, and a tradition that we still try to foster in England today. A study of these diaries, in so far as they outline the characters of the people concerned – admittedly they are all dead now, but others just like them fill their places – will greatly enlighten the colossal problems now to be faced.

Although the Central Provinces was only a very small part of the Indian scene, it is a microcosm of the Government of India, yet studying it in detail is much the same as studying a bacillus through a microscope. By an examination of a very small detail, one can gain insight into the workings of the whole. During the time of Sir Hyde's governorship, many events of worldwide importance took place, but the time frame is too short and their spread too parochial for the Central Provinces to rank in the main line of history. His diaries contain notes of all sorts of occurrences in his daily life, though he has kept them fairly strictly to the official line, except when really roused.

James only transcribed those parts of the original diaries which he considered to bear on the Indian character; however his son Timothy has included it all, without any deletions even if Europeans are denigrated for such faults as drunkenness or incompetence. Scholars of Indian independence may find the diary entries in 1937 particularly interesting as the India Act of 1935 was implemented.

3. India and Religion

To begin to show some of the differences, some of the huge gulfs to be crossed before one can reach understanding of the diaries written between 1933 and 1938, one must start with greatest, single area of difference between India and almost the whole of the rest of the world, at that time; the people's attitude to religion. It is difficult to realize the way in which, and the extent to which, Indian thought, at the time, was permeated by religious beliefs. To most Europeans religion is a matter of belief, circumscribed dogma and occasional observance. Even in the early days of this century, when far more English people "believed" than do now, when heaven and hell were fairly real concepts only just beginning to questioned, religion was even then very much of a Sundays only affair and, though it set the tone for our morals and caused many people to lead moral lives – in the hope of ultimate reward or fear of damnation – it cannot be said that, except for a very few people, religion meant much in one's day to day life.

Not so the Hindu. To him religion is a way of life, pervading every corner of daily existence, social relations and personal thought. Marriage in Hindu society, for instance, is not merely sanctified by a religious rite, it is regulated by complex social rules inextricably entangled with religious belief. Religion prescribes attitudes towards certain animals, certain objects, certain occupations. It provides its own fabric of personal law. The caste system is integral to Hinduism. No Hindu but has his caste, low or high, which is part of him from birth to grave, and to which he succeeds without choice and from which he cannot escape; and his caste regulates his religious observances his social relationship, and in a general way his occupation and livelihood. Indian Mohammedanism also has some of the character of the religious society in which it has been embedded. It, too, is a way of life, more rigid than Hinduism in some ways, such as fasting and respect for holy writ, less rigid in others. It, too, prescribes certain attitudes towards ordinary creatures and events, besides enjoining observances, practices and taboos, some of which are repugnant to Hindu neighbours, as some Hindu customs are to Muslims.

A quotation from H. V. Hodson in *The Great Divide*: "So here we have two great groups of people, living together in one country, ethnically not distinct yet separated by whole modes of life and attitudes of mind, each a permanent hereditary group, without intermarriage or mutual absorption."

A remark in the India Office List of 1936 puts the matter fairly succinctly: "Nowhere else in the world do we find the population of a large subcontinent broken up into an infinite number of mutually exclusive aggregates, the members of which are forbidden by an inexorable social law to marry outside the group to which they themselves belong." The whole provides a framework for conflict that makes Northern Ireland seem tame by comparison, in fact Sir Hyde makes the remark in one place, "The more I see of the Indians, the more I am reminded of the Irish."

As to the Muslims, they go even further in bringing their religious beliefs into the domestic and political life. The idea of Islam goes far beyond religion, in the sense that Christians use the term. The basic tenet of the Muslim is that Islam is a polity, a system of Government, a State. To govern a country correctly, one only has to read the Koran and apply the precepts. Of course that ideal, the pure State of Islam, was unobtainable as long as the Muslims only inhabited part of India, and as long as the British governed the country as a whole, with Delhi as the capital, but as soon as the British started to withdraw, having found no single Authority to which to hand over power, and thus were forced to form the state of Pakistan, the Muslims were able to found a state run on that precept, reliance on the law as laid down in the Koran, although there are some nods in the direction of a secular state. The result was that the Muslims, saw no alternative to partition, whatever its shortcomings economically and however traumatic its formation. They realised that here was the chance to create a state on the principles of their deepest beliefs and thus in a way, rather relished the prospect. In this sense Iran and Pakistan are very similar, in that they are both fundamentalist, Islamic Creations. To what extent they will in the long run succeed has yet to be discovered.

4. Hinduism and India

It is impossible to understand how religion works fully unless one has lived in a "religious" country, a country such as India, where people run their entire lives on a truly religious basis. A priestly taboo to an Indian is as inhibiting as a brick wall to us, and a priestly command as binding as a shackle.

A Brahmin or high caste Hindu would in no circumstances eat food that had been rendered "unclean" by the shadow of an untouchable passing over it, even if he were starving. To eat such food would jeopardise his chances of salvation and his passage into the hereafter. Safe passage into the hereafter is far more important than prolonging life on this earth. By the same token, an Indian, however poor, will always give money for the glorification of his god. In the beautiful temple in Tanjore there is a gold and diamond brooch worth thousands of pounds given in the 1970s to the temple God by the coastal villagers of the area, and there is no poorer village in the world than an Indian fishing village. At one Anna a time, or even a few Pisah, they had collected together this large sum of money to buy a jewel, beautiful by any standard, for the god to wear on his feast day. The glorification of their god was far more important to these people than their earthly needs. To cap the lot, the jewels of that temple must be worth some millions of pounds, secure in what we condescend to call an

23

undeveloped country; yet no one would think of selling them, not ever. Religious needs and religious observances rank far higher than any mere earthly function.

But the Hindu religion is not merely a matter of temples and priests. Every trade, every job even has its caste. Sometimes, if you enter a village with a vile and revolting smell, you will know it belongs to the lowest caste of all, in fact to one of the "outcastes", who alone are allowed to take on the unclean work of handling meat, cutting up the carcases, rendering the horns and hooves and curing the hides. But the caste system even extends into the household where the strictures of the demarcation lines between each job would make our trade unionists green with envy, and idea of the English multi-skilled operative is completely foreign to them. This is one of the reasons, coupled of course with the cheapness of labour, that domestic staffs, both in Indian and European households, are so numerous. Each man has his own special job and cannot do any other; to change jobs would be to transgress the binding laws of caste.

On occasion this can give rise to near chaos. If a dead bird falls on the verandah, anything dead being automatically unclean and dead feathers especially so, you call the bearer, your personal servant, who says he cannot touch it, unless he happens to be Goanese and therefore Christian. The bearer will call the butler, who calls the next one down the scale until the mehatar or sweeper, whose normal job is to clean out the thunderboxes, who is sufficiently unclean himself to remove the offending feathered friend. But the mehatar will certainly live outside your compound and may live down in the bazaar so the removal may take quite a long time.

One of the reasons we know so little of Hinduism is that they have no record of proselytizing, no desire to force their ideas on other people – one of the more unfortunate aspects of Christianity. If anyone wants to be a Hindu, he can come into the fold; though the converse is not true; once you are born a Hindu, you are a Hindu forever and may never leave. If a Hindu has ideas other than the strictly orthodox, he is free to found his own sect. The Jains and the Sikhs, for instance, both Hindu sects, at their beginning went through none of the traumatic upheavals that marked the growth of Protestantism. In this field it is well within the terms of the paradox mentioned above that the Hindu, tolerant to the formation of new sects and therefore of aberrant forms of worship, is fiercely intolerant when considering the dogma of the castes within his own community; for instance, an untouchable or one of the 'Scheduled Castes' as they are euphemistically known, is accepted anywhere in the world, except among caste Hindus, and though Christians are generally accepted, especially in Southern India, a Hindu-Muslem riot in the Central Provinces would spring up at the drop of a pagri.

It is interesting to note in passing that a lot of their religious ceremonies are carried on in a language so old that its meaning has often been completely forgotten and even the priests do not understand the words they utter.

Perhaps the most perverse part of the Hindu religion touches this question of Outcastes, who are rejected by all caste Hindus, thrown out of the religion, yet must for ever remain Hindus. No one but an Indian could see the logic of that but to the Indian it is perfectly right and proper, even to those who are cast out. Since the Hindus believe in the transmigration of souls – they think that this life is now lived only in preparation for the next which will be lived in some other form on this earth – they believe that if you live a good life in this life, you move up a notch in the caste hierarchy when you return next time, eventually reaching complete unity with the godhead, which is their form of heaven, and conversely, if you lead a bad life on earth, you go down a peg for the next life becoming progressively an outcaste and eventually an animal, and one could think of no more perfect form of hell than to be a bullock belonging to a Hindu or to a Tonga-Wallah. On this basis, the caste of 'outcaste' represents very much what we would term Purgatory.

But the point is that they are still Hindus. They cannot move off and become Muslims, though in fact, there is considerable inducement for them to change their religion, and many Christian converts have come from the ranks of the outcastes. But only the Hindu could think up a religion where some of its members are banned from the temple rites, banned from all but the most menial and "unclean" jobs, kept in perpetual servitude, and yet are forbidden to find a better life and greater freedom elsewhere. The justification of it all is, of course, that this life is only one of many and, when put into that perspective, the fate is not so terrible. The whole question of the outcastes throws a light on the Indian mind, not least in the fact that the outcastes accept their lot. Only enormous pressures by people like Dr. Ambedkar have managed to make any changes and still the laws passed in the Lok Sabah are more often observed in the breach than their observance. As it is said elsewhere, the Indian has an enormous appreciation of authoritarian rule, and for obedience to tradition.

No apology is offered for dwelling at some length on the religious side of the Indian scene, since it forms such a very large part of the Indian character. To try to understand the Indian mind without describing at some length this side of it would be like trying to understand the English countryside without speaking of fields. Although the religious side of the Indian character is not brought out in the diaries, that is only because it is so innate, so much an integral part of the scene, that Sir Hyde never thought of mentioning it; it was part of his basic understanding and not a special event; part of what anyone who knew his India, as Sir Hyde did, knew automatically and therefore did not need specific mention.

5. Colonel Sleeman and the Thugs

To appreciate the lengths to which the Indian will take obedience to tradition and religious idealism, if that is the right word, one must read the astonishing story of Col. Sleeman and The Thugs. This remarkable story first came to light with a reference in the diaries to the village of Sleemanabad, (in the C.P. not far from Nagpur) where burnt an eternal flame in honour of its founder. Why should a village in India be named after a Sahib and what had that Sahib done to deserve commemoration by an eternal flame? Colonel Sleeman must surely rank as one of the greatest but least known of Englishmen who ever worked in India.

The story, as given by Sir Francis Tucker in "The Yellow Scarf" runs roughly as follows.

Major General Sir W.H. Sleeman, K.C.B., to give him the style and title he held when he died in 1856 after 47 years' service in the Army and Political Service, was known as "Thuggee" Sleeman for the ruthless way he pursued and finally exterminated almost single handed that curious and malevolent tribe known as the Thugs (pronounced T'ug) who were nothing other than a tribe of professional murderers. Thuggee is a concept which we in England find difficult to grasp. We know about thieves and we know about murderers, the former usually working in small gangs or alone, the latter being incidental to the former, or else committing their act in a moment of passion. But in India, Thuggee was a trade carried on in the name of religion, in honour of Kali, the Black Goddess, consort of Siva, the God of destruction. Every murder, according to the Thugs, benefited three people: Kali, to whom a sacrifice had been made; themselves, both in that they were one step nearer to paradise and also that they naturally increased their store of this world's goods by appropriating those of the people they murder; and, ironically, the victim, as their belief held that, by being murdered in the name of the god, he at once went straight to paradise.

We find it hard to think of gangs of fifty or so, sometimes accompanied by their women and even children, moving around the country murdering anyone who was unwary enough to stray into their path, taking their goods and then retiring during the hot weather to rest up as presumably respectable citizens in their own villages.

The murders were done with the utmost precision, every move being carefully thought out and rehearsed according to a strict ritual. Omens were observed, the sacred pickaxe, which flew to the hand of the thug when he commanded, was taken, and "sotha" (deceivers) were sent out to ingratiate themselves with potential victims – all thugs were accomplished musicians and singers and it was with music and song that they usually made their first approaches and set the scene for the crime. When the "sotha" were ready, "feles" or scouts went out to select the mango grove where the deed would take place, and to dig the graves in advance, hence the pick-axe, which, incidentally, they worshipped daily.

At the appointed moment, the leader would give the "Jhirni" the death call usually with a shout of "Tamakhu - Kha-loj" (Smoke Tobacco) the "bhurotes" (stranglers) each sitting next to a victim, would produce a yellow or sometimes white "rumal" (scarf) and with at least three accomplices strangle the victim who died of a broken neck within minutes. It was all completely rehearsed and no-one was allowed to escape, wives, children, servants all died so no tales were told, they simply disappeared. The victims were then stabbed, so that their body would not swell, and then buried; the tribe shared out the "garbhang" or booty, and moved on to find their next victims.

Sleeman first got on to the Thugs when he noticed that some of the soldiers of his regiment disappeared just like that. His regiment was stationed near Lucknow just south of the Kingdom of Oudh. The normal terms of recruitment in the army then were for each man to sign on for three years, serve two and then be granted a period of leave, during which he returned to his village, to his wife and family and tilled his crops like a good rayat (farmer). But they always returned to their regiment at the end of the year's chutti; to desert was almost unheard of. Sleeman, however, noticed that it was some of his best soldiers who went missing and that could only mean one thing, that they were dead. But why no news from the village? Other soldiers returning reported that So-and-so had left the village at the appointed time, intending to rejoin the regiment, so his non-arrival was a mystery.

Sleeman became sure that they must have been waylaid somehow, somewhere, and it was his original investigations into their disappearance that led him to the whole story. Sleeman reckoned that in the 300 years prior to 1830 when he started his anti-Thug campaign, 40,000 people a year were killed by Thugs, all in the name of religion. By 1848 under his guidance, 4,000 Thugs had been convicted, of which the greater number were hanged, transported or imprisoned, for which he took almost entire responsibility.

Since then Thuggee has been almost entirely absent from India, no one being more grateful for his services than the Indians.

One of Sleeman's most difficult tasks was retraining the children, especially since the parents were justly incensed at the thought of their children learning an honest trade such as bricklaying or carpentry. Murder was their trade, passed down from father to son and sometimes even to daughters. It was a holy trade carried on in the name of their god, and Sleeman had to work very hard to steer the children into the paths of righteousness.

To complete the story, Col. Sleeman had used as his headquarters a small village in the southern Central Provinces near which was a very ancient shrine. As part of his campaign, he had managed to induce the Government to make a grant of 96 acres of land to rehabilitate some of his reformed but landless murderers and one day took his wife on a tour of the area. He had married some four years earlier but as yet he had no heir which, to an Indian peasant, is the darkest calamity. Being met by the Brahmin in charge of the shrine, he and his wife were conducted thither with the urgent inducement that anyone who visited it would have a son. Sleeman said he would give a present of money to the shrine if it so happened. The following year he returned to the shrine to fulfil his promise, his wife having produced the son which the Brahmin prophesied. The village by then was prospering and, in honour of his work against the Thugs and the fact that he founded it in the first place, they renamed it 'Sleemanabad' a name it bears to this day. Not only that but the Brahmin lit a flame in the temple which was certainly burning 103 years later (though the sceptics say the old wallah had lit it the day before!) when Sleeman's grandson went to see it, the visit being reported by Sir Hyde Gowan in a letter to Sir Ernest Burdon of The Knights of St. John of Jerusalem dated 3rd March 1937:

" Dear Sir Ernest,
Sleeman .... had a positively royal reception at Sleemanabad, where the villagers came a mile down the road to meet him and escorted him in triumph to see the sacred fire which had been burning since the days of his grandfather."
s g . Hyde Gowan.

6. Indian Cows

Returning to the original theme, a prime example of the way in which the Indian can turn a thing upside down and make a nonsense of it is in their attitude towards cattle. The well-known sacredness of the Indian cow is not a basic and fundamental tenet of Hinduism, in fact, in Asiatic terms, it is a fairly modern development. It was found that the cow was a good and useful animal giving work, meat, milk, dung and several other blessings, so the cow was made sacred. But if the cow was sacred, it could not be killed and had to be left to die from natural causes.

Unwanted cattle were simply left tied up in the sun to die from thirst, lowing piteously. Of course this debarred the cow as a source of food, of much needed protein. Not only that but, as it was sacred, only the priest could oversee the breeding. However, the priests got their basic stock by way of gifts from the faithful, who naturally handed over their poorest beasts; one could not expect an Indian to give away his best animals, as there is a limit to what the faithful will do. So the priests, head cattle breeders, were bound to breed from the poorest and scraggiest beasts in the area. Thus, although the Brahmini Indian cattle can be bred into some of the finest stock in the world, the herds in an ordinary Hindu village are poor in the extreme.

7. Indian Wells

A small sidelight on the Indian's ability to do things in other than the obvious way, is in the question of digging wells. In any area of the country where the soil is rather light and sandy, and the water table high, an Indian does not dig a well in the way we would expect him to, by digging a hole and lining it as he goes down. He builds a tower and lets it sink. James told a story that he was passing through such an area once and noticed a dozen or so round towers scattered over the terrain. He asked the local Commissioner what they were and he said: "wells". James told him to pull the other one as it had bells on it, but he explained the principle. They build the tower of local brick up to some twenty feet high and, as the weight of the tower gets greater, it slowly sinks into the soil. As it goes down, more bricks are added to the top and the mud scooped out from inside, till the required depth is reached. The only thing the Commissioner did not explain was how they stopped it sinking when it got to the correct depth, though there was obviously an answer to that somewhere.

8. Tanks

There are several references in the Diaries to Tanks. James gives this explanation as their significance:

A 'tank' is a reservoir for catching water from the rains and holding it as long as possible. In certain parts of India, especially in the South, the land is more than ⅔ covered by Tanks, some quite small and temporary. They fill up in the rains and then slowly dry out during the following months, so that in the dry months, villages are sometimes as much as ten miles from a water supply. When full, the tanks often mysteriously contain fish which have survived dormant in the dry mud for up to nine months and come alive again when the rains come each year. One can sometimes see a fisherman casting his net and catching fish from a pool not much larger than a dining table. The fish are small, very small, and probably taste very muddy, but they are edible and at least form a small source of protein. As the tanks dry out and the water recedes, a good covering of grass is left, making a rich pasture for the cattle. Throughout the whole of the peninsular of India, tanks form an essential element in holding the rains for use in agriculture. There is also some very good duck shooting to be had in the season.

9. Tigers

Sir Hyde loved being invited on Tiger Shoots. The best story of all time about tigers, and one which, Sir Hyde used to tell with some relish, concerns a young subaltern on his first posting to his regiment from England. As was usual, the C.O. told the Senior Lieutenant to go and meet him in Bombay and bring him up to the regiment, so the Senior Lieut., being a man of good connections and some wealth, promptly booked forty-eight hours leave, got in touch with a friend of his, the Resident of a Princely State, and asked if there was any shooting to be had. He was in luck and was able to greet his new fellow officer on the quay at Bombay; "Come on, young 'un. I've got you a day's tiger shooting, borrowed a gun and we are all set. The train leaves in an hour."

At the Rajah's Palace, after a night's rest, the young officer was instructed in the ethics of tiger shooting with beaters and given the strictest instructions. Of course he was put in the end machán at the far end of the line of guns, so the likelihood of his seeing anything was small. However, he was told: "Tiger and only Tiger! You'll see pig and peacock, deer and Lord knows what all come by, but you're to let them all pass. Shoot at nothing but Tiger. If you shoot at anything else, you'll scare all the tigers into the next province." In the macháns, the line of guns could just hear the beaters, who kick up a heck of a racket in order to scare the tigers away from themselves, coming towards them, when suddenly, from the far wing:

BANG!

"What the devil's that young fool up to? We told him to shoot only at tiger and the beaters are miles away yet":

BANG! BANG!

"What in the sacred name of thunder?".

BANG! BANG!

"Oh, God. There'll be no tigers on this beat!"

BANG!

Up came the beaters; down climbed the shooters; they waited in a furious knot at the Rajah's machán, their faces black with anger – it was hard to know whose was the blackest. Up came the culprit, gun on shoulder, a grin on his face:

"Hello, you chaps. How many have you got? I got six."

And by the snakes he had. A mother and five grown cubs had tried to sneak past on the wing and he had bagged the lot.

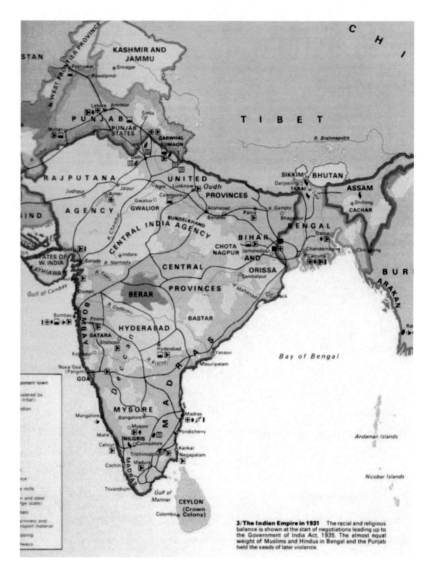

3/The Indian Empire in 1931 The racial and religious balance is shown at the start of negotiations leading up to the Government of India Act, 1935. The almost equal weight of Muslims and Hindus in Bengal and the Punjab held the seeds of later violence.

10. Maps of India 1933

This map shows the location of the Central Provinces, and Berar – the area over which Sir Hyde was responsible as Governor.

Central Provinces as its name tells us, is right in the middle of India, centred on Nagpur. Sir Hyde split his time between Nagpur and Jubblepore (now Jabalpur) and when it was too hot went to Pachmarhi. Jubb. (as in the diary) was where the Indian Army had its Central Provinces base. After Indian independence in 1947 the C.P. ceased to exist and was split up between Madhya Pradesh and Maharashtra. The district of Berar, over which Sir Hyde assumed the Governorship during his term following the successful negotiation of a treaty with the Nizam of Hyderabad, lay between the C.P. and Hyderabad.

11. Languages

English is the official language of India and that all, or at any rate most, of the speeches in the Lok Sabha, the Parliament, are made in English. The reason is the very, very simple one that India has so many languages and English is the only language that everyone understands. The most widely known of the original Indian languages is Hindi, derived from Sanskrit, one of the most ancient languages of which we have record. Hindi is spoken over the Central Indian Plateau, the Deccan.

Down to the South and along the coasts, are a group of Dravidian languages, all of extreme antiquity, each different widely from the others even to the extent of each having its own script. In the South the main languages are Tamil, Telegu, Kanarese, and Malayalam. Some of these are similar like Tamil, spoken in the South-East and Malayalam, spoken in Kerala. The language spoken by all the educated people is English.

In the North the position was made more complicated by the Persian invaders in the eleventh century who bought their languages with them. These languages had Scythian, Arabian and Persian roots with Arabic-type scripts, and it is versions of these that form the modern Northern languages, Pushto, Punjabi and Balogh to name but three. In the middle where Punjabi met Hindi a union occurred giving birth to a sort of universal, all-purpose "dialect" called Urdu. Indians themselves usually spoke either one or the other of the main elements, but as a fusion language Urdu was the one used by the English as their way of speaking to their Indian subordinates. Urdu can be written in either Persian or Devanagari (Nagri) script and Indians learned it in order to speak to the English, and the English, in turn were often given monetary rewards for facility in Urdu. In some cases it was compulsory to be able to speak it reasonably fluently. However, Urdu was only useful in the North of British India. In the South – anywhere South of the Central Provinces – it was fairly useless.

In the Central Provinces, there were half a dozen languages: the Indo-aryan group comprising Western Hindi, Eastern Hindi and Marathi each spoken by about 5 million people, and the Dravidian group, Dondi spoken by about a million, with Dakhani, spoken by the Muslims of the Deccan and Ramasi, a remnant of the Thuggs.

Sir Hyde spoke fluent Hindi and good Urdu. It is to be expected that he had a few words in all the languages he encountered in his Province.

Before the war a simplified Hindustani for the ladies was invented; it had about eight to ten essential words.

Ao = Come here   Jao = Go away   Lao = Bring it
Mez = Table   Kahna = Food   Jeldi = Quickly
Pine ka pani = Drinking water

With a few more nouns this got the Memsahib everything she needed.

12. Newspapers

On the subject of newspapers in India, at the time in question there were three major papers, all owned and edited by Englishmen (or Scotsmen). The biggest of them and the one with the greatest prestige, was the "Times of India", published in Bombay, a "quality" newspaper. Close behind was the Calcutta "Statesman" which, though quite as serious as the Times, was rather dull and more concerned with business and the jute trade than politics. One of the oddities of India was that it was the only country in the world that I know of, where you could buy that paragon of all knowledge, that dream of punters the world over, tomorrow's newspaper! Wednesday's Times was printed on Tuesday and was on sale in the streets of Bombay by three o'clock that afternoon, just in time to catch the Mail Train for Delhi which left about then. In

Delhi, it was on sale on the stated day but, traveling further up the line, it got to Benares on Thursday and Calcutta on Friday morning. And the Statesman did the same thing in the opposite direction. Of course, it is all altered now, if only with the coming of the aeroplane. The third paper, the smallest and most readable, somewhat reminiscent of the London evening papers, was the "Civil & Military Gazette", published in Lahore and circulating throughout the Punjab and north-west. These were all printed in English.

Beyond this was a plethora of local papers of all grades, some printed in English – in Nagpur were Hitavada (Hit. in the Diaries) and the Daily News (D.N.) – but the majority in the local language. To say that many were 'scurrilous' would, from the English point of view, be putting it mildly, but as very few people took any notice, it did not matter much. Any Indian who felt he had something to say, and they are an articulate nation, and who had a few rupees to hire a press, would start up a paper and keep it going on a circulation of a few thousand copies! Any town of any size had more than one paper. Nagpur, whose population in 1935 numbered a quarter of a million people, not really large by any standard, had several in both Hindi and Marathi, including Kedar's paper, The People's Voice. One notices how one of the leaders of the Government runs his own information service.

There was one other paper, an attempt at a 'glossy', but the printing and style were much closer to that of Comic Cuts, published weekly. Its main claim to fame was a Competition Crossword offering probably the biggest money prizes in the whole world, it was always a very easy crossword but containing a large number of alternatives, and the clues gave little indication of which alternative gave the right answer. So they published a subsidiary seriously discussing the merits of the various alternatives! The prizes were so big that Tata, the steel people, once thought of buying up a whole issue, which would give them enough copies to cover every alternative and thus make them certain to win all the prizes. They calculated that the return would be better than that that they could get on the normal money market and thus would be a good investment! But it did not come off.

13. Some History

At the time Sir Hyde took over, India was a country of some 400 million people with two basic religions, Hindu and Muslim, the former being divided into castes and several sub-religions of which the Sikhs were the most important. The people spoke twenty different languages with two hundred dialects and at least half a dozen scripts. To find one's way round India, speaking the "baht" or local language or dialect was, and is, a feat more difficult than to travel round Europe. Customs varied from district to district, with different methods of cultivation, systems of land tenure, ways of building houses, and variety of food eaten; in fact the whole country was divided into a mass of small enclaves and it is a measure of the Englishman's organizing ability that he even managed to get any sort of cohesion into the country at all. In that he was helped by the Indian's general feudal structure that was found to be existing, the Indian's instinctive knowledge of who was ruler and who was ruled, but as the aim was to wean them away from such a structure towards democracy, the matter was not easy.

By the end of the first millennium A.D., India had been a very old, static, peaceful country, almost entirely Hindu, divided up on a linguistic and feudal basis with a considerable wealth of culture. All the great temples of South India were built at the beginning of the first millennium B.C. or, with the second revival around the end of the first millennium A.D.. In 1018 A.D. Mahmoud Ghazui came down from the North through the Khyber Pass and conquered the Punjab, the Country of the Five Rivers, and in 1192 the Muslim leader Mohammed Ghori defeated Prithviraj, and the Muslims followed up with the conquest of the Ganges Valley and Bengal. This influx of Persian and Turkish invaders brought the religion of Islam and alien tongues into the whole of the North of the Continent, pushing the original Aryan and Dravidian inhabitants down to the South. This great empire of the Moguls broke up after the death of Aurungzebe in 1707, leaving a chain of satrapies and petty princes which, coupled with the remains of the other empires such as the Mahrattas, came to form the Princely States. With these, first the East India Company and later the British Government came to various agreements, conquering where it could and forming alliances with the more powerful of the Princes. Thus at the beginning of the twentieth century, the country was divided into British India, containing some 320m. people, of whom 24% were Muslims, mostly in the North, and over 600 Indian States, with a total population of some 80m. of whom 13% were Muslims. Of this, the Central Provinces and Berar accounted for about 16m. people of whom 4.7% were Muslims. The Muslim population of the Central Provinces was not large but was enough to have a high riot potential.

14. The Entry of the British

The entry of the British into this story falls into two parts, the first, quite frankly self-seeking and secondly, in the interests of trade, the later stages were transformed into something greater and much less mercenary. During the second half of our stay, we gave to India something that the Indians, at that time and on their own, could never have achieved, the fruits of which are with them to this day. The aims of both Englishmen and Indians were basically the same; reference the Montagu-Chelmsford report of 1918: "Indians must be enabled, in so far as they attain responsibility, to determine for themselves what they want done. The process will begin in local affairs. It will proceed to the complete control of provincial matters, and thence, in the course of time and subject to the proper discharge of Imperial responsibilities, to the control of matters concerning India." On which Mr. W. V. Hodson comments: "Despite the paternalistic caution and the note (not discordant in the 1920s) of overriding imperial duty, from then on it was a question of time and methods, not of ultimate objective."

Thus the real difficulty was not the aim, on which all were agreed, but the "How?" How was it going to be possible to transfer power to a country as diverse as India, with no definable nexus who could receive that power when transferred? The problem of India was essentially one of imperialism, nationalism and internal disunity, not of race or colour. The Government of India Act 1935 was an attempt to implement the Montagu-Chelmsford report and the difficulty of persuading the Congress Party to participate in the government their own country forms a large part of the diary in 1937 and 1938.

15. Congress

Congress was formed, oddly enough, by a Scotsman, Allan Octavian Hume in 1885, to discuss social rather than political matters, and was founded with the full support and active help of the then Viceroy, Lord Dufferin. For twenty years the keynote of the organization was "unswerving loyalty to the British Crown". The Congress leaders, all Indians, believed that the continued affiliation of India to Great Britain was absolutely essential to the interests of our own Nation's development. Its aims, according to Hume, in 1888, were threefold. First: the fusion into one national whole of all the different and until recently discordant elements that constitute the population of India; second: the gradual regeneration along all lines, mental, floral, social and political, of the nation thus evolved; and third: the consolidation of the union between England and India by securing the modification of such conditions as may be unjust or injurious to the latter country.

From the first, Congress never intended to make itself a merely Hindu organ. In 1886 the president was a Parsi, Dadabhai Naroji, four Englishmen have been among the presidents, and up to the 7th July, 1946 the president was A.K. Azad, a Muslim and even the great Mahomet Ali Jinnah himself, eventual founder of Pakistan, was in his early days the devoted disciple of another great Hindu and Congress leader, Gopal Krishna Gokhale. Right up to the time of partition it was trying to speak for all India and was supported by many Muslims and people other than Hindus, though it must be remembered that it never spoke for more than a small proportion of the total Indian population. However, there was a serious split in Congress in 1908, when the moderates parted from the extremists, causing the Muslims to lose faith in it and from then on Muslim separatism grew.

The second party in the constitution was that of the Muslims, but they were hopelessly divided. Their real problem was the same as of all minorities. If they fought the Congress, they could not hope to win, numbering as they did less than a quarter of the population. They could win locally, in the North and in East Bengal for instance, where they were in a majority, but never on a National scale. If they joined with Congress, then only compliant Muslims, "Congress Men" as they were called, would be elected to whatever positions of power there were and they could not hope to have a real voice in Government.

This is where the British Raj gave their greatest services to India; District Commissioners, appointed by the Government throughout the length and breadth of British India could act as judge, land assayer, settler of disputes over debts, inheritance and every sort of squabble. All provinces had either a Muslim or a Hindu minority and the Commissioners were trusted by both; a Muslim would never have accepted a Hindu's judgment, nor a Hindu that of a Muslim, but all trusted the D.C. or Sahib. They appreciated his intelligence and trusted his impartiality. The Pax Britannica was a very real thing in India for this reason of trust.

16. Partition

One further relationship is important. The Muslims were either rulers or peasants. They had arrived by conquest, were good fighters, knew how to till the land, but they had no middle class. All the junior administrators, the manufacturers, the shop-keepers, the money-lenders, were Hindus; educated Muslims were very sparse on the ground. The result was that the means and methods by which the Muslim minorities might be assimilated into the administration, whatever it might be, were far from obvious.

There is a popular opinion which says that Partition should never have happened but it seems that Jinnah was forced into it by circumstances. Partition was suggested not very seriously in1930 by Dr. Mohammed Iqbal, but the idea never took shape till Jinnah returned to India in 1935, and even then it was never treated as a really serious goal for many years. It came about simply because there was no acceptable alternative.

17.Money

At the time the diaries were written the Rupee was stabilised at 13 to the Pound. (In the mid 1970s it was about 75 rupees = £1.00)

3 pies = 1 pice

4 pice = 1 anna

16 annas = 1 rupee (roughly 1s and 6d in old money ie. 1930s)

100,000 rupees = 1 lakh

10,000,000 rupees = 1 crore

18. The Diaries

The position in India in 1933 when Sir Hyde's narrative starts was that the British wanted to decrease their governance in India but were completely stumped when it came to the question of: "How, do we transfer Power and to whom?'. The Congress wanted the British to leave India, but could no more answer the essential question than the British could. They tried to speak for all India, but failed. The man who probably had the greatest influence, Mahatma Gandhi, stood aside for a long period, having no official connection with it at all but who called the shots with his ally Nehru from the wings. The Muslims were even more divided than Congress, some being in Congress, some in the Muslim League and some belonging to neither faction. The Princes, on the whole, supported the Raj.

For many years, Ghandi settled his headquarters at Wardha in the Central Provinces a few miles South of Nagpur. Sir Hyde had more contact with Ghandi than almost any other representative of the British Government in India, although in the diaries he does not mention that he met him during his term as Governor. There are lots of "Ghandi" quotes, mostly uncomplimentary and showing Ghandi up in a poor light.

At the local level in the Central Provinces, there was a provincial, mainly Hindu, Ministry which was on the whole on very good terms with the Raj and only refused co-operation when personalities changed after the elections in 1936, and the Congress members were then commanded by Congress itself. This relationship is very clearly brought out in his diaries.

Sir Hyde's hardest task during his term as Governor was in inaugurating and operating the Government of India Act, 1935, by which power was transferred at the Provincial level from British to Indian hands. The core of the Act was the establishment of autonomy, with a representative parliamentary system of government, for the eleven British-Indian Provinces, within their defined provincial powers. The Act intended that these Provinces should become components of an all-India federation including the Princely states. In the cold weather of 1936/7, elections to the Provincial Legislatures were held throughout India to enable the new constitution of India to become a reality. The Congress Party won a majority in most Provinces including the Central Provinces, but the Congress Leaders refused to allow their people to take office for a time as they were unsure that the Governor, who was still in post, would not overrule actions which the new Ministry wanted to put in place. After a political struggle, Congress gave way and their local leaders took up their posts in the Provincial Government. Sir Hyde was instrumental in assisting in the provision of the solution to the political impasse.

19. The Government of the Central Provinces

The India Office list of 1943 defines the general situation as follows:

The Government of the Central Provinces consists of The Governor, an Executive council of two members and two Indian Ministers. There is a Secretariat. The Province is divided into four Divisions and 19 Districts. The Legislative Council which came into being in 1921, numbers 73 of whom 55 are elected. The Judicial commissioner is the highest court of appeal and is assisted by four additional commissioners, two from the C.P. and two from Berar.

There are complicated arrangements set out for Land Revenue collection.

Overall policy was dictated from Whitehall – The India Office and under them the Government of India in Delhi.

The India Office is referred to in the diaries as S/S.

The Secretary of State for India	1933/34/35	Sir Samuel Hoare
	1936/37/38	The Marquis of Zetland
Parliamentary Under Secretary		R.A Butler

The Government of India

Located in Delhi in winter and in Simla in summer.
(G/I in the diaries)

His Excellency the Viceroy and Governor General
(H.E. or H.E. the V. or the V.)

to April 1936 – Lord Willingdon

after April 1936 – Lord Linlithgow

The Council of State

President — Sir Manekji Dadabhoy

Nominated member for C.P. & Berar — Ganesh Srikrishna Khaparde

Elected member for C.P. & Berar — V.V. Kalikar

Legislative Assembly

Nominated Member for C.P. — H.C. Greenfield

Nominated Member for Berar — S.G.Job

Elected Member for C.P. — Sir Hari Singh Gour

Elected member for Berar — Seth Lalidar

When Sir Hyde arrived in **1933** the people in post and mentioned in the diary who (with Sir H.) were actually running the C.P. were as follows:

Private Secretary	C.C. Morrison
A.D.C.	A.M. Holmes

Executive Council

Police, Judicial & Jails (Home Member)	E. Raghavendra Rao
Revenue & Finance	Eyre Gordon
	(referred to as Eyre, Gordon,
	G., R.M. or H.M.R.)
Ministers: Education & L.S.G	Mahomed Yusuf Sharif
Ag., Excise, P.W. & Industry	Vital Banhuji Chaubal
Chief Secretary	Noel James Roughton
	(referred to as Noel or N.J.
	or Noel James)
Revenue Secretary	Rabindranath Bannerji
Legal Secretary (Officiating)	C.R. Hemeon (L.R.)
Education Secretary	C.E.W. Jones
Secretary P.W.D.	H.C. Hyde
President to the Legislative Council	Sir Ahmad Rizvi (H.P.)

By **1935** the following changes had been made:

Private Secretary	Mr Cole
Ministers. Education & LSG	Khaparde
Ag. Excise, P.W. & Industries	Naidu

1936 & 1937

Private Secretary	Captain J.H. Caesar M.C.
A.D.C	W.F.M.Davies

1938

Military Secretary	Captain J.H.Caesar M.C.
A.D.C.	R.F.McKeever
Private Secretary	R.Bannerji
Financial Commissioner	Sir Geoffrey Burton
Ministers:	
Prime Minister & Home	Dr Narayan Bhaskar Khare
Education	Pandit Ravai Shanker Shukla
L.S.G	Pandit Dwarker Prasad Misra
PublicWorks	Mahomed Yusuf Sharif
Finance	Durgashanker Kripasanker Mehta
Revenue	Prushottam Balwant Gole

Legislative Assembly:	
Speaker	Gupta

Indian Police, Central Intelligence Officer	T.H. Collins

CHAPTER 3

1933
SEPTEMBER - DECEMBER

Pachmarhi.

Sept. 16th 1933.

– being my first day of office as Governor. Having been called
unexpectedly take over the reins from a wise and sagacious chief, and
having a genuine mistrust of my ability to follow him with success, I
intend to set down here such events of my term of office as bear upon
my conduct of it. The record is solely for my own use, to enable me to
appreciate the extent to which I have fulfilled my trust, and the extent
to which I have failed.

H.G.

Tuesday Sept. 19th

My first day with Secs.. Eyre, who was to have gone to Hyderabad for
the last stage of the Berar talks, has been stopped at the last moment by
a wire saying that they had been concluded. The G/I are naturally
concerned with what they call "the broad view" – in other words,

getting H.E.H. *(The Nizam of Hyderabad)* into the federation net – and are apt to forget that it's we and the Beraris who've got to lie on the bed that they're making. The Beraris complain with reason that they're being treated like cattle, and we have protested, and shall continue to do so. It seems that Hydari *(Finance Minister to H.E.H.)* is insisting on durbars. I can't understand how he fails to see the danger, for H.E.H. as well as for us. If the Beraris get what they think a square deal in the new arrangements, the Hindus will have no use for the Nizam, and the durbars will be left for the Mussalmans. H.E.H. won't like that, and he'll say we've queered his pitch. Trouble at once. But if the durbars are successful and well attended, they will become a focus and centre of intrigue for all the disgruntled elements in the place. Worse trouble. H.E.H. gets a finger in our administrative pie, which is exactly what that cunning old fellow Hydari wants. The more we think of the idea, the less we all like it. And is the Nizam to make his own durbaris? And to take nazarana? And to announce boons? The difficulties are endless.

Note (JHBG):

Durbar, Durbaris

'Durbar' is the State Government, and a durbar is the Government holding a ceremony for the purpose of governing. In fact it means a ceremonial levee at which the (Nizam) accepts gifts, pronounces laws and hears petitions. The Durbaris are selected by Government according to the best Eastern principles, but in the C.P. have no overt function.

Wrote my first letter to H.E. the V. about Gordon's appointment. It's hard to have to recommend the passing over of an old friend like Irwin, but I simply must have the man who will be most help to me, and in the end G. is he. He's shrewd and quick witted. Whereas I. is slow in the uptake and rather ponderous and his wife can always be relied to put her foot in it. Everyone likes and trusts G..

Hemeon brought me the latest council grouping. About as much coherence, I should say, as the segments of a kaleidoscope. If provincial autonomy is not to be with us till Jan. '36, what about prolonging the life of the Council? It's a long extra lease. But elections are expensive and unsettling and a new Council might contain obstructive elements. Some of the present members nearly staged a walk-out at my swearing-in, because they were put at the back of their own Council Hall, after the crowd of durbaris. Rather childish, but understandable, and anyhow they were nice about it in the end. Noel must have used his best blarney. But the matter wants putting right. A Governor's relations with his Council are much closer than with his durbaris, who belong to a past order of things.

Wed. Sept. 20th

Talked things over with Eyre and Chambal. The latter thinks the Council may give the Ministry a run, but the make-up of the Coalition party hardly inspires confidence. On the other hand, the opposition – orthodox Brahmin with rabid anti-Brahmin – is an unholy alliance, and is not likely to be effective. Chambal tells me that land is fetching no better prices in Berar. I can't make out why some of the big men don't seize the chance and buy. But it's a good thing they haven't. "Latifundia perdidere Italiam."

Thurs. Sept. 21st

My pet baby, debt conciliation, is said to be making a good start in Khurai, but to be thriving poorly in Seoni. If the Seoni people don't want it, we'll move the Board elsewhere. Shall we take over Jiwandass' estate? It would be liquidation, really, not C/W management, and as a revenue officer I have always said "no". But public sentiment would like it done, and I know Rao thinks the effect would be good. Need one stick pedantically (?) to the strict canons of revenue administration?

I should like to do something for the old man. We seem to be in hot water with the G/I. over the Road Development Fund, and I'm not surprised. We've not stuck to the main objective – spending our ordinary grant – but have shilly-shallied over our programme and have asked for money from the reserve before most of the ordinary grant is even allocated. I've tried to ginger Hyde up. The powers above are curiously distrustful of the transfer of law and order, and are trying to hedge it round with safeguards. N. S. B. If you make the transfer a sham by taking the Police more or less out of the power of the Minister you'll get no money from the Council. They are not going to pay for a sort of Praetorian Guard. As M.B. *(Sir Montague Butler, his predecessor)* wrote, "Confidence begets confidence, but a transfer that's a sham will merely invite trouble".

Mond. Sept. 25th

Meeting of Govt.. We decided to have a shot at pulling Jiwandass' estate out of the mess it's in. I think the move is sound. We can't do anyone any harm, and if only prices will improve, we may do good. Anyway, people will see that we're trying to help a man whose father helped us and the public, and who has been loyal to us. The question of prolonging the life of the Council is to wait till Nov., when the V. may give us a lead over the Assembly. Our electoral rolls are out of date, and would take 6 months to renew, so we couldn't have an election till next year at any rate. And we're quite happy without the Congress Members!

Wed. 27th

Have protested to G/I about H.E.H.'s durbars in Berar. H.M.H. has pointed out further difficulties. Will H.E.H. appoint his durbaris and announce concessions, as is usual at a State durbar? And take 'nazar', as is ditto? And will the Govt. be asked to attend – a hopeless idea – as the Resident does? And what happens if the Council passes a token cut refusing funds? And so on – the objections are endless.

M.B. has left me a nasty case. Last year we sacked Behere, Head of Tatwardhan High School, because he wrote in a Bombay paper an article (poem) glorifying the Sholapur murderers. The University have elected him now to their Court, and the Vice-Ch. (Nyogi A.J.C.) on his own authority has appointed him head of the Marathi department. "Only a very little one", said N. in self-defence to M.B.. Reminds one of the house-maid's baby! M.B. has left it to me to decide whether the G. in C. should fight the University, or I, as Chancellor, should fight the Vice-Ch., or we should do nothing. He put Nyogi heavily on the mat, and left N. with the impression that he was sore because he hadn't been given an LLD. The situation gets piquancy from the fact that N. is standing for re-election, and being a Govt. servant is afraid Govt. may put a spoke in his wheel. I believe N. is very anxious to interview me, and Rao is going to ask him up for a week-end, and send him along. Jones thinks the matter barely worth fighting, and points out the danger of Govt. appearing to interfere in the internal affairs of the University. Agreed; but it's embarrassing for me to have as my Vice-Ch. a Govt. servant who takes under his wing a man who extols the murderers of Govt. servants. We'll see what N. says, if he comes. Anyway we must make it a condition of any Govt. servant taking up a job like this in future that he does nothing to embarrass Govt. It's not playing the game – at least not cricket, though it may be "Kho-Kho"!

Friday Sept 29th

Gave my first official dinner last night. All the Govt. Secs., Heads of Depts. plus the Commandant and R.A.M.C. Doctor. Walked very warily and decided to avoid all chance of heart-burning among people who think that these things matter by having one long table in the ball-room – officially "Durbar Hall"! With everyone in strict order of precedence both as to place and partner. Had the family joke – my mid-Victorian épergne out and really on the long table flanked by its two supporters and two large rosebowls of E.'s it looked very well. W.J.P. said he'd never seen a G.H. table look prettier. At any rate there were no silver bridges or pile drivers or caskets. It was the first try-out of the establishment. And Yesu gave us an excellent dinner and everything went off without a hitch, except that someone has filled a bottle of J. & B. that I bought with peach brandy or some such witches brew. I suppose they think that one doesn't know the difference; just as when they doctored the G.H. Whiskey, John Begg's best Gold Cap, and Tom Kelly never spotted it. After dinner I talked to every lady in turn – exhausting, but I gather today that people really enjoyed the party which is encouraging.

Oct. 4th

The wisdom of Monty. "My own attitude in these matters is to let people suffer the disqualification their conduct brings upon them, when that conduct is deliberate and not due to some accident or misadventure, but I never push principles to extremes." From a file about disqualification for munl. Service of persons convicted of c.d..

Thurs. Oct. 5th.

The Raju case has come up – a pitiable business. A fellow Mason, and a philosopher of repute, with no vices that I know of, but with an utter lack of financial sense and financial morality. He seems to have cast his net far and wide, and to have obtained money from any likely quarter, by methods for which "dubious" is a kind epithet. The Minister seems chary of tackling him because he hears that he is being backed by titled persons in England. I've told him that if the whole peerage backed R., that could make no difference to the way we've got to tackle the case; but these cases against men whom one has known and respected are pretty hateful. At present we've got to make further enquiries.

Sat Oct 7th

I wish they would make up their minds about Irwin and Gordon. Mrs. I. has written out to say they're receiving letters of congratulation, but I don't know whether the news is true or not, and don't know what plans to make. I hope there hasn't been any queer work at home; but I'm sure they wouldn't override both Monty and my clearly expressed opinion without saying something first. And I've a second shot in the locker for them suggesting that the appointment remain temporary until the new era. M.'s wisdom again. They've hustled through the Berar negotiations with indecent haste, and the Resident has initialled an agreement which is open to objection on several points, as we see it. We've told the Govt. so, but these politicals don't give a hoot about the C.P. or the Beraris, so long as they get their agreement; and I am not sanguine as to the result.

Thurs. Oct. 12th

A further batch of papers from the G/I about Berar. The Nizam now wants a dual oath of allegiance, or his name mentioned as part-authority in legislative acts. All wrong. Many Beraris are genuine British subjects, and the dual oath will be repugnant to many more who are not. And the whole idea is opposed to the facts. No Berari is subject to the Nizam's laws, nor is he bound to obey any order of H.E.H. . He owes no real allegiance to H.E.H., nor does the legislature derive the sanction for its acts from him – vide Art. I of the Agreement and Proposal 74 in the White Paper, which put the King's authority beyond reach of doubt.

To give a geographical note:

Berar, which will often be mentioned, is a region, a lot smaller than the C.P. lying to the south-west and bordering on Hyderabad. H.E.H. – which refers to His Exalted Highness the

Nizam of Hyderabad, Nawab Sir Mir Osman Ali Khan, G.C.S.I., G.B.E., sometimes referred to irreverently in Delhi as 'His Exhausted Highness', but who, in his day, was said to be the richest man in the world, and who, as far as this narrative is concerned, usually spoke through his Finance Minister, Sir Akbar Hydari – considered it to be part of his domain and its exact status was in dispute up to the early '30's. The Berar Agreement which had already been a long time in the making, was supposed to be signed on the 19th. September 1933, (see the very beginning these diaries), but was not in fact signed till the 16th. November 1936. By this, the Nizam retained titular sovereignty over Berar, but its administration was taken over entirely by the Central Provinces. The real point is that Berar is a grain and cotton producing area, richer than the rest of the C.P. and therefore able to contribute substantially to the C.P. Exchequer, which, of course, was a slightly sore point with the Beraris.

On a slightly lighter note, in the Legislative Assembly one time, the Member for Berar gave a long and impassioned speech, about three-quarters of an hour, intended for the ear of the C.P. Minister of Finance, pleading the cause of Berar. But the Finance Minister was very deaf and towards the end of the harangue, leant over to his Secretary and asked: "What does he want?" The Secretary shouted: "He wants more money for Berar!" "Tell him he can't have it". Such is politics!

Sund. Oct. 15th

Vide Sept. 27th – Nyogi came and saw me today. He was apologetic but pointed out that the post he'd given Behere was one of little influence compared with his position as an elected member of the Ex. Council. Also that he couldn't cancel the appointment now without arousing sympathy for Behere, who as a matter of fact appears to be alienating it for himself. N. promised to give me an undertaking in writing not to make such an appointment again, and professed himself genuinely anxious to maintain cordial relations with his Chancellor. As soon as this election for V. Ch. is over, I'm going to issue orders that all Govt. servants must obtain Govt.'s approval before standing for election. (Note: 'Done. H.G.') G.S.C. Rule 15 is quite clear on the point and I do not know why it has not been enforced. I hope the Behere incident is not closed. N. has been very decent over postponing Convocation for a week, so that I shall not have to curtail my time at Jubb. (Rao says the Behere solution is "very satisfactory.")

Have had two invitations – to Savangarh to shoot duck, and to Bhopal to be a guest of H.H.. E. will enjoy them both.

Friday Oct. 20th

What queer proposals one has to deal with in this queer country! The Inter-University Board wants us to recognise all degrees as equal in value. That would mean that the incentive to increasing the value of the degree from any University would disappear, and each body would compete in cheapening its degrees. At least that's the plain meaning. It's like putting a car into reverse and expecting it to go forwards. And anyhow why should we tie our hands? Many candidates go deliberately to Universities where the fees are small and the degrees easy, and it would be absurd to put them on the same footing as men from the better Universities. I have said so, and am waiting to hear what the others say. Then again there's Gidney going off at a tangent with a proposal which would mean that any pure European who had been born in India and who came to serve or work in India would have to vote as an Anglo-Indian in the new constitution e.g. if James had entered an Indian Service he'd have had to vote as an Anglo-Indian! Curious failure to think straight. In a different class is a proposal by Pandit Rao Deshmukh (late Min.) for starting a Sports Association. Needless to say, there are no visible funds, and Govt. is to give a grant which will cover about three-fourths of the exs.. Equally of course the latter will consist mostly of the salary of the "Secretary", an M.B. who is said to be known to the Police, and whose idea in starting the Association is said to be to federate all the Hindu akharas in Berar, with the notorious Hanuman Vyagamshala of Amraoti at the head. It's all just like Patwardhan ("Lieut.") and his egregious Flying Club.

Mon. Oct. 23rd

Deshmukh and Dravid have both been to see me about the above, and say that they are trying to wean the Hanuman V. from its association with politics. They are both serious, I think, and if they succeed the Sports association idea may be worth encouraging. Anything that will get these people to see that physical culture and politics have nothing to do with one another is worth trying.

Tues. Oct. 24th

Two matters settled as I hoped. The S/S agrees to Gordon's appointment on conditions which G. has accepted – I am sure wisely. Had he refused, he'd have nothing to look forward to but Ch. Sec. or Commissioner – and how long will Commissioners last in the new regime? On the other hand I shall be surprised if there is no special post into which he can be fitted. Anyhow it is a great relief to think that I shall have him as R.M. these next two years. Next a letter from Nyogi about the Behere business – the "amende honorable" complete, as far as was possible. He promises that there shall be no repetition of the incident, and thanks me for the way I treated the matter. A nice letter. But the main point is that the incident is closed without a row, and with no damage done to either party.

Thurs. Oct. 26th

R.M. Deshmukh has sent the S/S an ungrammatical and inaccurate pamphlet about Berar and it has been sent down to us with laconic request that we should say that we think there ought to be any special provisions, financial or legislative, in the Act about Berar. In the first place, this isn't in the least what D. is driving at. And, secondly, the reference, made in this casual fashion, opens up the whole question of the future joint administration of the province. Louis Kershaw at the I.O. admitted to me frankly that they did not know there was such a thing as a Berar financial question; but N.J. tells me that when he was giving evidence before the financial committee he started to explain our problems and L.K. shut him up, as "the matter was parochial". He asked me why we hadn't represented our difficulties, and seemed surprised when I said that we could hardly discuss C.P. cum Berar finance openly when we were not supposed to know that the C.P. might not be divorced from Berar. They do not seem to have tumbled to the fact that the C.P.-Berar settlement has an important bearing on federal finance; because if Berar gets the major part of its revenues for itself, the C.P. will become yet another deficit province, and another burden is added to the weary camel, the federal budget. The problem this reference raises is difficult – how can you reconcile a separate budget with a joint administration? On the other hand, how can you leave the settlement to a sort of gentleman's agreement like the Sim Settlement, when there is no semi-irresponsible authority in the Govt. as there is at present to enforce execution? I have tried to clarify the issues, and must wait and see what the others say.

An invitation to go to the Vice-Regal Lodge Feb 3rd to 6th. Very kind of them to ask us so early.

Sat. 28th Oct.

Sharif made an astonishing remark to me. The Raipur Dt. Cl. has been superseded for the past two years, and Hamilton is very anxious for the period to be extended. Sharif thinks this illegal, and I'm inclined to agree with him. But I said that I should have to circulate the file, and probably Rao, who knows the country, would be able to give us good advice. Whereon S. burst in – "Don't trust his advice. He is a cunning and crafty man, and I cannot make out why people don't see through him." I was not surprised by the opinion so much as by S.'s sudden candour. But if Rao knows that he holds it, things will become difficult in government. That's the worst of these people, they all distrust each other so heartily.

Friday Nov. 3rd

Mark Patrick and wife have been here for four days. He told me that the S/S had no use for half measures over the transfer of the Police (vide Sept 21st above) and wants us all to strengthen his hand against the right wingers. He had been talking to Smyth, who told me much of what I've written above. I had a long talk with him about Berar and explained our point of view about durbars and the dual oath, and he seemed to agree. He said that he had only met two officials in India so far who'd dammed the White paper. I gather from him that there's little chance of the Bill going through before March '35 which means Jan '36 at the earliest for the new regime. Lady Evelyn paid Yesu the compliment of saying that he was as good as the Viceroy's cook and was only beaten by the C-in-C.'s man, whom she calls a super-cook. Better not tell Yesu or he will want more wages.

Nov. 6th Jubbulpore.

A somewhat hectic three weeks in front of me, during which I've got to try and entertain all the station – some 250 odd, civil and military –

without treading on anyone's toes. And I'm worried to death about E., who had been having fever before she sailed and oughtn't to have started. I don't know how she will stand all this racketing.

Difficulties ahead over Gandhi. He's having a Harijan meeting in Nagpur on the 8th, and we've said that Govt. servants are not to contribute to the funds, as we've no guarantee that they wouldn't go to G.'s c.d. activities. At the last moment, in the fashion of this country, the organizers sprang on the Minister a request for the use of Patwardhan H.S. playground. His position was strong. He'd only got to say he must take my orders, which were obviously necessary in any matter connected with G., as we never know we mayn't be creating an awkward precedent both for ourselves and for other Provs.. Instead of doing so, he and his colleague swapped polite notes to each other – quite against the B.R.'s – and he decided to let the organisers have the playground, and presented me with a "fait accompli". I have ordered a discussion at the next meeting of Govt. on our general line of action re Gandhi. I am inclined to think we must block subs. from Govt. servants, for the reason above, but must do nothing which might be construed into impeding the Harijan movement on the mere ground that G. is still a potential c.d.'ite. For one thing, the more G. gets absorbed in Harijans, the less likely he is to meddle in politics and disturb the present peace.

Tues Nov 8th

Patrick writes – "It is a great comfort to hear someone who knows the province as you do, with reasonable confidence in the future I should like to attach Winston, Page, Croft and Alfred Knox to you for a month or two for a course in a sense of proportion"! The thought of having Winsome Winnie for a chela takes me back to college days when I heard him speak as the chief guest at a dinner of the Strafford club. (High Church and Tory) very much on his present tack. He's boxed the compass since then.

Sat Nov 11th

Armistice Day and I got through my first public function (not counting my swearing-in) without doing anything silly. After an open-air service at which we did <u>not</u> have "O valiant hearts" we went to the Cenotaph, where I laid a wreath; and later on the troops marched past and I took the salute. Very fine they looked – except the King's, whom I thought undersized, though they swung along stoutly enough. Standing before the Cenotaph the sun was a bit hot but just as the first bead started a little breeze sprang up and all was well. I have refused to go to the Armistice Ball. I never did like ending the day of commemoration with a beano, and every year that passes shows how little cause we have for rejoicing. I protested mildly to the Bishop at dinner the other night against the omission of "O valiant hearts" from the services. It's a fine tune and the words express the spirit of the occasion so the C. of E. with its flair for the banal, missed it out and give us "O God our help" – which on this particular occasion means precisely nothing.

Sunday Nov 12th

It is said that Lord Chelmsford, during his tour of the provinces inquired somewhat plaintively why the G/I was so unpopular with the local Govts.. We have just had an instance of the sort of thing that would have given his Lordship his answer. We asked for Powell as I.G.C.H. plus D.P.H.. He knows the province and has the diploma of Public Health. Instead they send us Wilson, (Civil Surgeon of Delhi, mark you) who is, I believe an excellent fellow but has not got the diploma and has never set foot in the C.P.. A sheer ramp on the part of the D.G.I.M.S. – and that, too, on top of their planting "Lung" Wilson on us last time. Reasons given? 1. Powell would supercede a large number of senior officers; 2. The amalgamation of the two depts. has only been sanctioned until 1934, and the diploma isn't necessary. But <u>one</u> - Wilson is only a year senior to Powell and the other two officers whom they offered to us as alternatives are of the same year as he and <u>two</u> the suggestion that we shall be able to separate the two departments in 1934 is purely childish. If an Under Sec. used arguments like that to me, I'd ask him which district he'd like to be posted to. The Politicals are very nearly as bad at insisting on their own way, without caring a hoot what effect it may have in the provinces. They have just said that they consider the C.P. Govt. "unduly apprehensive" over the dangers of allowing the Nizam to hold durbars in Berar, as some of them were "not likely to occur in actual practice". We probably know a bit more about that likelihood than they do! In the same breath they've practically admitted we are right by saying that the programmes of a durbar must be approved by the V. after consultation with us. Monty always thought it unlikely that H.E.H. would ever hold a durbar and this makes it more so. At any rate I hope so. They've not said anything yet about the dual oath and the joint authority matter.

Friday Nov. 17th

The announcement about Berar is to be made when H.E. the V. goes to Hyderabad shortly. In the "contents" of the announcement nothing is to be said about durbars or other terms.

Gandhi's Harijan tour has given us a problem. Ordinarily we should bless any movement that aimed at raising a part of the community. But it is clear now that the movement is arousing strong opposition among the orthodox Hindus. We have already settled that Govt. servants cannot be allowed to subscribe to G. because even if such gifts were devoted to Harijan work, they would release funds for c.d. work. Are we to allow them to attend meetings? And are we to give schools, playgrounds etc. for meetings? We all say "no". The movement has now entered the sphere of controversy, and we must be neutral, as usual. If we backed it, the orthodox could charge us rightly with "downing" them. The situation is, as so often happens in this land, Gilbertian – Gandhi, the declared enemy of Govt., touring the country on a mission of social reform, and his friends asking Govt. to help it by the loan of playgrounds for meetings, and roads for welcome arches, and by allowing its servants to attend the enemy's meetings and subscribe to his funds. Meanwhile, Govt. can't help a movement for social reform because a part of the community says it's against their religion. One thing is clear – we must not be forced into the position of backing G. against the Sanatanists.

Monday Nov. 20th

The G/I have backed us over the dual oath and authority for legislation, which is something to the good. They must realise, I think, the difficulties in which we shall be landed if any substance is given to the shadow of H.E.H's sovereignty. Gordon and I have whacked out together a very difficult draft over the question whether the Constitution Act should include special provision for dealing with Berar finance and legislation. We see no alternative but to give the Governor a special responsibility for securing to the Beraris "a fair share" of Berar revenues – a commission to be appointed from time to time to determine that the fair share is. I do not envy myself the task, but there is no way out that we can see.

I've discovered that I'm the only governor who has no A.D.C.. All of them have at least one, plus several Hons.. I don't think the present arrangement works well as the P.S. cannot attend to my wife as well as to me. I am going to look for one. As D.R. says "you must choose an A.D.C. as carefully as you'd choose a wife".

Nov 30th

Back in Nagpur. Jubblepore has been a strenuous but cheerful show, and everyone was very good to us. I don't think I had an early bed for a fortnight, what with our own dinners and the Burtons' and the Lings'.

I think the visits achieved something practical, as I got to know all the soldier men, and that is good for liaison. And I saw the schools and hospitals and they seemed to appreciate it – especially the consequential gifts from the discretionary grant! And were very friendly. But I must learn how to go round a school. At present my remarks are rather fatuous. I must also learn something about Boy Scouts. I committed a 'faux pas' at my first rally by shaking hands with my right hand it appears that a good scout salutes with his right and shakes with his left!

Saturday Dec. 3rd

My first public show since I was sworn in – Convocation. Raman stayed with us, an interesting man, but he talks so much at meals that one never gets through them! I only made a few remarks in introducing him. He gave a v.g. address, his main point being that while passion and sentiment may give incentive and driving force to our lives, reason and logic must be their guide. He also pleaded against the commercial spirit in science, pointing out that all great discoveries which had been commercial successes have come to scientists in the ordinary course of their work, and not because they were searching deliberately for a commercial proposition. The students behaved very well, and I liked especially the way they applauded the women graduates.

At night dined at Lodge Corinth. The Lodge was packed and they received me in due form, and gave me my patent as P.D.S.G.W. . Then a first, well done. Hill of the B.N. Rly is the driving force evidently. Parakh made a good speech in proposing my health – fluent and in good taste. I was relieved, as I had to keep him in order in the Vicaji case in 1922, when I was put on to hold the enquiry. And of course we're old foes in Council, since he became a tub-thumper. It shows what masonry can do.

Thurs. Dec. 7th

The G/I have approved our instructions re Gandhi – "No comments to make." Bon! One never quite knows how they'll take these things – and indeed it's difficult to know how to take them oneself. (The Indian is a master hand at making things awkward.) So when there's agreement it's a relief.

Fri Dec 9th

Back from Amraoti, where I attended the 10th anniversary of the K. E. M. College, a good show. Little Tosty was in great form – though he did give us a 25 minute speech – and all the students seemed happy and cheerful. I was very pleased when a crowd of them who had gathered near my car gave me three cheers off their own bat as I drove off. At the meeting I made a short speech which seemed to me to be tripe. I can talk about facts and policies, but talking by and large is much more difficult.

Monday Dec 11th

E. and I went to Raipur yesterday, for my swan song as President of the Gen. Council of the Raj Kumar Coll.. "Dana" Gibson our commissioner is A.G.G. in charge of stakes and I took the opportunity of mentioning the vamp which was when they tagged the P.A.'s post from us and refused to take a man with it. We offered them Grigson, who is a long way junior to Drake, the P.A., and they said he would "go over the heads of 74 officers of the Political Department". They said nothing of the fact that those 74 officers would each get one step up (unearned). The G/I are positively childish at times. The Raipur show was another piece of the good staff work. The Smith Pearces were very hospitable and we enjoyed the day greatly. There was an air of keenness and alertness about the boys that I liked they all seemed happy and unselfconscious and were terribly pleased when I went and talked to them after the prize giving and got them three days holiday. I managed to stop any formal speech making and only spoke for five minutes myself. It will be one of my aims while in office to discourage chin wagging except of the briefest!

Dec. 16th

Vide Oct. 26th I have forgotten to record the solution we reached after much discussion and redrafting. We stuck to the joint budget, rejected the idea of dealing with the matter in the Act, either directly or by appointment of a Commission to adjudicate, and put the onus on the Governor as a "special responsibility", which he will discharge on the advice of a Commission. An alternative to include it in his Instrument of Instructions was rejected because there would be no sanction with which they could enforce his orders.

Thank goodness Gandhi has left us. Crowds have flocked to see him, attracted by his personality. But he grumbles everywhere about the smallness of the purses presented to him, and it remains to be seen how he will use the money. His interest in the Harijans has so far been mainly verbal, and though he has said he is leaving 75% of the contributions behind for local work, we have not heard yet of anything being done with the money. "Graeculus esuriens", the local Congress-wala, is hardly a safe banker. The other 25% goes presumably to Congress funds. It remains to be seen if G. will return to Wardha. Chote Lal thinks not, but Jamanlal Bajaz will probably try to keep him. If he does, there's sure to be trouble after August, when his suspended sentence expires.

Sunday Dec. 17th

University sport yesterday. Some good performances but the last two years when one College – Morris last year, Robertson this – has swept the board and that takes a bit of the interest out. I refuse to stay put, and went down to see the start, and spent my time among the judges and competitors. I am not going to be an animated dummy more than I can help. One does much more good by mixing freely with people than by sitting in a chair and talking stuff to a string of people who are bought formerly up to one.

This extract from the Raipur fortnightly (Intelligence) report. "It seems doubtful if Gandhi's reputation has been enhanced by this tour. His contact with the depressed classes was of the slightest and a good many people seem to have been disgusted with the commercial spirit of the whole business. It appears to many to have been a purely money-making proposition, and the people are sceptical as to the destination of the funds collected." Our "saint"!

CHAPTER 4

1934
JANUARY - JUNE

Tuesday January 9th 1934

There has been nothing of interest to record for a long time. Xmas camp was a good show, though the three Tiger that Rukhar provided eluded us. In the first beat there were Ma ("Old Mahogany" we called her) and a cub. Ma was missed by Morrison and the cub got out unseen. In the second Ma galloped past the end machán out of range, and Pa leapt back over the heads of the beaters. In the third, two Tiger came back and devoured the first kill which hadn't been eaten at the time, but de-camped at once, and we saw nothing. Party: Jack and Dorothy N. Walker, Hydes from Seoni, Lawrence Mason and our 5 selves. They all said they'd love it. Hyde let his rifle, an old Winchester, off by accident after the first Tiger beat, and on the last day he left a cartridge in the barrel and his chuprassi let it off while cleaning it in his tent. On neither occasion did he hit anyone, but I told him he couldn't expect such luck to hold. As Jack said "any man can make a mistake, but only a fool makes the same mistake twice".

A propos of the last entry (Dec. 17th) we are finding great difficulty in locating that any money has been left behind by G., except a trifling sum in one district.

Tambe came to see me this morning, and tried to pump me about the orders re: Berar. I told him, quite truthfully, that nothing was settled finally, and that I could not tell what S/S would decide, either as regards the Nizam's privileges of as regards finance. He professed to think that if Berar became a definite part of B.I., and if the feeling of separateness no longer had the present anomalous legal position to keep it alive, the demand for financial satisfaction would die down in Berar. In my first address to the Council, just drafted, I have asked both parties to come together and try for an agreed settlement, otherwise I foresee endless bickerings, and a packet of trouble for the Governor who has to settle the matter.

Thurs 11th

Lodge St Andrews gave a banquet last night. I was much struck with the excellence of the work in Lodge – a third, finishing with a closing in full form. Spence D.S.M., wants to come to Nagpur and bid farewell to us all. I hope we shall be able to bring it off. He will be a great loss.

Note (JHBG):

Sir Hyde, though he preferred to speak extempore, found it necessary to work to a written text, so that his exact words could be referred to later to prevent misunderstanding. His Ministers collected these texts and had them bound and published quite on their own initiative. They presented a copy to Sir Hyde, who asked why they had done this thing. The reply was: "So that we may refer to them and be guided by them", which, in view of all things, was really rather a pretty compliment. Actually they finally ran to two volumes of speeches and an 'Appreciation' after his death. Certain excerpts are reprinted with this document, but the full texts are available if required, and form a separate printed file.

Below is his first speech.

Speech at the opening of the session of the Legislative Council on Thursday, the 18th January 1934

Mr. President, and Gentlemen of the Council,—Before I commence my address to you today, I should like to express what I know is in the hearts of you all—a sense of the great loss that our province has sustained in the passing away of Sir Bipin Krishna Bose. When I first came to the province over thirty years ago, he was one of the leading figures in its public life, and each year as it passed added something to the work which he accomplished for the public good, and something to the esteem in which he was held by all manner of men, whether of high or of low estate. No request for his assistance in public affairs ever went unregarded, and even in his declining years, when his strength was no longer sufficient for active work, men turned to him instinctively for advice—for the shrewd and practical advice which he seemed always to have at his command. Though death has taken a great figure from our midst, we have been left the richer by the example of a life devoted to none but the highest ideals, and by the memory of a kindly and gentle spirit.

When I had finished piloting my first budget through the Council in the session of last March it must have been far from the thoughts of any member present—it was certainly very far from mine—that on the next occasion on which I spoke to you I should be addressing you as your Governor. I cannot begin what I have to say to you today more fittingly than by paying a brief tribute to the memory of the wise and far-seeing man whose place I have been called upon to fill. I was privileged to observe him during nearly all the years of his rule at closer quarters, possibly, than any other person in the province, and this I can tell you, that he never faltered in his desire to see our province march forward steadily on the path of constitutional progress, and spared no effort to achieve that end. If you wish to judge the measure of his success, you have only to read his first address to this Council in 1925 and to compare it with his last. The heritage which he took up was one of strife, of frayed nerves, and of warring antipathies. The heritage which he hands on to his successor is, I think I may fairly say, one of peace, of sympathy, and of genuine effort towards mutual understanding. I count myself fortunate, gentlemen, that I have received such a heritage, and my one hope is that when in the fullness of time I come to lay down my office, my successor may be able to say of me that the torch is burning as brightly as when it was given into my hands, and that I have done nothing to dim its flame. No one knows better than I do the weight of the responsibility which rests upon me, and how hard it will be for me to fulfil worthily the trust which has been placed in me. There is only one means by which I can hope to succeed, and that is by your help, and I appeal to you all as old friends—for I know that I may count you as such—to give me that help in full measure, bearing always in mind that we are both striving for a common object, the good of our province—you for your home-land, and I for the land to which I have given the best years of my life. There is an old adage which says—"He hath a good judgment who relieth not solely on his own". I shall rely upon the help of your judgment in all matters with which you and I have to deal. There is another matter on which I should like to touch, in view of the large part which Service questions play in your proceedings. As you know, a special responsibility is laid upon the Governor to protect the legitimate interests of the Government Services. While firmly adhering to the principle that the Services exist for the administration, and not the administration for the Services, Sir Montagu never faltered in his determination to see that every man had his due. When Service economies and reductions of establishment were unavoidable, he considered their reactions, to my certain knowledge, with the most anxious care, and with the sole desire of giving effect to the wishes of your Council to the farthest extent that was compatible with justice to individuals and with the needs of sound administration. To those principles I intend to adhere, so far as strength lies in me.

One final point. My predecessor was deeply impressed with the value of your Council as a meeting-place for the official and the non-official points of view. To me these past few years, during which it has been my privilege to work in this House, have been years of learning. I remember that many years ago, in fact in my first year of service, my Commissioner concluded a trenchant piece of advice to me as follows—"You will find that in this country you have never ceased learning; and you will find that there is no one, from the highest official down to the humblest patwari, from whom you cannot learn something". I have always been thankful for that advice, and during these latter years especially I have endeavoured to turn it to good account. To grasp the trend of political thought, and to understand the hopes and aspirations of its leaders; to get into the mind of an opponent, and to find out what there is in it with which you can agree, what you must oppose, and in what you can afford to compromise; to put forward your case temperately, and in such a way as to conciliate opposition and not to arouse it; to stand undismayed before a fire of questions, often awkward and embarrassing; to be more wide-awake than sometimes you appear to be—these and many other lessons are to be learnt on the floor of this House. I have endeavoured to learn them myself, and I commend them to all officers of Government who are members of it; for I believe firmly that they can have no more valuable experience.

Gentlemen, I have dwelt at some length on the personal note, because I take it that a Governor's first speech must be largely an occasion for revealing what manner of man he is, or wishes to be accounted. I will now deal with two matters which are of first importance to us all at the moment. The first is our economic situation. On the facts of that situation there is no need for me to dwell. With prices at their present level, and with a cotton crop which is no more than fair, the agriculturist, already sorely tried, has still to face an array of difficulties. But if there has been no marked improvement since you met last, on the other hand there has been no marked deterioration, and though we still have to tighten our belts, the future is not without hope. Elsewhere in the world there is a feeling that the darkest hour has passed, and that the faint streaks of light which are on the horizon presage the dawn. I will not trespass on what the Hon'ble the Finance Member will have to say to you on a later occasion, but I can tell you that we hope to balance our budget both in this year and the next, and pay back some of our overdraft of previous years; and that in itself is no mean achievement in these days. Meanwhile, as you know, my Government continues to watch and is ready to adopt any measure of relief that is within its means and offers any hope of success. In passing the Debt Conciliation Act we made an attempt of the success of which we were by no means confident, but we made it because we felt that we must explore every avenue that was open to us. I am glad to be able to tell you that the two Boards which are working have made a promising start, and that we hope to create a third Board almost at once. When the Act has been extended to Berar we shall start work in that division as well. Here I should like to pay a tribute to the work of the non-official members of the Boards. Their services have involved a heavy sacrifice of time and trouble. The sacrifice has been made without remuneration and has been made ungrudgingly. In order to relieve the burden to some extent, you will be asked in this session to pass an amendment of the Act increasing the maximum number of members of the Boards from five to nine. We shall also ask you to consider in this session two Bills which are designed directly to relieve the agriculturist. One is the Usurious Loans Bill, which is designed to remove certain difficulties experienced in working the Usurious Loans Act—the difficulty, in particular, of adjudging when rates of interest are excessive. The other is the Money-lenders Bill, the object of which is to regulate the transactions of moneylenders and to ensure a fair deal for debtors. I need not say that we shall welcome any advice or suggestions for further relief. But I would ask you not to consider any remedy which is impracticable on the face of it, but to concentrate on what is feasible in the present state of our finances.

The second matter on which I wish to touch is the question of Berar. I regret to say that I am not in a position to tell you more than you know already, namely, that Berar is to be administered, as now, jointly with the Central Provinces. But whatever may be the exact nature of the arrangements which may be made for the future governance of our province, they can make little difference to what is, when all is said and done, the one problem which concerns us vitally, namely, the financial relations between the two parts of the province; and it is because I am convinced that the future happiness of our household under the new constitution will depend very largely on the right solution of that problem that I wish to state it to you quite bluntly and plainly today. The problem is this. One area of a joint administration claims, for reasons the weight of which it is needless to discuss now, that the revenue derived from it should be spent wholly or mainly in it. Those who disagree with this view say that under any unified administration it is in the common interest that the rich area should pay for the poor area, just as the rich man pays taxes for the benefit of his poorer brethren. I shall not attempt to give any indication as to what should be the solution of that problem, beyond saying that my Government has endeavoured to lay the case of both parties as fairly as it could before those in whose hands the framing of the new constitution lies. What I do wish to place before you is this. Firstly, a house divided against itself cannot stand, but must surely fall; and secondly, a solution which is agreed upon between the parties is, generally speaking, better than a solution which is imposed from outside. The province is handicapped already by the small number of seats allotted by the White Paper to it in the Federal Assembly; do not let us weaken ourselves still further in the counsels of the nation by divided interests. Am I expecting too much if I ask the leaders of all parties in the House to get together before the new constitution comes into being, and to agree amongst themselves on a solution of the problem which will be satisfactory and honourable to both sides?

In conclusion, Mr. President, permit me to offer you my congratulations on the honour which has been conferred upon you. And to you, gentlemen of the Council, I extend the greetings of the New Year, with the hope that before it ends the sun may break through the clouds that have overhung us for so long, and shine once more upon our fortunes. As you know, I have extended the life of the present Council because of the great constitutional changes which are impending, in the face of which an election would have been a fruitless waste of energy and money. I am confident that this fresh term of life will be put to good use.

Diary Continues

Thursday January 18th

Got through my first address to the Council. I hate reading a set address, and for two pins I'd break with precedent next time and make them a speech. I suppose I could not do that really, because every word a Governor utters is scanned and weighed with meticulous care, to see whether there's some deep and hidden meaning in it − which there very seldom is! − and one couldn't take the risk of making some unguarded statement. But I have no use for paper oratory. Mitchell told Edna afterwards that it was "Masterly"!

Jan 22nd

The M.C.C. have come and gone, and the C.P. did very much better than anyone expected them to do. Their bowling was never collared, even by Barnett who made 140 in the M.C.C. first innings. The C.P. lost by six wickets − 195 and 188 against 261 and 125 for 4. The match went to the full three days − and we thought that it might be over before tea on the second. Giardini Ricketts (Manager) and Ballantyne stayed with us. J. had rather a good opinion of himself, which isn't surprising, but is very charming and has a pleasant, quiet manner. He's mad keen to shoot a Tiger, and as soon as the match was over we sent him off to Bastar with Ratnam. Bastar is the most likely spot and even there you can't turn tigers out at a moment's notice, I don't imagine. The other two guests are also extremely nice and it has been great fun altogether. Last night we had a dinner first, with all the leading Indian lights of Nagpur, and a reception in the garden afterwards – the Council complete, the C.P. Eleven, all the members of the club and their guests about 300 in all. The garden and house looked lovely lit up, but there was rather a cold breeze blowing, and those who were wise put on overcoats and wraps.

The address has been well received which is a relief. One never quite knows how one's own ideas will appeal to other people, and as I dwelt largely on a personal note I wasn't quite sure whether it would come off. The Hit. complains that I didn't tell them enough secrets – they seemed to think the Berar announcement ought to come from me!! But is otherwise cordial and the Daily News even more so. The bubble popularity. Thank goodness I've never cared for it, and have not consciously sought it. One of his team told us that Jardine refuses deliberately to be popular with them, or at any rate with the professionals because he thinks he can get better work out of them if he isn't. That seems to me to be wrong psychologically.

Thursday January 25th

Laid the cornerstone of a Muslim sarai, and made a short speech. He said as I sat down "nice, human, and not political". I must beware of my fatal facility for stringing words together into what I fondly imagine is picturesque English, or I shall get sloppy and highfalutin. It does seem to me though, that we lack the human touch so terribly in all our official speeches and writings; and that lack reacts upon our work.

Sharif is in great alarm about the "Ministry". He rang me up last night and told me Kedar (leader of the Coalition) would like to see me. K. came this morning. He has dropped his censure motion on the President. It was indefensible from any point of view, and the party have over-ruled him. But he thinks that Rao and the President (close friends) are combining to get the ministry into trouble. The President won't give him the seating his party wants in the hall. (I must say I think Rizvi foolish in this, and wrong. But I'm not butting in.) Also, K. says that the Independents like Manmohan Singh, B.P.Pujasi, Dwarkanath Singh, and so on, are "moving about", and trying to stir up trouble for the party, and that they must be getting their inspiration from Rao. Where else? Because that little crowd doesn't make any move on its own. I know Rao and Sharif distrust each other, but they've always been perfectly friendly at Govt. meetings, and I can't believe that Rao is not playing straight. He has nothing to gain by a change of ministers. Anyhow I talked to Rao, and merely said that this Council mustn't go and spoil the effect of having kept the last Ministry going for 2½ years by chopping and changing as they used to do, and that if he found that the Hindi members were up to any tricks he must try and keep them straight. He assured me quite frankly that the "Coalition" party were so uncoalited, so to speak, that they were always on the jump about possible break-aways, and that as a matter of fact the danger of an attack on the Ministry had passed for this session. Hemeon has just rung up to say that there's no no-confidence motion in for today.

Friday Jan. 26th

A string of "beggars". First Seth Thackurdas Goverdhandas, the Council bore, wanting a title for himself. I'll ask Burton. Then Sir M.B. Dadabhoy pressing once more the claims of Sir Biseshwardas to a K.C.I.E. I'd love to get it for him, because I think he deserves it, but the difficulty is that the recommendation has been made at least twice already, and not accepted. Should I let that deter me from making a recommendation that I believe to be right? The answer is in the negative. Then came Jaiswal, wanting me to back him in applying for a license to start a distillery in Delhi, save the mark! I told him my position in such matters was a delicate one, but if etc. etc. He told me one or two interesting things. Apparently the Hindu Mahasabha, Munje's show, is the devil behind the scenes at present. It doesn't like the fact that the President and Vice-President of the Council, the Pres. of the M.C., Nagpur, and one of the Ministers, are all Muslims. So first they instigated Kedar, leader of the Coalition, to draft a motion for Rizvi's (the H.P.'s) removal. That would have been a bad move – bad if it was (as it wasn't) a genuine attack on him for giving a ruling that K. didn't like, because the passing of such a motion would make the position of the chair impossible; and worse, if it was (as it would have been) a mere move in the party game, because the chair must be outside that game. Luckily K. thought better of the matter. So now the Sabha is proceeding to try and break up the Coalition, and from the result of what was regarded as a test division yesterday, they are succeeding. It is unlikely that any move against the Ministry will be made today, but it's pretty clear that an attack will come in the budget session. N.B. Some of the nominated members and Independents voted with the Nationalists, as Kedar told me that they would do yesterday. Jaiswal also tells me that the Chhattisgarhi members only stick to Naidu because Rao has told them to do so. And Naidu is the leader (with Khaparde) of the Opposition. They're a funny crowd – each playing for his own hand, and with as much cohesion as grains of dry sand. Even the Muslims, a small band of seven, who one would have thought, would have banded together in self-defence, are as disunited as the rest, and after having yowled for a Muslim minister can't stick him now they have got him. And among them all moves Pande, like a mischievous schoolboy, posing always as the champion of the oppressed rayat (peasant), (whose cause he hinders by his inability to distinguish between fact and fancy) and always out to create trouble for someone. He has a keen nose for garbage.

The Bihar earthquake is a terrible business; the more one feels a bit, the worse it grows. I issued an appeal backing up H.E. the V's and Commissioners have been told to get up local committees. Unfortunately we already had to relieve our own local unfortunates after the September flood and funds are low and now there's news of frost in the northern districts. It really does seem as if things could not go right. The rati crops were excellent before this.

Sat. Jan 27th

Rizvi came and had a talk this morning. He says the Council spared the Ministry largely because it was felt not to be fair that I should have to tackle the formation of a new Ministry at once. But there is little chance of the Ministry surviving the budget - not because they've done anything wrong, but merely because their selection as Ministers by M.B. was unexpected, and they have no particular personal following. Gordon, who was also here, thinks that his colleague is clearly planning his political future far ahead, and is arranging the board as he thinks will suit him best. Meanwhile we're going to look into the idea of having a 5-crore loan to enable rayats to compound their debts at -/8/-. I can't imagine that it will be feasible. I'm also going to have my idea examined, of Govt. taking the present chance of buying up landlords cheap and turning their villages into rayatwari. I'm convinced that we could have no finer investment. But it's obviously a matter in which one would have to proceed with great caution.

Note (JHBG):

5-crores of Rupees was worth about £3¾ m.
-/8/- means 8as in the rupee, or 50%.

Sat. Feb. 3rd

The last day of a very pleasant and interesting four days as the guest of the Nawab of Bhopal – a man of great character and an attractive personality. He has been the best of hosts, and everything has been done for us that we could want. Tuesday he had a 10 ft. 5 in. tiger for us – and Morrison, my P.S., shot at and wounded it, just as it had got to the spot which I had marked down as the first target, and was drawing a bead on it! (He and Holmes, A.D.C., were in the same machán as I was) Said I took so long to shoot that he thought he'd better! As he made no attempt to apologise, I had him up in the evening and drove it into his head *(adjective 'thick' crossed out! J.G.)* that the tiger was being brought out for me, and that my P.S. had no business to shoot before me, however long I might be in firing. It took quite a long time to make him see that H.H.s don't arrange tiger shoots for the benefit of P.S.s. It's not pleasant having to din that sort of thing into a man and come the Governor over him, but he forced me to it by being so stupid. It's just the same over the household expenses; unless I drive into it he never thinks about economy where my money is concerned. I love entertaining and it's a great pleasure to be able to give people a good time, but I do not like seeing money thrown down the drain. Wed. We had a sand grouse shoot, great fun, though I shot badly and only got 23 birds. Malcolm got 24 and H.H. 29 but I had much the best stand. But I haven't had much chance to keep my eye in during the past 15 years in Nagpur. Yesterday we went out to Chiklod, where H.H. is building himself a retreat-lake, swimming baths, squash court, gymnasium even a digging pit, where H.H. keeps himself fit – an example we might all follow. What with the above and lunches and dinners each day we have had a busy and most enjoyable visit Col Lucas Mil. Sec. was kindness itself.

Friday Feb 9th

Back in Nagpur after three most interesting and enjoyable days at the

Viceroy's house – an amazing building beyond the reach of criticism. The gardens, ending in the beautiful sunken garden were perfect in design and a dream of colour, and I'd sooner stand looking up through them at the serene and flawless outline of the great house beyond them before any other man-made view that I have seen as yet — even including the Taj, which is petty in comparison. Their Excellencies were kindness itself, and one couldn't have wished for more charming hosts. A first visit of such a nature is bound to be rather alarming in prospect, but they made us feel from the start that we were honoured guests whom they were glad to see, and when we were going Lady W. astonished E. by kissing her and saying she was sorry we were going away. And then of course no one can help liking E.. I've made one friend, I think, General Sir N.M. Eastern Command. He put it across me badly on the Lodhi links and is now under solemn obligation to pay us a visit next October in Pachmarhi, and give me my revenge on my home course. According to what Sir N.M. told me is a daily custom, we dined out every night, the Bhores (he stayed with me when the Simon Commission came to Nagpur), the C. in C. (who has the best chef in India), and in the Haigs (he was at New College with me). We met a number of very nice people, but I do long to be able to go and talk to whom I want to, instead of having a string of good ladies brought up to make conversation for a stated period! One of the little drawbacks of my position that I've got to get used to. At the C. In C.'s dinner we had one real treat – besides the dinner and an excellent champagne Victor Cazalet, a wandering M.P. of great parts, sat down and played to us on the piano – just things that wandered into his head, it seemed. Lady M. (wife of the above), who was talking to me at the time and who is a trained pianist, went into rhapsodies "listen to that! I played that once at a concert in Brussels. He's got no business to be able to do all these things so well". We also lunched with the Grahams, where we met our very old friends the Mitchells, whom I hadn't seen for many years, and with the Schusters, another old New College man. In between all this and the inevitable sight-seeing I had interviews with Glancy, Haig and Schuster. Glancy, who seemed rather tired (he was dealing with the Princes Protection Bill in the L. A.) was not informative as to the main point over the future of Berar, namely whether it is to be administered as British India, the present legal fictions being swept away. He surprised me by saying that he had warned Hydari about the dangers of durbars, and thought they shouldn't be allowed. I hadn't expected that after the G/I left, saying that our fears were misplaced. When I talked to him about the Finance problem, he seemed inclined to think that it was a matter for the F.D. – which it is, of course, partly, but it's the political Department which has to settle what the constitution is going to say about finance. I asked Haig about a High Court, and he says that we could have it when we were able to pay for it. Goodness knows when that will be. But if Orissa gets one with the aid of its subsidy, we shall have to claim help too. He told me that the G/I quite approved of the line we took over Gandhi, though they thought it wise not to tie the hands of other provinces by telling them to do likewise. Schuster and J.D. Taylor were very helpful over the main problem – how to get the present cheap money down to the agriculturalist so as to relieve the burden of debt. I gather that they'll let us have what money we want, within reason, if we can evolve a scheme. As regards the C.P. the idea that I want tested is to let the malguzars have loans under security of their villages, both to pay off their own debts and possibly also (though Gordon sees difficulty in this) to gain cheap loans to tenants. In Berar the only course seems to be to start land mortgage banks, on much less stringent conditions than we have imposed so far. The two banks we started recently have done nothing because the conditions are too severe. S. asked me if it would be any good giving out a large loan for road and bridge building both to put money into the countryside and ultimately to improve our resources. The first reason is good – but the burden of interest and maintenance would be crushing. The second would have no effect on the present crisis no amount of new roads would ease the burden of debt.

I had an interview with H.E. on my last evening. He was very charming and finished up by saying I was a most satisfactory governor – because I had asked him for nothing! Not likely that I should, until I'm much more sure of my standing than I am at present. He talked to me chiefly of certain happenings which do not concern this record, but the moral was –" don't ask for yourself; and if you don't get what you want don't squeal". I suppose the squealers think that the chance of getting their prize is worth the sacrifice of pride. But if they haven't been chosen in the first place, what chance have they not getting the decision reversed? The only occasion when I've ever known it to come off - (deleted) appointment as C.C.F. has been a cause of much groaning ever since. A mule in a fog.

Tuesday Feb. 13th

Dr. Munje has just been to see me about his "Military Academy". Apparently it is to coach boys for Dehra Dun, but as there are not likely to be more than 2 or 3 vacancies a year for the C.P., the others will go into the I.C.S., the Police, "or any other Service" – the usual vagueness. I pointed out to him that, so far as I knew, military institutions were run in every country by the State, and not by private individuals, and he admitted practically that the objective was camouflage, designed to attract pupils and to foster a spirit of discipline – sadly wanted. I told him that we should sympathise with any effort to improve physique and, or morale, and asked him how much money he had got to start his school. The sum – also vague – appeared to be about Rs. 5,000, whereas to start and run such a show properly he would need nearer 5 lakhs! The cat, of course, came out of the bag a day or two later, when Macnee told me that M. had asked him if Govt. would object to his appointing

Behere (vide Wed. 27th Sept. above) headmaster. Really the inhabitants of this country amaze me sometimes. Here is the leading spirit of the Hindu Mahasabha, a rabidly communal organization, asking Govt. to smile upon an institution which usurps one of the chief functions of Govt., and is to be under the headship of a man who has been sacked from Govt. service for extolling the murderers of Govt. officers. It's worse than Kokar Dekar and his Sports Association, or the egregious Patwardhan (ex R.F.C. mechanic and builder of hotels) and his Flying Club. Their intriguing reminds me of the burrowing moles – the only person who is in the dark is the mole.

The Ministers had a bad break while I was away. The Dt. Councils in Berar (and elsewhere) are due for re-election, and they got hold of Chaubal and got him to persuade Sharif to agree to a prolongation of their lives. I heard of this as soon as I returned, and called a meeting of Govt. at once. We had recently given the Bilaspur Council a fresh lease of life, for very special reasons connected with law and order in that somewhat "difficile" tract; but that decision was a different matter to a general prolongation. Sharif was forced to admit that a general order would be illegal, and would certainly be attacked, and I put it to them both that they were playing a dangerous game in allowing it to be said that they were violating the law in order to benefit their own friends. Then they gave in. But I do not think the better of them for their effort. It's funny how ready a lawyer is to drive a coach and four through the law as soon as it suits his purpose to do so.

Sund. Feb. 25th

Kedar came and saw me this morning. He seems to think the Ministry may survive. If it doesn't, he talked about an alliance between his followers, numbering 16, and the 11 Nationalists, which he said would be "absolutely unbreakable". Huh! I gather that at the moment they are all buzzing about, intriguing, bargaining. Of real complaint against the Ministry they have none, except that they are trying to get at Sharif because of our circular saying that local bodies shouldn't let their servants join Rashtryia Swagam Sewak Sangh. On that we are on safe ground – or at any rate on ground which we cannot surrender. The R.S.S.S. is a rabidly communal organization – Munje's, needless to say – the proclaimed object of which is to train Hindu youths on Nazi lines and make the caste Hindus supreme in the commonwealth. And no government which draws its money from the general taxpayer can allow its servants to a show like that, or let the servants of local bodies join it. But the whole problem of our control over these men is a very difficult one. Our powers are indefinite, and we are always in danger of being drawn into that worst of errors – threatening things that we cannot enforce. As, for instance, when they employ c.d. convicts.

Wed Feb 28th

E. is trying to help on Mrs Seaman's scheme for village nursing. Wilson, the new I.G.C.H. has written a note crabbing it. We had him up and talked to him and tried to convey to him as gently as possible that I had no use for the crabbers. The main thing if you want to get anything done is to try, and if one remedy – whether for the apathy or unavoidable suffering in a village or for the deities of a countryside – doesn't succeed, to try another. E. and I both feel that G., good as he is, is a bit inclined sometimes to get into the "I feel that this is impractical" tack. It's one of the main sources of the unpopularity of my service with many people – we're too critical of other people's efforts.

Sund. March 4th

The budget session is in full swing, and the main interest is the fate of the Ministry. The first attack came on Co-Op. Credit, when there was a lot of mud-slinging – it's a pretty rotten show, from top to bottom – and the voting was equal, the President giving his casting vote for Govt.

The next was on Industries, and the Ministry won by 3 votes. Yesterday it was the turn of the P.W.D., and they won by 7 votes. "From strength to strength!" All the little dummy voters, the sais, the barber, the gaoli, the lawyer's clerk, and so on, are being canvassed and petted and coaxed. A degrading spectacle. Rao is being accused right and left of working against the Ministry, but I don't intend to take any notice. He has never shown the slightest hostility to the Ministry in the Cabinet; on the contrary, he has taken upon his own shoulders the task of facing the music over the R.S.S.S. circular, which will not add to his popularity. And Gordon says that he has exerted himself personally in Council to get votes for the Ministers. Kedar is the moving spirit behind the suggestions. I had a letter from Monty the other day, reminding me of Ps.120 -"Deliver my soul, O Lord, from lying lips, and from the deceitful tongue... ...Woe is me, that I dwell in Meseck, that I sojourn in the tents of Kedar"!!

We've had the house full of soldiers lately – General Geoffreys, S. Command, General Baird, Secunderabad Division and Brig. Ling from Jubb. All bringing a breath from the outside world into the somewhat stifling atmosphere of Nagpur. Yesterday Sir R. Spence D.G.M. came to bid us a formal goodbye. He will be much missed – a genial and kindly personality with a heart as big as his body; one of the not very large number of persons who live Masonically.

Monday March 5th

The plot thickens. Kedar rang up last night to ask if he could see me this morning. It appears that the members spent yesterday in pulling wires, telling tales, and generally buzzing about. Some people for their own ends want to drag Rao and even Gordon into the vortex of intrigue that is going on, and have been inventing ridiculous stories of Rao having promised one man a title and another an H. Magistracy, and so on, if they would vote against the Ministry. Sharif and Chaubal came to see me just when Kedar was expected and were evidently prepared to chuck their hands in. When they told me the stories that were going about, I asked if they had any proof, and they suggested that I should send for the persons concerned. I then asked them if they thought it would be right for me to hold a sort of departmental enquiry into the conduct of one of my own colleagues, and they admitted that it would not. Then I sent for Rao and Gordon, and in the meantime saw Kedar, who told me he hadn't slept a wink all night because of what was going on. He being in the thick of it – he hates Rao – I am not surprised. He repeated the same stories, but he had no proof except what A said to E, and C overheard D say to E, and so on. When Rao and Gordon came, I put the matter straight to them, and Rao said at once quite frankly that various people had been to him to ask which way they should vote, that it was all very embarrassing to him, and that he had tried to steer clear of being mixed up in the business as far as possible. I then called the Ministers in, and told them as above, and suggested to them that everyone seemed to be losing their heads a bit over the canards that are flying around, and that until (a) they receive an adverse vote in the Council, or (b) they can point to some definite act on the part of the reserved side of Govt. which impedes them in the discharge of the obligations, they should keep calm and not get flurried. They seemed to agree. I also pointed out to them that there were just as many people interested in getting at Rao as at them, and that, while they could defend themselves, he was tongue-tied through being Member, and could not take an active part in party politics. They should therefore discount any tale which brought him into the arena of intrigue. Once again they agreed. But goodness knows how long they'll keep it up. Sharif is not self-seeking, and is quite likely to throw his hand in through disgust. Chaubal is young and has yet to find his feet, and he too may easily (be) stampeded by Kedar. The truth is that this Council is past its best, and I wish I could dissolve it and get a new one.

Tues. March 6th

"Lord, what fools these mortals be!" Two cuts both of an obvious nature, were carried under demand No. 30, Misc. Trans., under which come grants to local bodies, about 6.17 lakhs. Members wanted to call attention to the inadequacy of the grants, now that they have been reduced by F.D.. Everyone knows the local bodies want more money, and the Ministers didn't challenge the division. "Cui bono?" Annoyed at this, the Council chucked out the whole demand by 34 to 32, and now local bodies will get no grants at all! I cannot "authorise" under the G/I Act unless an "emergency" exists, so the only chance of the L.B.'s getting their money is if we put in a fresh demand at the August session. Sharif came to see me this morning again, and asked what he should do. I said, "Do nothing, until the Council has passed a clear vote of no confidence". The Council's action is the worst piece of political tactics I've seen it perform. Everyone seems to be so bemused with intriguing and lack of sleep that they've lost their heads. The majority included Rodgers, P.S.Deskmukh, and Jaiswal, all of whom ought to have known better.

Thurs. March 8th

No cuts against the Ministers on Tuesday, and in an Excise division yesterday they won by 2 votes. A resolution to do away with Commrs. was defeated by 29 votes to 16! Marvellous! Noel says that all those who aspire to the Ministry abstained from voting against the Govt.. What a child's game it all is - just about as much reality or seriousness. Hemeon says there are four "no confidence" motions tabled for today, which is the last budget day. They will probably be taken tomorrow, after the Tobacco Bill. I gather that the members have not yet woken up to their responsibility for demand No. 30. The L.B.'s will jog them sooner or later, and meanwhile we shall make no move.

Kanitkar came to me yesterday and asked me (a) if the resignation of one Minister alone would be accepted and (b) if a combination of the Nationalists and People's Party (old) would be acceptable. I told him that (a) I could not answer hypothetical questions, but (b) if the Ministry fell, I should be prepared to deal with any party that I thought stable.

A lot of twaddle was talked yesterday over the R.S.S.S. circular. Rao is stout, and our position is clear. Govt. has taken no action against the Sangh. It has merely declared that, in view of the open statements of its leaders, it would be embarrassing for Govt. servants to be members of it, and L.B. servants should toe the same line. The point is that we know – and they know that we know – that the Sangh's activities are anything but innocent, and they're afraid that our interdict on Govt. servants is the prelude to more serious action. Which led to a lot of sentimental tosh about improving the physical standard of Indian youth and similar camouflage. Mrs. Tambe was almost tearful, they say. It is a curious thing that these people can never run a show that might be of real benefit to the general physique without directing it against someone — the Hanuman Vayaganishala against Govt., the R.S.S.S. against non-Hindus, the Mahommedan akhoras against Hindus, and so on. They must always be up against someone or something. The longer I live, the more striking does the similarity between the Indian and the Irishman seem to me to be.

Wed. March 14th

The Ministry has fallen. After they had got all demands through except No.30 (above), they had to face two motions of "no confidence". The first, vs. Sharif, was a tie, 34 all, and the president very rightly gave his casting vote against the motion. At the same time he made some remarks about the awkwardness of his position, and the need for the Mins. to consider theirs, which were injudicious. The second, vs. Chaubal, was carried by 35 — 34, Mrs. Tambe being the odd vote, and

Sharif forgetting to vote for his colleague! Both of them, with Kedar, came to me the same evening (9th.) and asked what they should do. Here I nearly made a bad mistake; it was after dinner! I said that all supplies had been voted (except one which did not matter), that the votes of n.c. were practically a drawn battle, and that I saw no reason for them to resign on the spot. Luckily I safeguarded myself by saying that I must both think the matter over and talk it over with Rao and Gordon. The more I thought, the more I failed to see how one could get over the one solid fact that a motion of n.c. had been carried against one of the pair, and that they held office on joint responsibility. To invite them to continue in office would expose me to the charge of having flouted the vote of the Council, and in August the Ministry, instead of marching out with the honours of war (as they have now), would be put to a sticky and ignominious end. R. and G. both agreed without a blink, so I sent for the Mins. (this was the 10th) and put the above to them. They were very decent about it, and agreed that their proper course was to resign. Then I sent for Khaparde, Naidu, and Kedar. K. came first, and said that he was going to join up with Khaparde. Kh. and N. came together, and said that they had no intention of unlinking. So I told them all to send me lists of their followers. From K. I heard nothing more, but next morning Kh. and N. sent me a list which gave them a clear majority in the Council. I have never agreed with the practice of appointing Ministers from among the followers of a party. It is not in accordance with English practice, and has the disadvantage that Ministers are not in the position of authority in their party that a member of Govt, ought to be. So I sent for Kh. and N., and asked them if they would be prepared to accept posts under the usual condition of reasonable support to Govt., and they both accepted without a moment's hesitation. Kedar's organ, "The People's Voice", is furious over the Ministry's downfall and accuses Rao of all sorts machinations. How much truth there is in the stories, no one knows except Rao.

There is the question that to have a Home Member who is an active politician leads to awkward situations. However much he may try, he can't keep clear of all the numberless intrigues that are going on, and much mud is bound to be thrown at him. Generally speaking, the Ministry has been well received by the Press, especially Khaparde.

Jubb. March 20th

A brief tour Dhuti, Seoni, Jubb., and Saugor to get away from Nagpur which is unpleasant in March and kill time before Pachmarhi – as I don't like going there more than a day or two before Secs.. Seems like taking an advantage of them. Incidentally I am learning how to catch mahseer, as to which everyone tells me something different – and finding out at first-hand what people think of debt conciliation. The tour has had an unexpected result. I have decided to change my P.S.. Morrison seems to have made himself generally disliked because of his failure to look after my guests properly and after all the trouble trying to instil some sense and energy and initiative into him, this is the last straw. (I hear that the lads at Saugor are planning to get him up on a steed that will shake his liver up good and proper!) I wish though I could get rid of my dislike of giving people the sack. It is a weakness which causes me a lot of worry that I could save myself if only I were a bit more ruthless.

Pachmarhi April 4th

There has been nothing of any interest to record during the past fortnight, except that as soon as I got here I had it out with M.. And he agreed that the best thing for him to do was to go back to his regiment. The whole business has been a lesson to me, never to take on a man on trust; but it never occurred to me that anyone especially a man like Tom Kelly, would dream of landing Monty with someone so utterly unsuited to be a P.S.. I'm now going to try one of my own men,

Cole who is reported to be a good man, and who impressed me quite favourably at Jubb., though I'm not sure that he isn't a bit soft. Anyhow I shall be glad of the chance to be giving promotion to one of our own men, as they are rather badly blocked at the moment.

I do wish these politicians would not behave like schoolboys. Kedar and Sharif have gone squealing to Delhi, to interview H.E. and complain presumably of the machinations of Rao. The P.S.V. wired to me yesterday to know if H.E. should see them, and I replied "No". They should come to me first, and if they've got any allegations to make supported by facts and are not mere bazaar gup, I'll hear them. But so far all they have been able to say in substance is that various people gathered at Rao's house during the session. And on that they seem to expect me to impeach my Home Member. Fiddlesticks! They should learn to take defeat sportingly. I had a talk with Rao this morning and told him all that was going on, and he laughed and said he wasn't going to take any notice. But I am becoming seriously concerned about what should be done if they turn the new Ministry out in August. One can't carry on with such a hopeless lot, and I can see no alternative but to dissolve the Council and try and see if one can get a Council that is not so utterly swayed by personal intrigues and wranglings as the present one is. Rao thinks that that will be the best course. But the G/I will simply hate the idea of one Province acting on its own.

There are all the signs of a real stiff hot-weather. I had a fan going on March 30th and on the 1st the maximum was 96 . Not a cloud in the sky, and a heavy haze everywhere. I can't read for half an hour without falling asleep. Luckily the volcano is quiescent for the moment – not even a rumble. The "Berar All-Parties' Conference" – how they do love pretentious titles! – has met under the presidency of that grubby little creature M.S. Aney, and has passed the usual resolutions in favour of separation and so on. No one takes them very seriously now-a-days. But it has been a great mistake to delay the settlement and its announcement so long.

Wednesday, April 11th

G. came back from Delhi without, I am afraid, having gained much inspiration from the surfeit of talk that went on. He says that the U.P. was the only province that has definite ideas but those all seemed to be on the lines of drastic and compulsory debt cancellation; the sacrifice of the creditor to the debtor. All very well but the debtor is as at least as much to be blamed for thriftlessness as the creditor is for bleeding him, and no settlement is any good that does not give both sides a square deal. As for other provinces, we have gone further than any of them, he says, in thinking things out – in fact some of them seem to think that there's no serious problem to be faced; e.g. Bombay says its land revenue is coming in well. We shall know more about it all when the programmes are out.

Cypher from G/I about Gandhi's volte face and the probability of the Swarajists coming into the Councils. They take the right view that we must do everything we can to encourage it, and lift the ban on Congress. All here agree. We shall never get the show running properly until Congress are back in the fold. We may have trouble with them, but better that than go on in our present way, with Achilles sulking in his tent.

G. Says that Kedar and Sharif went buzzing about Delhi, and that Haig saw them and sent them away with a flea in their collective ear. It would be difficult to imagine anything more undignified – especially as it's Sharif's own fault that the Ministry fell. Hemeon says we could get a new Council elected within four to five months of a dissolution. August to January – just time enough, if need be.

Thursday April 12th

After what I said yesterday it is amusing to hear that Hailey has returned the United Provinces Agricultural Relief Bill to the Council, pointing out that they can't play fast and loose with the existing system of credit without running the risk of making things worse than they are at present. I quite agree. There are far too many half–baked ideas about debt cancellation going about.

Yesterday I came across the third "job" perpetrated by Chaubal in his last few days as Minister. He seems to have spent his time trying to gain favour by reinstating people. Unfortunately he chose the worst possible cases, and wasn't clever enough to write an order that was even passably convincing. I have had to upset every case. It's just what Kedar did at the end of his Ministry. What are things going to be like under the new Constitution? "If this ye do in the green tree, what will ye do in the dry?"

Wednesday 18th April.

A difficult meeting of Govt. got over safely. Last year the G/I proposed that we should make Govt. servants responsible for the political misbehaviour of their dependants, and we agreed. The rules came down a short time ago, and both the Ministers disagreed. Khaparde urged that the order was neither reasonable nor capable of enforcement, and that it was a mistake to put Govt. servants' backs up at the moment, when everything is peaceful. G. and I both thought there was a good deal in what he said (The G/I reference was made while I was at home). On the other hand we and Rao all felt (a) that we couldn't back out now and (b) that Govt. must be master in its own house, and has a right to insist that its servants shall be above suspicion, and shall not embarrass it, either personally or through their dependents – and we all know how embarrassing the Nyogi and Munji cases were in 1931. After a little talk, the Ministers agreed that the rules would have to be published for the reserved departments, and that in the circumstances the transferred departments couldn't stand out – and all was well.

I have been suffering lately from people who can't draft, who don't seem to be able to visualise, as they write a letter, what effect it will have on the man at the other end. It always seems to me to be the first requisite in a really good officer that he should have imagination and a sense of form for humanity, call it what you will. So much of our work in this country, excellent in quality as it is, loses its effect because it is mechanical, and infused by human feeling. And it's a toilsome business having to rewrite as many drafts as I do. I suppose I'm too pernickety.

Yet another case of the administration existing for the services instead of vice versa. Two C.C.F.s are wanted, the Punjab in August and the C.P. now. Whitehead of the U.P. (cheek by jowl with the Punjab) is senior, and a year junior come Parker and Bell in that order. We pressed hard for Bell (C.P.), because we must have a man who knows our problems and troubles, especially after the prominent part which foment grievances played in the troubles of 1930 and '31. But no. Seniority is all that matters in the eyes of the G/I and we are to have Whitehead thrust upon us. As the G/I blandly remarks "he has served for a time in Jhandi where conditions are not dissimilar to those in the C.P." A sheer incitement to profanity. The whole matter is that in the I.F.S. as in the I.M.S., they don't care two hoots about sacrificing a man's knowledge and experience – including the ability to speak the local tongue – nor about the good of the provinces. All that matters is that there should be an even flow of promotion among the grey-heads. Some day when I'm feeling in real fighting trim I'm going to put the whole case before the G/I, and try and get them to see what a scandal it all is. But I haven't a hope that I shall do any good. An ear is not, I believe, one of the organs with which a barnacle is blessed.

Sat April 28th

Human nature is a strange thing. Dendy (G.S.O.I. Secunderabad) tells me that C.M.'s regiment had no more use for him than I had so then why did Tom Kelly try to plant him on the Butlers? The longer I live the surer I am that although the second thoughts are best in the most things, in judgements of men first impressions are the ones to go by.

When I first set eyes on my late P.S. – at a lunch at the Savoy to which I had asked him – I said to myself "that is not my man" and should have saved myself much worry if I'd acted on that.

Sunday April 29th

A small piece of encouragement for the last three years the appointment has – "more Indico" – in any matter of acute political controversy. There is a good man in the Department whom every official knows to be the man for the job, but for some unknown reason the politicians were up against him. The case has dragged on, and last November I had to refuse to override the Minister, who wanted to turn Bál (our man) down and get a man from Bengal. Luckily the latter eventually refused to come and the case has to be started all over again, (how typical that is of an official methods!) and now Khaparde, the present Minister has come out with a slashing note, in which he refuses to hear of the appointment of anyone save Bál! A sign of grace. In my note on the case I took the opportunity of saying that it was a thousand pities that a purely departmental affair like this should have been allowed to become a political issue. Place hunting and job hunting – I'm afraid they are the strongest influences in the C.P. world of politics.

The "People's Voice" – run by a sanctimonious M.B. who has as much real sympathy with democracy as a mediaeval baron – asks why Sharif "was compelled to come out of office", when the n.c. vote was passed against Chaubal only, and points to the case when R.M. Deshmukh resigned, and Rao didn't. There is, of course, no similarity between the cases. R.M.D. resigned because he had quarrelled with his leader. But apart from that, the idea that Sharif could remain in office without Chaubal, when Ch's downfall had been caused by Sh's failure to record his vote, shows how little these people know of even the A.B.C. of sportsmanship. I will do Sharif the credit of saying that he never suggested such an idea himself, and fully admitted the principle of joint responsibility.

Monday April 30th

I seem to have much to learn in regard to the capacity of human nature for springing surprises on one – also as to how to treat a woman! Doris B. who is always crusading on behalf of someone, found a hair-dresser in Jubb.. A widow woman with children, who was losing all her trade in the hot weather, and can see it the brilliant idea of getting up to Pachmarhi, and letting them use the G.H. electric installation. (Imagine the look of disgust and annoyance that would have spread over Monty's face if such a proposition had been made to him!) So she makes things up with Malcolm Holmes the A.D.C. and this morning she wrote to M. with final suggestions. Unfortunately it hadn't occurred to either of them, that we might object to having a part of G.H. turned into a barber's shop with cars coming in and out at all hours of the day, and Malcolm who is not very far seeing, was quite surprised when I turned the idea down flat. I always tease Doris about her "bossiness", because it is merely an energetic person trying to help other people – she does more good work than most of the other wives of officers put together – but this time I had to explode. I wrote and said "Definitely nothing doing".

Wednesday May 2nd

The male hand is rougher than it realised. I had an abject letter of apology from D. yesterday, and she told me afterwards that when she got my letter she burst into tears, and could barely get her face right in time for tennis! She made me feel a beast, and set me wondering whether I had been right in my refusal. But I know I was and E. agrees. However one may wish to ease off the grimness of G.H. , one cannot have it turned into a place of public resort. And a few tears never did anyone any harm.

It's an exciting job keeping these Ministers away from pitfalls. Today a petition came in, asking Govt., to upset in revision an order of the D.C. Amraoti, refusing to postpone certain proceedings in connection with the Dt. Cl. election, which were due to take place at noon today. There was nothing to show the locus standi of the petitioner no statement of the facts of the case, not even a copy of the order appealed against. And yet the Ministers wanted to interfere, because they had inside knowledge of what was going on, and were afraid that their party interests would be prejudiced. I put it to them – and Rao and G. backed me up stoutly – that Govt., couldn't go off half-cock like that, on the basis of a document that no revisional court, whether criminal, civil or revenue, would even look at; and that if it did, the Minister would find it very difficult to face the music in Council. Eventually they saw the wisdom of keeping their feet out of the tarmac, and said that they were willing to leave the matter to my discretion – which I exercised by turning the petition down offhand. They seem a reasonable pair, and Kh. has passed at any rate one really good order.

Cypher from H.E. yesterday. Wheat prices are expected to break still further, and he suggests a conference to see if anything can be done to stop the fall. It does seem as if things never could get better for the wretched tiller of the soil. ODTAA.

Wednesday May 9th

See Wed. 2nd May. We had a lucky escape. In spite of our refusal to interfere, the Ministers' party (Nationalist) carried the day at the L.B. elections, and the Shetkari Sangh (P.S. Deshmukh's lot) were discomforted. P.S.D., who is up here for a Select Comm., told G. that what really annoyed them was that Govt. has refused to interfere, "because then they'd have had a real good grievance!" So my instinct was correct. Not that the whole business wasn't pretty obvious. What astonishes me is that a wily old bird like Khaparde can't see when there's a pitfall like that in front of him.

A bombshell from the G/I. The U.P. have a wonderful plan for creating a new Heaven and a new Earth. Unfortunately it involves borrowing 10 crores from the G/I for loans to encumbered Estates, and the G/I have shied clean off the course, and have written round to us all to say that if we want to get money for this purpose we must raise it by issuing provincial bonds in the local money market. That knocks our scheme for buying up indebted landlords on the head, because I am quite certain we couldn't raise the money locally at sufficiently low rates to make it worth our while.

Thursday May 10th

Whitehead the new C.C.F. came to see me this morning – quiet and rather shy, but struck me as having character, and obviously a vast improvement on his predecessor. I told him I'd like to see the C.C.F. become what it was in the days of George Sankey Hart. He's drifted at present into being merely the administrative head of the Forestry Department, instead of being Government's technical informant and adviser, as he was intended to be. He showed signs of jibbing at my pet scheme of confining the Forest Act and the activities of the Department to high forestry areas, or at any rate areas in which tree culture is the first consideration. But I'm certain that the idea is sound from every point of view, financial, administrative, and political, and I intend to go ahead.

The decision of the Swarajists to enter the Assembly and there to damn the White Paper has had an amusing effect in the Liberal camp. Hitherto the Liberals, in the approved huckster fashion, have said that the W.P. scheme was worthless, and utterly insufficient to satisfy the "national demand" – how they love these bombastic cant phrases! All they want, of course, is to extort more, like any bazaar banya. Now they see the Diehards gaining strength every day in England, and a new cloud arising on the Indian horizon, and they are getting frightened lest between the two forces of reaction and extremism, the forces of sober progress may suffer defeat. So they're beginning to hedge, and to say that although the W.P. is a poor scheme, "of course we'll accept it and make the best of it." Vide the Daily News, Leader, Hitavada, and I daresay others. Tragic as any disaster to the W.P. would be, I'd dearly love to see the face of Sapici or Sitalvad or Shastri when he heard that it had been wrecked. And it would have been their own fault entirely. Had they acknowledged the essential merits of the scheme from the start like honest men, they'd have taken away from the Diehards one of their most potent weapons – the taunt that we're trying to force on India a constitution no Indian is ready to accept.

Sat May 12th

I suppose that after 20 pretty strenuous years one ought really to be grateful for an easy time. But at present I'm getting about 2 to 3 hours work a day, and sometimes barely as much as that, and I find it frankly boresome. At any other time of the year I shouldn't mind, as I should go out of doors. No one can do that now and the consequence is that all afternoon I sit in an armchair and fall asleep while trying to read – which is bad for both body and soul.

An amusing instance of how ridicule will sometimes affect one's object where reason has failed. The secretary of the Golf Club is one of those persons who have an inverted sense of humour, and it occurred to him that it would be amusing to build a bunker just out of sight over the brow of the hill at the third, and then listen to what people said when they found a real good looking drive trapped (as a fact I have cleared the hill several times by 6 to 8 feet, only to find my ball in the bunker). Everybody said what a rotten bunker they thought it, but the committee whose knowledge of golf architecture is not extensive would do nothing. So I christened the bunker "Murcot's Folly". And yesterday the men were at work pulling it down! By tomorrow we shall be rid of an offence and an eyesore.

Wednesday May 23rd

Some time ago I went into the question (confidentially) of the length of time it would take to get a new council elected if I dissolved this one in August. I found it would take seven months, which was too long, so I chucked the idea. But I left the file openly on my shelves, and now "our Pachmarhi correspondent" informs the Statesman that the council is to be dissolved in August! Shouting it from the house tops is not the only way of getting an idea abroad – and it won't do the Council any harm to think that they are not there for keeps.

The question of the extent to which we should object to local bodies employing political exconvicts is always with us. Today we discussed a proposal to prohibit it by law, as Bengal have done. But the Bengal problem is v. different to ours, as our local bodies don't employ terrorists and murderers, and we all agreed that the proper way to deal with the matter was to take each case on its merits, and not go in for any legal fulminations. The whole business of our relationships with local bodies is a wearisome and distasteful one to me. They seem utterly unable to realise how inefficient & blatant they are – and how corrupt.

Friday May 25th

The G/I have at any rate one God-like attribute. They are always on the side of the big battalions. The smaller provinces have complained that the road fund should be used for the development of road in tracks where they are wanted, instead of being largely devoted to subsidising the provinces where cities are many and big, and petrol consumption disproportionately large. The G/I practically admit the fairness of our claim, but turn it down because they say the bigger provinces would object. That's the spirit that a man should show! Meanwhile when they want us to take Bengal terrorists or Afghan detainees off their hands nothing is too nice for them to say. They're trying to land us with five of the latter at the moment.

CHAPTER 4

Sat May 26th

My dear E. has gone home for five months, and I shall miss her as much as I always do. She has been splendid in her part, and couldn't have played it better. But she made me sad the other night by telling me that my five years in this job would put ten years onto her age, because she had wanted very badly to go for good next year, when I had always intended to retire, and hated the thought of three more restless and unsettled years, by the end of which she would be 60. I know just what she feels, and I dislike the thought of them myself; in fact the only things that will keep me out here are the need to save a little money, of which I've acquired parlous little so far, and one's natural dislike of chucking a job that has been entrusted to one.

Tues. May 29th

Rao came and had a talk this morning. He thinks they may attack the Ministry in the next session, but won't get the 22 necessary members to stand up for the n.c. motion. Khaparde is secure enough, but the Hindu members are fed up with Naidu because he was appointed instead of one of them. There's been more talk in the papers about Council being dissolved, and Rao says it all started with a chance question I put to Fulay when he came and saw me last month. It must have been something quite innocuous, because I have no recollection of putting it, but these people fasten on one's every word, spoken or written, in order to discover what deep significance lies behind it – the answer in most cases is exactly nix!

Rao says that when the new constitution comes in, the Council will probably agree to the first Pach. season, but not to the October one. If they do, it would not be possible to resist them. Pach. is doubtless very pleasant at that time of year, but no one can possibly maintain that work in Nagpur is intolerable then. And I'm not sure it won't be rather pleasant to be saved the additional house-shifting. One could perfectly

104

well come up here for a time on tour, without all the elaborate bandobast that the second season involves at present. Marnabb, A.G.G. Indore, has just come for a week's visit. I like getting into personal touch with those with whom we have to deal as our official neighbours. It saves a lot of misunderstanding sometimes, and incidentally brings one into contact with some charming and interesting people.

Tues. June 5th

Yesterday was amusing, if somewhat tiring day. We started with the annual civil versus military golf match (on handicap) 22 a side. Singles in the morning and they were one up. Foursomes in the afternoon and we were two up, and just scraped home. A great fight especially as a large number of matches went to the last green. I won both my matches there – two up against Maurice Wright, and two up with Eyre against M.W and Col. Pearson. And then in the evening came the birthday dinner which was quite a good show. I said I'd ask 40 which is usually the G.H. limit and then other people turned up whom I wanted to ask and we expanded to 46. Macnair amused me "jolly good dinner" he said " usually at these shows one gets hold of a tough bit of meat of some sort that one can't get one's teeth into, but they gave me some chickeny stuff that I thought was first rate". It was Pyrke's best pheasant! After dinner I did my duty and talked to all the Indian officers, but I always feel that the effort is a failure. When one has spent one's service among the soft races of the C.P. it is very hard to enter into the thoughts and ideas of a P.M., Risaldar, or a Havildar from Nepal. Still, they were all very nice and all had a nice firm hand grip.

Friday June 8th

People by their gratitude make one feel ashamed sometimes of the cheap and easy way in which one earns it – merely by spending on them a certain portion of one's abundant salary. Macnabb after thanking me for his visit, says "and may I add as an outsider, that it did not take me long to realise how very appreciative people were of your unusual kindness to the younger and more hard up".

I have been uneasy sometime over our policy of telling local bodies not to employ c.d. convicts on pain of having their grants docked. The Jubb. M.C., whose president is Misra, Govind Das's "friend", have defied us, and we have cut their grants. Tomorrow we are issuing orders taking the ban off Congress organizations, and c.d. will be then be dead officially. These c.d. convicts have committed no criminal offence in any but a technical sense; how then can one refuse to allow their employment on the ground that they belong to a movement which has ceased to exist? Further, I dislike issuing an order which I am not in a position to enforce by law or rule. I sent for the ministers this morning, and found we all thought alike. Then I sent for Rao and G. and they too agreed that we should take the opportunity to withdraw the ban in this particular case. (We don't want to lay down any principles, but just to deal with each case as it arises, e.g. some of the Nagpur conspiracy case men might come into the question later on. That would be a different matter.)

Mond. June 11th

Had a meeting of Govt. this morning, and we decided to cancel the order about grants to the Jubb. M.C. At the same time they have appointed a Sec. without our sanction, and on that we've got to stand no nonsense, as the law is behind us. I shall be glad when the Jubb. business is over. Misra is the type of man who makes one feel contaminated when one has to deal with him.

Saturday June 16th

In the last of my string of visitors has gone. It has been very nice having them, but I think I overdid it this year. At any rate it is a relief to be alone – except for Waterfall, who has just come back from leave and is to take N.J.'s place, and has come for a day or two. Next year I shall concentrate more – have the house quite full for 10 days and empty for a week.

We're writing to the G/I to persuade them to let us have money to lend to malguzars and to buy up villages with. It's seldom that one is in the position of scoring whatever happens. If the malgos. repay their loans, well and good: we've saved our agriculturalist. If they don't equally well and good. We've got rid of an incubus. Only along the line of the gradual expropriation of the malguzar is there any real chance of bettering our finances. And the going will never be as good as it is now, with money cheap and land values at rock-bottom.

Friday June 22nd

These politicians really are a priceless lot. "The People's Voice", having hotly attacked the Ministry for the order stopping the Jubb. M.C's. grants (see Friday, June 8th) now turn round and attack it equally hotly – and incidentally me, for not dismissing the Ministers – because the order has been withdrawn, simultaneously with the withdrawal of the ban on Congress. "Lowering the prestige of Govt.", "encouraging every local body to resist Govt.", and so on – bless me, the most sundried bureaucrat of us all couldn't have done better! The truth is that they had hoped to have the order as a stick to beat the Ministry with at the next session, and are now very cross because it's been taken out of their hands. "Woe is me that I sojourn in Merek, that I dwell in the tents of Kadar" said the Psalmist; and then "I am for peace but when I speak they are for war". But it's disheartening to think that one has got to spend four more years in this atmosphere. "Deliver my soul, O Lord, from lying lips, and from a deceitful tongue." Monty's psalm comes in useful.

CHAPTER 4

Tuesday June 26th

The Jubb M.C. have caved in over the matter of the Secretary. We told the Imperial Bank, which holds the Municipal funds, that they paid money out to the new Secretary at their own risk, and they promptly stopped paying. That brought Misra to his senses, and he caved in. The Hit. says that the withdrawal of Govt's order has been a "victory" for the "National Press". Needless to say, there's no acknowledgment of Government's response to a popular wish. The local press is not exactly famous for the generosity of its spirit.

A more refreshing matter is a meeting of the All-India co-operative workers at Amraoti, where Khaparde made a very sensible speech, and where there was much evidence of a refusal to lose faith in the movement, and a general wish to overcome present difficulties and pull the movement round. Abuses, failures, recurring crises, and the usual inability of the Indian to keep business away from politics have driven Government into a very critical attitude with regard to the whole structure of co-operative credit – more especially in view of the determined effort made by Kelkar, the first Minister, to pervert it to political uses – but one must have faith and do what one can to help those who are genuinely trying to pull the movement round. Bramha's the best of them. Some people say that we ought to let the movement collapse. But anything in the nature of a crash could bring great suffering, and I am sure that our right policy is to avoid it at all costs.

The monsoon broke on the 19th – in the moon's first quarter, which will please the cultivator. He still retains the belief that any process connected with growth must be done under the waxing moon, and not the waning. Signs are propitious so far. But we have had five good monsoons running, and five harvests spoilt to a greater or less degree by calamities in the cold weather; and it makes one anxious when one thinks how small a reserve we have for meeting even a partial failure of the rains.

Wed. June 27th

I had a talk with Rao this morning on the situation in general. Today Reuter says that the Constitution Act won't be passed till the end of 1935 – which means Nov. '36 at the earliest for the new order of things. We shall have to have a Council election before then, surely. Rao thinks, and I agree, that it would be a good thing to get the Congress back into the Council before the new Act comes into force. They will then have got over their first exuberance, and will treat the new constitution soberly, whereas if they and it come in together, they will be above themselves altogether, and will kick their heels up too freely. He thinks the Ministry is safe for the present, and was greatly tickled by the die-hard leader in the P.V. about the Jubb. case. He said at once, as I did, that they're cross because they've lost the stick with which they hoped to beat the Ministers. He described Kedar as a man with plenty of brains and no judgment. I agree – though I should add to the negatives! He (Rao) says that congress is now very keen to get into the Council, and that there is simply nothing moving politically in the province except K.P. Pande's effort to stir up agrarian trouble and Shukla's attempt to work up an agitation against irrigation rates. We are going to meet the former by levelling down high rents in Jubb. and Narsinghpur; and as for the latter, if Sh. can succeed in raising a genuine outcry against rates which are the lightest in India, and less than half those of the Punjab, he'll be a cleverer men than I take him to be.

CHAPTER 5

1934
JULY - DECEMBER

Sunday July 8ᵗʰ

The Daily News (Nagpur) of this day held the following article:

VIII
C. P. BECOMES A MODEL!

Apropos the Government review on the working of the Debt
Conciliation Act in the Central Provinces, which was referred
to in this paper last week, it is interesting to note that the
Governments of Madras and the Punjab have taken our Act as a
model for their local legislation. This beneficent piece of
legislation was, perhaps, the most important measure carried by
our present Governor in the Legislative Council as Revenue
Member. Sir Hyde Gowan was specially fitted for piloting such
a measure by virtue of his intimate knowledge of rural economy
as Settlement Officer of the Hoshangabad district where debt
conciliation work had been done after the great famine. There
is a general feeling that the benefits of the Act should be

extended to a wider circle of agriculturists. Any measures taken to relieve the economic depression on a larger scale will be, in our opinion, a more perennial monument to the work of a Governor, than a well-chiselled marble. We hope the Government will extend the field of their activities.

[*The Daily News (Nagpur) 8th July 1934*]

Thurs. July 5th

We got back to Nagpur on Tuesday. How Monty used to endure Pach. for a fortnight after we'd gone down I can't imagine – dull, wet, and gloomy. Yesterday, by a coincidence my birthday, the D.N. had a laudatory article on me going for those who after losing office couldn't take this defeat like gentlemen. "Be in opposition and criticise but do it decently". They said I had acted with perfect constitutional propriety both in the ministerial crisis and in the Jubb. business, and ended up – "There is nothing that our province cannot accomplish under our present Governor"!! Today the Hit. raises its eyebrows and enquires "Why this thusness?". "Our role has never been to advise on our contemporaries but to read them and wonder why so many strange things are being said in them". De Haut en bas! "The article indicates there is a strange lull in the political world. Is it a lull that is very prelude to the storm?" – a dark, mysterious hint in true Oriental style! It is likely that one doesn't take what any of the rags say seriously – sweet as can be one day, vitriolic the next. I always want to make the editors an annual present of a dozen boxes of Carter's Little Liver Pills. Of much more value to me was the way in which they drank my health at a little dinner I gave – musical honours with a zest that almost brought tears to my eyes but how long will it last? I have always feared and mistrusted popularity.

Tuesday July 10th

It will be interesting to see the fate of our two taxation Bills – Court Fees and Tobacco. The former is to raise money for Rao's pet scheme, a High Court. In my own mind I have no doubt that the sole justification for this scheme is –

i.   that if every other Province has one, we should too, and –
ii. that the H.C. will be independent of the Ministers
     under the new Constitution.

At present and under the present constitution it's a costly luxury. Rao is wise in saying we should get the change through now, but the P.V., which is run by people who turned down our Chief Court scheme in 1929 (or thereabouts) because they said we must have an H.C., is howling about the waste of money. The Tobacco Bill we shall probably put off till Jan., by which time the agitation stirred up by the 'bidi' merchants will have died down. They collected 10,000/- for propaganda. We shall go on at it until the Council eventually sees sense and accepts it.

The monsoon has started well, and we are now having a timely break which should please everyone.

Thurs. July 12th

Gandhi says he's going to do a week's fast next month at Wardha, because one of his followers hit a Sanatanist or some such nonsense. The fast doesn't matter; the place does. Apparently we are to have him back in the C.P., where he has no affinities except his friendship with J. Bajaj. And we shall have the task of dealing with him, if he decides to return to "his spiritual home" in prison. Well, Gandhi - incarcerations have a recognized technique by now, and we must just follow it.

Rather annoying – a knee's gone wrong, and Logan says I'm being affected with 'spirochetes' from a tooth which has got to come out –

and it's a very nice tooth! – and I've got to have all sorts of drastic treatments. I hate being messed about, especially when I'm feeling perfectly fit, but L. knows what he's talking about.

Naidu, the Minister, is setting about his job in earnest, and is trying to get waterwork schemes going. How far he will succeed when Govt. hasn't a bob I don't know. There are no signs of dissension in the Ministry yet, and in fact the five of us work together very harmoniously, and so far – touching wood, and so on – we've had no disagreements of any kind. Rao is particularly accommodating, and is always ready to make things easy for me.

Tues. July 17th

I'm not quite so sure about Naidu. Recently I had the appellate and revisional procedures of the various Members and Ministers put on a proper legal and constitutional basis. This meant that the Minister no longer issues revisional or appellate orders on his own, as they're the orders of Govt., i.e., the Governor acting with his Minister. Some busybody has got hold of this and writes to the Hit. saying that the power of Ministers is being curtailed. It's Naidu who is chiefly affected, and it looks as if he had given the information away and had inspired the canard. He's not very bright, and it's quite likely that he didn't appreciate what was going on when the matter was under consideration in the Cabinet. But all of them are adept at getting hold of the tarred end of the stick, and quite ready to accept an explanation when given, and it may be as well to issue a brief correction. Will discuss it tomorrow.

We've definitely postponed the Tobacco Bill until Jan.

Wed July 18th

We decided that it was not worth while doing any 'dementi' work unless and until the matter is brought up in Council. Jaiswal, ex-minister, who is responsible for practically all the Council questions that have come in so far, is trying to embarrass the Ministry over the R.S.S.S. Circular. The reply will be that the circular was advisory; and if they ask us what will happen to local bodies which disobey: "Wait and See".

The G/I have sent us a peremptory order from the S/S to re-appoint a D.P.H.. There has evidently been pressure brought to bear, probably by the B.M.A. and it is a transferred dept.. It is improbable that we shall take the matter lying down, if we can find any effective means of protest. The letter gives no resources – merely says that the S/S has decided that he can no longer allow the present arrangement to continue. I regard this as a marked discourtesy. But the G/I will never, never grow out of their school-mastering methods of dealing with the provinces.

Friday July 20th

It really is a mistake to take anything that these politicians say or do seriously. After making a perfect ass of himself by his trip to Delhi, and after being responsible, as one of the directors of the rag, for the article in the P.V. referred to on June 22nd, and, Sharif came to me today and said he had two favours to ask – one about some land he wants for the Anjuman H.S., and one about C/W subs. to his new sarai. I laughed, and asked him why he had been behaving as he had; as regards the Delhi visit he said quite frankly that they thought I was too new to my job to want to break with Rao, and they were determined to get at R. somehow or other. As regards the article, he admitted it was a bad effort, but Mangalmurti had issued it without showing it him or to Kedar. Hum! Anyhow, I twitted him with letting his paper become bureaucratic, and said that the next time any of them accused Govt. of being unresponsive they ran the risk of having the article cast in their teeth. Then, because it is useless, as I say, to treat these people as other than schoolboys, I told him I'd help him as far as could over his land and his subs., and we parted on the friendliest of terms. He doesn't think there's any chance of the Ministry going unattacked next month. It's all rather disgusting, this frenzied place-hunting.

Friday July 27th

I think that I have made – or been largely responsible for the making of – a mistake. In order to save money we discontinued taking I.N.A. Telegrams, which rarely contained anything of interest, and we're usually not even punctual. But the result has been that they (The Associated Press) have given confidential instructions to their local correspondent that no publicity work is to be done for this Government and on the other hand that anything which is embarrassing to it should be broadcast. It's a form of blackmail, of course, and a peculiarly unfair one at that, in as much as our action was solely dictated by a desire for economy. But the question is whether it is worthwhile is antagonising the A.P. (which has Reuters behind it) for the sake of saving four or five thousand rupees. I am going to have it discussed at the meeting tomorrow which I have had to call to consider what action we shall take over the D.P.H. question. Khaparde & Waterfall want to protest, and asked for reconsideration. But the G/I has already passed similar orders for Bombay, on the ground that the doubling up excludes I.M.S. Officers who haven't got the P.H. diploma from appointment as I.G.C.H. and I don't think we any hope of being listened to. It's just another case of the Administration being sacrificed to the services.

We've had a strike on at the Empress Mills for three months. It's just been settled. Gordon and Shrobert have done some very good work especially S. It was all stirred up by Bombay Communists.

Sat July 28th

We decided to show the G/I that we were carrying out their orders about the D.P.H. but at the same time to put in a strong a protest as we could, explaining the difficulties into which we shall be landed with the Council, and pointing out that the latter will almost certainly turn down our two taxation bills (Tobacco and Court Fees) on the ground that they won't let us raise fresh money to be spent on restoring service posts.

The wicked thing is that other departments I.C.S, P.W.D, police, have lost numbers of prize posts. Why should the I.M.S. be specially favoured? Too easy with the B.M.A. behind them! It's disheartening work trying to economise. And we cut down I.N.A. telegrams and we get blackmailed. We cart over our own files between Nagpur and Pach. saving 60% in cost & 50% in time – and we get asked by Dehli what the deuce we mean by defrauding the Post Office. We amalgamate departments and we get to curtly told by the G/I to put them apart again. In the files of the secretariat there is a scheme which I worked out for reducing b... useless hordes of menials by half. I was told that I was going against the customs of the country and had better leave the thing alone which I did. And so on N.S.B.

Thursday Aug. 2nd

Wilson has told me what is probably behind the D.P.H. Business – besides service interests of course. He says that Megaw late D.G.I.M.S. and now Medical adviser at the I.O. is a keen Sanitarian, & that he has almost certainly advised the G/I to put a stop to the policy of economising on D.P.H.s. It just shows how little people like M. realise that there is such a thing as a transferred department. The whole thing is a farce.

Kedar has brought in a resolution asking for an enquiry into Rao's conduct in working to upset the late Ministry. Manglemurti and Parakh have brought similar ones. What an unsporting lot they are! They don't mind how much dirty linen they wash in public, if only they can get their defeat avenged. I would disallow the resolutions if I could, but I have no power to do so. The charge is a grave one, and having now been made openly must either be proved or disproved. I have an uneasy feeling that Rao must have been indiscreet in what he said and did last session; otherwise it is difficult to account for this excess of vindictiveness even in a man like Kedar.

Sat. Aug 4th

A slight difficulty with the Minister, soon surmounted. The Asst. to the Civil Surgeon here had to be transferred hurriedly, and a temporary man was put in for a few weeks pending the permanent man's arrival. He proceeded to bring a sick and dying uncle to the Mayo, and then, when his successor arrived, protested loudly against being transferred. The uncle, of course, turned out to be an ex-D.C. and close friend of Naidu, and Naidu persuaded Khaparde to cancel the transfer. Talk about the administration existing for the Services! We've a cholera outbreak on, and at all times the Asst. to the C.S. has an important and hard-worked post. And a temporary man was to be allowed to hold it, merely in order that he might look after his sick uncle! Thoroughly Indian. However, I got hold of Khaparde, and he agreed to the obvious solution – that the permanent man should take over, and the stop-gap be allowed to stay on in Nagpur, either on special duty or on leave.

Missionaries are queer folk. Talking of Father Elwyn,

Note (JHBG):

This refers to Verrier Elwyn, the author who spent his life among the Baiga, a tribe of Gonds living in the eastern C.P. and who finally married a Gond wife called 'Cosy'!.

Monty once said that these holy men seemed to think themselves absolved from the canons of straightforwardness that meaner men observe. The British & Foreign Bible Society have started a branch here, and some time ago I had a letter from the Bishop, saying that under their auspices he was going to give a lecture on rock inscriptions at Nakr-el-Kelb as they affected the Bible, and asking me to preside. I said I would with pleasure, and invitations were sent out to attend a lecture, H.E. in the chair. Yesterday, up comes one of the B.F.B.S. people with the request that I would first deliver an address on the work of the

Society, or in the alternative that I would call upon the Rev. Snooks to do so! I said quite firmly – nothing doing. I'm very glad to preside at the lecture, as the Bish. is a very old friend. But it's not my business to preside at propagandist meetings, and they had no business to try and trap me into doing it. Norman says the good lady went away looking rather crestfallen. How queer people are! Why couldn't they have said from the start that what they really wished to do was to advertise the work of the Society, and that the lecture was merely a bait to get people to turn up?

Tue Aug 7th

All went well. I told them the story of Dr Temple at speech day – "Ye don't come here to hear me. Ye come to hear the boys", and then said a few words about the B.&F.B.S. and finished with a quotation from "The Bible in Spain". Mrs Wood thanked me effusively for giving them such an excellent start so I suppose I must have said what they wanted brief though it was.

A front tooth out (pyorrhaea) and a plate in. I hate losing my own good teeth and being "made up".

Wed. Aug 8th

The "Regent" (the local picture-house) had its second birthday yesterday, and I took a party to it. Naidu, the Manager, is one of the few level-headed and enterprising men of business that the C.P. possesses – one of the very few who realise that it has nothing to do with politics. He came up with drinks at the interval, and an enormous garland.

Rao was away from today's meeting of Govt., ill, so I couldn't discuss with him this resolution against him. The more I think it over the more I'm convinced that I should do far more harm by disallowing it, and letting people say that a scandal was being suppressed, than by letting it go on. With this exception, the list of resolutions is a harmless one.

Seth Thakurdas, the Council bore, who asked me the other day to give him a title, wants to cut all our salaries 20%. He can whistle for his title!

Friday August 10th

An informative letter from H.E. the V. (Acting). It appears that the J.S.C.'s report is coming out on the 20th Nov. and that it will contain proposals which fall considerably short of the white paper so that there will be wrath in India. The G/I have been told that if the elections to the L.A. are held after Nov. 20th, Congress will sweep the board. We are therefor to hold them as soon as we possibly can, but the fact that there is any connection between this decision and the J.S.C. Report is to be kept a secret. Machiavelli is not dead.

Today is the first really wet day we have had this monsoon. Crops are excellent so far, but tanks in Nagpur low, and we want a downpour to wash the cholera away.

Wed. Aug 15th

A hectic day. Yesterday Rao came and saw me, and urged very strongly that this resolution of Kedar's is ultra vires, as "the Government" cannot appoint a committee to enquire into the conduct of one of its own members, in view of the protection given by para. 110, G/I Act. No committee could be appointed to whose authority he would be amenable. The constitutional position is so obscure that after a long discussion with him and G. I decided in the end that we must refer it to the G/I. – the point being that a decision will be a precedent, both here and in other provinces. In the meantime premature discussion of the resolution would plainly be against the public interest, and I must therefore veto the moving of it. I dislike having to stifle discussion at this early stage in my career of office, but I can see no alternative. Kedar came to see me before the above discussion, and said they would not move the resolution if I would agree to hold an enquiry myself – absurd!

I put various questions to him, and found, as I had expected, that they were all woolly-headed about the implications of their proposal. They couldn't say what sort of committee they wanted, nor what authority it would have, nor what offence of which cognizance could be taken they wished to prove. I learnt afterwards from G. that Rao was also approached, and told that the resolution would not be moved if he would agree to withdraw his support from the present Ministry. Could political cynicism go further? Their pretence of outraged morality is the purest bunk. It's all a move in the political game.

The C.in C. has arrived to stay. I was rather dreading his visit, as I haven't much in common with the Cavalry leader type of man, but they have both of them been charming, & very easy to get on with.

Thurs. Aug 16th

It is difficult to deal with these people. After appearing to concur in yesterday's solution, Rao returned my draft, saying that as I couldn't accept his arguments and veto the resolution off-hand, he would be "most grateful" to me if I would allow it to take its course. Well, I simply cannot say that a discussion of the matter would be "detrimental to the Public Interest" – and that G. and Hemeon (L.R) both agree with me. And to say that the conduct of one of its members "is not primarily the concern of local government" is a paradox of positively Chestertonian proportions.

Talking to me after dinner last night, Pam Stent told me that there is great bitterness among the Indian members of the Commission against the English members. She's inclined to draw a long bow, but I must find out if there is any truth in it. The difficulty is that among the senior Indian members of the Commission there are a number of men of the five-foot-three type – little men who in the old days would never have got beyond the Provincial service and whose social attractions are small. These make me think that they ought to be entertained and made friends of by the Europeans, and have the curious aptitude of the oversexed for construing everything as a slight. The result is inevitable – awkwardness and restraint, an Englishman's bugbears in his private life. Chitham told me a few days ago of a Brahmin D.S.P. – member of an old Nagpur family – who had just asked him for a transfer to a district with an English D.C. because he was sick of the intrigues that go on under the Indians. His then D.C. was one of the five-foot-three-ers I was thinking about. There is another point about Rao's affair. Members are appointed by the Crown. How can a Governor come to any decision himself which directly affects their position and prerogatives? Obviously the only authority competent to do that is the Crown.

Note (JHBG):

Just to show the attitude of the Indian towards Government Service and the type of men who tried to get into it, below is a transcript of an application received at some time; Sir Hyde copied it out as being worthy of note but did not date it. It is timeless.

"With kind permission of your Excellency, may I state that during my career as a student, as I was busy with many responsible duties, I could find almost no time for my studies, hence my failure" ....asking for interviews he continues "I must get myself settled for life in some Government post before I get on the wrong side of 25".

Sat Aug 18th

A letter has just come in ordering all local Governments to cease carrying their own dák. One more instance of the scandalous way in which the provinces are sacrificed to Simla. Not a word about the time which we save. The arguments are simply (i) that these short distance services are lucrative to the P.O. which cannot afford to lose them, and (ii) that para 4(b) of the P.O. Act, which exempts matters that concern solely the receiver and sender, doesn't mean anything. Govt. cannot be both receiver and sender. Fiddlesticks! It can and is.

Col. Russell, apparently head sanitary man in Simla, came to see me this morning, and admitted that he was the man responsible for our having a D.P.H. forced on us. I told him that Simla seemed to have forgotten that there was such a thing as a transferred department. He also assured me that service considerations had nothing to do with the decision. I said in that case the G/I's letters were unfortunately worded.

After that a Council about the Rao resolution. Rao at the last moment jibbed at the matter being referred to anyone, and asked that if I felt myself unable to veto the resolution outright it should be allowed to take its course. Well, I can't, for reasons already explained. The Ministers urged that as we know the charges are false – do we? What about "Not proven"? – I should be entitled to say that discussion is against the public interest. It took me a terrible time to make them as that would be prejudging the issue with a vengeance – and even then I got it under Naidu's skin. And he was Public Prosecutor for years at Wardha. These people do not care two hoots for the principles of the law the moment they find them inconvenient. Apparently my seeing Kedar the other day has given rise to all sorts of rumours. Having been given to understand that I thought he was playing a pretty poor sort of game and one that he hadn't even taken the trouble to understand, K. apparently went off and said that I was all on the side of the People's Party. Pah!

Sund. Aug 19th

I gather that the atmosphere in Council is entirely friendly, and pretty dull. K.P.Pande brought in a bill to abolish the power of arrest for arrears of land revenue, and we first of all carried a compromise, and then actually defeated the bill itself.

One longs sometimes to be able to tell the Indian newspapers editor just what one thinks of his ways. He has such a jaundiced and ungracious mind. Some time ago one Batchelor, who got booted out of the I.C.S. in this province because he was an incorrigible lunatic, wrote an article in the D.N about making power alcohol from mahua, (or mowra, Bassia Latifolia, the 'Indian Butter Tree.') and the D.N. took it up and talked a lot of twaddle about "the C.P.'s gold mine". It had always seemed to me that we were wasting our substance as regards mahua, and I specially ordered the thing to be looked into – with the result that we found it was one of those attractive-looking propositions which on close examination turn out to be commercial duds. We then published the figures in full. The D.N. remarks today: "But it (Govt.) puts forth various small difficulties (sic) which are not insurmountable. We cannot accept as final the opinions of I.C.S. officers – Jacks-of-Trades but masters of none." The "small difficulties" were the complete impossibility of producing alcohol at a price at which it could compete (a) with petrol, and (b) with alcohol produced from the huge quantities of molasses which are a by-product of the sugar factories. And "the opinions" were those of the trade, and were fortified by the complete failure of a similar experiment in Hyderabad!

Very interesting letter from N.J., who says that he has seen Rab Butler, and learns that they are inserting a clause in the new Act laying upon the Governor of the C.P. a special responsibility to see that Berar gets its "fair share" of the joint revenues (vide Nov. 20th). He will have a Committee to help him. So they seem to have accepted our proposals. The Govr., he thinks, is to have a sort of "Super Chief Secretary and a Superior Private Secretary "; but these matters are to be settled by the G.G. in C., and it seems that we shall not have any difficulty in getting a Financial Commissioner to deal with appeals. Indirect elections to the Federal Assembly are to be adopted. He doesn't think the Act will get to the Lords before July, and as their Lordships refuse to work to a time-table no one knows how long they will take. "Nothing can be done to expedite matters from our side, as the Commons are very jealous of any action being taken until they have given their approval to the legislation." That doesn't look as if Jan '36 would see the new constitution functioning, does it?

Wed. Aug. 22nd

The new regiment at Kampti, the Yorks & Lancs seem a queer lot. I dined with them last night. The only person present to receive me was the Adjt. & he took me along to the mess-room where the C.O. greeted me in a casual sort of way and asked me if I'd have a drink. He introduced me to General Nicholson from Secunderabad to whom he had been talking, but to none of the other officers present and then went on talking to General N., while Ling the Brigadeer at Jubb., came and talked to me. It would have been a weird way of receiving a Governor if I'd known the regiment for years, but in a regiment new to the place it was inexcusable. (This was all changed when the Col. in question went. The others were first class.)

Kedar evidently funks his resolution against Rao, and the Council plainly don't want to get to it. They talked for 3 hours on Monday on a matter that they could have finished in half-an-hour; and yesterday K. brought in a motion of no-confidence against the President – the usual bilge, which so far as the H.P.'s conduct in the House goes we have no hesitation in opposing. But they've produced letters (a gross breach of confidence, but that doesn't worry a man like Jaiwal, the addressee) showing that he has been dabbling in politics outside the House, and at a meeting of Govt. this morning, I refused to countenance the saying of anything on behalf of Govt. which could be taken as approving of such conduct. I have little doubt in my own mind that Rao and Rizvi are both thoroughly well mixed up in all the political moves that are going on, and though that's only in accord with what every other C.P. politician would do in their place, there are times when it's embarrassing.

The G/I have written us a very polite letter about the D.P.H. but they say it's no good us asking the S/S to reconsider the matter and blurt out the fact the real reason why they won't do so is that the C.P. is a danger to the other provinces in the matter of epidemic disease. This is a serious charge which no-one has ever suggested before, and I am having the matter investigated. If we can show that the charge is unfounded I shall let fly. If not, the sooner we set our house in order the better. The council will have to play if we can make them see the position.

Thurs. 23rd Aug.

The motion against the H.P. found only 6 supporters, including the mover, and I gather that the total strength of the so-called "People's Party" is now only 10 at the most. Many people would hide their diminished heads in shame, but I don't suppose for a moment that our Mr. Kedar will. Preparing for a speech in answer to an address at Akola, I read Monty's speech there in 1925 – a perfect masterpiece of suave and high-sounding phrases which mean exactly nil! He had to perfection the art of saying nothing while appearing to say everything.

Friday Aug. 24th

If there is anyone in this world more unreasonable than Indian newspaper editor, I have yet to meet him. The D.N this morning says that my giving Kedar an interview was "open to misconstruction". In other words, if the leader of the opposition attacks a member of the Govt., I am to refuse to see him – even for the purpose of telling him what I think of him! I'm afraid that I take a very different view of my duty. But that's the way of these people. The one maxim they really understand and appreciate is the old gag – Orthodoxy is my doxy. Heterodoxy is your doxy."

Sat. Aug. 25th

See Friday 22nd June. Mangalmurti (the fat one) came and saw me this morning, and astonished me by apologising for the P.V.'s article on the Jubb. case. He said, of course, like the others that the editor wrote the article on his own and that no-one else saw it – hum! I told him that what he should blame the editor for was not the attack on me, but his astonishing bad tactics in slating Govt. for being for once responsive and indifferent to its "prestige". He is an amusing fellow. Always seems to find a joke in things – and is reputed to be the biggest intriguer in the province. I do not persuade myself that the P.V. now has "an humble and a contrite heart", but at any rate it's a sign of grace that M. should have come.

Thur Sept 6th

Just back from an exhausting tour in Berar – Amraoti & Akola. They are wonderfully hospitable in that part of the world, and I was kept going from morning till evening. The details, I suppose, were very much those of any other gubernatorial tour, and I shall not bother to record them. On Aug 29th I made a little bit of a golf history for myself, as I did the 9th hole at Amraoti in one – distance 231 yards, hole if anything slightly higher than the tee. Several angels must have watched over the ball, as the approach to the green is rough, and the green itself not the truest. Unfortunately in my position I cannot write to Kroflik's and say "What about a ball or two?"! Had an interesting meeting at Lodge, where a young mason read a thoughtful paper about Masonic origins which inspired me to get up and talk on the same subject – though I haven't touched it for years.

A letter from H.E. saying that the Royal Assent to the Constitution Bill is expected either in Aug '35 or, more probably, Oct-Nov '35, and asking whether on the former supposition we could get a new Council elected by Jan-March following. It's all deadly secret, but I must get details from Deshmukh, our franchise pandit, and consult Rao and G.. At first sight the idea seems fantastic. But having delayed things so terribly at home they're now, of course, getting the wind up about any further postponements.

Tue Sept 11th

After getting all the details & talking the matter over as above, I've told H.E. that I consider it quite impossible to hold elections in Jan–March '36. We worked out that 10 months at least would be required from the date of Royal Assent to the announcement of the election results, even if we don't have a delimiting commission, which I personally don't think is necessary. That takes us to June, and of course May–June is a hopeless time for that game. Even if it could be done by March, the budget would have to be put through in December – most unwise – and the usual cold weather work of the revenue staff would go to pot. We have told them that the biggest electorate we can cope with is 1½ million. We're going to get 1¾ m shoved upon us, and if the arrangements break down there will be a terrible mess. Far better to take the thing calmly and make sure of the job.

Friday Sept 20th

Got to Pach. on the 12th much regretting that I had decided to come up by train. The 210 mile road journey may be tedious, but at any rate you can get into a car and have – with luck – no further bother until you arrive; whereas by train you have a lot of fuss, unpacking and repacking, jolting & jarring, and a bad night's sleep into the bargain. The road for me in future.

A puzzling letter from H.E.. The G/I after having the assembly eating out of their hand for the past few years, are now horrified at the thought that they may get a Congress-Nationalist majority against them after the forthcoming elections, in which event their position would become "extremely difficult". They recognise that Govt. may not rig the elections; but nevertheless I am asked (i) to use my influence with the ministers to make them support pro-government candidates and (ii) to give the people advice as to the selection of loyalist candidates, and (iii) pull the string in various other ways. I showed the letter to G. and our reactions were identical. (a) We haven't the slightest sympathy with the G/I. It will do them all the good in the world to face the music, as we in the provinces have had to do in the past 14 years. Once again they show how little they appreciate the meaning of responsible government, the moment their own interests are affected. (b) A Governor should not be asked to do covertly what is against the spirit of the G.S.C. Rules, and to compromise his position by giving any single person cause to say that he is interfering in favour of one party in the elections. But it is not going to be easy to answer the letter, as of course all the above is to be uttered on no account. A soft answer, I suppose. But it goes against the grain.

Monday Sept 24th

In very truth the G/I are an inspiration and a guide! When we want to open up through communications, they veto our proposals because at some point or other the road concerned, touches a railway. When we try to economise by doing without a D.P.H., they make us have one, and tell us that we're a danger to other provinces. (We're pickling a rod for them over that.) When we carry our official dák from Nagpur to Pachmarhi at half the cost and in half the time that the P.O. demands and takes, we're told that we're poaching on their royal preserves. And when we want to borrow money from the Provincial Loan Fund in order to give loans to save indebted malguzars (selected cases only, and on the security of whole villages, which can turn into a raiyatwari if the malguzars don't pay up), they say there's nothing doing. If any province succeeds in devising means to put its agriculturalists and its finances on their feet again, it will be entitled to the full credit. All we've had from G/I is talk and cold water. This latest is from Alan Parsons, Montagu's blue-eyed boy. It ends with a little sermon on the need for caution in our plan for buying up proprietary rights! And at the same moment they're wringing their hands over the prospect that Congress may get a majority in the Assembly next November, and that that body will no longer eat out of their hand. So they, implore us to do what we can to get good candidates put up, who will back Govt., and to get the Ministers to make speeches on their behalf. (This in a personal letter from H.E. to me.) We who have faced the music in the provinces for 15 years can hardly be expected to have much sympathy for them, and I must confess to being extremely surprised, in view of the way we're forbidden to meddle in politics by the G.S. Conduct Rules, at being asked to sail as near the wind as I can, merely to prevent the G/I realizing what representative government means.

Sat Sept 29th

Yet another instance of the way in which the interests of the provinces are disregarded. We rely on the railways – Eastern group – to buy our Jál, for the production of which we have spent a lot of money, & which is of excellent quality for sleepers. The Railway Board have now taken to getting the sleepers by competitive tender, for the sake of economy. Well and good – though the word "economy " seems out of place in connection with railways that pay the preposterous rates for work that ours pay. But what is the result? The tenders go to private contractors who are out for a gamble, & will neglect no means however shady, of getting their timber cheap; or to private owners of forests who will have no scruple in cutting their jungle to pieces. Meanwhile we (i.e. The State) will lose 2 lakhs of revenue at a time when we want every bob, and all our work and organisation goes for nothing. And the share of the total contract that we want is a very small one. We have protested once more. It's Edlands again – a bad department so I have no great hopes. But there is one thing on which I have made up my mind. I will not be deterred from telling the G/I what I believe to be the truth of a case merely because they may turn us down. I remember many years ago when the health of the C.C. was being proposed at a Commission dinner, the proposer congratulating him on being free from "the administrative squint – one eye on Nagpur and one on Simla" which had marked his next-before. May I be kept free from a similar optical blemish! There is no reason to suppose that there is any heaven-sent wisdom descends upon the barnacular colony of Simla & if our views differ, ours are as likely to be right as theirs. So I have never been able to see any disgrace, as some people have seemed to, of being turned down.

Thurs Oct 4th

M.L.Darling of the Punjab has come to stay and advise about Land Mortgage Banks. I have a shrewd suspicion that when put to the acid test, the ideas that cheap money is obtainable for everyone who wants it and that land is purchasable for a song, don't pass unscathed. We are shaping a scheme for buying up villages and turning them into rayatwari. But we find that to make it a business proposition we can't afford to pay more than 15 times the l.v.. From the wails of the landlords we had gathered that they might be obtainable at 5. Not a hope. Enquiries are not complete yet, but it looks as if we should have to pay more like 20. Then the L.M Banks. G. says that if we are to do any good to the men we want to help – the sound men who have been hit badly by the slump – we mustn't charge more than 8% for loans. Bhalja says if that is so, we can't afford to pay more than 4½% on the Bank's debentures. (It's the Bank that pays, of course. We only guarantee.) Khaparde says – if that is so we risk not getting the debentures taken up. And where does the cheap money idea go to? Kh. of course wants to get the debentures out at a comfortable rate of interest, so as to put a good security on the market. But they are all looking through the wrong end of the telescope. The objective is to help the cultivator. The first thing that we must consider is the rate we are to make him pay; and if we can't raise money at a rate which suits that rate, the whole thing goes West. They're a genial pair of fellows, these Ministers. Things are brewing up.

Sund. Oct.7th

As I thought. Naidu came to me yesterday, and asked me to drive a coach and four right through the L.S.G. Act. The Act forbids a Dt. Cl. to cut the pay of certain of its higher employees, without our <u>previous</u> sanction. As usual, the Councils make a habit of applying for it six months late, and Naidu wants to accord sanction by a curiously flagrant piece of hair-splitting. I pointed out to him that nothing of that sort could get over the plain wording of the section, and he gave that ground up. Then he said that these cases were so "awkward" and so numerous, that he must sanction. I told him that if he once started hanky-pankying with the law his doom was sealed and that his only safe course lay in saying: "There's the law. I must enforce it. If the consequence is awkward for you, that's your fault and not mine". He seems quite ready to accept advice in these matters, and he said he'd follow mine. Then Khaparde. First he tries to snaffle C.P.Dufferin grants for Berar, on the basis of some silly 'naksha' that one of his pals made out for him. I talked to him about it, and pointed out that it was a bad line to raise a controversy of that sort, and he said he'd be content if we'd give Berar more money. G., who is Chairman of the Fund, has written a very firm note of protest. Next he tries to get an M.B. friend of his – a flabby, disloyal creature who hasn't even the guts to stick to his disloyalty – past the efficiency bar, on the ground that "there is nothing on record against him", when his last report says that he is useless, unqualified, and unfit for promotion! I wrote on the file that the report had evidently not been brought to H.M.'s notice, and what about it?, and am waiting for a reply. Next he vetoed certain transfers which the I.G.C.H. proposed in accordance with our settled policy of not keeping a man too long in one place. Reason – to keep an Indian friend in Akola, where the C.S. has a large private practice, instead of the senior man in the cadre, who has a claim to go there, and who happens to be an Englishman. I have asked him if he wishes Govt. to make a change of policy. I intend to make it quite clear to Kh. that so long as he is my Minister he has got to run straight. He is shrewd enough to understand the alternative without my saying anything about it. The difficulty is that like all his kind he doesn't know a straight line when he sees it.

Gandhi is keeping quiet in Wardha. It seems to be pretty clear now that he's not going to do anything foolish in the C.P., at any rate for the present. Congress is slowly realising what a will o' the wisp he is – an "ignis fatuus."

Monday Oct 8th

"Il sit bien qui sit le dernier." Misra (June 8th) wanted us to remove his disqualifications as a candidate for the Assembly, so that he could stand along with his "friend" Govind Das. We have removed G.D.'s, but Misra's is a different matter. He is not a C.P. man; he is mixed up with revolutionaries; and he has been a public scandal as Pres. of the Jubb.M.C.. So we recommended to G/I Home that they should refuse his application, and they have agreed. (There is no Bajpai in the H.D., thank goodness.) I wish one hadn't to deal with creatures of the Misra type. They make one shudder.

Friday Oct 12th

E. has arrived – great joy. Everybody loves her and is glad to see her back.

It is amusing to hear the Congress people on the subject of Misra being disqualified. The more excitable element is flapping its hands about, talking, of "an all-India insult" – rubbish! – and calling on the leaders to withdraw all Congress candidates. The leaders have got other fish to fry, and care nothing for Misra, so they're telling the tic-tackers to keep cool. You never can tell, of course, in this amazing country what the repercussions of such an action will be – nor, beyond a certain point, ought you to consider them. Rao advised us to bar Misra, G. and I both agreed, and it was plainly the right thing to do, so we shall stick to it at all costs. Meanwhile a letter has come from Binney recommending the suspension of the Jubb.M.C.. We sent them a list of their financial iniquities and gave them four months in which to put them right, and I gather that they haven't moved a finger – could not, probably because M. as President never calls meetings!

Sat Oct 13th

I was rather touched last night. At the end of dinner, Norman – inspired by the Pol Roger – got up and asked the house party to drink our health, and they gave us musical honours, a tribute chiefly to E.. The Lansdown Week is on & we have the Patersons, George (the holder), Clive Rich & Gabrielle Smith, who came out with E., staying with us. A party as nice as one could wish for. I've said very little about the social side of a Governor's life, because that only bears indirectly on the judgement that I am trying to form on the way I fulfil my offices; and if one deals with social matters one is apt to wander into trivialities.

Wed. Oct. 17th

Letters from G/I and from H.E. about publicity (a) general, with special reference to the Congress and Communist programmes, (b) specific, to boost the J.S.C.'s report. We have never been very fond of publicity in the C.P.. If you go beyond what may be called authoritative exposition, plus the placing of articles in the papers, you get entangled in argument and controversy, and in that sphere a Govt. servant has the dice loaded against him, and is likely to do much more harm than good. That was what we found in the Non-Co-op. days. Haney has developed some wonderful system in the U.P., chiefly by appealing to the big landlord class. We have no such class here, and have never felt the need of his district "amán sabhas". Rao dislikes the whole idea, and points out that if we train the lower ranks of Govt. servants to propagandize for Govt. now, when the Reforms come in every Ministry will use the permanent staff to maintain itself in power. There seems to me to be much sense in that view.

Wed. Oct. 24th

Naidu, the Minister, has just been to see me. Misra is defying our orders to reinstate the Secretary, and has also done nothing to comply with the four-months' ultimatum which we gave the Committee in April to put its house in order on pain of dissolution. He has not yet called a meeting of the Comm. to deal with the matter of the Sec., and we have given him 15 days in which to do it. The elections are due in Jan., and Naidu is funking doing what he ought to do, for fear it will arouse sympathy for Misra. I told him straight out that so long as I was head of the province I would not agree to any course of action which allowed any person or body to refuse to carry out an order of Govt. passed in execution of the law. It would mean that our authority over local bodies would be at an end. Binney (Commr.) and Banerji (R.S.) were present. I suggested to him that we should get everything in train for an order dissolving the Committee on financial grounds, and should discuss further action at our first meeting in Jubb. on Nov. 10th, and he agreed. Meanwhile some of the members of the Comm. have requisitioned a meeting, and it is to be held on the 31st. If they decide to reinstate Sharma, well and good. It will be a sign of grace, and we can then consider what to do about the financial case, which is of purely local interest, whereas the case of the Sec. affects the whole of our l.s.g. administration. If they support the President, we can dissolve them without hesitation.

I am worried about a letter from H.E. proposing that for next year's twenty-fifth anniversary celebrations an all-India subscription shall be raised for the Red Cross & Dufferin Funds, to be used, so far as G. and I gather largely in creating central posts. Frankly we have no use for the idea. The Red Cross will make no sort of appeal in the C.P., & for the Dufferin what we want is buildings, not posts. But the difficulty is that buildings – e.g. for Amraoti & Jubb. where the present buildings are a disgrace – will make only a local appeal in its narrowest sense. What we want, it seems to me is something which will make a provincial appeal, like a tuberculosis hospital. I must talk to Wilson.

Genl. Macmullen, G.O.C. Eastern Command, has just spent four days with us. He beat me at golf at Delhi, & I said that he must come here and give me my revenge. I beat him 2 up one day, giving him his 5 strokes. Next day he did 12 bogeys *(?Birdies TJG?)* (Handicap 13!) and mopped the floor with me. A man of many talents. One of the bright spots of this job that it brings one into contact with really interesting people, and helps one to be less parochial.

Sat. Oct. 27th

Misra has called a meeting for the 12th. The requisition was signed by 20 members, i.e. a majority, and M. says that if they vote to reinstate Sharma he will resist by force. If he does, he puts himself in our hands.

"Congressmen cannot get rid of artificiality and corruption, and of the almost overpowering desire to wrangle." Thus Gandhi! "Oh! wad some God the giftie gie us, etc." But they never will. They're as full of bombast and self-conceit as a balloon is of gas. All the hot air about the terrible things they were going to do because of the refusal to enfranchise Misra seem to have evaporated.

Sunday Nov. 11th Jubb

We left Pach. on the 4th and had a delightful, if rapid, visit to Indore to stay with Col. Macnabb. Thence to Mandhu, a city of departed splendours, where one could spend a week wandering among to ruins and looking at the marvellous views. The dhar people received us most hospitably – and what a lunch! Turtle soup, four lordly salmon, cold grouse, & so on, consumed under the vaulted dome of an old Mahommedan tomb. The Residence at Indore makes my two G.H.s look poor and countryfied. It's solid and English, both outside and inside.

Jubb. is hectic. I've already opened a new hospital – a really good piece of work by the Cantt. Board and in my speech I commended it and its officers especially Kennedy and Marshall as a good example to other local bodies. (E. said the speech was "good English" which pleased one from so competent a critic). Then the Armistice Ball, a boy Scout Rally, and a long meeting of Government at which we got through some useful work. Roughton has taken over from G. and we continue, I think, to be a harmonious team, with a will to be accommodating. I have never regretted my decision to have the captains as ministers not the subalterns.

The Jubb.M.C. affair progresses "according to plan". We have found a way of getting rid of the President, without dissolving the Committee. But the whole affair is a sad commentary on Congress mentality. God help the country if people like Misra become top dogs in the new Constitution!

Thurs Nov 22nd

The J.S.C.'s report is out at last, and after going through the differences from the W.P. which was sent me with it I cannot find anything much on which I can comment, except that they have made no provision for our revenue appellate authority. The Govt. is to be charged with a special responsibility for seeing that Berar gets a "reasonable share" of our joint revenues. Not quite the same thing as a "fair share" which was our wording. But that is all that is said about Berar, except that it is now to be "a part" of the C.P. whereas formerly it was only administered along with the C.P.. Presumably that means that it will be deemed to be part of B.I. which I regard as the first essential step towards the unification in sentiment and in fact of the two parts of the province. Whether the fissiparous tendency of Berar will now disappear remains to be seen. There is nothing vital in any of the other differences.

Fri. Nov. 23rd

My first serious difference of opinion – happily soon composed – with the other members of Govt. It seemed to me that we ought to issue a statement about the Jubb. business, and Naidu agreed. So I drafted one myself, making it clear that our quarrel with the President was due solely to his refusal to carry out an order of Govt. issued in execution of its legal powers. That to my mind is the one plain and simple issue – the need for Govt., to put down a calculated and deliberate defiance if its legal authority, which, if not dealt firmly with, would lead to chaos in local self-government. Naidu didn't like facing the issue, and drafted a statement making out that Govt. had interfered to enforce the wishes of a majority party in the Committee, a "rump" consisting of 18 out of 35 members. The suggestion seemed to be wrong in fact and in principle, but to my surprise Roughton backed it, and the other two followed him. So I called them all together, and put my point of view forward as forcibly as I could, and they agreed, subject to some minor modifications in my draft, which has now been sent for issue. I hope I did not overbear them, but I told them straight out that what we must have is the whole truth and nothing but it, and that it would be a subterfuge for us to pretend we were backing the majority party, when we had made up our minds to dissolve the Committee if it didn't back us up and if it supported the President's defiance. It's never any good skirting the real issue, and in this case it was simply whether the King's writ was to run in Jubb. M.C. or not. I think they felt that I was right. What they were out for was a tactical move.

Thursday Nov. 29th

Delicious! When the communique was issued, side by side with it in the D.N. was a letter "from a correspondent", which was Naidu's draft verbatim! Reading it over again I was thankful I had opposed its issue – a farrago of petty detail, written to tickle the ears of the groundlings. I hope the whole disgusting business will now be dropped. But they'll probably attack the Ministry next session. The P.V. excels it itself as usual. "The new constitution lays on the Governor the duty of protecting the oppressed. Why didn't H.E. intervene to save Misra from being bullied by the Minister?" Oh! These democrats! And they can't see how funny they are.

Speech at the opening of the Constables' Training School, Nagpur, on Monday, the 3rd December 1934

Mr. Chitham, Ladies and Gentlemen,—The ancients had a saying—it occurs, I believe, in one of the books of the Sybilline oracle—that the mills of God grind slowly. What would they have said if they had heard, as we all did just now, that the project which is coming to fruition today was first mooted in 1902, more than a generation ago? They would have said among themselves, I think "Verily Jupiter has a rival in the Government of the Central Provinces"! But out of evil cometh good, and out of this great delay has come a practical advantage, that those to whom the credit of starting this school must be given—Mr. Morony, Mr. Chitham, Mr. Duke, and last but not least my hon'ble friend the Home Member, who has convoyed the scheme safely past the Cerberus who stands at the doors of the Finance Department—have been able to take as their model similar schools which have been started in other parts of India, and to profit by their experience.

Many years ago I had an experience which is rare for officers of my service. I served for a year in the Police Force, a year which I have never regretted. It was a very happy year. But it was more than that, because it taught me one of the most valuable lessons which a young magistrate can learn, the lesson that he must look at the administration of justice from two sides—not merely from the point of view, of the man who sits comfortably at his desk and sends the criminal to jail, or acquits him, possibly with scathing remarks about the failure of the prosecution, but also from the point of view of the man who has to do what we call "the dirty work", who has to find and catch the criminal, very often at great personal risk, and too frequently handicapped in his task by lack of training. Only when he appreciates both points of view will he be able to hold the scales of justice even.

Any person who knows the history of our province for the past fifteen years knows that during that time the Police Force has been called upon to face almost every form of civic disturbance. It has had to contend patiently and good-humouredly with satyagrahis; to face the riotous mobs of the days of non-co-operation and civil disobedience; to deal with what was practically

139

open rebellion among forest tribes; and – the hardest task of all – to stand firm and impartial when communal passions were blazing around it. It has faced these tasks with a loyalty and a steadfast courage which is worthy of all praise, and its record is one of which any Force might be proud.

But that record has been earned in times of stress. In ordinary daily work, such as the prevention and detection of crime, traffic regulation, and so on, the tale is somewhat different. No Police Force can function to its fullest efficiency until it has gained the confidence of the general public, and has taught the public to regard it as an ally against the evildoer, and not as an enemy to the innocent. And in our province the criticism is heard frequently, both within and outside the walls of the Council Hall, that this confidence can never be gained until the general standard of intelligence and training in the lower ranks has been raised.

To meet and remove this criticism two things are essential. The first is that the men of the Force should be adequately paid and properly housed; for thus only can we attract the type of man that is required, and I commend the fact to those who hold the purse-strings with another saying of the ancients – that to the wise man a word is enough. The other need we are supplying today by the opening of this school, where, having got the man we want, we can train him in the way we wish him to go. I can wish the school nothing better than that its finished product may do credit to those who have sponsored it.

Friday Dec 7th

I hope we shall have a little peace at last. We returned here a week ago, and Convocation was on the 1st. It went off quite well, though it's always a dull show. One of the newspaper men complimented me on having smiled and looked genial, & and said that I didn't seem to be as stand-offish as Monty. With memories of Encoenia, how can one take a show like that with one's nose in the air? When Tookey asked if some graduant might be "omitted" instead of "admitted", I grinned frankly. Since then there has been a four-day Commission Week, an experiment which owes its origin to the enthusiastic John Stent, and has been a great success. There had been no Week for 13 years, largely owing to Indianisation, the C.P. Club dispute & similar reasons. In that time the character of the Commission has changed completely, and those who remembered the old genial Weeks were few. So when the idea of renewing the institution was started the promoters were able to start "de novo", on a new kind of Week in which the Dinner would be in Talankhen, an evening show at the V.T.I., gymkhana on the cricket ground, tennis match at G.H., & so on and it all panned out very well, with lots of fraternisation and plenty of bonhomie. I had to speak at the dinner, so I told them a funny story or two which put them in a good humour, & then put the serious stuff across – changes in Commn., changes in conditions of service, but no change in tradition was the main idea. And as examples of the tradition I took Lely's words about the Banyan tree. Shirt sleeves and "the hearts of the simple loving people among whom we dwell", and Foxy's "administrative squint", adding a few words about not climbing, because if you climb you don't do it on the stepping stone of your dead self – pace Tennyson – but on the living bodies of your fellow officers. They seemed to like it all. I captained the cricket team, was not out for 3, and played in the tennis with Rustram. After being 2 sets to nil up, 5-2 and 40-15 on my service we frittered that set (9-7) away, and lost the fourth when I was tiring, one point off an easy victory. Still it was great fun.

The Bill has come, and I've Just finished my comments, Rao having given me valuable help. Why this secrecy about the very fact that the Bill is in existence, I simply can't imagine. Everyone knew it was going to be put into shape the moment the report was out. They've cut out all provision for leave of Governors, and if they go sick they're to get no pay! Inhuman and unwise. I suppose they'll want me to start the show. Query – will my five years run from 1933 or 1936 (the start of the new show)? If the latter, I shall say "no, thank you". I have no intention of staying beyond 1938 – I want to go and play golf or grow apples! If they won't let me go then, I shall go in 1936. Never could I lick my chops, to put it vulgarly, over being Governor in the way that some people have done. It has far too many drawbacks in the way of isolation, conspicuousness, pomp, and boresome public duties for my taste. I'd like to get the new constitution started, because I probably know more about the technique of the business than others. After that I should lay down my office with few regrets, especially as I know that E.'s one desire is to be quit of the country, and settle down in England.

Wed. Dec. 12th

At a meeting of Govt. this morning, I said I'd had a letter from H.E. the V. about discussions of the Report in the Leg. Councils, and proposed to give a day for it. Rao said – "Go steady". Apparently there are great dissensions about the communal award, and by no means any unanimity about the Report itself, and many of the members are afraid that if the Report is discussed these little rifts within the lute will be shown up. So we're going to leave a day free and they'll get their discussion only if they ask for it. Meanwhile the Berar leaders have met together and asked again for Berar as a separate federating unit. They also want the agreement with H.E.H. to be published as soon as possible, & I quite agree with them, and am writing to H.E. to ask if there is any news of its publication. It is difficult to see why it should not have come out with the report.

This is the sort of thing one has to contend with. When the P.W.D. was reorganised Dube was sent off with a pension & we told the G/S he was not fit to be C.E. Now his pension cash has come up and the Minister wants to give him an extra pension for the periods when he officiated as C.E. on the ground that his work was "up to the required standard". Unfortunately for technical reasons the G.S.'s sanction is required, & I jibbed hard at recommending for an extra pension a man whom we had booked as unfit. But they said that although he may not have been fit in 1932, his work as C.E. in 1926 and '30 was good. So I said I'd agree if they could put me up a draft that wouldn't make us look foolish.

I wish I could get a decent P.S.. Cole is better than Chas. Morrison because he's not such a simpleton, and is quite pleasant. But he's got the back-bone of a jellyfish, and the powers of observation of an owl in daylight – which he resembles facially – & the initiative of a tortoise. He's always registering "surprise" at this and that and that's as far as he ever gets. It's very trying. The post is a very lucrative one, but all the young Civilians whom I might have are married – and a married P.S. is out of the question.

Friday Dec. 14th

The Malguzar of Kelod, who owns 20 villages, made an interesting statement to me this morning. He said that the tenantry were coming to regard the malguzars, not as their landlords, as they used to do, but as brokers who intercepted 50% of their rent-roll on its way to Govt. As this is the literal truth of the position, it seems that the tenants are waking up. But at whose teaching? Govt. has said nothing. It sounds like some "Kishán Sabha" business.

What is one to do about these "Opening speeches"? How is it possible to make a different speech for each hospital – that is to say a speech that is worth listening to? I don't see how it can be done. One must just say a few ordinary things, suitable to the particular occasion and give up searching for "Great Thoughts".

I met Parakh at the Quadrangular yesterday, and he talked about the Jubb. show. He quite agreed that Govt. could not be expected to knuckle under to any local Hitler; but he said that what got at him as a lawyer was the Minister reviewing his predecessor's order on a question of fact. I could not tell him that the reason was that Sharif's order had been passed against the L.R's advice. It's the weak point in the case, of course, but as Naidu passed the order entirely on his own, it's up to him to face the music.

Thurs. Dec. 20th 1934.

Speech at the opening of the American Mission School at Dhamtari on Thursday, the 20th December 1934

Mr. Miller, Mr. Brunk, Ladies and Gentlemen,—When I accepted your very kind invitation to open this building today, I had no idea that you were going to give me a chance of saying a few words on what, as the result of 32 years of work in this country, I believe to be one of the most vital of its problems— far more important for the vast mass of the people than any change of constitution. For constitutions come and go, and leave the villager practically untouched, wrapped in that pathetic contentment which is only content because it knows nothing better.

Many years ago I had the good fortune to be appointed to do the settlement of a district, and during four most interesting years I worked among the cultivators, hearing their joys and sorrows, the details of their quarrels, the treatment which they received from landlord and from moneylender, the way in which they contracted their debts, the way in which those debts grew from pebbles to millstones hanging round their necks. And I can say this without fear of contradiction, that of all the calamities against which they have to contend, famine and flood and pestilence, the cruelty of nature and the cruelty of man, by far the greatest is ignorance—ignorance of the new methods which science is teaching, ignorance of their rights, ignorance of the very contents of the bonds which they sign, ignorance of the way in which their debts grow until they find themselves loaded with a weight under which they sink. I am, of course, painting the darkest side of the picture, but it is a side so large that frequently it overshadows every other side, especially in such years of calamity as we have been passing through recently. And so, when you tell me that the aim and object of your work is to prepare young men for rural life and leadership, to turn out workers who will serve in the villages, and not budding B. A.'s who will go to the towns and swell the great army of the unemployed, I say to you that you are working on lines the soundness of which no well-wisher of India can deny. It is not my business to criticize the educational policy which Government has pursued for many years, but in this province that policy has had one most regrettable effect to which no one can be blind. In a land where three-fourths of the people are agriculturists, it has drawn the best brains of the countryside away from the villages into the cities, and has taught them to use their pens and their tongues instead of the plough-share upon which the very life of our province depends. Signs are not wanting that we are beginning to recognise the disastrous effects of that policy and to turn our thoughts to what we call the problem of rural reconstruction—a phrase the mere use of which is an accusation, because it implies that we have got to rebuild that which we have allowed to fall into disrepair. It is my earnest hope that in the new order of things which lies before us we shall divert our energies more and more to the countryside; for, while politicians scheme and lawyers argue, it is on the prosperity and content of the villages that the real happiness of our province is based.

And so to you, and to all who think and work as you do, I say "God speed you in your task". May I ask you to convey to all those far-distant friends in America and Canada who have helped you to raise this building the deep and abiding gratitude of those who, like myself, have the good of our countryside very much at heart? They have raised an enduring monument.

Dec 24th Monday Camp Khitoli

Just finished a four day visit to Raipur, where I opened a hospital – and in so doing received the most gorgeous "láv" I've ever seen. E. also getting the same – and took the opportunity of saying the first word about the Silver Jubilee Fund. I think this "Láv" business is being overdone. I don't know what the things are worth, but it is a good number of rupees, and they're agin the spirit of the G.S.C. rules, therefore E. and I have now a collection of 30 or 40 of them. The most beautiful we have put on the walls of the drawing room, & the rest we shall give to hospitals. People at Raipur were very cordial, & I had to refuse several functions that they wanted to get up. One day we motored to Dhamtari & I opened a mission school which is to train the villagers to stay on the land, & not to be budding B.A.s, & I took the chance of getting one in about our educational policy – drawing the best brains of the countryside into the cities, to swell the great army of the unemployed. An American Bishop came up to me afterwards and thanked me for my "inspiring words". I thought it would be rather fun to put in a touch (no more) of hot gospelling, to see if I could stir people out of their self-complacency – and asking if he could reproduce my speech in his American Church Journal, I said "of course" (the speech being a public one). The D.N. gave me a pat on the back, the Leader said that no Nationalist could have damned Govt.'s policy more trenchantly, but no-one else took any notice!

My visit happened to coincide with an athletic meeting got up by the District Schools Association and they asked me to give the prizes away. There was a big crowd there, and it was altogether a good show. But no boys from Dt. Council schools, the reason being that Ravi Shanker Shukla, Chairman of the Council, had forbidden them to attend. Such is the Congress mentality. The chance of spiting me – which was a signally damp squib – was to be preferred to the physical welfare and the enjoyment of the schoolboys. I attended Lodge Chhattisgarh and (on the way to Katrui) Lodge Heart of India, both good meetings. At H. of I. I took the opportunity of telling them that no good Mason squabbles over office-hunting – a fact they had forgotten of recent years. And now for a rest. The party is the N. Walkers and the Hennessys, complete with two children, a baby, & a doctor sister of Mrs. H.'s – four doctors in the camp!

1935
JANUARY - JUNE

Nagpur. Sunday Jan 6th 1935

The camp was very pleasant, though we had no tiger kills, and only got a panther and a sambhar. But we had a lot of small game – peacock, partridge, jungle fowl, hares and so on – and lived well, and that's the main point of a Christmas camp! And the sál jungle was beautiful. There were stretches on the river which runs into the tank that might have been England.

The Liberals have used the holidays to damn the I.P.C. Report with a shrieking chorus of vituperation, in which catch-phrases like "blackmail" and "kissing Sir Austen's baby" take the place of sober reasoning. They're a poor lot – hermaphrodites who don't know which sex they belong to, and are continually wailing what friends they are of Govt. – because they haven't the guts to be anything else? And at the same time damning everything that Govt. does or says. If such as these be our friends, God save us! They have behaved just the same at every crisis in Indian affairs that has occurred since I've been in the country.

Tues Jan 8th

I set the ball rolling for the Silver Jubilee Fund this morning with a meeting at G.H., at which we appointed a Committee and explained the plan of campaign. It's going to be hard work collecting funds with a bad cotton crop and everyone pretty well broke, but we shall do what we can. Hari Singh Gour, whom we had not put on the committee, got up and suggested that that body should have power to add to its members, to which we agreed. But I reminded them of the saying that the best committee is one which consists of three experts, of whom two are dead.

Friday January 11th 1935

Attended an Indian circus, which had one-third of its takings for the night to the S.J. Fund. The place was packed with Indians, and when I came in they all clapped. I was much touched. E. & I seem to be popular, but I rather dread it, because I know what a bubble popularity is, and how easily it is pricked. Still I suppose it is better to be that after one's first year than the reverse, provided one doesn't allow one's head to be turned. And I think that I'm a bit to hard-boiled for that.

Speech in reply to an address from the Anjuman Hami-e-Islam (at the Silver Jubilee Celebration) at Nagpur on Friday, the 18th January 1935

Khan Sahib Siddique Ali Khan and Members of the Anjuman Hami-e-Islam,—I am deeply sensible of the compliment that you have paid me in asking me to accept an address from you on the occasion of the silver jubilee of your institution, and I can assure you that it gave me great pleasure to accede to your request. The growth of your institution from a small night-class conducted by voluntary teachers to a flourishing group of schools with nearly 500 pupils affords a striking example of what a community can accomplish when it is determined to work out its own salvation. You have paid a tribute in your address to the encouragement which you received from all my predecessors in furthering the objects of your society, and you may rest assured that I shall always be as ready as they were to help your community to take the place which rightfully belongs to it. One of the best known of your modern poets, Maulvi Altaf Husain Ansari, who wrote under the *nom de plume* of Hali, has written forcibly of the need for that "ilm" which education alone can impart. A friend of mine has translated two of his quatrains, the thirty-ninth and fortieth, as follows:

"Fair Knowledge! By whose favour whole nations riches gain,
While swift decay hath stricken those who Thy arts disdain;
Thou dost disclose the secrets of this World's treasure house
To those far-sighted peoples who of Thy lore are fain

"Hail Knowledge! Of joy's storehouse Thou art the magic key;
Of all delights the fountain, source of prosperity;
Rest Here and Rest Hereafter are found beneath Thy shade;
Provider in this Lifetime, Guide to the Life to Be."

If you will let the work of your institution be infused by that spirit, the key to the future will be in your hands. You have made in your address, gentlemen, certain requests on behalf of your institution, and although I cannot, of course, give you any definite promises, I can assure you that they will all be examined carefully and sympathetically. As you know, the path of one who would like to be a benefactor is a hard one at present, for though the spirit may be strong and willing, the financial

Cerberus begins to growl as soon as the faintest whisper that resembles the word "expenditure" is heard. Specially do I appreciate the need which you, like so many other institutions in Nagpur, feel for more space for playing-grounds, and I will look personally into the question of helping you. And now, gentlemen, it only remains for me to thank you once more for your kindness in presenting this address to me. Your record both in the class-room and on the playing field already gives you legitimate cause for pride, and in congratulating you on attaining your first jubilee I wish you all prosperity for the future. May you preserve intact the ideals which inspired those who founded your society, and build up a strong and enduring tradition of service to your community and to the State.

Note (JHBG):

An interesting point arises here. To the question: Why did the two quatrains quoted above have to be translated in to English and were not given in the local 'baht', the answer probably lies in the statement: "A friend of mine has translated ..." The author of the poem, Maulvi Altaf Husain Ansari, was in all probability from North India, so the original of his poems would likely have been unintelligible in Nagpur. Sir Hyde spoke fluent Hindi and good Urdu, (Urdu is a mixture of Hindi and Punjabi), and, since he had to have the poem translated, it was therefore not written in one of those, so, as usual, it had to be translated into English, the lingua franca of the whole of India. One does wonder, however, what the Nagpuri made of 'nom de plume'!

Sat. Jan 19th

Manekji Dadabhoy threw an enormous dinner-party on Thursday for us – 96 in all, a very pleasant gathering, and lashings of a very good brand of champagne. Of course he got up and said lots of nice things about E. and me and of course I got up and said lots of nice things about him, & what a difficult task I was likely to have under the reforms, & what a good boy I intended to be. The editor of the D.N. was there, and it all appeared print next day, bowdlerised, so as to make one cry – really I should never speak "ex tempore" without sending to the Press a draft of what I actually did say! This was followed by a leading article, saying that they had no doubt that Sir H.G. would be a good boy – quite a good boy – but what they are afraid of was the bad boys who might follow him!

There's no doubt they simply hate the idea that if they play the fool we shall in the last resort be able to put a stop to it. However light they know the hand on the bridle will be, they can't bear the notion that there's a bit at all. At the back of their minds is a Hindu saying: "Timukárá nakel hamáre háth mei hai".

Thank goodness I've finished my Council address, not an easy one to write, with all this invective against the Report. I've stuck to explanation and eschewed controversy as far as I could. Rao says: " If I may be permitted to say so, it reads very well", so I hope it will go down. That it will convince anyone is more than one can hope for.

Tues. Jan. 22nd

Dadabhoy, who was dining with us last night, explained the matter of the bowdlerised speech. It seems he had provided his own stenographer to record speeches, and supply a report to the D.N. Unfortunately D.'s liquor was so good that the stenographer got drunk, and when the speeches came on was "non compos"! So D.'s purple patches and my somewhat less serious effort go unrecorded because of the redness of the wine. I told him Benson's story of Curzon, who at a complimentary dinner attributed his success to the fact that he made it a practice to associate only with his intellectual superiors. Whereon Lord Houghton woke from a doze and exclaimed – "By God, that wouldn't be difficult".

I said I wouldn't copy C. because Chitty might wake up and say something equally disconcerting. They laughed. Then I embroidered a little tale about Scylla and Charybdis – the twin dangers that will beset the Governor whose grasp of the helm is too slack, & him whose grasp is too firm; & pointed out that the ship would only get through if all the crew from Number One downwards, helped the Captain to keep on a steady course, and so on. I've never been so thankful for a classical education as since I became Governor. Whatever its drawbacks may be, it does help one to see and illuminate a point, and thereby, one hopes, to make others see it graphically too.

Yesterday Gour and others came to see me re the C.P. Flying Club. We are in a vicious circle at present. The club can't raise subscriptions until it is assured of an aerodrome. An aerodrome can't be constructed until Govt. is sure that the club can be financed; and Govt. can't be assured of this until subscriptions have been raised. Apparently the G/I are thinking of making an aerodrome, and there's money ear-marked for it. We simply must make certain that an aerodrome is possible on the trap and mud of Nagpur, & I promised that we'd ask the G/I to send a man to settle this question once and for all. Then we can get ahead – or not.

Friday Jan. 25th.
Speech at the Legislative Council on Friday,
the 25th January 1935

Mr. President, and Gentlemen of the Council,— It must needs be that to those who stand at the gateway of great changes the story of the immediate past loses much of its savour and interest. Nevertheless the months which have elapsed since I last addressed you provide food for much serious thought, and I should be doing less than my duty if, before dealing with what lies beyond the gateway, I did not give you some account of the efforts which Government has been making to grapple with the one problem which is of vital importance to us in this province at present—the problem of giving relief to the agriculturist from the burden of debt which is weighing him down. None of you will disagree with me when I say that it is upon the right solution of this problem that the whole future happiness of our province depends. If we are to find a permanent solution of it, we must travel through three stages—first, the diminution of existing debt; second, the provision of means for the liquidation of what remains; and third, the prevention of further indebtedness. I propose to deal with each of these in turn, as briefly as I can. As you know, the whole field of agricultural economic development was surveyed by the Economic Conference which met at Delhi in April of last year, and the conclusions at which it arrived have been of the greatest practical value to us.

With the steps which we are taking to deal with existing debt you are all familiar. We have amended the Usurious Loans Act so as to limit the interest which may be charged to what is just and reasonable, and have passed an Act to control and regulate the dealings of money-lenders. We have also passed an Act which, while it avoids anything approaching confiscatory measures, yet offers considerable inducement to the creditor to agree to the reduction of capital debt. The results of the working of the conciliation boards are made known to you from time to time, and I need not say more than that we have every reason to be satisfied with the progress of what has been an entirely new experiment, so far as legislative action is concerned. But here I must enter a *caveat.* At my recent visit to Raipur, where there is no conciliation board, I was told by malguzars from a certain tract that the report that Government had passed an Act for the partial cancellation of debt, and intended to pass another providing for a moratorium for all debts, had actually resulted in the stoppage of all agricultural credit; and this statement was confirmed to me later by certain sahukars. The rumour about Government's intention is, of course, entirely baseless; but I mention the incident to you to show how delicate the situation is, and in view of what has been happening elsewhere to remind you of the danger which is inherent in all legislation of this character in which compulsion figures—the danger that it may recoil on the heads of the very persons for whose benefit it is intended.

The second stage is the provision of means to enable the agriculturist to pay his debts. Here we were confronted with the phenomenon of a plentiful supply of cheap money in the money market, contrasted with a dearth of money and consequent high rates of interest in the countryside; and our problem was, to adopt a familiar metaphor, to construct channels from the tank to the fields, so that the refreshing water of cheap capital might be brought to them and endow them with new life. The method which after much thought we have decided to adopt for this purpose is the creation of land mortgage banks with debenture capital, the interest on the debentures being guaranteed by Government. I may say in passing that we have also under consideration the question whether Government should guarantee the capital as well. Further, we are introducing legislation to facilitate the operation of the banks in the Central Provinces by making occupancy holdings transferable in their favour. We have, however, been confronted by an unexpected difficulty. We found on enquiry that neither was the supply of money as cheap, nor was the rate of interest charged to those who have good security to offer—the class which it is our main object to benefit—as excessive as we had been lead to expect; in fact, that when the rate of interest at which we could raise debentures had been added to the expenses of management and the profit due to the Provincial Co-operative Bank, which will issue the debentures, the resultant rate of interest to be charged to the mortgagee was barely low enough to be attractive to him. I need not enter into details here. I have explained the general position to show you the practical difficulties which inevitably arise in the solution of a problem of this nature.

There is yet another expedient which we have been examining carefully, and of which I think that you should be informed. There is a general complaint that the selling value of villages is very low, and it has been suggested that Government should enter the market, and offer to buy up whole villages belonging to indebted landlords, the necessary funds being provided by long-term loans. The effect of this step would be threefold. It would stimulate the market; it would give relief, which we were credibly informed would be welcomed in many cases, to landlords who honestly wished to liquidate their debts, and were ready to sell a portion of their estate for the purpose; and it would increase the capital value of Government's rayatwari estate. The scheme sounds attractive; but here again we were met with a practical difficulty. After making all allowances for drawbacks to patels, cesses, and so on, we concluded that as a business proposition we could not afford to pay more as purchase price than 12 to 15 times the land revenue; whereas the figures of actual sales in our possession showed that it was unlikely that these figures would be sufficient except in a comparatively small number of cases. The scheme is there, and if the opportunity arises and you, gentlemen are willing to provide the funds we shall proceed with it; but once again reality seems to throw cold water upon expectation.

I turn now to the third stage, the prevention of debt. I need no excuse for dealing with this matter, because it is one that affects the foundation of our prosperity as a province, and one on which no one who has had real experience of agricultural conditions can help feeling deeply. The measures which we have been considering, so far are not curative; they are no more than palliative. Nor can we ever hope for a permanent cure until we effect a revolution in the countryside and our methods of treating it. As I pointed out in a recent public speech, in a province where three-fourths of the inhabitants are agriculturists the tendency of our educational system is to draw the best brains of the villages into the towns, where they swell the army of the unemployed instead of doing their appointed work in their own homes. When we have reversed this process and have educated the natural leaders of the countryside to lead and reorganize their own heritage; when, further, we have effected a radical alteration in the social customs which compel the tiller of the soil to incur for ceremonial purposes debts which are far beyond his capacity to repay; and when, finally, we have freed him from the ignorance which at present rivets his chains upon him; then, and then only, can we hope to have found the solution of our problem. Signs are not wanting that a new spirit is abroad. Village uplift and village reconstruction are becoming watchwords. And when we have more money to spend on them, and more especially when under the new constitution the increased voting-power of the countryside begins to make itself felt, it is my earnest hope that we shall devote ever-increasing attention to the welfare of those who till the land, which is the real source of our wealth in this province.

And now let me turn for a moment to another spirit which has arisen during the past year and has a close bearing on what

I have just been saying. I refer to the demand for what is called a plan for economic development, something on the lines of the two Russian Five-Year Plans. You are going to discuss this matter shortly, and I shall not say more than that I welcome the discussion, and hope that some fruitful suggestions will emerge from it. During the past year all departments, both agricultural and industrial, have had various plans under execution or investigation, plans for the provision of cheap seed; for the regulation of markets so as to ensure that the cultivator gets a fair price for his produce; for the substitution of profitable crops for those less profitable; for the reclassification of forests so as to improve grazing facilities and to explore the possibilities of rayatwari colonisation; for the adaptation of education to rural needs; for limiting usury and regulating money-lenders; for the production of industrial alcohol from Mahua and for village uplift. We have also prepared a comprehensive scheme for the building of roads and bridges by means of a loan which will be repaid from our annual share of the Road Fund. You will agree, I hope, that we have not been idle. I cannot conclude this part of my address without making a brief reference to the valuable consolidation work which is being carried on in Chhattisgarh. The area dealt with covers half a million acres, in which 11 million holdings have been reduced to 1½ million at a cost of 1½ lakhs of rupees. Villages are now clamouring to be taken in hand, and a second working party has been formed. You may be interested to learn that recently we have had enquiries from the Straits Settlements as to our methods of work—a sure tribute to the value of what we are trying to do.

And now, gentlemen, I shall ask you to step with me beyond the gateway, and to take a brief glimpse into the future. It is not for me to discuss on this occasion those aspects of the new constitution which concern the centre. It is my intention only to try and make clear to you how the changes which are under discussion will affect in actual practice the governance of this province; and if, when you have heard me, you say that I have told you nothing that you did not know already, I shall not be displeased, for I shall know then that you at any rate have "read, marked, and inwardly digested" the Joint Select Committee's Report. I shall only consider that I have failed in my task if I do not succeed in making plain to you the substantial and, in practice almost complete, liberty in the management of the affairs of the province which will be yours under the new Act.

I must first say a brief word on two matters which are not directly administrative, the system of election and the franchise. Great disappointment has been expressed that the system of indirect election to the Federal Legislature has been preferred. But when we look back over the discussions, and think on the array of arguments that was marshalled on either side, does not a suspicion come over us that a great many of them were after all somewhat theoretical and academic? That it is very difficult to find any one of them which outweighs the plain blunt fact emphasised in the Report, namely, that under a system of direct election for the huge constituencies which are to be created candidates could neither canvass their supporters nor keep in touch with them when elected? And that anyhow the results will be pretty much the same whichever system we adopt? I confess that that is how the matter presents itself to me, and if anyone is prepared to "tear a passion to tatters" over the decision, I envy him his power of blind devotion to a dogma.

Next, the franchise. It is a curious thing that, so far as I have been able to discover, those persons who say that they would prefer to remain as we are now have made no reference to the promised enfranchisement of some 21 million men and 5½ million women who have no political rights at present. In our own province the electorate will be raised, so far as we can calculate, from 200,000 to roughly 1¾ million, and a particular feature of the increase will be the very large extension of the female electorate. I would ask you all not to allow your perfectly legitimate desire for the extension of your own political liberty to make you forget these millions of your fellow-citizens, to whom the passing of the Act will mean the dawn of political freedom and responsibility.

I come now to the kernel of my subject, and the one matter which above all others is of practical daily importance to us, namely, the actual governance of the province. And first I would call your attention to a fundamental and vital change which the Act will make. At present the Government of each province exercises, as the Report points out, "a devolved and not an original authority", and the Central Government exercises an extensive and very real authority over it. This latter authority will now cease in all ordinary matters of administration, and the whole executive power and authority of the province will be vested constitutionally in the Governor himself as the representative of the King, and in practice, with certain safeguards, in the Council of Ministers. Now I suggest to you that even if the form of the provincial Government were to remain as it is now, this one change alone would make a large advance towards that solid and tangible goal, the power to manage your own provincial affairs in your own way. And when I add that the present Executive Council is to be removed, and all departments are to be placed in charge of responsible ministers upon whose advice the Governor will act in all ordinary circumstances, I make the further suggestion that for all practical purposes your goal will have been attained. I need not remind you of that fable of Aesop which suggests that it is wiser to hold the substance than to grasp at the shadow.

I shall be told, of course, that the Governor is armed with so many special powers that the powers of ministers will be illusory. Before I deal with that point I should like to make two observations. The first is that I would have you clear away from your minds an analogy which has frequently been used in order to describe these special powers or safeguards. They have been compared to the brakes which are used to keep a motor car under control. That analogy seems to me to be as untrue to fact as it is unsound in suggestion, untrue to fact because the intention of their designers is not to slow down the rate of progress; and unsound in suggestion because brakes are in constant use, while any idea that the safeguards will be used habitually in practice, instead of being reserved for cases of emergency, ignores the very pertinent fact that a Governor holds office only during His Majesty's pleasure. Rather would I put the position thus. Before us stretches a fair high road, down which the car of the State may travel on its lawful occasions without danger and without let or hindrance. But to each side there are occasional turnings, and these turnings lead to bad country, to *cul de sacs,* sometimes to deadly peril. In front of each of these turnings is placed a warning notice and a bar; but if the car is steered straight, not one of these bars will ever be brought into action. And the second observation is this. Are not those who would sweep away the safeguards upon the horns of a dilemma? As I shall suggest to you later, every one of these safeguards is devised to protect some vital interest of the State; and if that interest is imperilled, no sensible man would deny that there

161

must be some means of saving it from being wrecked. But if our affairs are so conducted that no such peril arises, the safeguards will never be used, and to fear them is to be affrighted by a bogey. To those who say that they would prefer to remain under the present Act I would make one further observation. I can assure them that even if these safeguards were employed regularly and to the full, they would provide the so-called "irresponsible" element in the Government—the element which has never exercised its influence except on the side of sanity and moderation—with not one tithe of the power over the whole field of administration that it possesses at present, either directly, or indirectly by its control of finance, or in its capacity as the agent of the central Government.

Let us turn now to the safeguards themselves. In the time at my disposal it is impossible for me to discuss point by point the various "special responsibilities" which are to be laid upon the Governor. You will find them stated in detail in paragraph 78 of the Report, and all I can do is to call your attention to the area which they cover, and to try and show you how limited it is, as compared with the total area of Government's activities. So long as no grave menace arises to the peace and tranquillity of the province; so long as justice is done to the weaker communities who cannot protect themselves; so long as the mistake is not made of shaking the confidence and impairing the efficiency of the public-services by unfair treatment; so long as discrimination is not exercised against those who have laid the foundations of India's commercial prosperity, and non-Indian traders are treated with the same impartiality as Indian traders are claiming for themselves in Burma; so long as due obedience is rendered to the orders of the Governor-General in matters in which general interests are at stake; so long will the special powers of the Governor remain inoperative, and the sword of which so much fear has been expressed will be allowed to rust peacefully in its scabbard. In our province the Governor has an additional responsibility due to the position of Berar, and with that I will deal later. But when all these matters have been added together, no person who is conversant in practice with the work of Government will be prepared to join issue with me when I say that the sum total represents no more than a negligible proportion of the daily work of any member of the Cabinet. I do not intend to deal in detail with the various means, both executive and legislative, which have been devised to ensure that in case of need the Governor's discharge of his special responsibilities shall be real and effective. If they are criticized as too drastic, the reply is two-fold; first, that these safeguards are not playthings, and that a safeguard which is not armed "cap a pie" is no safeguard; second, that their operation is confined normally to the sphere, the strictly limited sphere, of the Governor's special responsibilities.

Here, then, you have the position. A Government of five, in which all the essential departments—finance, revenue, and law and order—are in the portfolios of persons who are not responsible to you for the manner in which they discharge their duties, will give place to a Government in which the minister in charge of every department must render his account to you. The Governor will have certain real and definite powers of intervention, but in a strictly limited field; while in the rest of the field he will be guided in all ordinary circumstances by the advice of his ministers. And here I wish to press one point home with all the emphasis of which I am capable. If we are to judge by what we have heard and read recently, there are some people who picture the future Governor, at the worst as a sort of

Frankenstein's monster, a dreadful Robot-man who will bestride the stage, brow-beating ministers, defying the legislature, and trampling underfoot the new-found liberties of the people; and at the best as an irresponsible autocrat, who will hold those liberties in the hollow of his hand. I can assure you, gentlemen, that there is neither jot nor tittle of justification for either picture. I have reminded you that the powers of the Governor will be small compared to those which he exercises, or can cause to be exercised, at present; and as to the personality of the Governor himself, I would ask what reason has any man for saying that he will be other than what he has been hitherto—a somewhat solitary person, who endeavours to observe the constitution according to the instructions which he has received, to be the friend and counsellor of his ministers, to work harmoniously with his council, and to steer a steady and even course amidst the pitfalls, the discords, and the personal animosities that surround him. Atlas himself had no more grievous burden to bear than that which will lie upon the shoulders of any Governor who fails to live at peace with his ministers and his legislature and to win the support of public opinion; and to suggest that he will court that burden except for the gravest of reasons is to ignore the fact that at heart he is just an ordinary human man, to whom the idea of being a second Athanasius *contra Mundum* makes no kind of appeal. As the Report has pointed out, "the success of the constitution depends far more upon the manner and spirit in which it is worked than upon its formal provisions"; and if those of you to whom it will fall to administer the new Act will display the spirit of trust which you claim that others should display, you need have no fear of any autocracy.

You will expect me, gentlemen, to say something about our special local problem, that of Berar. Unfortunately I am not in a position at present to tell you anything more than you can see for yourselves in paragraphs 61 and 83 of the Report. We have spared no effort to make the true position clear to those in higher authority, and, in especial, to ensure that there should no misunderstanding as to the reality of Berar sentiment. On the financial question, the decision is that the Governor should be given a special responsibility for seeing that Berar gets what is described as "a reasonable share" of the joint revenues, and that, if our present arrangements are thought unsuitable, he shall appoint an impartial committee to advise him in the matter. I have seen it said that this decision delivers Berar bound hand and foot to the tender mercies of the Governor. Nothing, gentlemen, could be further from the truth, for the simple reason that in any decision at which he may arrive the, Governor must inevitably follow, unless he has the gravest of reasons for not doing so, the advice given to him by the committee which is to be appointed if the present arrangements are to be scrapped. But that, gentlemen, is not the vital point. What really matters is this – that the decision implies that we have to settle our problem for ourselves. I can do no more than repeat to you the suggestion which I made last year, that the leaders of both parts of the province should come together and endeavour to arrive at some amicable settlement before the Act comes into force. After that event has happened it will be the Governor's duty in the discharge of his responsibility to take the task of settlement upon himself, and the time for mutual friendly arrangement will have passed.

I am afraid, gentlemen, that I have occupied much of your time. My excuse must be that I have dealt with no subject which was not in my opinion of first-rate importance to us. As practical men of the world, you will permit me to suggest that what really matters to you is the extent to which in future you will be able to manage your own provincial affairs, and that in this respect you need have no misgivings. In wishing you the best of fortune during the ensuing year, I would ask to be allowed as an old friend to remind you of a sentence which William Penn, the Quaker, wrote in prison: "Nothing does reason more right than the coolness of those that offer it; for truth often suffers more by the heat of its defenders than from the arguments of its opposers."

Note (JHBG):

To underline the difficulties of agriculture in the Province, it is well worth noting that half a million acres had been divided into 11 million holdings, and, that even after the working party had completed its work, the average size of a holding was still only one third of an acre.

Sat. Jan 26ᵗʰ

My address to Council yesterday has been well received, which, is always a relief. But the D.N. say that however persuasively and eloquently I may put the case, I can't convert them, as they've made up their minds already! You might as well talk to the hinder end of a mule as try to change the mind of an Indian.

The "Statesman" paid me the compliment of reporting me in extenso with a black line extract at the head. It was very hot in Council, and my brow was like that of the bird in "Tit-Willow" I nearly laughed at the end, when I quoted William Penn's saying - "Nothing does reason more right than the <u>coolness</u> of those that offer it". At the exact moment a large drop fell plum on the right lens of my glasses.

N.J is being obstructive. We all want Govt. to guarantee the capital as well as the interest of these Land Mortgage Bank debentures we're going to issue. Bombay and Madras have both done it, and Darling, the

Punjab expert, has advised us to do it. The risk is trifling, as all loans are doubly covered by the security; and after all, we not only guarantee, we supply, the capital for <u>taecavi</u>, which is much the same sort of transaction. But Noel boggles – talks of the possibility of political pressure to prevent recovery and of extension of the liability and so on – the type of timidity that prevents anyone ever getting forrarder. As I said before, a brain, but with neither vision nor humanity to supply driving power. We had a meeting of Govt. yesterday to discuss his tremors, and I've told him to put them all on record.

Tues. Jan 29th

What might have been an unpleasant incident has closed satisfactorily. The H.P. (Rizvi) has apparently cherished the idea that Gordon was behind Kedar last August in bringing a vote of censure on him, (See August 22nd, 1934.) – this being because G. could not express open approval of what R. had been doing in Raipur. On Friday R. was congratulating N.J. on his promotion (acting). He (Rizvi) was also feeling none too well, owing to some liver complaint, I gather. So he spake thus – "I venture to say that he has been more popular than some of his predecessors in office ...... I hope he will try to revive the good example set by Sir Arthur Nelson whose conduct is a model for all the Services to follow." He also talked about N.J.'s being a future Governor, a matter entirely outside his brief. Now comparisons are always dangerous, and this one was particularly so, because the only H.M.Rs since old A'thur are myself and G. – the head of the province and the permanent Member. Personally I have always got on very well with R. (Rizvi) and have never had the semblance of a breeze; so I was rather hurt that the H.P. should have gone out of his way to make this gratuitous offensive. I got the full report last night, so this morning I sent for Rao and asked him what it all meant, and he said he was sure it was the H.P. trying to get a bit of his own back out of G.. I pointed out that whether the remarks were directed against me or against G. they were in bad taste, uncalled for, and unnecessary – in which he agreed, promising to speak to the H.P.. Ten minutes later the H.P. rang up and asked if he could see me in half an hour. When he came, he assured me at once that I had been miles from his mind when he spoke, and acknowledged straight that it was G. he was getting at. He promised to expunge the offending words from his report, said he quite saw how unwise they were, and asked me to accept his assurances etc., etc. "Tabula rása", I said, and the incident closed. But the scream is that although A'rthur, in his pleasant but rather gutless way, was liberal minded and got on well with the Indian politician N.J. was for years the chief motive force behind the well-meant but very ill-advised and injudicious activities of the E.G.S.A., which earned the Services an unpopularity that outweighed most of the good it did. He was a real Service die-hard, in fact – a bull in the political china shop of the early twenties. (One tactless effusion of his got stamped on heavily by the S/S.) So the H.P.'s appeal to a Nelson-Roughton tradition is not without humour.

Thurs. Jan. 31st.

The H.P. has been setting everyone's nerves on edge. He had to give a ruling on the point whether a select Committee on a Bill should report its proceedings in full, dealing with proposals rejected as well as those accepted, or should merely report what changes it recommends, and say nothing about its proceedings. The former appears to be the English practice; the latter the Indian (established by Sir F. Whyte and followed by Patel). Parakh was for the former, but the H.P. ruled for the latter, and so doing was frankly offensive to P., Kedar, the Mangelwurzel, and all those who had supported the no-confidence motion against him last August. The House tends often to lapse into a school debating society, with everyone interrupting everyone else – I'm not sure that's not an insult to the society; it would be to the R.S.D.S.! – and I know the H.P. wants to get it into order. But there's no need to be unpleasant about being firm; and it's a curious thing that since the House has had its nerves upset it has passed two pieces of legislation which are radically unsound. It has given malguzars a statutory power to take nazarana on the transfer of occupancy holdings to L.M. Banks; and it has sent to a select Committee Mangelwurzel's dreadful Bill for a three-year moratorium for the sale of agricultural land for debt. I'm amazed at the latter act of stupidity; but they must buy their experience.

Indian journalism is not without its better side. One "Chatterbox", who writes in the Hit. (now almost a Congress organ), puts the matter of the H.P.'s remarks about N.J. quite well. "If you are congratulating a man implicate other persons in your speech – particularly persons who were not present – it is slightly indiscreet, let alone unfair .... But it is not the voice of Esau that spoke. I quite understand that." (I wonder whose voice it is!) Then he becomes refreshingly candid. "Rizvi relies only on helpful precedents. He quoted Patel, but Patel was not an impartial Speaker. I do not want to speak disrespectfully of the dead, but fact demands that I should say that Patel was a partisan Speaker. He is not a model but a warning to other presidents." The first time I have ever heard an Indian have the courage to say what all of them know. He does me the compliment of saying: "I always look forward to any public utterance of the Governor, for all his utterances set up a high standard of literary performance."!!

Á propos of the courage of one's convictions, or the lack of it, the more one sees and hears what Indians write and say about the Report, the more one condemns them for levity and irresponsibility. I do not believe that more than one in ten of the writers and speakers have made any serious attempt to read and understand the report that they condemn so glibly. And although H.E. himself, Brabourne, Erskine, Haig, and I have all explained the great advance which the new constitution will bring, and quoted chapter and verse therefor, all we are told is that our arguments are "thin", "weak", "unconvincing" and so on, without one single effort at rebutting them. But, as I said before, one expects nothing else, so is not disappointed. "Chatterbox" tells me that I managed to avoid the trap into which Erskine and Brabourne fell, of giving "patronising" assurances that they would give assistance in working the constitution. It's terribly easy to fall into that trap unless you've spent many years in the country.

Thurs. Feb. 7th

The Council debate on the Reforms added nothing to its laurels. I gather from Rao that scarcely a man among them had made any effort to read the Report, and certainly none of them made any effort at fair and impartial appraisement of it. But with the inevitable exception of Kedar the debate was calm and good-tempered, and most if it was thinly attended and extremely dull. Even Parakh did not enliven it by his usual travesties of fact. He was merely frothy, and didn't give the Govt. benches, which were waiting for him, a chance. Rao made a very able and sensible speech. It must have been a hard business for him, for of course he thinks that the reforms are inadequate. But office has brought him much wisdom.

As soon as the chattering had ceased, N.J., Wilson & I took train to Raigarh en route to Sarangarh's famous duck shoot – a very enjoyable three days. On Sunday we split into three parties of 4 each, & shot snipe (mostly) between Raigarh & the Mahanaddi, getting to Sarangarh in time for dinner – total bag 136. Next day we shot the more distant tanks and got 201, including a record bag of 25 geese. The third day we shot the near tanks. S. was very keen to beat the record they set up the year Monty was there, 525, and we beat it fairly easily getting a total of 900 for the three days, the only really big shoot I've had in the C.P..

S. (Sarangarh, a Rajah and large landowner) is a most enlightened man, seeing that he is only a Raj Gond, and has never been to England. Everything in the Palace was spick and span, and during the whole of our stay we saw no one except him and his son (and the Rani for a few moments) – none of the usual underlings, hangers-on, and poor relations that one is accustomed to in such places. He was an excellent host. I wrote in the Visitor's Book: "It seldom falls to a man to assist in making a record and to take so small a personal part in the making, and at the same time to enjoy himself so thoroughly". The fly in the ointment was that a new gun for which I paid the A.&N. £40 in Oct. went wrong and I've had to send it back.

Thurs. Feb. 14th

A long week-end in the Banjar Valley, where I wanted to take E. because I knew it was the sort of thing she'd enjoy. And really it was attractive – 99 sq. m. of undulating forest and maidán, with low hills all round, and over the maidán the game wanders, - barasingh, cheetah, sambhar, pig, black-buck, (a few) and an occasional bear. But the numbers are nothing to what they used to be, and heads of any size are few. I am going to have the regulations tightened up. I found that a Mahommedan Army contractor in Jubb. had been given 11 licenses in one year in Molinala and other Mandla ranges! A scandal. Needless to say, the D.F.O. (an Imperial officer) who gave them was also a follower of the Prophet. The game is being exploited commercially – to an Army contractor the possession of game blocks into which he can take his "friends" is an asset of obvious value – but fortunately there is a definite urge at present towards preservation.

I really have been unlucky in my P.S.s. After ten months of him I have definitely had to admit defeat over Cole. He "deeply regrets" his mistakes – and repeats them the next day; says that he "feels ashamed of himself" for failing me – and makes not the smallest effort to do better;

admits with tears in his eyes that he has been slack and spineless – and does another flop an hour later. It's like trying to get life out of a jelly-fish, and I've told him that he must go on leave as soon as he can get a passage. Ling is getting me a man from the Shropshires whom he guarantees. His name is Caesar!

The naïveté of the Indian politician is beyond belief. Govt. vigorously opposed the Mangelwurzel's Bill for a moratorium, because it said it was a dangerous and unwise measure. Now he writes to me and asks me to break all precedent and give him a day in the budget meeting to get the Bill through. Reasons – the usual talk about the plight of the agriculturalist, about which M. cares not two hoots, and of which he knows nothing first hand. Unfortunately, he had omitted to take the precaution of asking that the Sel. Committee should report before the meeting, and as Rao had already summoned them for after the session, my reply was easy. But E. saw nothing strange in asking me to expedite a measure of which I have openly expressed disapproval. And the other day Sharif, whose bitterness towards Rao I have recorded, came to me and asked me to make him G.A., and later a High Court judge! I pointed out to him that as an ex-Minister he knew the position of the Home Member with regard to such appointments, and asked him if he thought that Rao was likely to back him. He grinned somewhat sheepishly. I wonder if he really thought that I should ask R. to agree to his appointment, knowing full well that R. would go off the deep end on the spot.

The G/I have made a great mistake, presumably under pressure from Whitehall. They have restored the 5% salary cut, and of course that forces us to do the same, thus converting our small budget surpluses for next year into a deficit. (Needless to say they refuse to give us a subsidy to cover the cost.) The move will not only make the Imperial Services still more the target of the agitator, but will put up the backs of all the commercial people, who have had a much harder time than we have had.   With Champagne dinners, Commission Weeks, & Police "Conferences", we cannot pretend to be suffering very seriously, and it is never worth receiving preferential treatment which makes everyone jealous of you.   But the G/I have little sense of reality.

Sunday March 3rd

A quite uneventful fortnight up to the 26th.   After that, hectic.   We motored to Jubb. that day, and in the evening opened a new wing at the St. Aloysius High School.   Took the opportunity of impressing on the A.I.s that although they would be under my wing in the new scheme, God helps those who help themselves, and no amount of special protection can keep a community that is not strong in itself alive indefinitely.

Next day (27th) their Excls. flew from Delhi to attend the Trooping of the Colour by the King's – their 250th anniversary.   They arrived punctually to the minute – 11.30 and were as delightful as ever.   He said he'd had a restful journey – read the paper from end to end, and had a good snooze.   The "Star of India" is certainly a beautiful plane, a four-engined monoplane, very comfortably fitted.   I drove with H.E. to the ground and E. with Lady W..   H.E. was very worried over the demarche of the Princes, who say that the G/I Bill & the draft Instrument of Accession are not in accordance with what they had agreed to.   H.E. is very worried, as he says that it puts the whole scheme in jeopardy, with the Princes holding all the trumps.   I am not surprised. It has always seemed to me to be a fatal mistake for us to build a constitution which depended in any way on the Princes, who are simply out for their own personal advantage.   We have governed B.I. now for the best part of a century without their taking part, and I can see no reason, apart from these infernal legal fictions about suzerainty and paramountcy & so on, why the grant of self-govt. to B.I. must mean bringing the Princes in.   Know the usual arguments about interconnection of interests etc., but that could all have come later, when we had got a reformed constitution going in B.I.. As it is, bringing the Princes in has delayed the reforms by years, and now at the last moment they look like upsetting the applecart.

But to return – the Trooping went off with machine-like precision. (Her Ex. stepped out in front of the Shauciana as the colours passed, & curtseyed low to them.) After that we took them to the C.H. for a few minutes rest and a glass of sherry before lunch. Her Ex. patted David (butler) on the shoulder and congratulated him on having been with us for 24 years. David is now a demi-god in the servants' quarters. Lunch at the Kings, a jolly party, as their Exs. have a wonderful way of getting rid of any atmosphere of restraint on these occasions. They delighted the N.C.O.s after lunch by being photographed with them, and promising to sign each copy. (The papers reported that it was me who had done this. We had to correct hastily!) At 2:30 (off) their Exc's left. All the King's officers & wives rushed down to the aerodrome & gave them a great send-off. They got back to Delhi well within the 4 hours. But I was glad when the plane was up. She seemed to clear two trees as the end of the aerodrome by not more than a few feet.

On the 28th I opened a new ward of the Victoria Hospital – another speech; how sick I am of making them! This one contained a real "gaffe". Wilson (I.G.C.H.) phoned me while I was writing it to say that one Dr. S.C. Barat was giving a large sum to build a new dispensary, and would I mention the fact? Now a doctor of the same name and initials was in the C.P. for many years ended up as a C.S. and retired in Jubb., so I talked about my old friend Dr Barat – only to discover to my horror that he had been dead three years and that the donor was his son, (though how the initials came to be the same I didn't discover).

To Nagpur on the 1st, and straight off to Dhantoli to hear Shrinivas Shastri open the Gokhale Library. He is a sick and weary man, and spoke sitting, but he spoke beautifully on the need for study and knowledge of books – the best speech I've heard in years.

Next morning (2nd) we went to a jubilee celebration of the New English High School – another speech! And in the evening Edna went to a show at the Parsi Girls' High School. We've been earning our pay lately.

Gordon comes back on the 8th, thank goodness. N.J. has not been much help as H.M.R.. He has opposed almost everything I have wanted to get done, and the only kind of action which seems to appeal to him is clamouring for financial help from the G/I – the sort of importunate protesting which got the E.G.S.A. such a bad name when he was its controlling spirit. And his budget speech was a perfect miracle of dullness.

Friday March 8th

Trouble in store. Grille came to me yesterday morning and asked about his confirmation as J.C.. Macnair having retired, there is now a clear vacancy, and the file about filling it came up a few days ago. We are hoping to get our High Court in Jan., and Rao proposed that as Grille cannot be C.J., being in the I.C.S., it would be better to let matters stand, and not confirm any one. I put on the file that this would not be fair to Grille, and was unnecessary, because G. had taken office on the clear understanding that judges of the J.C.'s court will have no hakk on judgeships in the new Court. Grille then saw Rao, and the latter told him (somewhat peevishly, so G. said) that if it was held that someone must be confirmed, he would have grave doubts about recommending him, because (a) he had been obstructive over the High Court proposals (b) he had shown racial prejudice over the question whether Hemeon should be confirmed before Shah, and (c) he had not stopped the Bar getting a budget cut brought about by his refusal to close the Courts on Abhyankar's death. (a) was an honest difference of opinion, and it is absurd to say that G. was obstructive. (b) again was a question whether merit should go before seniority, and there was no question where the merit lay. (c) was no business of Grille's, and I am surprised at Rao tackling him about it. The Abhyankar case was amazing. A blustering, ill-conditioned fellow, who had fought Govt. consistently, had gone to jail in the C.D. and been disbarred because of it, and had only just asked pardon and been allowed to resume practice. And when he dies, immediately after an election campaign that he had fought in the most scurrilous and unprincipled fashion, they want the Govt.'s Courts of Justice to be closed as a mark of respect! I disallowed a resolution on the subject, and now they've carried a token cut – as if in any case the thing had anything to do with the Council. They're an irresponsible lot, but I wish they'd redeem the fact by having some sense of humour.

Sund. March 10th

I spoke to Rao about the Grille business. Apparently G. was tactless enough to insist on seeing Rao at 1 p.m. on a Sunday during Council. A man who does that deserves all he gets, and Rao admits he was a bit short with him. He says that G. is not pulling his weight in the Court, but he doesn't want to be "difficile" over it. We are now to find out whether we must fill the post permanently or not.

One can't always have good days, and yesterday was one of the worser sort. First, a peremptory letter from some wooden-head in the F. and P., refusing to increase the allowances of some Afghan Sirdars, sons of an ex-Amir, whom the G/I planted on us two years ago. *(I have more papers on this if anyone is interested – TJG.)* After having impressed on us their royal lineage etc., they now tell us that they're ordinary British subjects, and that their allowances are higher than they'd get if they were generals in their own country. The answer is obvious. If they were generals in their country, their receipts would not be confined to their pay. Next, I went to lay a foundation stone at a school. The original programme included one speech from the Secretary. But at the New English H.S. the President had spoken as well, and the boys sang "Bande

Mataram" at the end; so these people added a second speech and B.M.. Now I have no objection to B.M.. The words are harmless, and the old disloyal associations are dead now. But I have no desire to have it thrust upon me wherever I go. It's a dull and dreary tune! So I said: "Stick to your original programme", the result being a distinct falling off in the usual audience! Third, I lent G.H. to the S.J. Fund Comm. for a fete. It was a well-run show, but only about half the number expected turned up, the rest being stopped, apparently, by the 1/- entrance fee. G.H. is not such a draw as the Comm. fondly imagined. I gather there is the usual amount of jealousy and underhand work going on over the Fund. One gets very tired of a life in which nothing is allowed to be simple and straightforward, every act is suspected to be a cloak for some deep-laid scheme, and every fact is distorted, and endowed with some sinister significance.

Chikalda. Thurs. March 14th

Here for a week, to get E. away from the heat till she sails. We've never seen the place before, and the views are wonderful – miles and miles of hill and valley and plain on all sides.

Yesterday I had a meeting of Govt. about the 5% cut in pay, which the G/I have restored. The Council have made a mess of things, as usual. Instead of registering their protest, in which I personally would gladly have joined them (!!), they have cut out the necessary supplies in certain depts., the remainder escaping under the guillotine. The result is that in the reserved depts. I must certify, and it was agreed that I should do this; and in the transferred depts. we must let the cut stand as regards those whose service commenced after 1.1.22. For those who were in service on that date the S/S's sanction is needed, and the Ministers had to scratch their heads very hard before they made up their minds to advise me that this should be applied for. They and Rao wanted to temporise and bargain, there being an idea that if we promised to restore part of the cut in the grants to Local Bodies, they (the Council) would pass a supplementary demand for the extra pay in Aug.. To me this is a piece of financial impropriety. We have said we can't restore the cut in the grant, and are only restoring the cut in the pay because we're compelled to. To do a thing which we know to be financially unsound merely to buy the Council's vote is nothing short of bribery, and I told Naidu so. (It's his idea, needless to say.) He grinned sheepishly. Finally they decided to take the hurdle.

Sat. March 16th

After I'd passed all the drafts and signed the necessary orders about the above, out comes a note from N.J. saying that Members and Ministers wanted more time to think the matter over. Considering the intellectual capacity of Indians, it is a constant source of amazement to me to see the time, the terrible long time, that it takes them to grasp the whole of a subject and to make up their minds about it. It is, of course, one of the reasons that we're in the country – their slowness of mind and lack of decision. It's annoying in this case, because we must get the S/S's orders before April 10th, if we are going to enforce the cut on May 1st. I suppose they're on the bargaining tack again. The Ministers are evidently not finding it easy to keep their party together. The Nationalists have insisted on Naidu handing L.S.G. over to Khaparde. Kh. came to me and said that he didn't think it fair that N. should have to stand all the fire (Excise cum L.S.G.), so he proposed to sacrifice himself for his colleague and take over L.S.G.. "Very noble of you, Mr. Khaparde", says I – not caring in the least which of them stands the battering, but being very fed up with the way in which Naidu has dealt with nominations to local bodies, which are now made on political grounds and no others. I wonder whether old Kh. really thought I should swallow his tale of altruism. The newspapers blew the gaff the very next day.

Sund. March 24ᵗʰ Nagpur.

An interesting meeting about the cut in pay. I told my colleagues:

i. that it was the Ministerial party which had landed us in our quandary, and must face the anticipated discontent in the Services;

ii. That although I had a special responsibility for the Services (Rao had underlined this) this did not extend to violating the constitution, which I should do if I allowed the transferred depts. to draw full pay;

iii. that in the case of the post-1922 men we should offend against the constitution if we paid them sums which the Council had specifically refused to vote, and in the case of the pre-1922 men if we did not take action at once to obtain the required orders of the S/S;

iv. that if allowed these two classes to draw full pay, trusting to a reverse vote on the Council in August and if the Council then stuck to its previous vote, the person who would be left holding the baby would be myself, and that in view of (i) above it was neither just nor fair to ask this of me. I left them in no doubt that a Governor could not possibly allow himself to be put at the mercy of the Council's vote in such a fashion. Rao and Gordon both agreed that my view of the situation was right. The Ministers plainly hated having to face the hurdle again, but they saw they had no option but to take it, in view of the plain facts of the Constitution, which they could not dispute. So they agreed that we should ask the S/S to sanction the cut for the pre-'22 men, telling him that we should, if feasible, ask the Cl. to reconsider the matter in August. The post-'22 of course cannot be paid till there is a fresh vote. The Ministers are divided between their dislike – which we all share – of giving back the 5%, and their fear of Service discontent. As in so many difficulties, the only sound course is to stick to the Constitution and one's Instructions whenever one is in doubt. They contain the final answer to all objections.

Monday April 8th

Nothing of any consequence has happened for a fortnight, which has been blessedly peaceful, and spent amidst the sight and scent of flowers. As the result of my insistence, my Pachmarhi garden is really beautiful this year – beautiful, that is, by comparison with the usual Indian landscape.

Last week I passed an order, on the Minister's advice, dismissing a rogue of a Municipal President about whose case there had been a lot of talk. In Thursday's issue of the Hit, I was astonished to see an article saying that the man was to be given a further hearing, and accusing me of unjustifiable interference with the Minister! I sent for the file at once, and was astonished once more to find that after I had passed my order the man had asked Khaparde for a further hearing, and he had granted it. He acted in all good faith, of course, and his sole idea was to make sure that the man had had every chance to present his case, but it had never occurred to him that when I had passed my order the case was finished, and could not be reopened without my consent. He offered to write to the Hit. and say he took the whole responsibility but I said 'No', partly because it doesn't really matter much what the Hit. says or thinks, and also it has always had its knife into Kh., and I don't want to give it an occasion for having another dig at him. "They say? What do they say? Let them say."

E. sailed on the 23rd, and I'm now in my dark half of the year – just as the Hindus divide each month into a dark and a light half, so I divide my year into the two halves, when E. is away and when she's with me. She had done same very good work – Girl Guides, Village Nursing Schemes, and Women's College – and has endeared herself greatly to everyone. I'm glad of it, because once she gets keen on these aspects of the life of a Governor's wife, she will cease to dislike her position quite as much as she did when it first fell to her!

Tues. April 9th

Really one need never go short of something to tickle one in this country. I've just had a request for the Home Membership (Rao's term ends in October) from, of all people, the Mangelwurzel, that glum-faced Pharisee and intriguer who is the real leader of the People's Party, and who, as editor of the now defunct "People's Voice", lost no opportunity of criticising me and embarrassing me. And he's got the brains of a rabbit. Of course he didn't come himself; he sent his smiling and genial younger brother, who is his chief jackal. I merely laughed, and said I hadn't really thought about the matter, but if that if etc., etc.. I'd have liked to say that if, every person eligible for the post refused it, I still wouldn't offer it to M. senior. It's amazing how many Indians there are who have an unfailing belief in their own capacity to fill any post, whatever degree of administrative ability or professional skill it may require, and have not the slightest compunction in asking for it, quite undeterred by any disservice they may have done to the person whose favour they seek. The most unforgiving and unforgetting of people, they nourish a grudge through generations, but have no shame or false pride about begging from a person whom a short time before they've been doing their best to annoy.

Monday April 15th

I was so cross about the G/Is orders re: the Afghans that I wrote to Glancey, the Foreign Secretary, and told him about what I thought about the way that the G/I had treated us. Yesterday I had a letter from Metcalf, the Dy. Sec., saying that he'd taken the file to the Viceroy, & H.E. had said that we were to have our way, for which I was very thankful. The Political department add a lot of stuff about the rapaciousness of the Sardars, of which – not being utter fools – we are as fully aware as they. The difference between us and the G/I is that when a man asks for a pound they say that a penny is ample, while we say "give him half-a-crown". Anyhow, H.E. has now allowed us enough for them so that we can tell them that they won't get any more.

Khaparde came to me a day or two ago to discuss a Committee that he wants to appoint to revise our system of local self-government. The Kelkar-Misra-Shukla school, which considers that local bodies should be under no control – or next to none – by the Govt. on whose bounty they exist, has been trying to organize a Federation of Local Bodies, and we are at a parting of the ways, where it is very necessary that our next steps shall be taken wisely and carefully. So when Naidu suggested a Committee composed of non-officials plus R.S. and the Minister, I jibbed. Fortunately there is an undoubted swing of the pendulum away from the K.M.S. crowd. People have been disgusted with the doings of local dictators and with the scandals which have been rife in the affairs of local bodies, and Khaparde thinks the Committee will remember that they themselves may shortly want to preach the official view, when they themselves are in charge of government – the official view being, of course, that bodies merely exercise a delegated power for certain definite and strictly local purposes. We have added L.R. and the D.C. Nagpur, and made a change or two in the non-officials, and I hope that everything will be well.

Tues. April 16th

For a man of brains N.J. sometimes shows a strange lack of tact and perception. Over this Silver Jubilee Medal a delicate situation has been created by the G/I suggesting that we should consider giving the medal to M.L.A.s and M.L.C.s. Some of them are disqualified at once on the ground of disloyalty. Are we to give it to the rest, including the dummies, simply as M.L.C.s? Common decency shouted "No"; so we wrote to the G/I (I drafted the letter myself) and said we thought medals should only be given on the grounds of public service, and not of membership of a legislative body. They agreed. The difficulty in the case is of course that the Medals are to be awarded by Govt., and not the Govr.. Party politics enter at once. Now it transpires that Commrs. have been asked not to include M.L.C.s in their lists, and N.J. puts me up a separate note on them, proposing that they should all get the medal except the dummies and the Congressmen. This puts us in the exact position which I wished to avoid. The proposal itself is bad, because there are many M.L.C.s whose loyalty is anything but unimpeachable, and many others who have done nothing whatever to deserve a Medal. And if we select, we fall straight into the mud. The only safe course is to keep M.L.C. business out altogether; and yet when the G/I has agreed to this, my simple-minded Chief Sec. goes straight off on the course against which I'd warned him!

Sunday April 21st

Rao has given in about Grille, and has agreed that we shall confirm him if he admits that this will give him no title to compensation if he gets less pay in the new High Court. So that's settled, so long as Grille agrees and he'll be a fool if he doesn't.

A very nice letter from H.E. about Rao's extension. As I feared I've put him in a difficulty, because he's already refused extensions in Bombay and Bengal. He gives us a locus penitential by suggesting that Rao would be much better employed after Oct., so far as his own future is concerned, by nursing his party and his constituency, & asking me to say whether that's so or not. The answer is of course "not"! Rao would never have agreed to my asking for an extension if it was likely to prejudice his future! I sent for him & had a talk, & he said his constituency was safe, & as H.M., M.L.C. and Leader of the House he was in a much better position to look after his future than as a plain Mr. R.. I replied to H.E. accordingly, but said that I quite understood his difficulty, and was content to leave the matter entirely in his hands.

Wed. April 24th

An amazing cable from the S/S about the cut in pay – rambling and incoherent. Starts by saying that he won't sanction the cut for the pre-'22 people ('22 we are now told should be '26) and seems to suggest that I should do the same with regard to the post -'26 people, though I've already told him that I can't "authorise". Then goes on to put two alternatives, one of which is that we should continue the cut without authority conferred by rule, and let ourselves be sued in Court – or else let Govt. servants appeal to me, in which case I shall allow the appeal, repudiating the action of my own Government! At least that is what we make out of the cable. Seldom can it have been suggested to a government by an authority like the S/S that it should deliberately do an act which it knows to be illegal and unconstitutional. Sir S.H. is ill at the moment, & we imagine that his advisers at the I.O. have got out of hand. The whole tone of the cable is, not that the wishes of the Council are entitled to the slightest respect, but that they must be made to vote the money by every possible means. We shall eventually come down to the bribe that I spoke of before. Another effort to economise gone west. Having been forced to have a separate D.P.H., we asked if the I.G.C.H. could do I.G Prisons. The usual reply from the G/I dictated by the Delhi Medico gang – a lot of twaddle about the efficiency of jail administration, modern methods, and so on. A lot of use "modern methods" are with the average Indian jail-bird! Meanwhile we've got to pay about 2000/- a month extra to keep an officer who's barely half employed. I am rapidly coming to the conclusion that it's a waste of time trying to be economical as long as the G/I is there to thwart one's every effort. They have never shown any knowledge of what real economy means, nor any sympathy with those who try to enforce it.

Sunday 28th April

I've finished the 5% cut business for the present. Much to my surprise, Gordon was anything but sound over it at first. He seemed to hold that the fact that Council had specifically refused funds for restoration was of no particular importance, so long as we didn't exceed the total grant. To my mind that is a bureaucratic constitutional heresy of the first water. He also maintained that if the S/S refused to issue rules continuing the cut, I should be bound to authorise at the end of the year. That is not only another b.c. heresy as to the nature of authorisation, but is directly opposed to the Act, which says that the use of the power lies in the discretion of the Governor. However, we thrashed the whole matter out at a meeting, and I wrote a draft to which they all agreed – G. ringing me up to say that he thought that the draft was the last word on the matter! But it's not an easy thing to tell the S/S that you don't like being asked to do illegal & unconstitutional acts. The curious thing is that there's apparently a lacuna in the constitution. The G/I Act gives the Council power to refuse funds for any particular item. And the classification rules (issued subsequently) give the S/S power to say that in certain circumstances that item must be incurred. But it never seems to have occurred to anyone that these powers might clash.

Sat. May 4th

If one gets kicked sometimes without deserving it, at other times one gets praise which is equally undeserved. I suppose the moral is that as one is not elated by the latter, one ought not to be irritated – as one often is – by the former. Here is the Hit. on our last Administration Report. "Those of us who were in close touch with ministerial politics in 1933-34 and the forces that were working against a stable Ministry cannot but give our approbation to the extremely tactful way in which H.E. Sir H.G., handled the situation, when a false step might have led to a serious crisis in our province. H.E. knows the men of our province well, a knowledge which Sir M.B. had and which was responsible for his success in our province." All I did was to stick strictly to the constitution and tell the defeated Ministry that it must resign, and then to appoint the leaders of the opposition, cursing the Council meanwhile for a set of inconstant knaves! I wish praise was always earned as easily as that!

The Jubilee Fund is going better that I hoped, and with luck we may get 2½ lakhs from the province.

A letter from H.E., in reply to one of mine, says that I can give the Council another year's life. They'll have had six years instead of three, and of course they have no shadow of a claim now to represent public opinion, but we think it better to keep them on than to let these wild and woolly Congressmen get in and make a mess of things. They are a dreadful crew – noisy, blustering, unpractical, not even honest (vide Gandhi), and we may as well have peace as long as we can.

Tues May 7th

The jubilee went off very well. The military had a small show of their own at dawn, not feeling able to put up a public show. 10.00 was parade service which was packed. I read the lessons, & had rather a start, as I suddenly felt giddy in the middle – the heat and heavy clothes I suppose, too soon after breakfast. But I took a strong pull at myself and got through without anyone noticing. In the afternoon we played the military at golf & had a great battle. 3 all and 2 halved. We played "Greensomes". Hennessey and I were round in 78, but lost on the last green 1 down. I had the members of Govt. & one or two others to dinner, and afterwards the whole station came to an "At Home", at which I gave away the Jubilee medals – a trying job, as they would not stick on the clasps. The garden was illuminated, & looked really beautiful. The Indian is a past-master in the art of illumination, and everyone seemed to enjoy the scene. I'm keeping the lights up today so that all the children can come in this evening and see them – this by special request.

Thurs. May 16th

An instance yesterday showed how the safeguards will be needed. We were discussing in the cabinet the appointments to be made to the High Court, and Rao very rightly proposed that we should accept the ordinary principle, viz. that until the claims of existing members of the C.S. had been worked off, the no. of I.C.S. judges should be 3, as at present. Naidu said he agreed to 3 this time, but would admit no future claims; and Khaparde wanted frankly to bag one I.C.S. post and give it to a pleader. When I pressed him for his reasons he could only say: "We ought to do it in order to encourage the Bar"! Like saying that you ought to allow a man to burgle your house in order to encourage the Thieves' Den! I told him straight out that it was just that attitude which made the Services so insistent on safeguards.

There is a gold mohur tree outside my office which is really beautiful – a perfect shape and a mass of golden-red bloom, which is at its best when the early morning sun strikes it. In spite of the heat, all the painters in Pachmarhi are homing to paint it.

Friday, May 24th

A terrible catastrophe. The whole of the top floor of the Sectt. has been burnt out, including all the C.I.D. records and the offices of half a dozen departments. The lower floor is not burnt and all the Govt. records have been saved, but goodness knows whether it is sufficiently sound to stand the upper floor being re-built on top of it. There is no news as to how the fire started. It had caught hold well before any one spotted it. Query – what were the chowkidars doing? But it looks as if it was the electric wiring that was at fault, and if that is so I shall want to know why my orders for regular inspection, issued after the narrow escape we had at G.H. last rains, have not been carried out. The way the P.W.D. allow the installations which are all 25 years old, to rot and become dangerous unattended is scandalous.

H.E. has agreed to an extension for Rao, for which I am thankful. It would have been silly to have made a change for one year. The date of the reforms – i.e. provincial autonomy – has now receded to April 1ˢᵗ '37. Well that's three more months' peace!

Tues. June 11ᵗʰ

There has been nothing of local interest to record. We have all been terribly shocked by the Quetta earthquake, and I've issued an appeal for funds, but I don't know how much will be forthcoming. The Province has just paid up extremely well for the Silver Jubilee Fund – 5¼ lakhs, half what the Punjab with four times our wealth has subscribed – so it's a bit hard to have to put its hand in its pocket again so soon. But the distress is awful, and we must do what we can. The S.J. result is more than double what I had hoped for.

Rao wants to leave Staples out in the appointments to the new High Court, & put Gruer in instead. I can't say I like the idea. S. may be no great shakes, but he's the senior of all the judges in length of service and Gruer is anything but impressive. We are suffering from the time, 15 to 25 years ago when no-one would go into the Judicial unless he was forced in. The result is that there isn't a single outstanding personality among the judges.

I gave a dance to the whole station on Saturday. Of course it rained – the only rain we've had for two months – and we had to have supper in the dining room and the verandah. But they all managed to squeeze in somehow, & they seem to have been quite happy.

Wed. June 26th

If it's a case of having to deal with a fool or a knave, give me the knave every time. We – that is Govt., the Municipal Committee, everybody – have been havering a long time over the question of new waterworks for Nagpur, the provision of which is a matter of the utmost urgency. We have a perfectly sound scheme, called the Kanhan Scheme, which won't cost more than 20 lakhs, can be finished in two years, will give us all the water we want now, and is capable of expansion. Naidu wants to spend three years investigating certain gravitation schemes which will cost double the amount, can't be completed – including the three years required for investigation in under 7 years, and will give no more water and be no cheaper to run. I simply could not make him see that if we start investigating the gravitation schemes we can't get on with the Kanhan scheme. He seemed to think we might carry the latter out at the same time spend a lakh or so on the other investigations. At length I asked him whether, in the face of everyone's statement that the present position is most dangerous, he was prepared to take the risk of saying that Nagpur shall have no more water for 7 years. Then he blenched and said 'no'. For a responsible politician he has a head of amazing thickness, and I can't make out how he manages to keep control of a party. In the present case I'm certain there's something behind his obduracy (today's discussion was the culminating point of nearly a year's noting and counter-noting in the Sectt.).

Just had a letter from H.E. saying that the S/S is agreeing to our proposal i.e. the 5% cut, viz. that he should pass no orders until after the August session. (See 28th April.) But he has sent a private telegram to H.E. that if the Council refuses to be good and vote funds, we mustn't imagine that the matter will be allowed to rest there – in other words, that he'll insist on the cut being restored. It will be interesting to see the text of the orders.

I see that I thought we should do well if we got 2½ lakhs for the S.J. Fund. We've got 5¼ ! The enthusiasm for the S.J., and the readiness to help the Fund, was beyond belief. In proportion to our resources we've done as well as any province in India, and better than most.

Saturday June 29th

The letters about the 5% cut are interesting. The G/I in a long letter to the S/S backed us up nobly, and said that we were right all through on the constitutional issue & that the various courses proposed by the S/S were imposs.. The S/S replied very briefly that he accepted our proposal that he should pass no orders till after the August session.

I had a private letter from Rab at the I.O. which said that they were going to agree to Rao's extension, of which I am glad. The local gossips are buzzing with excitement, of course, as to whether he is going to get it.

John Stent, Commr. of Nagpur, a reformer in a hurry, has sent up a great scheme for a Town Improvement Trust for Nagpur, which is to have a Mayor and Corporation. Except for the M. and C. idea, which is what the Indian editor loves to call "an eyewash", the scheme is a good one, and he's taken a lot of trouble over it. But he wants us to vet it, agree to it, settle its finances, and rush a Bill of 111 clauses through the August session, sending it direct to the Select Committee instead of circulating it for opinion. Not a hope. Nagpur is a curious place. It has "swelled visibly" in the past ten years, and has now nearly a quarter of a million inhabitants, but no one can quite make out why. Bar two cotton mills and a small Railway workshop it has no industrial shows of any size, there is no particular wealth in the place, and both it and its leading inhabitants are entirely undistinguished. Streets and buildings are mean and unimposing, and in fact it is very difficult to make out why it should have grown as it has or why it should be thought worthy to aspire to the dignity of a Mayor. I am by no means sure that Govt. will agree to forego half a lakh of revenue, and the citizens to pay a substantial sum in extra taxation for the luxury of this Trust.

CHAPTER 7

1935
JULY - DECEMBER

Sat. July 6th Nagpur

People are very nice sometimes. The 4th being my birthday, I asked a few Pachmarhi people in to a quiet dinner as I always do. At breakfast time I found my place laden with presents – a book rest from Julius, an electric toaster from Davey, a set of Bonzo tools from Betty Chance (engaged to J. and saying in the house), a dozen golf balls from Joe Hennessey (also staying with me), silk hankies from Sheila & David, Joe's two kids, and another from my very good friend Doris B. And at dinner my guests presented me with an autographed copy of Buchan's – "The King's Grace". I was touched beyond words. I suppose they all felt that they'd like to make some return for hospitality, but as I always tell people, I want no return. I'm overpaid – or certainly not underpaid! – and I ask people to stay with me because I like having people about me. I can't go to the Club, because people have to rise when I come, & there's too much fuss altogether. And as I'm a gregarious soul, liking well the company of my fellow-men, they must come to me instead – and I claim no merit for asking them. And there's another problem. I couldn't bear that an idea should get around that H.F. expects presents

– especially ones of some value. It would cramp my style and everyone else's. So I had a heart-to-heart talk with J., the keeper of my conscience, & explained to him exactly what I felt, and that I wanted him to let it be known in a quiet way that H.E. did <u>not</u> want anything ever beyond a sort of token present costing a very few rupees. That sort of thing always tends to spread, & I couldn't bear people to have the idea that I expected things.

Next day we came down to Nagpur via Chindwara. Never again in the rains. In the last 40 miles there are at least seven places, at any one of which one may be held up. Fourteen miles out we got a cloud burst, and sat for an hour watching the waters rise over an Irish bridge. (What bitter sarcasm in that name!) Then I got fed up and we went back to Savner, 6 miles away & had some tea and caught a train on the "chota line" that had not intended to start for two hours, but didn't seem to mind waking up earlier. The cars didn't get in till nearly midnight. I suppose I'm impatient, but sitting in a car without occupation of any sort, waiting for a stream to fall, would drive me frantic.

Mond. July 8th

I foresee we're going to have difficulties of the type usual in this country over the disposal of the S.J. Fund. Their Exs. propose to take 20 out of the 120 lakhs in the Fund for Quetta relief and to divide up the remainder eventually in the proportion of 30 to the centre and 70 to the provinces. As a start they are giving us 55 shortly. I asked Gordon and Staley (Sec. of our local branch) to come and talk things over, and they told me that the lawyers in the committee are beginning to haggle & to say that they'd been promised 70% of the total collections, and that they must have that, and that if anything is to be given to Quetta it must come out of the Centre's share. (Curiously enough, although the Bihar and Orissa disaster made a great appeal to C.P. people, Quetta has left them, almost unmoved – partly because they regard it as a military outpost, and the concern of the G/I; and partly because of the poisonous campaign which has been going on in a certain section of the Press against the refusal of the G/I to allow Congress volunteers and other busybodies to overrun the place, poke about among 20,000 buried corpses for other people's property, and generally get in the way. The Press (Indian) has shown a regrettable lack of responsibility over the business.

It is unthinkable, of course, that so long as all provinces are treated alike, there should be any disputing over their Ex.'s wishes as to the disposal of a charity fund, & I told G. and J. that I'd be no party to anything of the sort. (One can imagine the way that some of these lawyers will waggle their heads and raise "láv- pinto".) I have asked them to make out rough schemes as to the disposal of our share, and then to call a meeting of the Committee at which, as patron of the Fund, I shall preside. I doubt whether they will dare to haggle if I am there.

Mond. July 15th

I am having great difficulty in making my Secretaries realise that one of their first duties is to see that cases which I ought to see, either because the Business Rules say so or because common sense dictates it, come to me. The other day we got a real smack in the face from the H.D. because we boggled about paying for sending prisoners to the Andamans. I called for the papers, and found that the G. in C. (all three of us) had agreed to our original protest, on the representation of the I.G. Prisons. Then the G/I raised their eyebrows, and

i.   we reiterated our unwillingness to pay and

ii. subsequently, when they passed this over in silence, wrote and accused them of ignoring us. Their obvious reply was that they hadn't ignored us, but did not think it worthwhile arguing with such Jews – or words to that effect.

I found,

a. that the case had never come to me after the first letter

b. that at stage (i) the figures were re-examined, and anyone could see with half an eye that we ought to drop our protest

c. that owing to N.J. dropping the very sound practice by which Ch. Sec. drafts all letters to the G/I himself, the stage (ii) letter was passed by an U.S.!

It is difficult working with a Ch.S. who takes as little interest and pride in his work as N.J. does. Crossword puzzles and contract are what really interest him. And now another. I have said already (June 29th) that I think we've got to proceed cautiously over this Improvement Trust scheme. Yesterday I was astounded to find, not only that the Committee's report, which is of course a confidential document as yet, had been given to the public, but that we had published a long Press communiqué, at the end of which we say that Govt. should have no difficulty in shouldering the financial burden involved, and that the scheme is an excellent one! I rang up Bannerji, the Secretary concerned, and asked what had happened, and he said: "Oh! The communiqué merely summarises the Committee's report". I then read the two paras. in question out to him, and showed him that in that case the person who drafted it couldn't write English – which B. can't! – and he took refuge in sorrow. And yet B.'s the man who sends every footling case of nominations to Local Bodies, a matter which I always let the Minister make his own bed, up to me in a closed envelope, with another closed envelope attached to the file telling me all the inner history of the dirty intrigues that have gone on about the nominations. As if I cared two hoots! I suppose B., being an Indian, will never realise the difference in value between the two cases. I've now sent for the file, and must see what can be done.

The pending difficulty over the S.J. Fund has been solved. I had a letter from the Central Sec. saying that, as the Quetta Fund had progressed so well, it had been decided to drop the 20 lakhs idea – in other words, there have been protests against the proposal, on the lines, presumably of our local murmur. Meanwhile I've written a letter of thanks to our Committee, who really have achieved a fine result – 5¼ lakhs when I should have been pleased if we'd got 2½. The way the Jubilee caught the popular imagination at the end was astonishing. I'm inclined to think that the date, May 6th, which for obvious reasons was an awkward one in this country in many ways, had not a little to do with the success. Hot as it is, May is the month which marks the end of the harvest year and the beginning of the marriage season, and Indians always seem ready in May to turn to some form of excitement. Flag-waggers, satyagrahis, non-co-operators, et hoc genus omne, have always felt the gadfly most potently in May. So possibly the Jubilee formed a timely safety-valve this year.

Friday July 19th

In the end, I decided not to do anything about the N.I.T. business. It appears that Stent's draft was sent in to the Sectt. to be used, if Govt. had no objection, as a press note on which local editors could base their leaders if they liked, thus saving them the trouble of writing a leader for themselves. And the mutts in the Sectt. sent it out as a Govt. communiqué. But none of the editors seem to have thought Govt. was backing the scheme, so I decided to say nothing for the present.

The Council passed an Act recently for the registration of certain medical practitioners holding certificates from non-recognised institutions, and I was advised to give my assent to it. The G/I now points out that the giving of these certificates is illegal, and a penal offence! It seems impossible to expect our Sectt. to use ordinary vigilance or to help one to steer clear of pitfalls. I fear that they're taking their tone from their No. 1. Altogether things are not going too well at present. The report of the Sectt. fire is in, & I have not the smallest doubt that it was due to defective wiring. In Jan. last it was reported that the wiring needed complete renewal; so they sent in a demand for 500/- & this was whittled down to 144/- ! and I simply rammed it into Hyde, after the G.H. alarm, that every Govt. building must be tested thoroughly. He assured me that the P.W.D were perfectly competent to do it, & that it would be done. And now this! H. is an excellent executive officer but Sectt. work is beyond him, & I fear he's cracking under it.

Friday July 26th

The King has approved Rao's extension, so that's settled – a great relief. I'm sorry for one thing, it means that Gordon will not be V.P. of the Council next Oct. and will not act for me if I go on leave next year, but that's a minor matter. I told him yesterday, and he said that if I'd asked his advice, which he knew I couldn't, he'd have said that Rao ought certainly to stay. Who on earth I'd have got to replace him if the extension had been refused I haven't any idea! There's not a man in the Province who's really up to the job, though there are a dozen who think they are.

A nasty case. A man in the King's at Jubb. molested a girl in a village near the Ridge Lines and got hammered. Next night 30 or 40 men of the regiment went and beat up, not the village which did the hammering, but a neighbouring one. They killed one man, and injured twelve more. They've already put through two gangster outrages, and this puts the lid on it. The officers of the regiment are a first-class lot, but the men are mostly undersized Liverpool Irishmen, up to any rascality. We talked about it in Govt., and it was agreed that I should write privately to the C. in C. and ask if the regiment's transfer, which is due Feb. next, can't be ante-dated – which I've done, as tactfully as I could. Another problem. H.E. is getting exercised over this question of Indian officers not being allowed in European clubs. It has been raised by Nicholson, G.O.C. Secunderabad, where there are 3 Indianised regiments, in a letter which is a model of what such a letter should not be. The claim of Indian officers of the Imperial Services to be admitted ex-officio, so to speak, into European Clubs has been disputed in the past by no one more stoutly than by the Military. Now N. says that every Indian Officer has the right to come into any European Club, and that if he does not get that right his loyalty will be severely strained; and he complains that their entry is barred by "second-rate" civilians, "people who wouldn't be able to get into any decent English Club", or words to that effect. That sort of tone, of course, is just the thing to put every civilian's back up, and make him say that no General in the world has any right to force upon him anyone with whom he doesn't wish to associate in the free intimacy of Club life. The whole question is a terribly difficult one, but my opinion has always been that these matters must be settled by the Clubs themselves and that the less Governors and Governments interfere with them the less likely they (the G.'s & G.'s) are to get told to go to Hades. That was always Monty's line.

Wed. July 31st

(Concerning Land Mortgage Banks) Gordon, at my instigation, has just had some very instructive figures prepared. After sifting carefully all our sources on information, we find that although land may be going very cheap when the sale is a forced one, especially in places where there is little ready cash, if you want to buy a village in the ordinary way by private treaty you will have to pay, not as much as formerly, of course, but a multiple of the land revenue which puts Govt. right out of court as a bidder. In short, though inflated prices have been bust, the present price is reasonably good, and any idea that you can go round buying up land for a song, like Nicolai Gogol and his "Dead Souls", is pure moonshine. And there goes my pet scheme for adding to the rayatwari estate of Govt.. But we must take the first opportunity of shutting up the parrot cry that the cultivators are being ruined because they can get no price for their land. It's just like the cry that the price of grain is ruinously low. They've been so spoilt by the fancy prices of the early 'twenties that they quite forgot that present prices are little below the rate (12 seers a rupee) *(about ¼ p a lb.!)* at which we started to give <u>famine</u> allowances when I first came to the country! Of course rents and revenue have gone up since then, but in the C.P. they are still so light that little can be made out of that argument. Our present plight is almost entirely due to the fact that for the past five or six years and more we've not had, so far as I can remember, one really good wheat or cotton crop. Give us good crops, and we'll carry along with the present prices all right.

Tues. Aug. 6th

I've written to H.E. about the Club business, saying that I thought the matter was one in which every Club must work out its own salvation, and suggesting that at all costs the controversy should be kept off the damnable "civil vs. military" tack to which Nicholson's letter was plainly heading it. I shall probably hear about it when I go to Simla next month. The problem is a very difficult one for the army – but one can't help feeling a malicious joy in hearing them squeal now over what is largely the result of their own past diehardism.

Council is going, as far as one can see to be hard-worked but dull. The only interesting debates will be the one about the 5%, cut, which Rao thinks we shall get though "in spite of the Nationalists", (Khaparde's supporters), and the one on Delimitation, which may or may not produce some C.P. vs. Berar fireworks. If the Beraris had any political sagacity they'd chuck this anti-C.P. attitude. Under the new Act they've got to come in with the C.P., and the keeping alive of these regional animosities can do no one any good. If they antagonise the C.P. they'll simply form an ineffectual minority in the Assembly. But they simply cannot see how absurd is their claim to what I may call individuality. Neither historically nor ethnographically nor geographically nor any other "ally" have they any distinct entity, and if they were a poor tract instead of a rich one we should never hear a word about "Berar for the Beraris".

The only interesting resolution is one by a Mahommedan member whom the Council doesn't take very seriously, proposing that P.W.D. contracts shall be given out by auction instead of by tender. He has been put up to do this by Naidu, who is always getting hold of half-baked ideas like this, and quoting in support of them that he did as Pres. of the Vardha M.C.. Hyde and Chance go off the deep end when the idea is mentioned, anyone can see with half an eye the awful results which would happen – contractors outbidding each other, as the Excise contractors do; every possible badmashi employed in order to scrape a profit; contacts breaking down and work being condemned; and the lives of Govt. officers being made a burden by supplicants asking to be let off their contracts and their fines. In a country of born gamblers deliver me from the auction system in any matter which admits of roguery.

I have commented before on the deep significance which is read into one's simplest and most unthinking act. The King's assent to Rao's extension came along in the ordinary way; H.E. asked me when I'd like it announced; and I gave the obvious reply – "As soon as you like – say next Saturday". But listen to the Hit.: "The announcement of the extension must have deprived the Council of many interesting developments and combinations, and was certainly a clever tactical move which ensures that the session will be a peaceful Moharrum." Clever fiddlesticks!

Sunday 11th Aug.

It was not to be expected that K.P. Pande, the bad boy of the council, who comes from the Jubb. district, would lose the chance given him by the Jubb. affray, and yesterday he duly moved "that the House do adjourn". Hemeon says that the tone of the debate was "commendably restrained". That is correct, I gather; but as usual the actions of Govt. were subjected to a great deal of misrepresentation. The dual enquiry by the police and the military has been an extremely difficult and ticklish affair, and would have been ruined by any premature disclosure of what we were doing. And as a matter of fact there was nothing to tell about the actual happenings beyond what everyone knew from the start. But the fact that we had not issued a further communiqué full of the usual flap-doodle was used as a reason for saying that Govt. was doing nothing and that we were "indifferent" (E.S. Deshmukh, ex-Minister). Pande wanted to withdraw his resolution, having obtained from Rao an assurance that we had been, and were, doing everything we possibly could. But P.S.D. twitted him with not being sufficiently serious, and at that he dare not do anything but ask for a vote – which was bound to "aye" – none of them would have the courage to say "No" to a motion like that, however blameless they knew Govt. to be. Today the Hit. comes out with large headlines – "Govt. censured over the Jubb. incident" and so our dirty linen is hung out to dry before India.

Wed Aug. 14th

E.S. Deshmukh came and saw me yesterday morning. Having behaved as he did over the Jubb. case, there was nothing surprising in his asking me for the votes of Govt. for a Bill of his regulating Hindu religious endowments – at least he saw nothing strange therein! I told him we were going to let Govt. servants vote as they liked, and then went on to point out to him that as an ex-Minister he knew perfectly well that Govt. was not to blame over the Jubb. affair, and he'd got no business to get a vote of censure passed against it. He blustered a bit, but finally looked shamefaced and admitted I was right. Then I asked him why he and others like him found amusement in holding their province and its government up to the scorn of outsiders, and he blurted out: "Sir, these things must not be taken seriously. Seventy-five percent of the vote against Govt. was because we wanted to take the opportunity of getting a hit in at the Home Member." And there was the cat right out of the bag. But, as I couldn't help telling him, though that's a perfectly good reason in ninety-nine cases, in the hundredth case it is not. And the hundredth case is one which concerns the honour of Govt., and the way in which it discharges its most sacred duty of safeguarding the lives of its subjects. A case like that should not be the spirit of political tactics.

The Council is a funny mixture. The B.N. Zamindari has been grossly mismanaged and is overburdened with debt, and is now under the C/W. The only hope of solvency is to own part of it. But as it is impractical, that needs a Bill, and we brought one in. Two interests combined against it, the Zamindari, and the people who won't do anything which helps the banya. To them add those who were "influenced" by the Zamindar, and you get a majority against the Bill. The only thing we really care about is that we shall now have to release the estate as being beyond hope of saving, and the wretched tenants will be plundered by the Zamindar to get money to pay his debts. G. and I agreed that we should make our position clear – Govt. has no personal interest in the matter, so to speak. It's merely doing its best to save the tenants from oppression, and if the Council won't assist, then the responsibility is the Council's. N.B.G. They're a queer lot, very reasonable over some things, and like mules over others.

Thurs. Aug 15th

A very interesting report from the Intelligence Bureau. Talking of the recent Wardha meeting, when the Working Comm. of the Congress funked the question of acceptance of office, it says that it was Gandhi himself who put his foot down on any idea of acceptance. "The acceptance of office by a branch of the Congress would ruin his schemes by placing impediments in the way of the successful prosecution of the new civil disobedience movement which he proposes to launch at the end of 1936." "Babuji" amplified this by saying that Congress's best course was to support non-congressmen who would be ready to enter Govt. and obstruct it from within. That idea is altogether too clever. After all, a Minister's salary is worth having, and whatever Congressmen may do, other people are not going to throw away a good post merely for the pleasure of helping Congress by obstruction. Get men into the Cabinet, and I have no fear of their being in a hurry to quit. But what worries me more is the possibility that if Gandhi really does launch his new c.d. movement – and he's so fond of the limelight that he's quite capable of ignoring all the lessons of the past – his h.q. will probably be Wardha and the C.P. It's a curious thing that agrarian agitation is already being worked up in the district, and today we are expecting a mass deputation which says it's going to sit outside the Council Hall until it gets a debt conciliation board and a land mortgage bank. This habit of mass deputations during Council is getting a nuisance. Fortunately it is limited by considerations of space, but already we have had marches of two or three thousand apiece from Wardha, Bhadara, and Betul. The average Councillor, of course, could no more say "Boo!" to one of them than fly.

Hemeon has just rung up to say that Kedar, the egregious, has given notice of an adjournment motion because of Govt.'s refusal to hear a deputation from the above crowd. The answer is simple. Govt. hasn't. On the contrary, both H.M.R. (Gordon) and H.M.E. (Khaparde) have said that they will hear representatives of the marchers. But fancy bringing an adjournment motion over the question whether the people of a tahsil should get a board or a bank out of their turn! As I told

Deshmukh a day or two ago, the adjournment business has been so overdone that nobody cares too hoots about these motions now.

Mond. Aug. 19th

The motion wasn't brought, as both Gordon and Khaparde heard some of the marchers. G. says that the show was clearly worked by Congress. Its leader, "Baba Saheb" Deshmukh, was one of the leaders of the flag-waggers in the Nagpur c.d. of 1923. The fact is interesting in connection with Gandhi's reported intention to restart c.d in 1936, because the new movement is to be a mass movement among the peasantry.

Council has passed very well on the whole. The chief event from an immediate point of view was the passing of the supplementary demands for the restoration of the 5% cut. That puts an end to our difficulty with the S/S, thank goodness. The majority was unexpectedly large, 44 to 10. I gather that Rao did the trick by reminding them of the fate of Kelkar, one of the first two Ministers, who, being a tactless and uncivilised sort of creature, got the backs of all Govt. servants in his depts. up, and at the next election was routed ignominiously. It finished his career. Govt. servants have a great pull, such is the fear of that authority, especially of the petty brand, can do to annoy you if it likes. The last day was taken up with an acrimonious C.P. vs. Berar fight over delimitation. The C.P. carried an extreme resolution, to the effect that, as between C.P. and Berar, seats should go entirely by population, and there should be no weightage for wealth, which is the Berar claim. Then, in the delightful way of these people, they voted that Nagpur and Jubb. should get more seats than Chhattisgarh proportionately to population, because they are culturally and educationally more advanced! In other words, you may use your weights, but your opponent mayn't use his! The majorities were very small, 2 about, and the voting is of little moment.

Thurs. Aug. 22nd

I wish Naidu had a more liberal supply of Poirot's "little grey cells". I'm trying to induce him to see that his Excise Committee must report to us in proper time, because (a) our anti-bootlegging measures are causing unrest among the Gonds (b) we've got to know where we are before the Financial Committee comes round next cold weather (c) we want a decision before the budget, if possible. So I wrote a note suggesting that we should give them a definite date by which to report. All agreed except N., who made the amazing statement that the Council's prohibition resolution of 1921 was only a "pious wish", not intended to be taken seriously (I asked him if he'd dare repeat that statement in Council!), and in any case was really only a continuation of our previous policy of the maximum revenue with the minimum consumption. I explained to him that in our previous policy the "maximum revenue" was just as much an ingredient as the "minimum consumption", and asked him how he explained away such measures as making the Saugur district dry, and what consideration had been paid to revenue in raising the duties since the resolution was passed. But it was a long time before he could see how preposterous his position was. Finally he agreed to take the note away and reconsider it. But what is one to do with a Minister who runs off the rails out of sheer stupidity every five minutes'?

Friday Aug 23rd

I have had a cable to say that my dear old Dad died yesterday, painlessly. He was aged 84, and of late years had been rather cut off from us by deafness, and by asthma, which meant that he couldn't stand smoke. I shall always remember him as a man of great natural charm of manners, widely travelled, & with a first class brain. It is the first break in my own little family circle, and is very saddening. We boys always loved him & respected him, & though he interfered little with us he had twice the influence over us that my dear Victorian mother had. Requiescat.

Wed Aug 28th

After a great deal of hesitation, it has been decided to send the Jubb. case before a European magistrate. A.H.Q. at one time wanted to send it before a Court Martial, but we came to the conclusion that that would be dangerous. The evidence is very shaky, and acquittal is quite on the cards, and if that occurred in a military court, we would be accused promptly of having conspired let the men get off. As it is we can say that we gave the law every chance & that we can't order convictions.

The case is a thoroughly unsatisfactory one. Forty men in a regiment conspire together to beat up a village in order to avenge an attack on a comrade. They get hockey-sticks from the regimental stores, and they go out and beat the village up at night. It is easy to understand that identification won't be forthcoming from the villagers. But what were their N.C.O.'s doing? They must have heard what was going on in the Barrack-rooms. And who gave the hockey-sticks out to them and took them back? It shows the lengths to which a conspiracy of silence can go. The raiders are a gang of Southern Irish, the same lot that are the curse of Liverpool, Glasgow and every other place that they infest. How the Americans must have grinned when they put the immigration quota onto them!

Sat Aug 31st

The D.N. says that I who have the last word in matters military and racial have acted in the above case "with a strong sense of justice". Credit to whom credit is due – it was Rao who first stuck out for sending the case to a criminal court instead of a court-martial. But the main point is that people will now see that we did everything we could. "The decision" says the D.N. "effectively refutes the baseless accusation that Govt. was trying to hush up the affair.

Mond. Aug (Sept) 12th Pachmarhi.

Just back from a very interesting and delightful visit to their Excs. at Simla. As before, they were perfect hosts and the visit seemed to go like a flash. We left Nagpur on the 4th and thanks to these new "Dunlopillow" mattresses, had a comfy two days' journey, finishing up in the special railmotor up the hill – a sort of large saloon car on railway wheels. Her Ex. was in bed with a bad cold, having just performed the feat of getting to Delhi & back by car & plane in one day! She sent me a pencil note to say how sorry she was not to be there. That night I dined with Cyrus Greenslade at the Club, a very jolly little dinner, and a welcome change from formality. (Memo – whiskey after champagne is definitely <u>not</u> wise). On the 7th we lunched with the C. in C. who I thought looked very ill, but who gave us a marvellous lunch. Then a cocktail party at Craik's (Home Member) and a dinner of 60 at Viceregal Lodge, before which I had the unique experience of being winked at by one of the guests – a complete stranger – as I was being led round to shake hands. He did the same to H.E. when he came round later, and was subsequently removed blotto. And he was the head of a Dept! After dinner we went to the Council of State Hall which is attached to V. L. and saw their private cinema.

8th I went to church with their Excs. and heard a very good sermon on the place of suffering & sin in the world, on the grounds that without them we would all get soft and rather bored! Lunch with the Badenoshs, where I met Grigg, the new Finance Member, an amusing personality whose frankness has set a good many people by the ears, but has taught these unsporting Congressmen that it isn't everybody who will take their attacks without hitting back. The Congressman's idea of fair play is that he should be allowed to hit you – verbally, of course; he hasn't the guts to do it physically – as hard as he likes, above or below the belt, but that you should have at any rate one hand tied behind your back, and the other, if free, well padded. Anyone who hits back good and proper is "arrogant", "insolent", "lacking in statesmanship", (how they love that word!) and so on. But after these many years it has to be recorded, regretfully, that it is very hard to find any true sportsmanship in this country. You have only got to read the annals of any football season in Calcutta to realise that.

But to continue. That evening we dined with the Mitchells, who had thoughtfully asked some O.R.s to meet me. A quiet and very pleasant evening. On the 9th we lunched with Jagdish Prashad (Member, Edlands), who gave us a first-class lunch in interesting company. A man of parts, I should say. At night the U.S. Club gave a farewell dinner to H.E. and were kind enough to ask me. Glancy (Foreign Sec. and President of the Club) made one of the most amusing speeches I have ever listened to after dinner, though I think he was a bit hard on Irwin, who had, he said, left the ball in the rough and given H.E. the task of putting it back again on the fairway. He said some nice things about Lady W. & in his reply H.E. said "Your President has told you in such glowing terms what a wonderful woman my wife is that you will probably forget what a wonderful man I am (loud and prolonged applause) – to have survived for so many years with one whom I may rightly call a human dynamo" (shriek of delight). After dinner I played "goli-boli" with H.E. & Glancy and two others. Simla seems mad on it & it has emptied the bridge tables. I forgot to mention that H.E. spoke for 55 minutes, all very interesting. Next day we lunched with Emerson, whom I was very interested to meet, having corresponded much with him in the past – a fine tough character, I should think, and very able. That afternoon we started for Pach. after a very convivial farewell from their Excs. who have the supreme gift of making one feel that one has been welcome.

Tues Sept 17th

My coming to Pach in Sept. always seems to bring up one of these Bay storms, and today we are wrapped in Stygian gloom, electric lights everywhere and fires burning in every room. I had a talk with Gordon yesterday. He had been very good about Rao's extension meaning that Rao would officiate for me and not he, and quite recognises that that was a consideration which I could not take into account. But he did not agree straight away, as Rao did, that Burton should act for Rao, & not Roughton. He asked for time to think it over. He sees little of Roughton's work & has not had to do most of it for him, as I have had! I have no intention, unless I am actually forced to it of seeing R. marked down as G.'s eventual successor after the trouble that I have had in keeping him up to the mark. He is utterly lacking in imagination, vision & humanity, and takes little real interest in his work – that's the heart of the trouble.

The Benda (Jubb.) case is going much better than we expected. Three men have been sent to the Sessions for murder & 8 more on charges of rioting etc.. So no-one can say now that we haven't done our best.

Wed Sept 18th

This Abyssinian business is very worrying. E. is due to sail on Saturday, & thanks to the ghastly stupidity of our statesmen we may be at war any day after then. Christopher *(Note: Hyde's middle son)* in a letter to his mother says that he was playing tennis at Witherslack, the Stanley's place, & Stanley (apparently Oliver) said to him that it was astonishing how Mussolini had managed to get almost everyone united against him in support of such unutterably foul people as the Abyssinians. To me the line we have been taking seems to be madness. In the first place who are we to point the finger of shame at Italy for doing what we have done regularly ourselves for the past 200 years, and as late as the Boer War? Secondly, why should we imperil a single English life on behalf of "such unutterably foul people"? And thirdly, why should we with France as a doubtful and hesitant backer, take upon ourselves the whole burden of the League's police-work? It is pure idiocy to talk of a "League of Nations" which does not embrace three of the seven Great Powers (U.S.A., Germany, Japan) with a fourth (Italy) on the point of leaving, and a fifth (Russia) apparently passive. The League is now a mere Rump – England and France with a lot of little fellows saying "ji hán" – and it passes my understanding to see how we are justified in risking a European flare-up to preserve such a body. The matter is one of cold logic. Sanctions mean war. War means a European War, of that there is no possible doubt. A European war means the end to the League for a century. Why not let it die of inanition, rather than in flames and blood? This talk about "ideals of the League" is all quixotic nonsense in the present year of grace, whatever it may have been 15 years ago. On the wireless last night Mussolini is reported to have said in an interview that it was a great mistake to think he was bluffing. No sensible man had a right to think that. When a Dictator sets his hand to a show like this one, all history tells us that he's got to go through with it, coûte que coûte, or fall. All these attempts to conciliate him are puerile. They simply pander to his megalomania.

As for sanctions, with Germany, U.S.A & Japan not playing, such measures as an economic blockade would be about as effectual as the walls of Jerico were. The idea is puerile. But I cannot believe that we have any real intention of going to war. The V. told me in Simla that the S/S was refusing to let them get ahead on the frontier, where trouble has been brewing for some time, because he didn't want troops locked up. Then two days later the S/S wired that that they could go ahead, and now two divisions are engaged. That certainly doesn't look as if we were afraid of trouble elsewhere.

Thurs Sept 19th

G. told me yesterday that he'd talked matters over with Rao, and they both agreed that whatever might be said when the permanent choice comes to be made later on it would not be right to press R. upon me now. As R. *(Roughton)* acted for G. last cold weather, his appointment now would compromise the final choice, whereas Burton's can be justified on the grounds that last cold weather he was on leave, that R. was then wanted because of the budget, he being an ex-F.S. and that now B. is the senior Commr. and there is no particular reason to pass him over. There has been a tendency, put into words by the H.P. in last January's session of the Council, that R. is marked down as the coming man in the Province, and this will open some people's eyes. It is partly founded, I think, on the fact that R.'s humour is of the fifth form variety, as I have often told him, and that that type makes a peculiar appeal to our M.L.C.s who will roar with laughter at the most primitive jest, provided it has a personal flavour about it, but will receive a real witticism in dead and chilly silence. I have put all this down at some length because the choice is an important one for the Province, and I must endeavour to be absolutely fair – and above all not to be led away by the fact that Doris, his wife, the stout-hearted if occasionally erratic, crusader whom I have mentioned before, is my good and faithful friend. I shall be amused if after all the bother the G/I say that we're not to appoint an official.

Friday Sept. 27th

It is curious how two supposedly rational minds can sometimes look at what appears to be a question of pure logic in different ways. Under the Poona Pact certain general constituencies, besides electing to an unreserved seat, have also to elect a "hariján" to a reserved seat. These have been loosely called multi-member constituencies, though they are not genuinely such, because the two members represent divergent interests, and what is really being done is to hold two distinct elections at one and the same time, for the reason that the electorate is the same in both. Then comes the question of the mode of election – single vote (transferable or non-) distributive, or cumulative. I say – and the other members of Govt. agree with me, except Gordon – that the distributive vote is the only possible one, i.e. that each voter has two votes, one to be used in electing a candidate to the open seat, and the other ditto to the reserved seat. That seems to me to be the only system which fits the logic of the facts. Gordon, on the other land, wants the cumulative system, under which a voter is given two votes, and can use them as he likes, i.e., he can give the vote intended for the reserved seat to a candidate for the open seat. The whole arrangement, of course, is anomalous, like so many other arrangements that have been made in this "ultá-pultá-desh", and must therefore be dealt with strictly according to fact and intention; and to tell an elector that you're giving him a second vote so that he can elect a hariján, then to allow him to use it to elect an M.B. seems to me to be completely goofy. Further, it might upset the election for the open seat, because if two candidates for it, A & B, had, say, an equal number of supporters, A might get double the number of votes that B got, if his voters didn't play fair and used both their votes for the open seat, while B's played fair and gave one vote in the hariján election. But nothing I could say would make G. see it. I write this, not because I think Hammond's Committee will say I am right – however positive I am, it's quite likely that their brains may be made the same way as G.'s! – but merely to show in what curiously divergent ways two similarly trained minds can work.

I shall be glad when the next week is over. E. is coming out on the "Viceroy" and must now be in the Gulf of Lyons, and war between Italy and Abyssinia may break out any day, and when that happens goodness knows how long it will be before we're at war too, judging from the way our statesmen are heading. The London correspondent of the T/I said the other day, in a very thoughtful letter, that however the men on the street might approve in theory of all this talk about "the ideals of the League" and so on, there was no doubt the in his heart of hearts he was "desperately anxious" that we should not get involved in a war with Italy. David Smyth who certainly can't be accused of being a pacifist, said to me at dinner last night that he couldn't understand all this nonsense about war to end war. If we went to war to enforce the ideals of the League we were no better off if we hadn't a League at all. I quite agree. Meanwhile I shall be greatly relieved when I hear that the "Viceroy" is safely past Aden.

Friday Oct 4th

Our wedding day, one of the many anniversaries that we spend together once in a blue moon. As soon as I emerged into the veranda for chota hazri I was given a telegram from E. who said that she'd had an excellent voyage. That means she's passed Aden, which is a great relief, as war between Italy and Abyssinia is only a matter of days now. Scrapping seems to have begun already. We heard on the wireless the noise of the great Italian Fascist mobilisation at Rome. A roaring Babel of sound & then, clear and dominating, a rather pleasant voice declaiming two or three sentences. Frantic applause, followed by more declamation and more babel. "Il Duce" addressing his followers!

Mond Oct 7th

Fighting is going on hard & the League is now slowly scratching its head & wondering what it is going to do about it all. In this week's "Investors Review" Andrew Still says exactly what I thought when I read that part of Sammy Hoare's "famous" speech at Geneva in which he talked about the free distribution of raw materials among the countries which require them. "What arrant humbug! Can Sir S.H. mention one single colonial raw material or other exported produce which the foreign manufacturers cannot buy on exactly the same terms as the British manufacturer has to pay?" Exactly. It was a feeble effort, such an obvious slurring over of the real issue which is what the Italians want is <u>land</u>, and that is just what we, who own a fifth of the globe, won't help them to get!

Wed Oct 9th
(written in the diary as May 9th! – confused by the arrival of his wife?)

My beloved E. has come safely, and says that they had an absolutely tranquil voyage, and saw no sign of war, except half a dozen of the Fleet at Gib.. Even the Canal and the Red Sea were just as usual. But it is a great relief to have her here. We are a houseful – the Frankanes & Baxters from Nagpur, and Clive Rich from Bombay plus my own family party of five. E. has brought out Betty Hanbury, quite one of the most attractive of the modern generation that I have met, and charming in her manners to older people. A cheery party they are, & the golf week should be amusing.

A letter from the P.S.V. says that the S/S does not like our proposal to put Pollock into the new High Court over the head of Nyogi. It's Rao's idea, and neither Gordon nor I really like it, though we let Rao have his way. I've a shrewd suspicion that Pam Stent has worked it. Pollock is her boy-friend and the Stents are very much in Rao's pocket at present. I've had to put S. rather heavily on the mat. I asked the Ministers and him the other day to come and discuss informally with me the mess that the Nagpur people are making over their water supply & Town Improvement Trust schemes. It is obvious that the water supply must come first – how can an Improvement Trust function without water? – and the M.C. can finance it quite easily without extra taxation. But that would mean extra taxes – not at all heavy – for the I.T. which is Stent's baby. So what they have done is to put up a scheme for financing the I.T. from revenues, and hang the taxation round the water schemes. At once there's a hoo-ha from all who don't care a rap for what happens so long as they don't have to pay, or who want a stick with which to beat the party in office & the whole business is in a mess. Stent, <u>more suo</u>, pooh-poohs the opposition as fools, knaves or what-not, which I tell him he cannot do. His idea was that the water scheme would be strong enough to carry the taxes through – which again is a dangerous assumption. At the discussion I endeavoured to get all our ideas into the right perspective. It was a purely informal show, not intended to be recorded or to form the basis of decisions. But Stent thought otherwise and as soon as he got home wrote out a long and argumentative account of the discussion, giving my views somewhat briefly and often incorrectly – and his own (at great length!). To think that an officer of his experience would think he had any right to write an official account of a discussion with me without my orders was surprising. And it was still more to find this account put on the file without my permission & without my being given the chance of saying whether the account of my views was correct. I have told him so plainly. S. is a useful, if somewhat verbose officer, but his head gets inflated very quickly.

Thurs Oct 17th

The week went off very well, with some marvellous net scores. The course was at its best, and the bogey is too high. I gave the prizes away last night, & made a speech of the lighter variety, which E. said hit the right note. Julia and Davey each bought a 1st cup home, so G.H. did well. Today all our guests go off, and we shall be a quiet party for a week. Meanwhile it becomes more and more evident that the League is funking any sanctions which may lead to war, which is as it should be. On the other hand there are curious movements of troops going on which look very much as if the Italians were contemplating a march from Libya to the Suez Canal, and we were preparing to oppose them.

Thurs Oct 24ᵗʰ

The Jubb. case, which is now known throughout India as the Benda case, has ended satisfactorily. One of the King's men has got a life sentence and 9 others penal servitude for terms of 1½ to 4 years. It would be too much to hope that those members of the Council who censured Govt. for "inaction" feel ashamed of themselves. But they ought to.

I had a heartening letter from Dadabhoy yesterday. He presided at the meeting of all the leading people of Nagpur – the real solid men whose opinion is worth having – at which they passed a series of resolutions urging Govt. to get on with the Kanhan and Trust schemes. He sent me a copy of them, with a very nice letter. At the same time the D.N. bursts forth with an article in which it says that everyone is sick to death of the controversy, that the Kanhan scheme has been before the public for 14 years, that five Chief Engineers have approved of it, so for heaven's sake let the crowd of interested amateur critics shut up, and allow more sensible people to get a start on. A well-known pleader, who is one of the critics, writes that people who think like him are much handicapped by the fact that their opinion is not supported, as everyone knows, by "a very high-placed British officer, about whose fine manners and high sense of duty there can be no two opinions."! I'm glad to hear it. But it's a pretty caustic commentary on Nagpur mentality that there should be all this fuss about schemes that in a sensible and progressive town would have been put through 20 years ago. And these are the people who want a Mayor and Corporation! One gets pretty weary, sometimes, of dealing with such people. Nor do my present Ministers do much to lighten the burden. Yesterday I had to point both their noses in the right way. Kh., who is always charming to deal with, dug his toes in about a measure which the Central Cotton Comm. have been pressing on us – legislation to prevent the growing of Garrow Hill, which ruins the name in the market of any cotton grown in its neighbourhood. The C.C.C. have passed a resolution accusing us in so many words of failing to do our duty, and they're quite right! I asked Kh. how Berar dared to claim "weightage" before the Delimitation Committee on the ground of its superior culture if it adopted this reactionary attitude – the truth probably being that both Kh. and his friends have been sowing Garrow Hill themselves. Finally he agreed to the Bill against growing the stuff being circulated for public opinion.

And then Naidu. He wants to get an Executive Engr., a typical Indian wire-puller, into Nagpur, to replace a European who has only been there a year. Chance, Ch. Engr., opposes it and Naidu practically told Chance to take his note off the file. I haven't seen the file yet, but it was clear that Naidu had been exercising pressure to prevent a Sec. giving his opinion freely, so I had him up and put it to him that he couldn't do that sort of thing. His reply was: "Do you think that I would do it?" To which I answered that I could not say, but that was the impression he had left behind, and I hoped he would take an opportunity to remove it. His air was that of one who is slightly ashamed of himself. When one compares men like Kh. and N., one ceases to wonder at Brahmin domination.

Sat. Oct. 26th

Really one never knows what the dwellers in this amazing land will be up to next. American buck nigger called Gunboat Jack, champion boxer of India, runs a show in Nagpur which has always been known as reputable, and I very nearly went to it myself last rains to see a boxing match. On Wed. three persons calling themselves his counsel, manager and contractor came up here and asked me to be patron of a show which he intends to give in aid of Armistice Day funds. Suspecting nothing, and knowing that the show had been going for six months, I consented. Next day, I read in the paper that on Monday the Municipal Committee had had a stormy meeting and by a 2 to 1 majority had turned the show off the land leased to it, the chief ground being that gambling went on at it. Now, whatever the merits of that decision may be - and I gather that there is a lot behind it – it passes my understanding how these people could have had the cheek to come and ask for my patronage without saying a word of what had happened two days before. The "Counsel", incidentally, is Vice-President of the Committee! It is impossible, of course, for me to do anything which would allow people to say that I was setting myself up against the Committee, so I wired at once cancelling all orders, and have told Shoobert, the D.C., to let me know what is behind it all.

And another piece of impudence, one of Shoobert's chuprassis who is a relation of my head chuprassi, and whom I had allowed to stay in his house in the compound of G.H., Nagpur, has been discovered to be running an illicit still there – on the principle, I suppose, that the safest place to hide is at Police H.Q.. It just shows the lengths to which I.D. is getting. A propos of that, it seems to be clear that the Excise Committee really is coming round slowly to a reasonable view. The chief question is whether they'll have the guts to take the fence. And what Indian has the courage to form his own independent opinion and proclaim it aloud? Not one in ten thousand.

Friday Nov. 1st

No one, I suppose, ever gets over the temptation to say: "I told you so", and there are occasions when it has to be said – and this is one.

Note by JHBG

My mother's sister Evelyn had a rhyme:
"Of all the horrid, hideous tales of woe,
Sadder than owls' cry or the midnight blast,
Is that portentous phrase: "I told you so."

After a long and full debate, the M.C. Nagpur, by a majority of 28 - 20, have shelved the Kanhan scheme until the gravitation schemes have been examined, which means that Nagpur will get its extra water about 1945. And God help them if they get a short monsoon in the meanwhile. Stent worked very hard to mobilise sober opinion, and succeeded to a certain extent. But as usual in India the forces of ignorance and reaction have triumphed. (The only thing in which the Indian mind is instinctively progressive is the effort to grab something which belongs to someone else.) The Kanhan scheme, as I suspected, has proved unable to carry through the proposals for extra taxation, and now everything is in a mess. I shrewdly suspect Naidu of being at the back of the business. The real secret of the whole business is that there will be a much bigger rake-off from a 50 lakh work than from a 20 lakh one. That's the only possible way in which one can explain the curious dead weight of opposition, of refusal to acknowledge plain facts and to face up to real dangers, which the Kanhan scheme has encountered.

Sat. Nov. 9th Jubb.

We came here on the 2nd for our usual November stay, which is always a pleasant time, though this year all the regiments seem to be changing at once, and all our old friends in the military have gone except the Lings. I've just been to a jubilee at the Anjuman, where I took the opportunity of pointing out to the Muslims how their internal dissensions are weakening their hands. They're almost as quarrelsome as the Hindus – and that's saying a lot.

One needs the patience of Job to keep Ministers straight. I have no doubt whatever that in the case I wrote about on Oct. 24th Naidu practically told Chance to write a note embodying N.'s, and not Chance's, views, so that I would pass it; and when Chance refused and repeated his previous recommendations, N. turned nasty and accused him of insubordination. Unfortunately Ch. had made the mistake of criticising a member of Govt.'s wishes, and I had to tick him off. But I told N. that if in future he didn't agree with a Sec. he should pass orders himself, and leave the Sec. to lay the matter before me if the rules required it. I was also able to get N., who is sadly lacking in "the little grey cells", to see that his proposed transfer was going to put three people's backs up, and please no one, and at last he agreed to drop the matter. In the course of our talks he gave the whole show away. "Mayn't I", he said, "transfer people as I like?" To which I replied "No. That's what the Presidents of Local Bodies do," (he's an ex-President himself of long standing) "and that's why Local Fund Service is so bad and so unpopular." He seemed quite astonished when I assured him that so far at any rate as the posting of Imperial Officers is concerned, it was my bounden duty to see that he did not make transfers arbitrarily and unjustly. But he saw I meant business and collapsed.

And Khaparde is just as bad, though he's so suave and agreeable that I hate opposing him. But he wanted to appoint an Indian as Head of the Agricultural College who has no single qualification for the post, over the head of a European who has acted in the post previously, and did very well in it – a most unjust proposal, and question him as I would I could get out of Kh. no real reason in support of it. Finally I said to him: "This case will go to the P.S.C. and the G/I.. Here are five solid reasons why C. (the Englishman) should be preferred to D.. Before I agree to D., you must give me five equally solid reasons in his favour which I can present to the P.S.C.." Of course he couldn't, and said he'd take the file away and reconsider it. Next day it came back – "C. may be appointed". But one feels all the time that one is dealing with a pair of irresponsibles, and that there's no knowing what they won't be up to as soon as one's back is turned.

Thurs. Dec 5th Nagpur

I have written nothing for some time. Our month at Jubb. was pleasant and amusing socially, though the fact that three of the regiments had only just arrived meant that things were a bit disorganised. Officially it was blessedly uneventful. We got here on 29th, and on 1st the delimitation Committee arrived. Laurie Hammond, the President and Laithwaite the Sec. are staying with us. Poor people, they have a desperate task, trying to cram six months work into three, and knowing that then anything may happen to prevent our getting the elections through next cold weather. The more one thinks of it, the more difficult does it seem for us to do our part of the job in less than a year. And as the Comm.'s report cannot reach England till the beginning of Feb. & the Order in Council has then to be drafted and put through Parliament, there will be precious little time to spare. L.H. is a charming person, full of talk and always amusing.

I am overburdened at present with speeches, of which I have to make 9 in the next six weeks. And my brain doesn't feel in the mood for sparkling these days. I want my leave I suppose.

Note (JHBG):

In order to write his speeches it was his habit to get up at 4.30 a.m. and don a pair of loose, towelling pyjamas, like the modern track-suit, that he had specially made for the job. His day would then proceed:

5:00 Draft speech
7.30 Shave and breakfast.
9.30 Office.
1.00 'Tiffin'
Afternoon, Interviews.
4.30 Tennis or golf.
8.00 Dinner
After which, he would sometimes have a game of bridge, but more often than not was asleep in his chair by 9.30. Who can blame him?

Yesterday I became wrathful. The election of the Vice-Chancellor is on the 6th, and I have studiously refrained from having anything to do with it, or from expressing any views on the candidates. But the "Hit." said that members of Govt. were canvassing for one of them, and that Govt. intended to issue a whip. There was a meeting of Govt. on, so I let forth on the subject, and was assured that none of my colleagues had been canvassing. The article had finished by saying that we'd better amend the University Act, and give the whole power of appointing the Vice Ch. to the Chancellor. So I told Roughton to send for the editor, and tell him that it was scandalous he should say such things without a vestige of justification for them, and that if he didn't withdraw I should probably signalise my aloofness from University politics by refusing to attend Convocation on the 7th. He curled up, and promised to do as he was told. Whether he will we shall see tomorrow. The paper prints on its first page a pretentious motto — something about "being in the right with two or three." Apparently truth doesn't come within their definition of the right.

Speech at the Convocation of the Nagpur University, on Saturday, the 7th December 1935

Mr. Vice-Chancellor and Members of the University, —Once again there falls to me the duty of beginning my speech by paying a last sad tribute to departed merit. "This fell sergeant, Death, Is strict in his arrest", and today we miss from among our company the familiar figure of our late Treasurer, Diwan Bahadur V.M. Kelkar. In 1923 he became the first Treasurer of the University, and continued to hold the post until his death. Your Executive Council has already passed a resolution of condolence, in which his work has been eulogised in eloquent terms, and I will not say more here than that he set to all of us the supreme example of a man who never wearied of public service, who never said to himself, as so many people do, "I have earned my rest, and I will take it", but who died, as he had lived, harnessed to the task of helping his fellow-men. Let us think of him in the words of Matthew Arnold:

"For peace his soul was yearning,

And now peace laps him round."

My next duty is a less mournful one—to salute the out-going Vice-Chancellor, and to welcome Sir Hari Singh Gour who was chosen by the Court yesterday to fill his place. In saying an academic goodbye to you, Mr. Niyogi, I know that I shall be expressing the feelings of everyone here when I congratulate you on two fruitful and successful terms of office. During those four years much real work has been done. The number of colleges affiliated to the University has been raised from 8 to 12. In spite of "the law's delay", a scheme for the building of a Technological Institute with the funds of the Laminarayan Bequest has received practical shape. Special attention has been paid to the problem of physical welfare, and a Director of Physical Education has been appointed. A great step forward in female education has been taken by the starting of the Central College for Women and by the appointment—the first, I am told, in any Indian University—of three ladies as Heads of three of the University Departments of Studies. These are but a part of the tale of progress; and for all of that tale, as well as for your constant attention to the affairs of the University in spite of your heavy official duties, we owe you a debt of deep gratitude. May I add a personal note? You were my first Vice-Chancellor, and I shall not readily forget the kindly and courteous way in which you welcomed me to my office, and made my path easy before me. The ending of our association fills me with sincere regret.

Next, Mr. Vice-Chancellor, allow me to extend to you on

behalf of the University a sincere and hearty welcome on your election. The office to which you have succeeded is a great and honourable one, fraught with opportunities for doing good, as your predecessor has proved to us; and the progress of our University, the development for better or for worse of the intellects and characters of its students, will depend largely on the way in which you perform the duties which will fall to you. May you be given strength to "rise to the height of this great argument", and acquit yourself well of your task.

In Col. Kukday, our newly elected Treasurer, you will have a colleague who brings to his task, as his predecessor did, the ripe experience of a life-time of public service, and him too we congratulate on the happy choice which the University has made.

One more congratulation I have to offer—this time to ourselves, for our good fortune in securing Mr. Jayakar to deliver the convocation address today. As a student, professor and public speaker, he is worthy of your admiration and your emulation, as it was amongst students that he laid the foundations of that reputation for oratory which he has acquired so deservedly. His work as a patriot and a politician, specially at the Round Table Conference, is well known to all of you, and it will be of interest to you as students to know that he has no small claim to distinction in the academic world as well. As the founder of the Aryan Educational High School, as a Sanskrit scholar of repute and the editor of a book on Vedanta philosophy, and as a Professor of Law who was famous for his mastery of his subject and the clearness of his exposition, he has claims to address us which are quite apart from his political fame, and we are fortunate in having secured his presence today. I will now call upon him to deliver his address.

Mond Dec 9th

A spate of speechmaking, which will last to the end of the week. Sat. was Convocation, very crowded, and duller than ever. Next year they are going to have two convocations. I shall not attend more than one! Jayakar gave the address – very good, a thoughtful analysis of how a student should spend his time, especially in his social hours, with a suggestion that our educational system makes the mistake of not providing any stepping-off places, but is a series of steps up which a student has to climb till he gets to the top. He only stayed a few hours, as he had work in Bombay, but he struck me as being a man who would be worth knowing better, quiet and thoughtful and forceful. Today was the start of the Morris Coll. Jubilee celebrations, and Sir S. Radhakrishnan gave the address – a delight to listen to. "It's truth that you must follow and not tradition. If you profess democracy, you must give up rearing your children from infancy in caste and communal and regional prejudices. Don't imagine that you have any reason to complain against the British for ruling you. As Gandhi has told you, the fact that you are ruled is due to your shortcomings, your attitude towards sex, your inability to put the national cause above personalities. Until you get rid of them, you will not be ready for self-government; for you must first learn the true democracy, which means the abolition of subjection and of grinding poverty." If all Indian politicians were as clear-sighted, our path would be easy. But with most of them it's a case of – "Video meliora proboque Deteriora seguor". The students were very friendly and pleasant and I had to face a battery of their cameras.

CHAPTER 8

1936
JANUARY - MAY

Monday Jan 13th

I am afraid that I have let this record slide for a month, chiefly because the writing of the Xmas mail, followed by the answering of Xmas letters and sending thanks for gifts, has left me little inclination for further writing. The Heilop Coll. also celebrated its Jubilee last month & there was a large gathering and many speeches. I'm getting very tired of all this talking. After that, nothing particular happened till we went to Ghogra, on the Denwa below Pachmarhi, for Xmas. We were a party of 12, we five, 2 Gordons, 2 Coxes, Chitham, & 2 Maltbys (friends of Chithams). It was a jolly crowd and although we didn't get a tiger we had plenty of fun with Peacock and Jungle-cock, which were as elusive as ever.

Since we returned, things have been busy. On the 4th I went to Lodge Corinth, to receive congratulations on my Grand Lodge rank. Work done with a quiet dignity & efficiency which was most impressive.

On the 6th the Stones arrived. He's the new C.J.

The 9th was the opening of the High Court, a full-dress show which went off really well. The ceremony was simple and effective, and there were no hitches of any kind. The only blot was a cluster of empty chairs, due, more Indico, to the fact that several members of the Leg. Council arrived just as the show was starting, and were naturally kept out by the Police. Just like 'em! My address seemed to go down well enough, and I actually got applause at the end, which is a welcome break-away from the traditional stiffness of behaviour at full-dress shows in the C.P..

That evening we had a dinner of 42 to celebrate the great event. Rao was like a dog with two tails, terribly pleased over the finish-up of the whole show. And well he might be, because it's he that's done all the work and supplied the driving force. I acknowledged what he had done in my address, and he sent me afterwards a charming little note, saying that he had been deeply touched by what I had said.

Next day the Commission Week started, and has, I think, been a great success. The young Indians are very good about coming in, and enjoy it thoroughly – though I do wish their wives were less heavy in hand! How can Indians ever imagine that they will be welcome in European Clubs so long as the majority of their womenfolk are like wet blankets in general company?

The dinner was last night and I made yet another speech, I'm so sick of them that this morning I told Pat Hemeon that I was going to postpone addressing the Council, which I usually do in Jan., till Feb.. As a matter of fact there are other reasons. I'd much like to know what Hammond is going to say about Berar, and what line Niemeyer is taking over our finances, before speaking. Our budget this year is gloomier than ever. Really we can't go on like this. Year after year it's the same tale – nothing can be done for lack of funds, and all construction work is at a standstill. We are asking for a subsidy of 75 lakhs, but heaven knows how much of that we shall get. This perfectly useless creation of two new provinces will absorb most of the loaves and fishes. I was told the other day as a fact that the separation landslide was started by same big Raja from Orissa, who gave colossal parties to everyone at home, and when they were mellowed by his hospitality got them to agree to a separate Orissa – which of course, meant a separate Sind as well. And we – the other provinces of India – have now got to pay the bill! I never could make out why such a completely daft proposal was swallowed by everyone at home with so little fuss, but if the above story is true, it's easy to understand.

Note (JHBG):

The above matter of Finance and precedent led to considerable jealousy, a sample of which is given in the following correspondence:

A Matter of Precedence.

Letter from Sir Hyde Gowan
To:- H.T. Craik, Home Member of Council.
New Delhi.
25th January 1936.
My Dear Craik,

1. I have been pressed to make a request on behalf of the province in the matter about which there is considerable feeling here. In a letter of the 5th instant we represented to the Government of India the unfairness of the present position in which the Central Provinces is classed in the Warrant of Precedence with Assam and the new provinces, instead of with Bihar. But we gather that this matter was not discussed at the recent Conference and that there was a tendency to suggest that the Government of India should not be bothered with it at the moment. It is possible that the impression received was wrong; but as the present

revision of the Warrant seems to offer us the only opportunity of gaining our point, I hope you will forgive me if I write you a few personal lines, on the subject.

2. Whether it be right or wrong, there is a distinct impression that the position of a province in the Warrant of Precedence is apt to be reflected in the weight which is given to its opinions in the general counsels of India, and the question is therefore not merely one of prestige, but has a definite practical importance. Here in the Central Provinces we feel that our present position is out of accord with the facts. We are a developing province, and but for the fact that we have not had a normal harvest for ten years, we should have developed more rapidly than we have. In the letter quoted above we have already given a number of facts in support of our proposal, and I will not repeat them, except to stress the point that the geographical position of the province is bound to bring it willy-nilly more and more into the limelight. I should, however, like to add to them another of which I have just been reminded, namely, that whereas Bihar only has one Military Station (Dinanur), the Central Provinces has four, including Brigade Headquarters, the Central School of Musketry, and the All India School of Equitation. It has also been noted that our Chief Secretary is already ranked with the Chief Secretaries of the United Provinces, the Punjab, and Bihar. Small points, but of cumulative value.

3. I have tried to make it plain that our request is not based on mere local pride, nor on that desire for high places against which we are warned in the Scriptures, but springs from a definite feeling that it is unjust that we should be ranked in a group below Bihar, and that our present rank is prejudicial to our interests in practice. Our request does no harm to anyone else, and I do

hope that the Government of India will view it sympathetically. We are feeling so depressed after reading the facts set forth in our representation to Sir 0. Niemeyer that a little encouragement would do us a power of good!

Yours sincerely,
sg. H.G.

Tuesday Jan. 21st

The news of the Kings death came through this morning. Two days ago when H.E. cancelled his tour of Kathiawar, I knew things must be serious. But what a wonderful end! To finish his Jubilee year and then pass gently away in his own home – not a palace – with the chorus of loving homage from his subjects still fresh in his ears.

"So be my passing –
"My task accomplished, & the long day done
"Let me be gathered to the quiet west,
"The sunshine splendid and serene
"Death"

I don't suppose there is one of us that does not feel the poorer of his going – poorer for the loss of a simple and great-hearted man, to whom his subjects were as his own family.

When he gave me an audience in July '33, I was immensely struck with his directness and sincerity, and the way in which he turned what might have been a terrifying experience into a memorable occasion, and sent one away feeling that one had got something great to live up to & must try and be worthy of one's trust. He did not do it consciously of course. As a matter of fact the conversation was anything but serious – the amount one had to drink in India (hot tea had been his beverage) in order to counteract the dry heat, the silly game that Winston Churchill and Lord Lloyd were playing over the G/I Act (a hint there) and the speed with which two English prisoners released after the Russian sabotage trial were getting out of Russia. But that was the impression he left on me.

Note (JHBG):

According to the story he told after the audience, the conversation went something like this:

His Majesty. "Ha! India. Very hot there I gather. Sweat a lot, don't you?"

"Yes, Your Majesty, you do perspire somewhat."

"What do you do about it? Drink a lot?"

"Ah - yes, but tea and such things of course."

"Oh, yes. Of course. Tea. I didn't mean anything else!"

To give the recent history of the Governorship, the Governor from 1917-22, or there about, was Sir Frank Sly, a bachelor concerning whom the 'in' joke was: "Who is the best match in India?"

Answer: "Dear Sly", the Hindi word for a match, the striking sort, being 'diarselai'. Unfortunately he spent most of his off time down at the club and got a reputation for 'lifting the elbow'. Government House became a bit of a shambles and the reputation of the Raj declined.

The end was reached when a posse of young lieutenants from the local regiment raided a G.H. Ball and carried off half a dozen of the maidens. To remedy this state of affairs, Sir Monty was installed as H.E. with instructions to tighten things up a bit, which he did most ably, but G.H. now became a 'barn', to use Sir Hyde's phrase. Luckily for him, when Sir Hyde was appointed, it was ruled that the Governor could relax although he still went down to the club on occasion. A better balance was struck.

Friday Jan 31ˢᵗ

One more mark of the Council's instability. All along it has accepted the idea of building a new High Court as part of the scheme for having a C.J.. Yesterday we put in a token demand of Rs. to cover the pay of the architect whom we have brought out from England to draw up the plans. A section got up and opposed it. There had been no party meeting, and the opposition took everyone by surprise, with the result that after a lot of chattering Khaparde's followers, the Nationalists, voted against the demand, and it was thrown out by one vote. And now what are we to do? It is one of the absurdities of the present constitution that all buildings come under "41 – Civil Works – Transferred" which means that I can't certify, and that the transferred side can put the kybosh, if it wants, on any reserved side scheme which involves building. We shall have to give them another chance in Feb., but if they still remain obdurate the High Court will just have to stay in its present grubby location. They're a mean-spirited crowd to be able to accept that idea with complacency.

Sunday Feb. 2ⁿᵈ

Rao told me yesterday that the vote on the High Court was all the fault of the Ministers, who were caught napping. Some mischief-makers tried to stir up opposition to the demand, without imagining that they had any hope of success. Then the Ministers failed to turn up at the Party meeting which discussed the coming day's business, and the Party didn't know what to settle about it, and were also annoyed because the Ministers hadn't bothered to turn up. Then, when the demand came on and the opposition was pressed home, their pique took charge, and all Khaparde's nationalists went into the "No" lobby. That's just the way things are decided in this land. A moment's pique, a passing whim, and all considerations of reason or consistency go by the board.

We spent a gloomy morning yesterday over the budget. Everything in the way of new expenditure that isn't of the greatest urgency goes out. But I managed to save a grant for Edna's Women's College, without which it would probably have demised, and a grant for a settlement for the untainted children of lepers – the latter by promising to give up 5000/- out of my own building grant. It's a good scheme. Apart from its place in the leper problem, it will give us two new rayatwari villages, and a bazaar on that white elephant of ours the Raipur Forest Tramway.

Wed Feb 5th

The P.W.D. is a difficult dept. to manage these days. In spite of the mess in which it has landed us over irrigation works – our annual loss over our works, about 35 lakhs – costs as much as a famine! – and of the appalling expensiveness of all it does, it has a great opinion of itself, and when it gets a Minister like Naidu, who is one of these amateur engineers, and pig-headed to boot, the sparks are bound to fly. The moment the minister tells Hyde to take up one work in preference to another, little Fido comes running up to me with tears in his eyes, flings a lot of figures and papers at me, and asks what he is to do about it. Yesterday I got fed up and told him to go home and do what he was told, and not to come running to me every time the Minister passed an order that he didn't agree with. He's a funny little beggar – a great worker, but knows nothing of Secretarial methods & much too excitable for dealing with Ministers.

Thank goodness I've finished my address to the Council. I can't write what other people want me to say, so I write what I want to say, and in my own way. But I'm always rather afraid that it may be bilge. I advised E. to be an impartial critic, but she persisted in saying that I ought not to alter any of it, and that it was jolly good for people to be told things differently. All I've done under the "general" head is to point out the consequences of disunion (Berar vs. C.P. and co-operators vs.

Congress) as I see them, and to make an appeal for unity. The Berar question is hopeless if they persist in squabbling over the revised Sriu settlement and that is bound to have either Berar or the C.P. discontented. And as I have pointed out to them, if there is one thing more difficult to handle than a discontented minority it is a discontented majority! The Beraris haven't the wit to see that if they join in with the C.P. instead of fighting it, they could get a Maharashtra party which would dominate the Council; whereas if they antagonise the C.P. they will be in a perpetual minority.

Jubblepore Feb 12th Wed.

We are here for what should have been the Corps of Signals jubilee, but of course all the tamáshá part of it has been shut down. I got back from dining with the Leicesters last night to find a cable telling me of George's death. He struggled as far as Lausanne, but must have died almost as soon as he got there. His loss is a great grief. Our lots had lain in different parts of the world, and I have never seen very much of him, but he was "a lovable character", as Sir C. Butler his Chairman wrote to me. It's hard work when these things happen in this job of mine. One has to carry on and smile as if nothing had occurred.

Nagpur Fri Feb 14th

I think there must be something in the air of this country that turns the brain even of the Englishmen wrong. The Medical Board wired to Simla that Caesar must go home at once, & Simla arranged a passage for him on this mail. Yesterday he went to Gampti and got the umpteen papers in triplicate without which nothing can be done in the Army. An hour later he got a wire to say his passage was cancelled, & he must wait for a trooper on March 6th! Someone in Simla had pulled a string, I suppose, and bagged his passage. That's the way they do things there. Fancy keeping a man in his condition kicking his heels about in an unfavourable climate for a month, feeling that every day the disease was increasing its hold on him. Sheer brutality. So I got cross, cleared the line, and wired to the Q.M.S. what I thought about it. Four hours later I got a wire back, saying that C. should go to Bombay at once, and would be sent off either on this mail or the next. The passage had been cancelled "under the orders of the D.M.S." – and the D.M.S. was at the time on the Delhi-Madras mail, by which time Gordon was returning from seeing O. Niemeyer! Some underling, I suppose, thought he saw a chance of doing a job in No. 1's absence.

Sund. Feb 17th

The way we are getting bled of men is awful. Gordon has just been offered the reversion of Petrie's post as Chairman of the P.S.C. and has to go on leave next month. That means that Roughton must come into the Ex. Council as well as Burton and (as G. must resign the Service) the question whether B. or R. get the permanent post becomes immediate. I have written to H.E. asking to be allowed to make a temporary appointment while I think over the matter of the permanent one. For four months from the middle of May the Commissioners of the Berar, Jubb., & Chhatt. divisions will have 18, 15 & 15 years' service. Let's hope that they'll all turn out to be young Napoleons!

G. says that our case for help was the best put up, acc. to opinion in Delhi, & that we stand as good a chance as any province of getting something – though there is going to be precious little to get. He gathered that one or two provinces which had attempted to pull the wool over O.N. (Otto Niemeyer) by producing healthy deficits this year were likely to find the attempt expensive, O.N. being about the cutest thing alive at spotting the real facts of a case.

Wed. Feb. 19th

The question of local bodies flying the Congress flag has been brought up again in Council, in connection with that very damp squib, the Congress Jubilee. It has a curious history in the C.P.. In 1922 the D.C. Jubb. refused to let the Jubb.M.C. fly the flag to welcome a C.D. deputation, and Govt. approved. Next year I, as D.C. Nagpur, refused to let a crack-brained Parsi, "General" Awasi, carry the flag in procession through the Civil station, to the accompaniment of seditious songs, as a retaliation for the Jubb. incident. Again Govt. approved, and we had a Flag Satyagraha, during the course of which Govt. announced definitely that local bodies must not fly the flag, and that if they did, that grants would be cut.

Note (JGBG and TJG):

The flag in question was the white, green and red flag of Congress, embroidered with a 'chakra', or spinning wheel, which was Gandhi's symbol for 'harijan' or cottage industry, and of which I (TJG) still retain a specimen, taken by Sir Hyde from a procession of Gandhi's followers in Nagpur in 1923. It measures 23 by 13 inches. Here is a picture of the central device of the spinning wheel which Ghandi adopted.

Ghandi flag with "Chakra" confiscated by Mr Hyde Gowan from the procession in 1923.

In that year Sir Hyde had been lent to the Police for a year, and it was in that year that Gandhi, with his headquarters in Wardha, a few miles from Nagpur, was at his most active in Civil Disobedience. The edict had gone out that processions in the European quarter of Nagpur were forbidden, so it was the one aim of Gandhi's followers to hold such a procession.

To quote from the Daily News (Nagpur) of the 29th December 1937:-

It was a grilling Nagpur May afternoon in 1923 that I first saw Mr. Hyde Gowan (now His Excellency Sir Hyde Gowan). A large crowd had collected at the cross-roads near the Bansilal building in the civil station to watch the Congress flag procession march beyond the prohibited area and disobey an official order. About half a dozen 'Satyagrahis' constituted the procession every day and as soon as they advanced near the prohibited spot an Extra Assistant Commissioner used to declare that they were arrested. The crowd gradually melted away after shouting some slogans. Mr. Gowan, Deputy Commissioner, and Mr. D.A. Smyth, an Irishman with a strong sense of humour who was District Superintendent of Police, directed the whole operation. The flag procession usually came at about 4 o'clock in the afternoon but if it was delayed Mr. Gowan would get impatient for he insisted on having his tennis every evening. He would tell Mr. Smyth: "You see to it. I will go and have my tennis."

All very civilised and non-violent. That was in 1923.

Diary continues

Feb 19th

But some cynical people in Simla, amongst whom, I know, was my predecessor, scoffed at the fuss which we junglies of the C.P. had made over such a silly business as the hoisting of a flag, and when Monty came here he gave D.C.s to understand that they were to turn the blind eye to such things, "provided that they didn't form part of a general campaign," whatever that meant. More – he laid down that stoppage of grants merely enabled Congress L.B.s to stop essential services and lay the blame on Govt. In 1931 someone in C.P. wrote and told S/S that congress flags were being flown all over the place, and that C.P. Govt. was winking at it, and the S/S asked us for the facts. Knowing the way our knees had weakened, I put up a draft, making what I considered the truthful best of our case. The S/S's correspondent had overstated his case, of course, as such people always do, and Monty took advantage of this – said that he didn't like the apologetic tone of the draft, resented the insult to our loyalty, and thought we should give the S/S a bit of our mind. The G/I sent his letter on, but took occasion to point out that they disagreed entirely with his idea about stopping grants. Monty, too clever for once, had said it was falling into the Congress trap. The G/I said 'no'; on the contrary it was the only way to educate the electorate and teach them not to return such people at the polls, which is obviously the right view. Our present position, in which we allow anybody that wishes to fly the flag all the year round, and yet say that we shall stop it the moment it becomes "part of a campaign of lawlessness", is, of course, pure bunk. The campaign is going on insidiously the whole time, and the flag is part of it. If C.D. broke out again and we told the local bodies to fold up their congress flags, they'd hoot at us in derision. The mischief has been done, and cannot be undone.

Greenfield in his fortnightly from Berar, gives an amusing commentary on the sublime confidence which the average Indian feels in his ability to fill any post. "Discussing with a local politician the other day the way in which unlettered and thick-headed marathas stand for election to local bodies and other offices which they are not competent to fill I was told that Mr. Tambe's rise to the (Acting) Governorship was one of the principal reasons. Everyone said that if the Govt. itself could raise a hitherto unheard of Small Cause Court pleader to such heights any one could aspire to them!!

Joke by JHBG

On the subject of 'unlettered and thick headed Marathas' a good story was being told some years later in the country. Two colonels, one a Maratha and one a Gujerati in the Imperial Hotel in Delhi, each complaining about the thick-headedness of their respective bearers.

"No one is more foolish than a Maratha bearer, I tell you." said the former.

"He could not be so foolish as my bearer." said the Colonel from Gujerat. "Look, I show you"

Calling the Hotel bearer, he said: "Humara bearer ko bolao."

"Jihan, Sahib."

Up comes his personal bearer: "Sahib."

"Dekko. Bazaar ko jao, Take this ten rupee note. Buy me a new Hindustan motor-car. Sumajta?"

"Jihan, Sahib"

"Repeat to me what it is you have to do."

"Sahib. I am going down to bazaar taking this ten rupee note and buying you new Hindustan motor-car."

"Ache. Jao."

Turning to his fellow Colonel, the Gujerati said: "You see. He knows a new Hindustan motor costs Rs. 15,000 and he takes one ten rupee note for buying a whole motor-car. What could be more foolish than that?"

"That is nothing" said the Maratha "I show you the most foolish man in whole world; You see. − Bearer. Humara bearer ko bolao."

"Jihan, Sahib."

Up comes the Maratha bearer. "Bearer, Gymkhana Club ko jao, Secretary Sahib mehra salaam do. Go to Gymkhana Club and ask Secretary Sahib if I am in Club, and come back here and tell me.

Sumajta?"

"Jihan, Sahib." And off goes the other bearer.

"There, you see, the Maratha is the most foolish man in the world. Here am I sitting in the Imperial Hotel and he goes all the way down to Gymkhana Club to ask Secretary Sahib in the Club if I am there. What could be more foolish than that?"

So the two bearers meet outside. "Oh, these Gujaratis are such fools. Here is my Colonel Sahib, giving me ten rupee note and telling me to go and buy him a new motor in bazaar. He knows that Hindustan motor-cars are made in four colours, black, blue, red and white, but he does not tell me what colour he wants. How can I bring back to him new motor car, if he not telling me what colour bringing it in?"

"But that is not so foolish as my Colonel Sahib. I tell you, the Maratha are the most foolish of men. He tells me to go down to Gymkhana Club and ask Secretary Sahib if he is in Club. But he is sitting there right alongside telephone. Why can he not pick up telephone and ask Secretary Sahib himself if he is in Gymkhana Club?"

Speech at the budget session of the Legislative Council on Thursday, the 20th February 1936

Mr. President, and Gentlemen of the Council,— We meet today under the shadow of grief. To all his subjects the King who has been taken from us was not only a great man and a great gentleman; he was above all the very human father of his family, as he loved to call us. And to us in India, his loss brings a special sorrow. No one who had the honour and privilege of paying their homage to him in person could fail to be struck with his insight into all that concerned this country, his affection for its peoples, and his deep and abiding interest in their welfare. That is the foundation on which loyalty stands. And if you desire evidence of that, you will find it in the countless messages of sympathy which have poured in from every part of the province, from every class of its population, and from every school of political thought. For a brief space we stand together, with our heads bowed by a common sorrow, and with a common thought in every heart is it too much to hope that before the shadow passes we may have come to see the futility of most of our differences, and may achieve at any rate something of that unity which was the dearest wish of our late King's heart?

When I addressed you last year I tried to give you some account of the measures which we were taking to cope with the three aspects of our agricultural problem, the diminution of existing debt, the provision of means for the liquidation of what remains, and the prevention of further indebtedness; and my first task today must be to render to you a brief account of what we have been able to achieve. Once again fortune has frowned on us; the cotton crop has been below normal for the fourteenth year in succession, and the wheat crop for the tenth. What we have done, therefore, we have done in the teeth of a fate which could hardly have been more unrelenting. All who have had to deal with the first part of our problem have kept clearly before themselves one fact—that we were sailing in uncharted seas, and that we must therefore take careful soundings as we go, lest our good ship founder on unseen rocks. And what has been the result of those soundings? The time has come, I think, when we may say with some measure of confidence that we are set on a fair course, and that if the watch is vigilant and the helmsman steady of hand there is no reason why we should not sail on without fear into the dawn. By the end of the last revenue year,

11 Conciliation Boards had dealt with no fewer than 11,330 applications, involving debts of 1441 lakhs, of which 611 lakhs, or 42 per cent, had been remitted. You may say, of course, that most of the latter sum was in effect a paper debt, and never could nor would have been recovered. But whether that be true or not, the fact remains that the debt was there, a millstone round the raiyat's neck, and that when a man is carrying a millstone of 100 lbs. in weight and someone knocks 42 lbs. off it, his heart will be lightened, just as his body is. Recently we have received a donation from the Government of India which enables us to start five more Boards, and the keen demand for a Board from almost every part of the Province is proof positive that, whatever may be the verdict of the future on our experiment, its present effect has been to bring relief and fresh hope to the countryside. It was inevitable that the practical working of the Act should reveal defects, and these we are endeavouring to put right as they become plain; but its main structure, which is a combination of voluntary effort with the imposition of a discount on those who stand aloof, has come through its first year's test as well as we could have expected.

Next comes the provision of means for repayment of debt. Ten Land Mortgage Banks have now been established, and Government has guaranteed the principal of their debentures up to a limit of 50 lakhs, and has also guaranteed the interest on them. But here a curious situation seems likely to arise. There is no dearth of applications for loans. There is a certain class of debtor, who will swim in shoals after the bait of a loan at 7 per cent, but unfortunately he is not the class which a Bank dealing with Government-guaranteed capital wishes to attract. The class which it wants to attract is the class which can be relied on to pay its instalments on the due dates; and, here the warning which

I uttered last year seems likely to come true. What is happening is this: the Bank says, "We will charge you 7 per cent, but you must pay on the nail". The *bania* says, "9 per cent, and you may pay when convenient". In the mind of the debtor the small saving of interest is not big enough to outweigh the extra strictness, and he goes to the *bania.* Up to the end of December, the Provincial Bank had only received for sanction from the local banks 71 applications, totalling just under a lakh of rupees. It would, however, be both premature and unduly pessimistic to say that this part of our efforts has not been successful. If the Banks do nothing else, the mere knowledge that they are ready to give loans at 7 per cent keeps down the general rate of interest for solvent debtors; in the area of one Bank, in fact, we know that it has already caused the money-lenders to reduce their rate for mortgage-loans to 7 per cent. And there is another point which seems to emerge from our scrutiny of what is going on. The oft-expressed fear that the working of the Conciliation Boards would dry up the sources of agricultural credit has not been borne out by experience. In a country where the snare of the fowler, in the person of the village *bania,* is spread far too wide, such curtailment of his activities as has occurred in practice need cause no anxiety.

In dealing with the redemption of debt by the sale of land, the very careful enquiries which we set on foot have had one definite result. An analysis of the figures for a large number of sales has made it abundantly clear that, when abnormalities have been discarded, and the real selling value has been calculated, there is no foundation for the oft-repeated complaint that that value has fallen to a disastrously low figure. Replies received from revenue officers in all parts of the province, and especially from the Court of Wards and Land Acquisition officers, have shown that with rare exceptions the value of villages is far in excess of any figure at which Government could afford to enter the market. On this point, therefore, our minds can be set at rest, and I hope that we shall hear no more of the complaint. The return of normal prices after a boom is always unpleasant from the vendor's point of view, but to the community at large it is a sign of returning health. At the same time special instructions have been issued to the staff which deals with enforced sales of land—what we call Collector's cases—to ensure that valuations are made properly; and it is hoped that these instructions will secure the postponement of sale whenever possible, and when that is not possible will ensure that the debtor gets the best price which can be obtained. Measures have also been taken, in view of the overwhelming volume of this work, to strengthen the staff. If any of you wish to criticize the nature of those measures, I hope that you will bear in mind the great difficulty of the task, and how important it is for the sake of those of your friends who are in trouble that there should be no unreasonable delay nor bungling about its performance.

We come now to the third part of our problem, the prevention of debt. If you agree with me—and no one has yet told me that I am wrong—in saying that the root causes of debt are neither heavy rents and revenue nor bad harvests, but thriftlessness, ignorance, and the burden of ceremonial observances, then we shall all realise that our task is not of a day, but of a generation at least. While our finances are in their present crippled condition it is difficult to make an effective start on the work of adapting education to meet rural needs. We have however, done something. Agriculture is now being taught in eight selected middle schools; civics, gardening, and the elementary science of plant life has been included in the Normal School syllabus;

and we are trying out an experimental syllabus for rural children in primary schools which includes the teaching of citizenship, village handicrafts, and common village tasks like the measuring of land and the weighing of grain. Of more immediate benefit is the action which we have taken to ensure that the cultivator gets proper value for his crops by adapting the provisions of the Cotton Markets Act to all agricultural markets, so as to put a stop to some of the blatant malpractices by which he is cheated at present. We have also appointed a special marketing staff, which is engaged at the moment on intensive surveys for the marketing of fruit, grain, and live-stock. Thanks to a generous and most welcome grant of 5 lakhs from the Government of India—the first real spare cash which we have seen in this province for many years, we have been able not only to bring many amenities to villages, such as roads and water-supply but also to make a start on various experiments in rural reconstruction.

Finally, I should like once more to remind the more forgetful of our critics of the greatly increased liberality with which the question of suspensions and remissions of land revenue has been treated during the past two years. The major scale of relief has been applied to all tracts, whatever their history; and remission has been ordered of all suspended arrears in excess of one year's demand.

From this brief survey of our efforts to tackle the most vital of our problems I pass, gentlemen, to the future, and first to that aspect of the future which is our immediate and pressing concern, namely, our finances. It is common knowledge that our position is serious, and I can assure you that our case for assistance has been pleaded in the quarters concerned with all the eloquence and ability of which the Finance Department is capable. It is no secret that we are hoping for a modern *"deus ex machina"*, who will descend upon the stage and with the magic word "subvention" will solve all our troubles. Every Greek theatre, you know, had a hoisting machine as part of its furniture, and when the plot of the play had become tangled beyond hope of mortal solution, the appropriate god was let down upon the stage and in a few well-chosen words put everything straight. And this leads to the point which I wish to make. We have all been taught from our childhood to believe that God helps those who help themselves, and I would ask you what warranty we have for thinking that the particular deity for whose help we are asking today will not act upon the same maxim. In the past this Council has shown much understanding of the needs and embarrassments of Government, and a readiness on more than one occasion to assist it with fresh supplies; and I hope that when you come to consider the proposals for fresh taxation—that is, for helping ourselves— which will shortly be laid before you, you will believe that they have been dictated by nothing but the dire needs of the situation, and will keep in view, not the interests of any particular class, but the common good of the province, which is in trust with you. The fitness of any body of citizens for self-government must depend ultimately on its willingness to impose upon itself such taxes as its circumstances require; and there is no surer sign of civic progress than the readiness to face those taxes. If you will allow me to touch for a moment, contrary to my practice, upon the fringe of controversy, I would make one request of you. Oppose the measures which will be laid before you, if you feel that you must; but I would ask you most earnestly to do so on their merits, and not upon the basis of the argument that no fresh Taxation should be imposed so long as the public services get their pay in full. That argument is not a fair one; for every member of this Council knows that in this matter the hands of the local Government are not entirely free, and that local considerations form but a small part of the grounds on which decisions have to be based. The sole charge which can be laid at our door is that from first to last we have insisted upon the just principle of equality of treatment for all the higher services; and if that be an offence, then the government for which I am speaking is willing to plead guilty.

I do not intend, gentlemen, to add anything to what I said last year about the new constitution. It has now become law, and when "the tumult and the shouting" has died down and the calm, dispassionate verdict of history comes to be pronounced, those who have been responsible for the structure are confident that it will vindicate alike the honesty of their purpose, the liberality of their intentions, and the skill and wisdom of their craftsmanship. What I have to say to you is this. Before us lies a year of preparation; and according as each man of us prepares his heart and girds his loins, so will he acquit himself when the time comes for him to run his course. I have used those words advisedly, because the great danger which lies ahead of us in this province and threatens to wreck our future is essentially a matter of the heart. It is the danger of disunion, and I should be failing in my duty at this juncture, when we stand at the parting of several ways, if I did not put before you, as simply and as clearly as I can, how that danger presents itself to me.

It seems to me to take two forms, a local one and a more general one. I will deal with the local one first, and in what I have to say I will ask you all to believe that I am striving, as is my bounden duty, to be completely impartial, and that my one object is, not to prejudge any issue, but to point out to you the inevitable results of certain courses of action. We have all got to make up our minds to one fact. Under the new Act the Central Provinces and Berar is treated as one province, with a joint legislature dealing with all its affairs. You will grasp the implication. If the two parts of the province agree, I can see before us a prosperous future, in which Berar, as the largest of the divisions, and closely akin by race, language and geographical position to its neighbours in the next largest division, is cast to play a leading part. But if that agreement is not reached, and if a settlement has to be imposed from outside, then frankly, gentlemen, the outlook seems dark to me. If the last fifteen years have taught us any lesson, it is this, that it is beyond the wit of man to devise a financial arrangement which can be imposed on the two parties with any reasonable chance of satisfying both of them. Discontent will come either upon the majority or upon the minority; and if there is one thing more difficult to deal with than a discontented minority, it is a discontented majority. That is a hard fact, to which it is useless to close our eyes. All of you have seen at one time or another a curious sight upon our roads. A cart is being drawn by two bullocks, both of which are leaning outwards. Their one aim seems to be, not to get ahead, but to get as far away from each other as they can, and to pull the yoke in half. We may suppose that the cart gets to its journey's end sometime, but it must take a long time in doing so; and unless all parts of our province can agree to pull together, that is just what will happen to it; it will take a long time getting anywhere, and no one will envy the task of those who have to guide it. And you have all seen another sight, a pair of racing bullocks clad in gaily coloured coats, cantering down the roadside, while their driver shouts with the joy of their speed. Fancy may be carrying me away, but why should that not be a fair picture of our province if we can all pull together?

Finally I come to the more general form of disunion, which has been brought about by the action of those who for many years have stood aloof from the working of the present constitution, and have not made up their minds as yet as to the attitude which they will adopt to the new one. I would ask them to read the history of the past fifteen years, during which the present constitution has been worked, and worked successfully. It has stood unshaken, as a lighthouse stands unshaken in a storm, against all the attacks which have been launched against it; and there is no reason to suppose that the foundations of the new edifice have been laid less surely, or its walls built less stoutly. But one irrevocable harm can be done, not to the constitution itself, but to the people for whose welfare and advancement it has been created. If one considerable section of that people stands aloof from the proper task of every citizen, the whole work of the community must suffer. Not only is it deprived of some of the best of its man-power and its brain-power, but much of what power is available is wasted in the barren and profitless task of coping with disorder. I appeal, therefore, to everyone in this province to remember the words of the Archbishop of Canterbury. "Look forward", he said, "not to the shadows which you fear, but to the substance which you have gained." Those who seize that substance will find that in their hands is, not a stone, but in very truth bread. They will find also, as history has shown abundantly, that a view of government from the inside is apt to change many ideas which were held confidently when the outside only was visible. Above all they will find that the sober, constructive work which is involved in the governance of any State brings more comfort to the soul than any wanderings among the barren rocks of the wilderness, where no manna falls, and the water is bitter, like the waters of Marah. And if, before I lay down my office, I am privileged to see both parts of this province, and all classes of its political leaders, working together for the common good, I shall say my "*Nunc dimittis*" with a cheerful heart.

Note (JHBG):

One is forced to assume that the Indian Legislative Council knew what was the meaning of 'Nunc Dimittis'.

Friday Feb. 21st

I'm glad to say that the other members of Govt. agreed to my point of view about the flag, & we answered the question so as not to commit ourselves to any threats. The weakness of our position is this, as in so many other questions concerning local bodies, is that we have never insisted on the principle – or rather fact – that a local body is merely an offshoot of Govt., exercising certain delegated powers. We have weakly allowed them to arrogate to themselves a quasi-independent status instead of telling them that they could not expect grants from a Govt. against which they were plotting, and the next regime is going to have its work cut out to get the reins back into its own hands, as it will certainly want to do.

I addressed Council yesterday, chiefly a plea for union between the C.P. and Berar, and for the return of Congress to the fold. The D.N. and the Hit. received it well, and backed up what I said. My last speech for the present, thank goodness. I've had my fill of this cold weather.

Thursday Feb. 27th

The T/I gave me a short leader – and the Bombay Chronicle said I'd issued a "challenge" to Congress.

Fiddlesticks. All I said was that the old constitution had withstood attack, and there was no reason to suppose that the new one wouldn't. But there is a certain type of thwarted and perverted mentality in this country which construes every statement of fact or truth into a challenge or threat or an insult or something equally bombastic. A tiresome crowd. It is an irony of fate that I who, whatever my faults may be, do like cleanliness and order and straight-forward dealing should have had to spend my working life amidst dirt, disorder and intrigue. It's trying to the temper!

And the Council! If they weren't a public danger, they'd earn a fortune as comedians. Having chucked out our token demand for the High Court architect for this year (vide January 31st) they have now passed the demand for next year's work, including a new bungalow for the C.J., in full by 37 to 8! We are now going to be involved in technicalities over what to do for the small sum required this year, but the vote clears us completely vis-à-vis of Audit. It's just like the case of the Nagpur water-supply. The most serious and vital matters are decided by personal 'zidd', sudden pique, anything but the solid merits of the case. And as soon as any absurd decision is taken, the first thing people say is – "Oh! That means nothing. We'll get them to reconsider that". The effect is de-moralising. There is no feeling of finality. It's all a sort of children's game, and in the most serious matters – such, for instance, as our chronic deficits – there's always the idea that the G/I can never let a province go bankrupt, and that whenever anything goes wrong, Pop will put it right again.

Our finances are really worrying me. Gordon estimates that our normal expenditure is 45 lakhs less than revenue. *(On reading what follows, I can't help feeling he meant to say 'more' than revenue J.G.)*

If O.N. gives us nothing, I can see no possible alternative to a drastic reorganization of the whole of the public services — the new scales of pay which we give to new entrants to be applied to everyone, and a 10 to 15% cut on the Imperial Services. Something of that sort. But would they ever let us do it? Our C.P. history is rather like that of Lancashire. During the boom years after the war our Excise revenue under the iniquitous auction system soared to undreamed of heights – about 1,40 lakhs and we mortgaged it all by increased establishments and higher rates of pay. Then came the crash, accentuated by our weak-kneed acceptance of prohibition as our "ultimate goal". Down goes our excise to 60 lakhs and there's nothing left with which to meet our excess pay-bills. We make a great mistake in talking about our efficiency. Witness our irrigation. Panicked by the big famines, we calculated that each one of them cost us about 1½ crores, and we built a lot of "protective" works, as an "insurance". What is the present position? A famine now costs us about 40 lakhs one up to us, certainly, but we might have foreseen the possibility of reduction — and our annual loss on irrigation is 30 lakhs! In other words, we are paying an annual premium of £75 for a £100 policy! Thanks to drastic economies, we now cover working expenses with about 1 lakh to spare, but interest has to come from the budget. Two of our latest tanks cost us a lakh and a half annually to keep up and their receipts are a bare Rs. 10,000/-.

I have told the P.W.D. to look into the question of abandoning them altogether. It's the old fallacy of imagining that supply creates demand – that if you stick your wares under a man's nose, he will buy them. So he will in this country, provided you charge about a tenth of what they cost you. And then there's the Raipur Forest Tramway, another expensive white elephant. It cost us 19 lakhs, and we were told that the timber would come pouring out of the forest. We gave the managing agency to a Calcutta firm which turned out to be the principal exporting firm under another name; and we gave it on a fixed annual remuneration, so that they had no concern with our profits. At the same time there was a strong road competition, and the exporters were thus able to force our rates down. Result – we barely cover working expenses, and each year haver about closing the line down altogether. When we talk about efficiency, we're on very unsafe ground.

Tuesday March 3rd

The Council carried one of its perpetual adjournment motions yesterday. Some years ago a gang of sadhus settled at Sainkhera in Narsingpur, and there practised every kind of foul and loathly vice, with the result that they attracted people from all parts of the country – a typical "Mother India" show. We broke the gang up, and they went to Bhopal, where I think the head of them died. His chief chela has now returned to the provinces and settled at Khandwa, where, needless to say he once more attracts worshippers, including, we are told a number of "respectable" persons. (Among people who are perpetually howling about insults to their self-respect, "respectability" is no guarantee of morality.) The police went to his ashram to check up on its inhabitants, who were said to include a number of undesirables, and a small party was seized and ill-treated and had to be rescued by a second party with a lathi charge. The facts are not yet clear, but that matters nothing to the Council. Instead of getting on with their work of discussing the budget, they pass their time discussing this, that and the other, and they carried the adjournment motion by a very large majority. Today that nosey-parker Fulay has got a motion of adjournment because one of the School at Pachmarhi had a few words with a P.O. babu who was rude to him, and is said to have kicked him. "Urgent public importance."!!

Thursday March 5th

The budget got through, with no damage except a few token cuts and the loss of the demand for the Khandwa forest report, which did not surprise me. But the H.P. refused to let us put in again the demand for the High Court (February 7th) and now I've got to consider whether I should get the Council out of its tangle by authorising it. The choice lies between that and putting it in again at the August session. If they were to chuck it out then – and they're capable of anything – we should have to let it lie until Audit takes it up a year, or so hence. And that might possibly mean a surcharge against the members of Govt., which would raise all sorts of awkward questions.

Saturday March 7th

Held an Investiture today and gave E. her K-I-H Gold Medal – a well-earned distinction if ever there was one, because what she has done has been done in spite of her dislike for the country and her natural wish to be at home with her family. It's a sheer sense of duty which has pulled her through. The show was a quiet one, only the decorés being there. That was much to my regret, as I would have liked E. to have a real tamáshá but the orders re court mourning were strict.

The war clouds are gathering in Europe once more. Hitler's démarche has fairly upset the apple-cart. But I do not think that war will break out just yet, because Germany can't be really ready. I'm afraid my sympathies are with her, at any rate in denouncing the Versailles Treaty. That document was made to be denounced as soon as Germany was strong enough. As to the tearing up of the Locarno Pact, one can't judge not having seen it.

I am spending my time at present trying to get something out of the G/I about Gordon's going. His photo (complete with garland) actually appeared in today's T/I as Petrie's successor, but we're still without definite orders and everything is hung up. It must have leaked out from Delhi, which is a regular whispering gallery these days. One of my callers today, an ex-M.L.C., said that if anything got out in Nagpur it was always through the Ministers. That was no news to me!

Saturday, March 14th

I decided, all members of Govt. concurring, to cut the Gordian knot and "authorize" the expenditure for this year on the High Court, and I hope we've now finished with the silly episode.

It's a strange country. A leading, and supposedly very enlightened, Mahommedan R.C. has asked Rao to drop the prosecution of the "Bare Dada" (the sadhu in Sainkhera mentioned above) because he and many of his subjects are "interested" in him. A devotee of Islam intercedes on behalf of a Hindu sadhu who has been guilty in the past of the foulest malpractices! It beats me completely.

Wednesday March 18th Pachmarhi.

As do many other things. At present the only provision in the C.P. for higher female education is a few places in men's Colleges, and Women's College which has led a precarious existence for some years, and which E. is now trying to set firmly on its legs. But it is a thankless and disheartening job among these Nagpur people. The whole business is wrapped in a cloud of personal animosity and intrigue. Not one of them asks – which is the proper way to educate our women? They're all out to grind their own private axes. If I were E. I'd chuck the whole show and make them make their own mess in their own messy way. The Standing Comm. for Education proposed recently that the Men's college should no longer admit women. The principal and the advisor to Owen (D.P.I.) wrote opinions which simply disgusted me – Irrelevant diatribes unredeemed by any vestige of sober reasoning. There is something behind it which I cannot fathom – some local controversy of an unsavoury nature – which prevents any of them dealing with the matter from the sole point which ought to be considered, namely the good of the women.

We came up early this year to get away from the stifling airlessness of Nagpur. There never seems to be any oxygen in the air there. Here it is very peaceful and refreshing not a sound as I write but the song-birds in the garden.

Of one thing I am quite convinced. Hyderabad intends to make a determined effort, as soon as the new constitution comes in, to get its finger into the Berar pie. We have just had a case of deliberate interference by H.E.H.'s Govt. with the management of an 'Imam' which it has no possible concern with.

Monday March 30th.

I have now got a note by Shahani, the editor of the "Hit.", about the Women's College which confirms me in my disgust about the whole business – the venomous type of thing which the Indian writes when his personal 'zidd' has been aroused, without a trace, needless to say, of recognition of, or gratitude for, the efforts of those who are striving to do something for the women. But what the reason for his venom is he still does not disclose, and it's not worth bothering about. No honest man can hope to follow the tortuous burrowings of the Maharashtra Brahman's mind. Take dear old Khaparde, for instance. He's a sahib to his finger-tips, and very cultured; but I spend my time trying to prevent him busking cases in order to shield his pals and doing jobs in order to help others of them, and generally in getting him to see that as a member of Govt. he's got to consider Govt.'s reputation for straight and honest dealing. And then there's Naidu – a non-Brahman. He's been surcharged by the Auditor for various sums in connection with the Wardha Dt. Council, of which he was Chairman. And I've just received a sort of open letter from a man who was his overseer, making all sorts of allegations against his administration of the Council, all in detail. How much of it is true, goodness alone knows. But I'm afraid that very few people would risk their money in backing its falseness. Such are my Ministers.

One piece of good news. The Nagpur M.C. got Sir M. Visheshwarayya to examine the water-supply schemes, and he's told them straight out – at a fee of 5,000/- – just what we've been telling them for 14 years, that the Kanhan scheme is the only possible one, that their city is dirty and ill-drained, and that the sooner they undertake the Kanhan scheme, re-organise their drainage, and start an Improvement Trust, the sooner they will justify their presence on earth. So I hope we have now heard the last of Bachelor and Dube and their gravitation schemes, and can get to work. But fancy a city of a quarter of a million inhabitants listening for an instant to the schemes of a man who was made to leave the I.C.S. because

i. he was a looney and
ii. a man who was refused promotion as Chief Engineer because he was half dotty and was unfit to run the department.

Is there any country in the world where sober reason is at a greater discount?

At last my troubles over getting a P.S. seem likely to be solved. I had tried to get a War Block officer but got no applicants, because I could guarantee nothing about the pay of the post after 1.4.37, then a Major Pim turned up, who seems the very man I've been looking for for 2½ years – retired last Jan; wants work above all things & will leave me to settle the pay. Seems to know everyone and everyone says nice things about him. The Brigadier says I couldn't do better. So I hope we shall get on well together.

Wed. April 1st.

I've just heard that The Vice-Chairman and Sec. of the Amraoti Dt. Cl., whom Khaparde did his utmost to shield by saying that we should refuse sanction to their prosecution, have been convicted of bribery and given 6 months each. I hope that will choke him off his latest effort – trying to shield some Municipal people at Ellichpur from a prosecution for cheating, on the ground that the case would produce "local bitterness" and that the amount involved was small! "If this ye do in the green tree, what will ye do in the dry?" Heaven knows what these people will do a year hence.

We had a meeting of the Executive Council this morning, and I'm glad to say that Rao agreed with me that Burton should take precedence over Roughton. Gordon was doubtful, and said that he'd sooner have R. to advise him in difficulty than B.. But he agreed that B. had vision, humanity, & imagination, which R. has not, & said that as it is I who will have to be advised & not he, he did not wish to press the point. G.'s going will be a great loss. He and Rao have been as helpful of councillors as any man could have wished for.

Friday April 3rd

I mentioned on March 3rd that the Council had censured Govt. over the affair of Khandwa Ashram. Subsequent enquiries have shown that the place is just what we thought, a thoroughly disreputable show; and now Congress, whose votaries can never be accused of any exaggerated concern for public (or private) morality, have held a public meeting damning the Ashram and all its works. It just shows how much value is to be attached to the vote of Council.

Something has evidently been moving in higher circles about King George's Memorial. H.E. wrote and told us we could get up local memorials, as he was only going to do a local Delhi one. So I got going here, and gave my usual dollop to the fund. Now comes an intimation from H.E. that they are going to have a big memorial at Delhi – apparently of the statue cum groups of figures type – and will we stump up? I am surprised, because it is known that neither the King nor his father liked statues, and King George certainly always wanted money to be put to useful objects. As the thing has come, not personally, but merely as a printed notice with a formal slip from the P.D.V. I shall probably not endanger our Provincial Fund by taking any action on it. I feel strongly that in our present poverty every penny we can collect should be devoted to useful local objects.

Monday April 6th

I will say that Kh., although he's always trying to run off the track, is very ready to answer to the rein when it's used. He brought me today two cases in which I'd suggested that he was being flabby in dealing with defaulting Municipalities, and in both he agreed to stiffen things up. Our local Boards, and Bodies generally, are a hopeless lot – so bad that even Indian public opinion is condemning them openly. One of the most encouraging things I've seen was the report of a Committee which we set up last year to overhaul local self-government. It was a really sensible and responsible document, and will enable us, I hope, to put our Acts into really good shape. Kh. presided, and that's one up to him. Naidu had been presiding over an Excise Committee, which he is taking on joy-rides to Bhamragarh (where the locals go naked, or used to many years ago) and Anarkantak, the sacred spot where the Nerbudda rises. We are winking at it, because Council has said nothing about prohibition lately, and we hope the Committee will allow that most ill-advised policy to die a natural death. But it can't go on much longer. Even Naidu looked rather sheepish when I heard about the Amarkantak trip, and asked him what he thought he'd see there.

Thurs April 9th

There was some more veiled nastiness in the "Hit." about the Women's College, so I told E. I thought it was time she chucked the whole business, and said she'd do whatever I thought wise. Before coming to a final decision, I said I'd consult Rao and Khaparde, and they have "implored" me to treat Shahani with the contempt he deserved, and not to do anything, as E.'s resignation would wreck the College. So I shall hold my hand for the present; but if there's anything more of this sort I shall tell E. to cut out of the whole business, and leave the College to the tender mercies of the wrangling Indian. It wouldn't survive them long!

Friday April 10th

There is a significant article in today's Hit. about H.E.H.'s recent visit to Delhi. Their man writes from Delhi to say that H.E.H. is not anxious to join the Federation, and is stiffening his terms for Berar. The immemorial Eastern method. Recently in correspondence he raised the claim that the Govt. of the C.P. should be considered as his representative in Berar, and not H.M.'s. He is now stated to be claiming that currency, customs, and Post Offices in Berar should all be his. I have not heard a word about it from Delhi, which is queer, but typical of F. and P. methods. One thing is quite certain. I serve no man but H.M. and if there is any question of making the Govr. of the C.P. run Berar on behalf of H.E.H., I'm off home. The position would be quite impossible. If they are going to give way to H.E.H., they must run Berar as a separate unit, and put in a man who will be specifically Govr. per pro H.E.H., so to speak. No self-respecting man could occupy the high and honourable position of one of H.M.'s Govrs at one minute, and at the next have to carry out the behests of someone who is subordinate to the suzerain power.

April 16th Thurs

I wrote to H.E. the other day, a private letter of farewell, ending up "Better lo'ed ye canna be". I got back a most charming letter, thanking me for helping him, and for keeping the province quiet. (It's the province that's done that, not I.) And now we have had a wire "Goodbye, good luck, God bless you both. Lord & Lady Willingdon." I had no idea that it was possible for a Viceroy & his Governors to be on terms like that. It makes one feel that the world's a better place & one's job more worth doing. The W.s are leaving amidst a chorus of regret and affectionate farewells, the like of which I have never heard.

Not a dissentient note – except for the ill-mannered, unshaven congress gang – just a swelling paean of praise and god-speed. I do not envy their successors, who will have to show themselves very human if they are to earn a tithe of the love that the W.s are taking home with them.

Sat April 18th

The Nagpur M.C. have adopted the Kanhan scheme unanimously. So that's one thing to the good. Now they'll probably start wrangling as to who shall do the work – and get the pickings. They can settle it as they like. The English firm Williams & Temple, which has done the preliminary work is responsible for all the recent trouble, because Williams, instead of doing what he was told started a hare in the shape of a fresh gravitation scheme – to cost double the Kanhan scheme, of course. So I shan't stir a finger to help them.

H.E. has agreed that Burton should be made permanent in succession to Gordon. So that too is settled satisfactorily.

We had an amusing letter from Delhi the other day. We want to separate our Imperial Forest cadre from the General one, as Burma and Bombay have done, so as to have our own men and keep them. The present system of transferring conservators all over India is an administrative crime, as we've told the G/I often. We asked if it was any good raising the point, and they said we might, though we would be up against "vested interests". That's just it. Whenever you want to put anything right in this country you find that you are up against "vested interests". I wonder how the Ministers will deal with them next year. I cannot help feeling that some of them, such as the old scales of pay for the Provincial Services, will have short shrift. And honestly I shall not regret it. There is no question that the pay drawn by (Indian) Govt. servants is out of all proportion to reality now.

Tues. Ap. 21st

Mani, Asst. Ed. of the Hitavada came to see me this morning, so I told him quite plainly & frankly what I thought about the Hit's attitude to the Women's College – that to attack people who were trying, at considerable personal sacrifice, to do a public service was neither playing the game, nor worthy of a paper which called itself the organ of the "Servants of India". He is a nice little man and took it very well – said he had no idea that the Hit.'s attitude had caused us so much pain, and that in future the Hit. would leave the College alone. I hope he'll stick to that. I made it plain that if he did not, the College would be left to its fate & the Hit. would have to bear the blame.

Thurs. April 23rd

Gordon left today. He will be much missed, especially by me, as he has been invaluable as H.M.. There was a dinner at the Club to him on Tuesday, to which all members of Govt. went, and all the civil officers, English & Indian. It was a very cheerful affair. Last night we gave a dinner to his own particular friends. G. & I had agreed that there were to be no speeches, a great relief to both of us, and we enjoyed two very good dinners without having them overshadowed by the cloud of a coming speech. It is really absurd that one can't bid good-bye to an old friend without making a speech about it.

We are having a scrap with the Army about the plateau. The Civil Govt. bought it 70 years ago. The committee that managed it from the start was appointed by us, & all its officers were civilians. And we pay for the whole of the upkeep. But the Army claims an enormous area of it, over which it performs no functions beyond clearing the area for safety purposes on the few days in the year when there is field-firing in the Long Valley. And we know what Army control means. In 1896 they started cutting the jungle to pieces. In 1906 a ferocious General (Denning) came up here and commandeered the whole of the houses in Cantonments for his officers, though many of them had been occupied for many years by Secs. & Head of Depts.. In 1931 they dug trenches all about the North Valley, to the imminent danger of the people who ride there regularly. And in 1932 they sent emissaries to reconnoitre the Plateau and see whether they could cut enough fields of fire through the jungle to enable them to bring the Ahmednagar Machine Gun School here. And all this (as regards the last two instances) in areas in which we pay every cent of the piper's bill. The Cantt. does nothing for the plateau. The Civil Govt. gives the Municipality Rs.10,000/- a year, and keeps up the whole of the roads, bridle-paths & foot-paths besides any miscellaneous expenditure that comes along, like tree planting and care of avenues. The way that the Military Dept. snaffled other people's land in 1924 et seq. without usually as much as "by your leave" was one of the coolest pieces of official brigandage on record. At one time they actually ran their boundary through half the golf links and the polo grounds (built and maintained entirely from civil funds) and some young pup threatened to turn us out of a part of the Golf course! Of course as soon as we shouted they caved in and put their boundary back.

Wed. April 29th

How people do squeal when they find their own pet weapons being used against them! There's the usual trouble going on over the Jubb.M.C. after having had the electoral rolls revised, I think, four times. We get the elections through – result, Congress majority of 5. So H.M. nominated 6 "Independents". Then came the selections. The Independents ratted – every one rats in Jubb. as a matter of course – and 5 Congressmen were "selected" out of 6. Thereupon the Independent nominees appealed to the D.C. against the validity of the selection proceedings. He refused to hear them, so they appealed to H.M. who ordered the case to be heard. After the usual delays the D.C. rejected the petition; whereupon they came up to H.M. in revision. Meanwhile the election of office-bearers cannot be held, D.P. Misra cannot get his hand on the reins of office, and the papers are squealing

that all the delay is due (to) H.M. having a down on Misra. More –
Grigson writes in to say that according to common report it's Rao who
is egging on Khaparde because he hates Misra – pure nonsense. All
that's happened is that the beaten party (who are just as rascally as the
Congressites) are employing the usual Indian tactics, which we are
powerless to put a stop to, and the others are howling. This year's Local
Audit report is an amazing document. The only heartening thing about
(it) is that that it has been written by an Indian – one man with the
complete courage of his convictions. Punctual and honest budgeting is
almost unknown. Members take advances ad lib. from the Municipal
or Dt. Cl. treasury, nominally for works, but really for their own
purposes. Collection of taxes is slack and large arrears are due from
members. The staff is babied in every conceivable way. Embezzlements
are common. And soon – a rotten state of affairs. I wanted to issue a
resolution on the report, but Kh. funked it, needless to say – "too near
the elections, and members will complain of Govt's lack of sympathy
in cutting grants". As if that had anything to do with the rank
dishonesty and incompetence that is reported everywhere!

Thursday April 30th

Niemeyer's report is much what we expected – an 'ipse dixit'
production, which merely says what is to be, without explaining why. I
gather that it was on these terms that he took up the enquiry.
Apparently there is no financial bar to 1.4.37 as 'Dev Tag', though it is
quite clear that it will be some years before the Provinces get a look in
at the Income Tax. We are to get a small subsidy of 15 lakhs, in the
shape of a remission of capital debt paying that amount of interest. As
we have protested for years that we are being unjustly charged 8½ lakhs
p.a. for what is known as pre-reform irrigation debt, the concession
doesn't amount to much. But the G/I have a scheme for the
consolidation of debt which when F.D. have disentangled the figures,

may bring us in a bit more; and if we got our excise policy modified we may just attain to solvency.

Every day I live I become more convinced that the first thing we shall have to do under the new regime is to cut down the pay of our establishments. The standard of efficiency which we have enforced in the past, and the pay with which we have rewarded it, are alike far beyond the standard that the Indian likes and the pay that he thinks should be given.

I have been reading some very good articles that Christopher has written from France and Germany to Low (ed. T/I) who with his wife was staying with us last Oct. – a charming Scotch couple. In a letter in reply, Low says – "I hear the new Viceroy has created a tremendous stir in New Delhi and his direct methods have given the official world a fright. Everybody thinks that he has more drive even than Lady Willingdon!" I hope he is making some of the barnacles shake in their shells!

Our disastrous Excise policy has resulted in a positively appalling increase in excise crime. Instead of frankly acknowledging it and chucking the prohibition stunt, which is two thirds political, H.M.I. wants the Police to be turned on to help the Excise Dept.. This is against our declared policy, and Rao and I are strongly opposed to it, though we don't mind the Police to assist in a specific "drive". Just like N. to want someone to pull his chestnuts out of the fire for him.

Sat May 2nd

A splendid instance of the inner workings of that unholy alliance, a Brahmin cum non-Brahmin Ministry. From 1933 to '34 Naidu was Chairman of the Wardha Dt. Cl.. His predecessor, one Charde, a Brahmin, had let the Council go to pot – pounds and schools falling to pieces, salaries of teachers, pound-keepers, etc., unpaid while the head office staff got large increases, corruption and speculation everywhere.

Naidu tried to put matters right, but after a time the reforming energy of his party flagged, and things got so bad that H.M.E. wants to dissolve the Council. He sent up a proposal to that effect to me, and I ordered it to be circulated. Thereon H.M.I. wrote a long note opposing the idea (Both of them seem to have forgotten completely that they accepted office on joint responsibility!) Banerji, R.S., comments thus in a private note to me – "Charde, leader of the Brahmin party, has been bringing pressure to bear on H.M.E. for dissolution, and H.M.I.'s Party is looking up to him to save their face". All this wire-pulling has been responsible for the delay in H.M.E.'s making up his mind. Although he does not wish to offend H.M.I. he expects that dissolution may help the Brahmin party in the next general election. H.M.I. takes the threat as a condemnation of his administration and therefore as a blow to his prospects at the elections. It is possible that H.M.I thinks bona fide that he did his best to set things right while he was Chairman. The special audit for which he asked was turned down by the Sharif-Chambal Ministry to spite him: that is what he says. He is conscious, however, that his followers have recently "allowed things to drift." A pretty kettle of fish they are! Plain though it is that the new reforms are inevitable, I tremble sometimes to think what is going to happen.

Thurs May 7th

Yesterday was a contentious day. There was first of all our answer about the Niemeyer report. There was a lot of argument with N.J. as a sort of unofficial F.D. as to the exact amount which we benefit by. The capital heads of the debt account are difficult to understand. But it is clear that we benefit by at least another 10 lakhs, so far as our next few budgets go; and with 25 lakhs to the good, and our Excise and Tobacco Bill black marks against us, I said it was useless making any sort of protest. All agreed, & we merely cabled to the S/S that we hadn't got what we wanted but would do our best to get along with what there was.

Then Khaparde, wobble-knee'd as ever, wouldn't stick to our principle of taking penal interest when local bodies default in loan payments. Only a petty sum was involved, and on the other side was a principle, but I suppose someone had been getting at him. He spends his time being got at.

Then I had to hold the fort against five military officers, headed by the Brigadier, claiming that they owned the Dantt. area of the plateau here, but the whole of the rest of the plateau as well! When asked for their authority, they quoted facts which told, not for them but against them. However, I told them straight out that we could never admit their claim to the plateau but that on the other hand we knew that claims of defence must be paramount, and that if they'd shed the Hitler attitude and ask us nicely we'd do everything we could for them. At the end of two hours we came to an agreement which ought to satisfy all parties, and they went away quite pleased. That was a good thing because Burton, N.J. & G. had failed to arrive at anything satisfactory the day before. But goodness knows whether Simla shell-backs will approve.

Sunday May 10th

The Brig. produced a final draft of the plateau agreement. We are to let them extend their Cantt. boundaries & in return be given a lease of all areas not required for actual firing. We will maintain them as hitherto, clear the danger Zone when necessary, & give them $3/10$ of the forest income, as we do now. What they were afraid of was that they might find they had to extend the firing areas, and would have to purchase land from us for the purpose. They were therefore very relieved when we said we would give it to them. On the other hand, we will get what we want – control over the plateau amenities. I showed the scheme to Rao and he thoroughly agreed.

I asked Commrs. to let me have a forecast of the elections, as I'm bound to be questioned at the I.O., and I've had some interesting replies. Jubb. says that Congress will get about 17 out of the 27 general seats, Berar 4 or 5, Raipur 4 or 5. Stent from Nagpur (an arch-procrastinator) has not yet replied. Rao says he thinks Congress won't get more than 35 or 40 genuine Congress-men in, out of 120. There seems a general idea that if the locals are let alone, there will be no question of refusal of office. In fact D.P. Misra & R.S. Shukla are as keen as mustard to be Ministers.

Rao has given Betty who is to be married on Tuesday a lovely wedding-present, three silver dishes, one large, two small, quite plain & really good. That's because she's marrying a policeman. He's always doing something for the Police.

Note (TJG):

At this point Sir Hyde went on four months leave staying for at least some of the time at The Bungalow, Gummers How in the Lake District. Here he first met my mother, Lorna, then newly engaged to my father, James. They were married in October 1936 just after Sir Hyde returned to India. She remembered him as being very grand and their custom was to visit the Bungalow every morning for a formal start to the day.

CHAPTER 9

1936
SEPTEMBER - DECEMBER

Pachmarhi Sept 27th

Back from 4 months' leave, the record of which would not be germane
to the purpose of this diary. Rao, who acted for me, has done very well,
so everyone says, and he handed over to me a most complete note on
everything which had happened. If there was a certain amount of
blowing his own trumpet, and letting it be known what he was doing
and saying, that was perhaps inevitable in the circumstances. But he
would have had a fit if he could have seen the following extract from a
letter written to me by a friend soon after my return – "It is nice to feel
you are back in India again. I hope we shall see your photo as many
times as we saw the appalling man who was acting for you"! Rao is of
a curiously negroid type, and no beauty. Socially he has been very good,
and everyone has been pleased. The only fly in the ointment is Naidu,
who has been nosing in the muck-heaps, and has got hold of some
garbage about Bobby Logan, Civil Surgeon of Nagpur, and a nursing
sister. Naidu has a jackal at the Mayo Hospital named Dube, an Asst.
Surgeon, who has been mixed up with various political intrigues. He
instructed Dube, to have Logan watched. What will come out of the

case I don't know yet. Intrigues and slanderings are only too common a feature of work at the Mayo. That's the worst of India. So few people can stick to their jobs without poking their noses into other people's affairs. Most of the Nagpur doctors spend far more time in politics than in the practice of their profession.

Vide May 10th (Agreement with the Army) Simla has actually approved of the agreement. So now we have laid a hob-goblin that's been worrying us for years. Also the S/S has agree to the view that I and others took about Cabinet meetings under the new constitution. Though they will be called by the Chief Minister, time place and agenda must be approved by the Governor who will normally preside, at least at first. The S/S has cut down the elaborate set of Business Rules the G/I framed to about a dozen simple ones and the only thing done during my absence of which I disapprove was that we crabbed the new draft – a piece of mere dialectic for which N.J. was responsible. I have written to Craik saying I agree with the S/S.

It's very amusing how one gets kudos for things which seem obvious and cost no trouble, just as one often gets a kick in the pants without in any way meriting it. When we answered the reference about the Niemeyer Report, it seemed to me to be patent that it was an arbitral award, and that it was about as much use arguing about it as confuting the Ten Commandments. So we merely pointed out that we hadn't got all we asked for, but that the award gave us a sporting chance of pulling along & we'd make the best of it. What did other Govrs. do without exception? Each one of them wrote pages and pages to show how hardly little Tommy was being treated, & how empty his belly was going to be – much in the strain of the phrase one used to hear too often on settlement work "Pét ke wáste larná cháhige, Sáhib" (One must fight for one's belly's sake). Result – when I called at the I.O. Rab Butler and Man Parsons, beams all over their faces, and said that the C.P. Govt. was the only one in India which had behaved properly over the Report;

& Rab would have said it in the House, only he thought it would lead to trouble.

I had a wonderful leave. Why the dickens does one ever leave England? Six weeks of visits to various relations & friends, leaving undone all the things that I ought to have done, such as the I.C.S. & O.R. dinners, Empire Garden Party and so on. Then six weeks in E.'s bungalow on Windermere, with Christo, Antony & the grandchildren, while James & other members of the families appeared and disappeared at intervals. A joyous, care-free life with a car and an outboard motor, a tennis court, plenty of golf & the tarn & lake for fishing. E. has stayed at home, as James gets married on Oct 7th and next day Antony goes up to Hertford. She gets out in early Nov.

October 8th

We drank James and Lorna's health in style last night. It's very sad not to have been at the wedding, but James's prospects were not very definite while I was at home & they'd have been fools to tempt providence by being married then. In one way I've been exceptionally lucky – I've two of the nicest and comeliest daughters-in-law that you'd find in a long day's march.

Funny lot, these M.L.C.s. When the Ministry was formed, Naidu took L.S.G.. After a time the party got so fed up with the way he was gerrymandering nominations to Local Bodies that they insisted on L.S.G. going to Khaparde. Now Kh. is amending the L.S.G. Acts in accordance with the recommendations of a Committee which we appointed, and is effecting much-wanted tightening of control; whereupon a body of his supporters, labelled Nationalists, is demanding his head on a charger and asking for L.S.G. to go back to Naidu, and for Kh. to resign. Reason? Because, forsooth, the two leading ones in the gang were not put on to the Select Comm. to consider the Bills! Personal pride and personal pique – those are the strongest motives to action in this country. Principle comes in a bad last.

Friday Oct. 9th

By a coincidence, Rajorker, one of the pair referred to above, came and saw me today, and I tackled him about the newspaper report that he was going to bring a 'no confidence' motion. He assured me that it was a canard, and that if such a motion were brought he would oppose it. But, being Chairman of a District Council, he disliked the tightening of control. He may; but the fact is that it is needed is shown by the easy passage that the Bills have had. People are beginning to realise that there are limits to the extent to which they should "be allowed to make mistakes" – the parrot-cry of the half-baked radical. The process is permissible, so long as the lessons of those mistakes are marked and inwardly digested. But when over a long series of years the same mistakes repeated again and again – vide the annual reports – there comes a time when the permission must be withdrawn, here we are lucky in having got public opinion behind the withdrawal.

Wed Oct 14th

I forgot to record what was the most interesting experience I had at home. I went with Christo to a Scout show near Windermere when the Chief himself came down to take over a wooded hill-top which had been given to the Scouts for a camping-ground. At lunch in the messing hut I sat next to B.P. and told him that I had not been allowed to become a Boy Scout, although I was styled Provincial Chief Scout. He said that was nonsense, and after lunch collected some H.Q. people who were there, administered the oath to me, and put the badge on himself. So now I am both in the movement and of it. I was immensely impressed with B.P. whom I had never seen before. He made a charming speech at the flag-hoisting and afterwards at lunch told me about his plans for carrying on the movement after he could do it no longer. He said he had been astonished to find how many men – thousands of them – wanted to continue in the movement long after

271

they had ceased to be boys. I told him – what indeed is obvious, that it was because the movement appealed to the eternal boy who is in every healthy man.

I have had a disheartening experience. In Feb. last my P.S. who had the delicious name of (Capt.) Julius Caesar, was invalided suddenly home with alleged T.B. (when he got home the doctors said he hadn't a sign of it!). I then took on an "axed" officer, partly to redeem a promise I'd made to the late C. in C., Sir Philip Chetwood, that I'd help one of them if I could. He had a wife and child at home, the wife incidentally being a niece of a man who had held a very high position in this province, and one would have thought that no one could have a stronger reason for keeping straight than he. Rao agreed very nobly to keep him on, and it was a matter of honour that he should behave himself with an Indian Governor. When he met me in Bombay, I could see that he'd had a skinful, and it wasn't long before I was sure that he was drinking heavily. Meanwhile no one had said a word to me to give him away, and I take my hat off to Rao and Ted Pratt, the A.D.C for their loyalty. (Personally I think that our English notions of loyalty in such a serious matter as this, are as ill-conceived as many of our other notions, but that's another story.) At length I could stand it no longer, and tackled Rao and Ted. Then the whole story came out – not as a secret, but as a thing known to everyone except me. P. had been completely out of control while I was away, had been sodden on several occasions in public, was frequently unable to come to meals, and there were many complaints of his offensive behaviour to women. It's the sort of thing that makes one despair of a certain type of one's fellow-countrymen. Fortunately P. had the grace not to make any attempt to deny it. He said that he was bitterly ashamed of himself and agreed that he should resign.

Sund Oct 18th

The Berar Agreement is settled at last. There's been much haggling over the drafting, but the document holds nothing objectionable now except the provision about durbars. Monty used to say that we needn't worry about that, because "His Exhausted highness" as they call him at the I.O. would never face the music if there was any sign of trouble. I wonder. He's allowed to confer Berari titles, but I can't imagine that there'll be much rush for them. The Indian thinks little these days of anything but an English title!

The Lansdown Week is over & to my surprise I annexed two seconds – one in the Long Driving, because the real Long Drivers couldn't keep inside the course, and one in the mixed, because I'd snaffled the women's Champion, Grace Tucker who was staying with me. I had a very nice house-party, the Tuckers and Watsons, who were charmingly to me for having asked them, and really did seem to enjoy themselves. There was also Noel James, who ate and drank like a plough boy. It's a pity he's so uncouth socially as it puts people off.

Wed. Oct. 21st

I am wondering how long this unholy alliance between the two parties in the Ministry will last. Unless I've misread the signs, this next session will see the end of it. One of Naidu's lot has been accusing Brahmin pleaders of sending their wives to Sadhus, and the pleaders want us to prosecute him for stirring up class-hatred. Rao has ordered the matter to be taken up "after the Session," and when I said that I'd discuss the case in Govt. Naidu came and begged me to drop it . If fellows like N. get into power, justice will be administered, not in the Courts of Law, but in secret meetings of the Ministry.

There is a curious development coming to notice at present. The rains fell so opportunely that there has been much less weeding to be done for the kharif crop than usual, and there have been complaints from a large number of districts of distress among agricultural labourers, and also among Koshtis. There have been various mass demonstrations, quite peaceful, and some dacoities. We have opened a number of works, but they have never fitted and D.C.s say, of course, that the trouble is "grossly exaggerated", and largely the work of political agitators. That is all very well, but there's one point that not one of them has dealt with. Wages fell so low a short time ago that a man was getting 1 a. *(anna - about a penny(d.), ½p.)* a day, and a woman 9pies! And the question which I've asked is, how can you expect people to come and break gitti for such a wage? – especially as food-prices have risen, and an anna won't fill a man's stomach. Until I've had that question answered I shall refuse to go to sleep over the matter. When one sees a sign or portent, it's sheer folly to pooh-pooh it unless one has made quite sure that it doesn't mean anything.

Tuesday October 27th

I'm beginning to doubt whether the Ministry will survive the session. Khaparde is amending the L.S.G. Acts to carry out the recommendations of a Committee which consisted largely of members of the Council. One of the amendments takes control of teachers away from the Local Bodies and gives it to an Education Board – a salutary reform. Now the non-Brahmins, who have captured most of the Berar L.B.s, say that this robs them of the help of umpteen teachers. (Note that they all consider that L.B. servants are to be used for political purposes). Naidu's followers are ratting, and N. himself was reported to intend to ask me for permission to vote against the Bills! I sent for him as soon as I heard this, reminded him that he had taken office on joint responsibility and told him that the Bills were the work of his colleagues and the Council, and not of Govt., and that unless he and his colleagues were agreed on them I'd withdraw the lot. I'm not going to allow the Council to finish its work with a protracted and unseemly brawl between members of the Ministerial party – or rather parties. He sat hunched in his chair looking rather sheepish, and making no denials. So now he has gone to Nagpur to talk matters over with Kh.

Thursday 29th October.

As I thought. A letter from Naidu in which he says that he and Kh. are going to have a final meeting on the 28th, after which he hopes to let me have a definite recommendation about the Bills. Evidently they are not in agreement yet. They understand nothing about loyalty or joint responsibility.

Another thing they understand nothing about is not tampering with the course of justice. We are prosecuting a foul and loathsome crew who live in the Chote Dada's Ashram at Khandwa, and beat up some police officers who went to look into affairs at the Ashram. This crew have been a curse to us for several years. They're the filthiest lot imaginable. The "Dare Dada" was infinitely worse than anything that Katherine Mayo ever described. And yet when we ran them in we get protests from all sorts of quarters which ought to be ashamed even to know of the existence of these beastly people. And now the Council is to debate a resolution – sponsored, ye Gods! by the Rev. G.C. Rogers, an Anglo-Indian headmaster – asking us to withdraw the case. The legal sec. pointed out that the resolution was not admissible, as the matter was 'sub judice', but H.P. simply wrote on it "Admitted". They are a hopeless lot. At heart they have not yet got out of the jungle stage. Things that make a European shudder leave them completely unmoved. And their respect for the law and its forms is no more than skin-deep.

Sat Oct 31st

Just finished another House Party – Fitze, A.G.G. at Indore & his wife, Low, Editor of the Times of India, & his wife, & "Boots" Shoobert. A very easy party to manage, because they're all of them people who can talk about all sorts of subjects, and they all seemed to enjoy themselves. Entertaining such people is no effort. Low had a talk with me about things in general this morning, & I showed him the draft of my address for the 5th which he seemed to like. I've tried to clothe it with flesh and make it human. So many Gubernatorial efforts seem to me to be little more than bare bones – and I'd sooner that men said almost anything of me than that I was dull!

No further word from Naidu. I wonder if they've failed to reach agreement. The Muslims are the latest lot to start squabbling. Some of them, like silly fools, are coquetting – with Congress, regardless of the fact that the first thing Congress would do if it got into power would be to upset the Communal award. But the Muslims have never been noted for political wisdom.

5th November 1936. Speech to the legislative Council

Speech at the Legislative Council on Thursday, the 5th November 1936

Mr. President and Members of the Council,—I have asked you to come here today in order that we may spend a short time together in taking stock of what we have done in the past, in glancing briefly into the future, and finally in saying good-bye and God-speed to each other before we begin to prepare seriously for the great adventure which lies before us in the coming year. And because the bidding of good-byes is never a pleasant task, I shall be as brief as I can.

During the past three years the course of outside events has ordained that the life of the Council should be extended over a period which is twice its allotted span of years. It is a severe test for any elected body to be compelled willy-nilly to remain in office beyond the period for which it has been elected, and it is greatly to your credit that through all these years you have never allowed your zeal for your work to flag. Now, when you come to your final session, you can look back upon a record of legislation with which any Council in the land might feel well satisfied. The irrigation law has been codified. The problem of rural indebtedness has been dealt with in the Debt Conciliation Act and in its ancillary measure, the Land Mortgage Banks Act. Money-lenders and moneylending have been brought under control by the Usurious Loans Amendment Act, the Moneylenders Act and the Reduction of Interest Act. A much needed reform in our system of local self-government has been introduced by the Local Fund Audit Act; and during the present session you will be asked to pass into law a series of Bills dealing with local bodies, and thus to set the seal upon the work of a committee appointed largely from among your own members. Agriculturists have been assisted by a series of Acts designed to help and make easy the marketing of their produce, and to prevent the growing of inferior varieties of cotton. Industries have been encouraged by the State Aid to Industries Act, and labour by an Act dealing with the debts of industrial workers. The increasing dangers of road traffic have been dealt with by the Highway Act. And finally, in a somewhat different field the awakening of public consciousness in favour of the protection of our fauna has led to the passing of the Games Act and the amendment of the Wild Birds and Animals Protection Act. That is a record with which you have every reason to be content, and on behalf of Government I thank you for what you have done.

I turn now for a moment to the other main function which a legislature is called upon to perform, namely, the voting of supplies. Through every one of the past six years it has been our lot to face together a financial crisis of unparalleled severity, and instead of being able to spend our time in planning, constructing and developing, our task has been to prune and to retrench, to make shift with one man where we wanted two, to make five rupees do the work of ten. I acknowledge gratefully that in that sorry and thankless task my colleagues and I have always been able to count upon your active help and co-operation. We may have thought sometimes that that help went rather too far; but you have never refused us the supplies which we needed for keeping the machine running in good order. The Financial Committee, consisting of members of your House and officials, which my predecessor appointed in 1931, devised scales of pay for the provincial and subordinate services which were accepted by Government with certain modifications. The effect of these scales on our finances will be seen more clearly with each year that passes.

So far I have dealt with the material aspect of your work. Let me now deal for a moment with its less material side. No one who has been able to observe the work of the first reformed Council and compare it with that of the present Council, the fourth of the series, can fail to be struck by two changes. The first is a change of temper. There was a time when the proceedings of this House were marked by bitter and acrimonious attacks on Government, its Ministers and its officials, including those who were members of the House. Happily that phase has passed. Each side has come to recognise that, when all is said and done, each in its different way is working for the common good, and a spirit of mutual tolerance and understanding has gradually been developed. While you have remained, and rightly remained, keen and vigilant critics of the doings of Government, the old acerbities have died away, and I hope I may say that nowadays we all meet as friends. I hope also most sincerely that that same tolerant spirit will survive in the new Constitution. The second change is of no less importance. Fifteen years ago the idea that Ministers should be supported by a majority party, and should resign office as soon as they lost the confidence of that majority, obtained scant recognition in practice. It is now the established convention that the Ministry leads a party, accepts office on terms of joint responsibility, and resigns if its followers refuse their support. Much has still to be learnt about party discipline and the need for more stable loyalties; but the seed of party government has been sown and is bearing fruit already.

I cannot conclude this brief glance into the past better than by conveying my thanks, as the person who has been charged with the welfare of the province, to certain quarters where they are surely due. First, Mr. President, permit me to thank you not only for the way in which you have carried on the traditions laid down by your illustrious predecessors, but also for the invariable courtesy which you have displayed to me in all matters touching the business of the House. Under your guidance the House has established a tradition of dignified and orderly debate which may well serve as a model to its successor. Secondly, I should like to give public expression to my gratitude for the way in which my honourable friend and colleague, the Home Member, has filled his position as Leader of this House and custodian of Government business. He has carried out his trust worthily, and has brought to your debates a knowledge of constitutional law and parliamentary practice which have earned for him a name in places far beyond the walls of this House. And thirdly, I wish to pay a brief tribute to all those officers of the province who have worked with you. On the occasion of my first address to you I laid emphasis on the great benefit which Government officers derived from membership of your House. The other side of the picture is equally true. In days that are now happily past, the official *bloc* was called upon to listen to much provocative criticism, and to meet attacks which were frequently misinformed and sometimes not very generous. Retorts were strongly worded on occasion, as was bound to happen; but on the whole those attacks were met with patience and good humour. Official members have striven constantly to supply the Council with all such information as could reasonably be asked of them, to raise the tone of debate, and to maintain the dignity of the House. They have served the House well, and we shall all join readily in thanking them.

A word about the present. For some time past Government has been busy with preparations for the inception of the new order of things, perfecting the machinery of the departments so as to make smooth the path of the new ministry; and that work will continue till the appointed date. The most important change has been the creation of the High Court, which has completed the constitutional structure of the province. Plans have now been made for the strengthening of an over-worked Secretariat and for the provision of a court of revenue appeals; and I hope that when the new Ministers take office they will find ready for them in every department a list of its needs, with details of the schemes which must be put through before we can claim that our administration satisfies modern requirements. They will find that they need every rupee which they can extract from the Finance Department—and that in itself is the strongest incentive which they can have as a Government to sound and orthodox finance and the conservation of our revenues.

And now I shall ask you to take with me a brief glance into what lies before us. What is the task on which we are entering in India today? It is the task of building a new democracy at the very time when in the West the old democracies are approaching their hour of trial. Menaced on the one side by the iron growth of fascism and on the other by the blood-stained and impious tyrannies of communism, they stand as the last guardians of peace, the last bulwark of individual freedom and of liberty of thought and action. Already, if your ear is laid to the ground, you may hear the tramp of the marching legions rising above the clang of the forges. During the coming months it will be given to you to lay the foundations of a new democratic State, and it will be for you to choose whether you will build it upon sand, so that it will surely fall, or upon a rock, so that it will stand as a bulwark of our liberties. The concrete problem before you is this: instead of the present electorate of some 200,000 voters, you will have to deal with an electorate of over a million and a half. It is the sacred duty – the duty of everyone who styles himself a leader of the people – to educate that new electorate aright, and upon the way in which you fulfil that duty the fate of the new structure will depend. As you go forth into your constituencies, two paths will lie before you; one will be broad and easy, and the other straight and narrow. In the days of Rome's decline the populace clamoured for *"panein et circenses"*. The Emperors gave them what they asked—and Rome fell. You too, if you wish, can promise the new voters their dole of food and amusement, remissions of taxation, boons of various kinds, the coming of that millennium which in your hearts you know is not attainable. That is the broad and easy path, the slippery path that leads to destruction. Or, if you are so minded, you can go forth to educate, to teach every voter what are his duties as a citizen; to put before him no policy which is not compacted of sound finance, sound administration, and equal justice to all men, and to ask him to return to this House none but those who will work for the good of the State. As one of your own-countrymen said recently— "On the quality of our representatives we shall be judged for our capacity to govern ourselves". That is the straight and narrow path, the path that leads to salvation, and it is my earnest hope that it is the path which every one of you will choose. And, as you go forth to make your choice, I will ask you to remember one fact; do not let the critics of the new Constitution delude you into thinking that the responsibility which you will be called upon to bear is not real, and that you will be able to treat it lightly, and if need be to evade it by placing it on the shoulders of the Governor or of any other person. When in due time you come to grips with facts, you will find that no such course will be open to you, that the Governor's powers are indeed strictly limited, and that all real responsibility for the welfare and progress of your province will lie upon no shoulders but your own. As wise men, you will light your lamps and gird your loins while there is still time, so that the coming of your task may not find you unprepared.

And now, Mr. President and members of the House, I will say to all of you "Farewell and good luck during the coming months". It must needs be that some of you will fall by the way-side in the struggle, but I shall hope to see many of you back in this House, ready to carry into the new Assembly the spirit of goodwill which you have created in the present Council, and to enter "with a new faith, a new hope and a new confidence" upon your task of responsible government.

Nagpur Thurs Nov 5th

I delivered my address today. When I got home D. rang me up and said "It's a pleasure always to listen to your voice. Today you were marvellous. Is it cheek of me to tell you that?" I said "No, my dear, I'm very touched & grateful to you for liking it." Fortunately my dislike of the bother of making up speeches & the thought of having to deliver them is quite strong enough to act as an antidote to the nice things people sometimes say.

Khaparde is to introduce his Bills. I made Naidu face up to the issue, whether he was prepared to disown his colleague and refuse to support him. Needless to say, he refused the jump. Kh. is going to make it clear that there is no question of confidence. The Bills were the result of the work of non-officials. If the Council wants them, it can have them. If not let it say so at once, and not waste everyone's time arguing about a thing it doesn't want. Kh. has been a very good Minister, and is a charming man to work with – courtly, learned, kindly, and with plenty of common sense. He is the best speaker in the House.

Jubb Sun. Nov 8th

Stone – C.J. – came and saw me yesterday in Nagpur and presented me on behalf of the Judges of the High Court with a charming miniature of the casket in which the Seal of the Court is enclosed – a kindly thought. After that we fell to talking, and he told me that he wasn't very happy about the way in which my masterful Home Member turns down his proposals. He said he would like direct access to me, and I said he could come and see me whenever he liked, and I'd discuss matters with him personally before allowing his proposals to be vetoed. When you start a show like the H.C. there are bound to be growing pains at first. The L.G. is apt to be jealous of parting with power in day-to-day matters, and the C.J. to chafe at anything which savours of that fetish, "the independence of the Judiciary".

Tues Nov.10th

How far India is from being civilised was shown only too clearly in the debate on the "Chote Dada's" prosecution – vide 29th October. H.P. overruled the objection that the case was subjudice – goodness knows why. Then one member asked Govt. to withdraw the case "to soothe the religious feelings of the Hindus"; another said that is was Govt.'s duty "to protect saints"; another that "it should not prosecute a Swami; another that the prosecution was "an interference with the religious practices of the Hindus". And all this about a pack of foul, lascivious blackguards who have performed every kind of bestiality <u>coram populo</u>. It makes one quite sick.

Thurs. 12th November

The Council has finished its career like a pack of petulant schoolboys. Just because I told them in my address that I was grateful for their being friendly and amiable, they seem to have determined, in truly Indian fashion, to show that they could be quite the reverse. They threw out the Board of Revenue Bill by a 2 to 1 majority, which means that I have to create a Board to hear revenue appeals myself, under the authority given me by the Act. Rao told me over the telephone last night that a good deal of racial feeling had been imported into the matter, as the Bill in effect preserved for the I.C.S. a post on which the Bar had set their hungry eyes. Then the House and the Ministry combined made a real good mess of the L.S.G. Bills. First of all Kh. made a tactical error of letting it be known that there was to be no question of confidence (vide Nov. 5th). That of course roused the opposition to all the fury of baffled men. Then, when he presented the report of the Select Comm., he made no motion about it, and went on to deal with another Bill – reason, he had not yet made up his mind whether to go on with the Bills, and intended that the House should be adjourned till after Diwali, by which time he hoped to have come to some decision. That put the House in an uproar, and Kedar, leader of the Opposition, said that if the Bills were thrown out the House would consider it a matter of confidence. When Hemeon rang me up to tell me what was going on I cursed volubly and said that Kh. had had weeks to make up his mind and if he got an opportunity he was to breathe gently the news that H.E. wanted no more shillyshallying. Whether he did or not I shall hear later; but after a short adjournment which the H.P. gave in order to allow members to cool down, Kh. announced that he did not wish to proceed with the Bills, and the House was adjourned sine die. Thank goodness I'm saved a ministerial crisis. But the session seems to me to have done credit to no one. The bilge these people talk is beyond belief. H.M.H. explained that under the new G/I Act the Revenue Appellate Authority could be appointed either by the Bill before the House, or by the Governor under Section 296. If the House threw out the Bill, the Governor would have to exercise his powers. Thereupon Kedar – Bombastes Furioso, and in his own estimation our leading constitutional lawyer – "challenged the Governor to use his powers"; and Dr. Deshmukh, ex-Minister and soldier of fortune, said that that would be a good beginning to the new constitution. Neither pandit knew his law well enough to remember that the section is mandatory. The Governor has got to appoint a Board, , after consulting his ministers. Hemeon says these were chance remarks, and no one took any notice of them; but what bunkum people who ought to know better will talk.

Left to themselves, neither my Govt. nor the Council have done well. Goodness knows that will happen when they're all let loose on April 1st.

Sunday Nov. 15th

Doris Burton and Pam Stent have both come from Nagpur with tales about the Council. Doris wasn't there, but she says that all the Govt.

members were disgruntled and dispirited. Both of them say there was treachery in the camp – Naidu, needless to say. The name Naidu seems a bad one in Nagpur. The fellow who gave us all the trouble over the Kanhan scheme in the Municipality is a scally-wag pleader of that name. "C.K." the cricketer, was the evil genius of the Indian team which behaved so badly in England this summer – just a lot of jealous, quarrelsome schoolboys, so Britton Jones, the Manager, described them to me. And as for my hon. colleague, if it were not for the need for peace in the air at this juncture, I'd tell him that I have no further need of his services. Pam, who was at the debates, says that all her sympathies were with the opposition. Except for the brief flash of temper to which I have referred, and which seems to have attracted very little notice, Kedar and Deshmukh were calm and correct, while the Treasury Bench was just a wobbling jelly of indecision. Unfortunately Rao's jerky and abrupt delivery makes him curiously ineffective as a speaker, and on this occasion his tactic – he's the Leader of the House, and therefore in charge of all Govt. business – seem to have been sadly at fault. The last thing he should have allowed Khaparde to do was to give the opposition the chance of saying he was monkeying with the ordinary procedure. "Elementary, my dear Watson, elementary". Burton, of course, is new to the game, and doesn't carry enough of a broadside. Khaparde quakes with indecision, and can't make up his mind. And Naidu sits like a doltish lump, too stupid to do anything, but not too honest to work against his colleague behind his back. I must say my sympathies go to the opposition, if Pam's account is true.

Nov 16th Monday

Ever since last Tuesday, when E. arrived, as charming and good to look upon as ever, we've had a rainstorm a night. It won't do any harm in this part of the country, rather the reverse, but the cotton people will be groaning. There really seems to be an evil fate presiding over the cotton tract. This will be the eleventh crop running that has been below average. And if the weather had only stayed clear it would have been a bumper crop. We give a dance in the garden every year, and his year it was to have been on Wednesday, but now we will have to postpone it till after the Week.

Nagpur. Sat. Dec. 5th

The rest of the month at Jubb. was mostly taken up with the Week, dinners at Messes, our dance and various dinners and other engagements which were pleasant enough but not germane to the purpose of this diary. When the other members of Govt. came from Nagpur, I learn from them little about the Council meeting that I did not know before. Rao said the members were like a flock of sheep. Up to the night before the vote on the Board of Revenue Bill it was going to be passed, and then somebody stampeded them, and over the precipice they went like – no, it wasn't sheep that did that. It was all the fear of the elections. And having once panicked, the tactics of the Govt. bench over the L.S.G. Bills simply made them more uncontrollable than ever. They are a curious lot. Reason moves them not an inch, but some wave of feeling, some fear or suspicion, will send them, to use George Meredith's phrase, "sky-high, a rocket-headed horde."

The elections are not going to be without humour. Congress, that promoter of Satyagraha, that lover of truth, is seeking desperately for candidates who will pay their own expenses, and will be given the help of the Congress organization provided only they sign the Congress ticket "for the duration" of the election! They've been trying hard to get Khaparde to take the ticket, and stand for the Berar Landholders. He was talking to that grubby little man M.S. Aney the other day, and A. tried very hard to get him. I asked Kh. chaffingly if he was going to smash the new constitution, and he said, "Sir, you can take it from me that no one in this province intends seriously to wreck the constitution". And that, I think, is true; they're much too keen to be Ministers, so that they can (a) line their own pockets and the pockets of their bhai-bands (b) get their own back on their private enemies – the two objects dearest to the heart of the Indian politician. That is no mere piece of cynicism (a) is amply proved by the history of the past 16 years. I know one ex-Minister who, as a pleader, in his pre-Ministerial days, could never have earned more than Rs. 3,400/- a month, but who after a term of office threw a wedding-party which could not have cost less than Rs. 30,000/-. And (b) is proved by their own statements. B.S.Shukla in Raipur, when I went to visit the place, tried to deter people from coming to me by the threat, "You wait till I become Chief Minister. I'll 'see you' then.".

Equally desperate is the Congress hunt for alliances. In Nagpur they've tried to patch things up with the Nationalists, and in Berar with the Democratic Swarajists, who are much the same. But as this means allying themselves with people who are sworn to attack the Communal Award, which the Congress refuses to attack, the allies are likely to make uneasy bedfellows. Indeed, there were secessions as soon as the news of the pacts leaked out. The Congress High Command has issued a thunderous manifesto, saying that no candidate is to be adopted who is not a true-blue, dyed in the wool Congressman, but no one has taken any notice of them. The annoying thing about Congress is, not so much its creed and principles, as the fact that it's so d—d sanctimonious about them, and then goes and chucks them to the winds as soon as there is an advantage to be gained by doing so. At present I estimate that Congress will not get more than 40 out of our 112 seats. But Heaven knows what may occur between now and the elections to falsify that.

The Berar Agreement came out while we were at Jubb. – all as expected. It has not been well received, except by the small body of Berar Moslems. The Hindu Press follows the line that we in the C.P.

have always taken – that the Agreement gives H.E.H. dangerous openings for interference in the affairs of the province. H.E.H. and I exchanged the necessary telegrams; in the course of his he made a pointed reference to the pleasure he would have in inviting E. and me to visit him. Exactly.

The Telegrams Exchanged in the Berar Agreement.

i. Inter-Office minute: 16th November 1936.
From Sir Hyde.

Please send the following telegram, "clear the line."

His Exalted Highness the Nizam.
Hyderabad, Deccan
"On behalf of the Government of the Central Provinces and Berar, I send your Exalted Highness sincere good wishes and cordial greetings on the conclusion of the Berar Agreement Stop The Government of this province will faithfully discharge its obligations for the welfare of your Exalted Highness' territories in Berar.
Governor.

H.M.H. and H.M.R. have approved.
Then return to me .

Wire sent. returned to H.G. sg. H.G.

Telegram from the Nizam of Hyderabad.   19th November 1936

HIS EXCELLENCY GOVERNOR OF CENTRAL
PROVINCES AND BERAR. JUBBULPORE.

I MUCH APPRECIATE YOUR EXCELLENCY'S
TELEGRAM AND CORDIALLY RECIPROCATE THE
GREETINGS OF THE GOVERNMENT OF THE CENTRAL
PROVINCES AND BERAR I HAVE EVERY CONFIDENCE
THAT THE INTERESTS OF MY SUBJECTS OF BERAR
WILL BE IN SAFE KEEPING I LOOK FORWARD ON SOME
SUITABLE OCCASION TO WELCOMING LADY HYDE
GOWAN AND YOURSELF TO MY CAPITAL SO THAT THE
BONDS BETWEEN HYDERABAD AND MY TERRITORY
OF BERAR MAY BE FURTHER STRENGTHENED.

NIZAM.

My telegram and H.E.H.'s reply should be sent to the Press for
publication,
s g . H. G. etc. etc.

Note (TJG):
*The actual Treaty signed by The King, remained in Sir Hyde's possession
when he returned to UK in 1937, and was found among his papers.*

Sunday Dec. 6th
Another Convocation over, thank goodness. What dull shows they are!
The address this time was given by Mukerji, Vice-Chancellor of
Calcutta, a position which he is said to owe more to his father, Sir

Ashutosh, than to his own abilities. A brazen-throated Bengali, who mouthed out a lot of the usual platitudes in a loud voice, and scarcely said a thing that betrayed original thought. Boots said he wanted to throw something at him when he got onto the usual tack of Indian culture being stifled by Western education – completely ignoring as they always do, that our main difficulty lies in the fact that Indians have taken to a Western literary education as a duck takes to water, and can't be pulled out of it. That's the real secret of the present unemployment. Every landlord, every petty shop-keeper, every khidmatgar, wants to put his son to college so that he can take a degree, instead of following his father's footsteps.

We have just had serious news about the constitutional crisis. Abdication is evidently much more of a possibility than the papers will admit. A telegram from H.E. practically warns one to stand by.

Tuesday Dec. 8th

Trevor, the C.E. Forests came to see me yesterday, and I took the opportunity without mincing matters what we think of the way in which the G/I – or rather the department cliques which run the Forest and Medical services at Delhi – sacrifice all administrative considerations, all provincial interests, to the "vested rights" of the senior members of the two services. They are just sending us one Shebbeane – an excellent man for all we know, but a complete stranger to the Province – to learn the C.P. in his last two years of service. When Bill goes next year he will expect to be made C.C.F. without knowing a damned thing about the province or his work in it. I always feel that we Englishmen with our Service selfishness, our talk of efficiency which too frequently cloaks incompetence – witness our irrigation failure in the C.P. – and our inability to avoid flaunting our high standard of living before the eyes of the Indians, have only ourselves to thank for a great many of our troubles. Certainly I'd have given anything to break the

291

Simla gang. Bajpai is always said to be the arch intriguer. As to the future C.C.F. I obtained an admission from the Edlands Member, Jagdesh Prashad, that Shebeane's coming did not prejudice the question of the appointment, but that's worth precious little.

Naidu told me the other day that he was talking to Dr. Khare, the leading Nagpur Congressman, and asked him how he was going to set about wrecking the constitution. "He said pick quarrels with the Governor", said Khare, and make his position impossible. "But that's not wrecking", said Naidu, and got no reply. Khare is a perky, snub-nosed little creature, who thinks he's a wag, with about as much ability for leadership as a circus clown.

Friday Dec 11th

I had the sorrowful duty this morning of reading the abdication message to the members of Govt. & so on. It is a tragedy, not because Edward has had to renounce the throne, but because a man who was a true king in all respects but one could not stand the acid test, & threw everything up, every interest of his country and his people and his empire, in order to marry a twice-divorced vamp, an ornament of circles that decent people avoid. He's always had the yellow streak, and now it's done him in. Personally I think that his brother is more likely to grow up in the image of his revered father than he would ever have been. The calmness, the sobriety and the solidarity with which the nation has gone through the crisis have been amazing. Its stock has risen every day.

Tues Dec 15th

We proclaimed the new King in due form yesterday on the lawn at G.H.. We had two Guards of Honour and about 400 people turned up, pretty well all who were invited. We stage-managed it much better than the January one when we hadn't got our hand in, and everyone said it was very impressive. The Archbishop of Canterbury has spoken out, and said what a sad and sorrowful sight it was to see a throne abandoned for the sake of a woman who could not be married, according to Church ideas – a very outspoken speech. Edward had evidently got on the wrong side of the Church.

Sunday Dec. 20th

I can't resist putting in the extract from the Hit. below.

Hitavada. 18.12.36.

"Deeds And Not Words   *Advice To Students.*

The speeches which His Excellency Sir Hyde Gowan has been delivering in the province during his Governorship deserve to be collected in an anthology as they form the purple patches of the literature of the public life of the province. Being a student of the classics, Sir Hyde brings to bear a highly imaginative mind on public problems and whatever he speaks is in the language of the piquant phrase and the rounded sentence. In his address to the Rajukumar College, His Excellency spoke about men of words and deeds. One of the chief characteristics of His Excellency is his pellucid frankness which may be embarrassing to some.

When he addressed the local Legislative Council in November last, he told its members with staggering candour what they should do and should not do in the elections. The sensitive among them resented the advice but we felt that the advice was much-needed and that His Excellency's warning had not come a day too late. Similar is our view about the advice which he gave to the boys of the Rajukumar College. In India there are too many men of words but too few men of deeds. The man with the sharp tongue and the resonant voice will get the ear of the mob to the exclusion of those who toil in silence. It is hoped that in the new democracy which we are going to have on April 1, 1937, there will be more of deeds and less of talk. In the book of Fate it is written that only the nations which do instead of talk attain greatness.

I've evidently made them think, which is my chief object. The allusion to 'resentment', Rao tells me, is simply Kedar. In my Address, I gave thanks to Rao, as Leader of the House, but didn't mention Kedar, who has recently been Leader of the Opposition. (Why should I? The opposition has been anything but helpful, as a rule.) This piqued Kedar, and after my Address he said in the lobby that I'd talked to them like schoolboys. That was nonsense, & I gather that he has little support. All I'd done was to put before them the two courses which they could follow during their election campaigns – bribe the electorate with promises, or try and educate it; and I asked them to do the latter. If it isn't one of the duties of a Governor to put the truth before the people as he sees it, then I have misconceived my functions. As a matter of fact when Low saw my draft, he said he was glad I was going to say that because the Viceroy had told him that one of the great dangers he foresaw in these elections was spate of unfulfillable promises.

CHAPTER 10

1937
JANUARY - JUNE

Friday Jan 1ˢᵗ 1937

The first day of what promises to be an eventful year. We are just back from Xmas camp at Khapa, a very jolly party – the Cox's, Chitty and the Maltby's besides us five. Weather delicious, game – except tiger – plentiful, shooting not too good. Personally I was using a new gun & couldn't find out what I was doing wrong. The holiday was saddened for E. by the news of the death of her eldest sister, and of the approaching death of a brother-in-law, who can't live much longer, and was a favourite. We had visitors as soon as we arrived, a Dr. and Mrs. Anderson. He's Secretary of the B.M.A and a man of great charm.

Friday January 8ᵗʰ 1937.

The C.J. came and had a talk with me yesterday – I suppose it is inevitable that when a new man comes to a province to convert a semi-dependent show like a J.C.'s Court into an independent High Court, there is bound to be friction of a sort. Stone doesn't quite understand official ways, and is apt to take any disagreement as an insult, while Rao has treated him rather as the head of an ordinary dept., and I'm afraid I didn't spot in time the chance of offence being given. But Stone is a very able and reasonable man, and I think we shall arrive at a correct relationship without much difficulty. I shall be very interested to see what Rao does if he can form a majority in the Assembly, and I ask him to become Chief Minister. He has any amount of ideas; but I am not quite sure about the balance. His handicap is the thinness of his skin.

Sunday January 10th,1937.

Yesterday I laid the foundation stone of the new High Court, which promises to be a very fine building – and we haven't one in Nagpur for which I would give a cent. The Sectt. is in the ghastly, streaky-bacon, Butterworth style to be seen at Keble College and Rugby Chapel, with gawky angles and meaningless slits and holes in the walls. I insisted on doing the job in proper style, corner-stone at the N.E. coins buried under it, corn and water poured on it (ought to have been wine, of course, but I thought that unwise, and water stands equally well "for refreshment"). I dislike these ceremonies being treated in the perfunctory way in which they usually are, so I explained in a speech what this one meant. Masonry comes in useful sometimes.

Note (TJG:):
At the ceremony mentioned above Sir Hyde was presented with a very hansom silver tray photographed here It is in my possession.

We are in the middle of a strike on the B.N.R. Jarrad, the Agent wants us to prosecute individual strikers because they did not give personal notice. Technically right: but there's no question that the Rly. had ample notice of the upcoming strike, and can't say that a public service was disorganised suddenly through lack of notice. I'm very averse from evading straight issue by a legal quibble, as I think it may simply harden public opinion in favour of the men. But Rao is inclined to think that we should prosecute – though neither Bengal nor Bihar, which are more affected than we are, have moved.

The elections are beginning to cause interest, but it's distinctly lukewarm. Congress is disgusting – nothing but petty personal quarrels, protest resignations, and "save-face" compromises. And hunting desperately for allies among all sorts and conditions of men. It is barren of constructive policy, and barren of honesty.

Mond. Jan 11th

A pleasant occasion at the Club yesterday afternoon – the opening of the Bowie Memorial Swimming Bath, a long-wanted addition to the Club. E. pulled the cord, I declared the bath "open" dived in on the word and everyone else followed suit. Then we had tea on the veranda, the President made a short speech, and we played tennis, finishing the day with a dinner at Auntie Doris'. A pleasant day but the more I play Contract, the more I regret the waste of time.

Youth the Connoisseur! We wanted some bubbly at Jubb., so Malcolm signed a chit for "six bottles of Champagne" adding ("good brand"). Shades of all the epicures! I suppose Veuve Cliquot (which we got and I dislike) tastes just the same to them as Pol Roger or Heidsieck or that dreadful stuff Ayala.

Thurs Jan 14th

I cannot understand why it is that so many Europeans in this country never seem to realise that it is up to them to keep up the white man's credit. After the dreadful episode of my late P.S., comes another case – also, thank God, of an Irishman not an Englishman. Hemeon, the Legal Remembrancer, dined with the Dadabhoys on Jan 1st. C.D. is President of the Council of State, & they are very old friends of ours. He seems to have been drinking all the evening, and D.'s champagne at dinner finished him off. He got drunk as a Lord, went up into the drawing room and committed a nuisance on the floor. Revolting. Stone, C.J., wrote to me privately and asked if I'd heard about the affair. But like James Forsythe, "No-one ever tells me anything". So I tackled H. himself, & made him go and write an apology, which he had not done. He seemed to treat the whole affair with almost levity. I then wrote to Lady D. myself, to express my sorrow that one of my officers should have made such a beast of himself. The incident will be all over the City.

These cursed people like Pim & Hemeon never seem to remember how their conduct affects the good name of every Sahib in India, just at the time we want all the influence we can command.

Mrs. H is unfortunately getting up a concert for the King George V memorial Fund, and I had promised to be patron. I've written to call that off. I won't countenance such conduct by having my name associated in any way with the name of H..

Sunday, Jan 18th

Went to Khamgaon on Friday with E. to open a Women's Hospital – at least she did the opening – I did the speaking. The Beraris always give me a cordial welcome and they are a nice lot. The hospital was a treat to see, everything right and in its place. I told them that the term "Nation-building" depts. are misleading. No democratic nation can be built. It must build itself – must have the will to build. That is what is chiefly wrong with this country. It has neither the will to build, nor the will to respond to our efforts to build. Look at this Village Uplift business. We have been making an intensive effort for five years in the Piparya Circle, and the net result, so far as I can discover, is just exactly nil. An enthusiast gets things going, there's a great flourish of trumpets, & off we go on our latest stunt. The enthusiast departs, the fanfare dies away, and the east sinks back with a sigh of relief to its repose. Perhaps it's not quite as bad as that, but one does feel that a desperate amount of effort is always needed to secure a very small amount of permanent result.

I had a letter from Monty, in which he says that I need have no fears if the wild men try to break the constitution. They tried it on him, but soon gave up when he let it be known how much he enjoyed administering the transferred departments. I have no desire for the role of Mussolini, but it would be rather amusing for a time to go back to the old days of the Chief Commissioners.

Sat Jan 23rd

The Hemeon affair ended with my putting him heavily on the mat, and telling him that if he misbehaved again he'd be for the high jump. I cancelled my refusal to be patron of Mrs. H's show, as I wanted the beastly business forgotten. And on the heels of it comes a far worse business. A wife of C. a member of the Commission adopted a child 18 months ago. Recently anonymous letters have been sent alleging that the child is really the child of B., another member of the Commission, who lives with A. & C., and a person who received one came to me in great distress and said she knew for a fact that the statements in the letter were true, having been given the whole story by the woman who helped A. & who confessed to her because she was leaving India, knew that there'd be a blow-up sooner or later, and wished that one person at least should know the real facts. Before I write or do anything more about the matter I'm going to find out the

truth by asking Logan, the Doctor who is alleged to have attended A..
As if one hadn't enough official worries without these scandals! A. got
Edna and Rao to be the child's god-parents!

Sunday, Jan. 24th 1937.

We went to a very pleasant function last night. The Gondwana Club,
the Indian counterpart to the C.P. Club, has just got into a very fine
building on a site which I gave them, and which is one of the best sites
in Nagpur. In gratitude for this they asked me to dinner. There were
about 70 people dining, all Indians except Barts, who is staying with us,
the Stents, Irene Bose and ourselves. They gave a very good dinner, lots
of champagne and there was a general air of bonhomie which was very
refreshing. Sir M.B. proposed our health – rather a heavy speech, but
the poor man complained to me that he had been made to have it edited
and couldn't say what he wanted to. In reply I was purely frivolous, but
it seemed to amuse them. It was nice to see a Club House designed
and built by Indians in the best modern European style, quiet, simple
and dignified.

The Congress are getting very cross. We have run in some firebrands
in Akola who were using the election campaign to preach sedition. One
of them is Brijlal Biyanit who has just been elected to the Council of
State. We waited till the election was over, as we thought it was only
sporting to do so but instead of getting a good mark for that, we are
being told that it's a pure piece of spite because he won the election.
Yesterday, under the orders of the G/I, we banned the reading of the
1930 Independence Resolution, which was to have taken place on
Tuesday (26th). Luckily, a confidential circular of J. Nehru's got into
Govt.'s hands. I think they'll obey, because they don't want to fight until
the elections are over; and if they disobey, they know they're for trouble.

Wed. Jan. 27th

Independence Day went off without any untoward incident. J.N sent orders round that there was to be no disobedience, so that all hastily burnt their copies of the pledge, and except for a bit of harmless barking the day was flat. They're not ready for a showdown yet – much too keen on winning the elections.

Friday Jan 29th Jubb.

We're here for a few days to open the second Constables Training School. Had an interesting experience on Wed., when Dr Mott spoke at a meeting of the B.&I. Bible Soc. on the international situation. He said the main thing we wanted was fewer pacifist societies prating about the benefits of peace, and more people engaged in searching for and removing the causes of war – less condemnation of the League of Nations before it had had time to develop and get a firm hold on the minds of the Nations, and more international colleges and institutions, bringing people together so that they may understand each other. Incidentally he defined a pessimist as a man who blows a light out to see how dark it is: and again a man who, having the choice of two evils, seizes both and holds tight! He is a very impressive speaker with a fine presence and a fine voice.

Yesterday we went to the Robertson College, where they presented Barts with a souvenir Centenary album, and afterwards he made a nice little speech in reply. I played tennis with students, and saw a company of the U.T.C. drilling. Jolly good thing they were, much more of a click about it than the A.F.I..

Monday 1st Feb.

Had a topping day's shoot yesterday with Joe Henersey & Co., peafowl, jungle-fowl, partridges & green pigeon – total 48. Also saw a panther, and nearly got charged by an enormous boar, who cocked a wicked eye at me and dashed past with a grunt. It's funny how seldom a wild animal will touch a human being unless he's molested first.

Opened the School this morning in pouring rain, which rather dampened the proceedings. But they had got my big Durbar tent up, & we went through the business. The school is a good show, very well designed, plenty of room for all purposes, and in a good setting. The two schools together ought to make a wonderful difference to the Police before very long.

Rao left his electioneering campaign in Bilaspur to attend the function. I'm afraid he's going to have a tough fight there. The Congress are employing every dirty trick to do him down – lies, false promises, personal abuse, even threats of physical violence. In Nagpur they have promised every man who votes for Congress a free house.

Nagpur. Friday Feb. 15th

Polling started yesterday, and all reports are full of gloom. Superior organization and the big drum seem to be carrying the day. And Gandhi is still a name to conjure with. "Put your vote in the white box and help Gandhi", is the Congress slogan. Personally I don't much care what the result is. For one thing, politics in this country is utterly unreal. The rabid Congressman of one day becomes the staunch House Member of the next.

The man who was defeated by the Congress in the recent Berar election for the Council of State is today working for the Congress candidate in Amraoti. And so on. For another, I am inclined to agree with Brabourne, who told Francis Low the other day that he'd sooner have to deal with Congress as a Ministry than as a large and compact opposition. The other day the Hit. prophesied that Congress would take office, and would behave much like any other Ministry; and there's an even chance that they're right. On the other hand it's a dead cert that as a solid opposition they will be an infernal nuisance – and a noisy one. The only danger I foresee us that they may use their power to undermine law and order, and work the villagers up for revolution.

I've just had another instance of Delhi intrigue. That arch-wirepuller Bajpai is trying to foist a certain Col. Rai on us as I.G.C.H., against our express wish, as the fellow is a professor, and knows nothing about work in a Province. I've been on the point of writing to H.E. personally about it, but have decided to say nothing unless they actually appoint Rai. Delhi will always stink in the nostrils of the provinces so long as it is manned by barnacles like Noyce, who hasn't done an honest day's work in the plains since I can remember, and schemers like Bajpai, glib-tongued and shifty eyed.

Sund Feb 7th

Dined with the C.J. last night. I really shall have to give up bridge altogether. Whether it's contract or old age, I don't know, but every time I sit down to play I get more bored. It's a curious thing that it's almost dying out in the Clubs. In the C.P. Club they say that on many nights there isn't a single table going. So I don't seem to be singular. To me contract has made auction seem dull, but has given me instead nothing that I want – too much convention, too much calculation, too much sacrifice of a game of skill to a gamble on bidding.

Waterfall's face grows longer every day about the elections. He was gloom personified about the prospects of Rao in Bilaspur.

No Delhi Durbar this cold weather. I am disappointed as I was at neither the '02 one or the '11 one, and would like to have seen it. But I'm sure the decision is wise. Apart from the ostensible reasons – not overworking H.M. – it always seemed to me to be madness to make places for a Durbar before we know which way the cat is to jump over the new constitution. Goodness knows what trouble we have on our hands

Wed. Feb. 10th

I have just written to H.E. to tell him that I shouldn't be surprised if Congress got 65 - 70 seats. Everywhere the reports tell of a landslide in favour of "Gandhi". The present year, of course, coming at the end of a series of 10 years during which we have never had an average wheat or cotton crop, is just about as bad as could be for an election. The masses are ready to listen to anyone who will promise them the millennium. For one thing I am thankful. So far there has been no rowdyism, and the arrangements have worked without a hitch. But it has been extraordinary to hear dead certs. among the non-Congress-wallas getting defeated. There is just a chance that things mayn't be so bad when the votes are counted, but I set little store by it. Naidu, who was to have dined with us tonight, has just come back from his campaign, and has written to say he feels too tired and ill to come. Kedar was put up against him as a sort of forlorn hope, and is believed to have won.

Needless to say, the first thing that Congress does is to show its lack of any sense of reality. Nehru has written to provincial Congress Committees to tell them that they must let the A.I.C.C. have their <u>reasoned</u> opinions about accepting office by the third week in March. That means that we may expect their Lordships to give a decision by the beginning of April at the earliest. But there are quite a number of things, e.g. the Rules of Business, which have got to be discussed with Ministers before issue on April 1st, and it has always been contemplated that the Ministry will be formed unofficially early in March, so as to allow us to get a flying start on All Fools' Day. I shall send for their No. 1 as soon as the results are out, and make him face the hurdle at once, telling him plainly that the A.I.C.C. doesn't run this province as yet. One can rely without fear on Congress being what they call in Lancashire "awkward."

Monday Feb 15th (See Jan 23rd)

I've just had a letter from Logan saying that the story is true. Truth is often stranger than fiction. A. must have had the most amazing luck. She's very fat in ordinary life, and she determined to trade on this and trust to people merely saying that she was putting on weight. Then when her time came she sent her husband to stay with Rao in Pachmarhi. (I well remember saying that he was to be sent for to discuss a certain scheme and being told to my surprise that he was booked to come to Pach..) That done, she went to the flat of an American midwife & got Logan to attend her. But he, very correctly and wisely, refused to pay any clandestine visits and warned her that if he was asked officially whether he had delivered her of a baby, he would have to say 'yes' which he has done. Now what am I going to do? Edna says do nothing until there's an "escandle". It's a private affair. And I want to because the last thing I want at the moment is an action against one of my senior officers, which would be bound to set every tongue in the province wagging.

A long letter from H.E. about Secs. and Heads of Depts. and their right of access to the Governor – all very much on the lines of what we've been doing in this province for the last 15 years. A few days ago I had a letter from him about Governors who are faced with Congress majorities all taking the same line of action. Again perfectly sound. I've written and told him what I propose to do, "as at present advised". But one can't help feeling that one is not likely to be left alone to work out one's own salvation! The news from the districts get worse and worse. Today it is said that Rao has been defeated by 5000 votes. Congress will caper for joy. They have never heard "Aeguam moments.. ....." or " Dellices doomed to die".

Friday 19th Feb.

Extracts from this fortnight's Secret Report – "The elections have proved that over much of the C.P. the simple and ignorant man in the fields or jungles was not ready for the extended franchise." "There is no doubt that money-lenders and the middle-class generally are getting restive over the multiplicity of measures designed to favour the poorer classes at their expense." The reference is to the Debt Conciliation Act. (my work), and to the various Acts like Usurious Loans, Moneylenders, etc. which Rao put through. And what gratitude has he or Govt. got from "the poorer classes"? Exactly none. He seems likely to lose his seat, and I am to be faced with a Congress Ministry. Lothian and his Committee who insisted on a franchise that we all warned them was dangerous, have fairly sold the fort. As the election results come in, it is clear that Congress is going to have an absolute majority.

Sunday Feb. 21st

The best news I've had for a long time – Rao has got in for Bilaspur. That means that he will be in the Assembly to lead the Opposition, and if I know anything of him it will not be long before he has gathered to his standard some of the pseudo-Congressmen who will see the sweets of office going to others – men like Kedar, Jakatdar, Kolhe and others who are no more genuine Congressmen than Rao himself. Otherwise the results are as bad as ever, and Congress will certainly have 2 - 1 majority. The Chindwara report says that the Congress slogan for the Seoni Gonds was – "Put your ticket in the box of your bhumiya (village headman) Gandhi, who starves like you and works for the poor and oppressed"! There is no doubt that the bad seasons of the past 10 years have prepared the ground only too well for the Congress success.

Lady Baden Powell has just come to stay with us for a Girl Guide all-India meeting – a delightful person. She says the Linlithgows are very difficult people to stay with, stiff and uninterested. As for the three girls, they make not the slightest effort to enjoy themselves or be pleasant to anyone, but spend their time moaning for Scotland.

That reminds me of a delicious story. On New Year's Day the Padre who preached in the Delhi Church said "As we look back on the Old Year we see before us a litter of blasted hopes" – and there were the three little Hope girls sitting in a row under his nose!

See Feb 10th (Rules of Business) H.E. is baulking at the idea of forcing the Congress hand. He wired a day or two ago saying "Go Slow". On thinking it over I am inclined to agree – but we'll see what he says in a letter which he promises. It will probably be better not to precipitate matters.

Monday Feb 22nd

It has come – "verbosa et grandis episttula", containing a lot of sound reflections on the present crisis, in which, as the H.E. says, "we are all feeling our way". But I think that I could have said it all in a third of the space! Apparently there has been a change in the situation about which the G/I has never told us. They suggested originally that the Reforms should be inaugurated with a formal meeting of the Assembly on April 1st, and it has always been understood that we should have everything ready – Business Rules & that sort of thing – by that date. But they seem to have made a 'chuk' in the Commencement Order, which provided for the election of members so as to be ready to meet as soon as the Act, Pt. III, comes into force (i.e. on April 1st), but contains no provision, so the pandits say, for summoning them to meet! So we can't have a meeting till about the 10th, and there's no particular hurry about anything. The Reforms Office has been overworked and a mistake like that is very easy to make – the omission is too pointless to have been intentional – but it's rather upset our ideas. However, there's no harm done.

Friday Feb 26th

Our Girl Guides have gone – Lady B.P. Lady Haig, Lady Arthur, Mrs.

Carey Morgan and "Rosalind". Such a charming lot they were, and the house seems very quiet and dull without them. They seemed to be very grateful for our having them, and said this was the friendliest G.H. they knew: "a home of welcome". I'd sooner hear that than almost anything. But E. is a charming hostess, and that makes it easy.

Friday March 5th

Back from a four day tour to Amraoti, to attend a Lodge meeting, Buldana to receive an address from the Dt. Cl. and lay a foundation, and Ajanta, to see the caves. At Buldana I took the opportunity to remind Congress that it really had got to govern now, and gave them an assurance that I should not use my special powers unless I'm forced to.

Note (TJG):

The following speech made at Buldana attracted much favourable notice and was one of the reasons why Congress was eventually persuaded to drop its objections and join the government.

Speech at the opening of the District Council Hall, Buldana on Monday, the 1st March 1937

Mr. Patil and Members of the District Council,— I thank you all most sincerely for the cordial welcome which you have extended to me today, and for the kindly references which you have made in your address to my work as a Member of the Government and later as its Head. I can assure you that it is a great pleasure to my wife and myself to come to your charming station; had I known, in fact, how charming it was I should certainly have paid you a much earlier visit.

Before I proceed, gentlemen, to answer the points raised in your address, I must make an apology. All of us have been extremely busy this last month with the elections and there has been little time for the ordinary business of life, such as the preparation of addresses and of replies to them. Incidentally, Mr. Chairman, I hope you will permit me to offer you my sincere congratulations on your election as a member of the new Assembly. I am quite sure that your constituents will find that they have elected a worthy representative, and one who will look after their interests faithfully and well. But the result of our pre-occupation has been that your address was not received in sufficient time to allow me to consult any of my Colleagues or Secretaries about its contents, and I am unable therefore to give you any definite undertakings on some of the points which you put forward. The only boon which I can bring to you is that of goodwill.

There is one definite assurance which I am fortunately in a position to make. You have expressed your confidence that the new constitution which comes into being in a month's time will be worked in the interests of the masses, by which I take you to mean the whole population of the province, whatever be its rank or circumstances in life. In addressing the Legislative Council I have endeavoured in the past to make three points clear beyond all manner of doubt. The first point is this. The one matter which vitally and above all other matters concerns the people of this province is the question how the new Act will affect their daily lives, what sort of Government it will give them, and whose hands it is that will control for the future their taxes, their schools, their roads and buildings, their law courts, their police, in fact every activity of the State with which they are brought into daily contact. The second point consists in the answer to that very question. It is that they themselves will govern through the medium of their chosen representatives, subject only to the safeguards laid down in the Act which, as I have repeatedly emphasised, cover only an extremely small fraction of the day's work. The third point consists in the assurance for which you ask, the assurance that the special powers of the Governor will only be used in the case of grave necessity and when his duty to his charge compels him to do so; while on the contrary his energies, his advice and his good offices will always be at the disposal of his Ministers, to whatever political party they may belong, provided always that their object is the same as his, namely, the good governance of the province and the prosperity and progress of its peoples. After 35 years of service amongst you, I am entitled to ask you to believe that those words are not spoken lightly, and that the future Ministers will find that in very truth they will be called upon to shoulder the whole burden of the responsibility for your welfare.

In two places in your address you have stressed the need for amending our Local Self-Government Acts so as to bring them into accord with modern needs and ideas. As you all know, the question of amending those Acts was taken up by Government at the express wish of the Legislative Council. A committee was formed consisting of members of the Council and representatives of local bodies, with a small number of officials, and bills were framed in conformity with their report. If those bills had been passed by the Council they would have effected a drastic reformation of our system. I need say nothing about the influences which led to their abandonment; let the dead past bury its dead. But I can assure you that the material which has been collected will not be wasted. The whole question will be placed before the new Ministry, which will be able to make use of the work that has been done when it frames its policy. I hope with you that the result will be seen in the removal of the many defects which according to modern ideas our present Acts contain.

The next matter to which you allude is the working of the Debt Conciliation Act. This is a matter in which, as the sponsor of the Act, I naturally take a great personal interest. I have never disguised the fact that the Act was an experiment; but we know enough about its working by now to be able to say that it has achieved a considerable measure of success, and the numerous requests like yours which we have received from all parts of the province for the starting of Conciliation Boards afford undoubted proof that, whatever its critics may say, it is at any rate popular. Throughout Berar the demand has been general, except in the Wun and Melghat taluqs. In the remaining 20 taluqs, proceedings have been completed in two, including Mehkar in your own district, and are in progress in 13, including your own taluqs of Malkapur and Chikhli. Government has decided to establish 10 new Boards with whole-time Chairmen next year, and the claims of Jalgaon and Khamgaon to one of these Boards will receive careful attention.

While on this subject I should like to say one word of a general nature. During the course of the recent election allegations were made in certain quarters that Government has done nothing for the tenantry. The kindest thing that can be said about people who say such things, even in the heat of an election, is that they have not read their briefs – that they have wilfully closed their eyes to what is being done around them. The real fact is that, ever since the depression, which is just passing away, began, Government has been using its utmost endeavours to devise means for improving the lot of the farmer. Rather more than a year ago, I thought that I would like a bird's-eye view of what we had been doing. So I had a list compiled.

It was headed "List of matters investigated or under investigation to improve the lot of cultivators and mitigate the effect of the depression". That list contains no quack nostrums, no wild confiscatory measures, no financial absurdities, and no impossible panaceas; but it does contain no less than 27 heads, covering almost every department of Government, and ranging from debt conciliation to the control of moneylenders, from the liberalisation of the rules for the remission of land revenue to the regulation and control of markets from land mortgage banks to the adaptation of education to rural needs, from village uplift to the suspension of grazing dues, from the consolidation of holdings to the development of agricultural industries. Not all the schemes which we investigated were found to be feasible, but wherever we found a measure that was practicable, we put it into practice, and I make bold to say that, if the new Ministers spend as much earnest thought on genuine measures for the improvement of the lot of the peasantry as the present Government has done during the past six years, they will establish their claim to the continued confidence of the electorate beyond any possibility of question. In Berar especially the voters can be relied upon to form a shrewd judgment of their acts.

And now, gentlemen, as one who has a peculiar fondness for people who do things for themselves, allow me to congratulate you most sincerely on the genuinely progressive work which you have done in this Council. The record which is given in your address is one of which you may well be proud, of which indeed any district in this province, however rich, might be proud. Only a few weeks ago my wife had the privilege of opening a model hospital for women at Khamgaon, and today she is to lay the foundation stone of a maternity ward at your hospital here. With those scenes in my memory and with your record before me I shall always think of the Buldana district as a place where they help themselves and get things done. And if in the new order of things it is ever within my power to do something for the interests of the district, you may rest assured that in gratitude I shall do it. In your address you make certain definite requests—for the expansion of your sources of income, for the increase in your grant for primary education, for the improvement of your water supply, for fresh means of communication, and for the transfer to you of buildings and roads. As I have already told you, your address did not reach me in time to enable me to have these points examined, but you may rest assured that this will be done, and that I shall do what I can to see that your needs receive sympathetic consideration from the new Ministry. On one point I can reassure you. On the representation of the Berar Joint Board, Government has recently decided to review the position regarding the assessment of income-bearing lands in the possession of District Councils, and has suspended the collection of such assessments pending further orders.

In conclusion, let me thank you once more for the cordial way in which you have welcomed my wife and myself to your charming station. I can say in all sincerity that every time I visit Berar I regret more keenly the fact that none of my service has been spent within its hospitable borders.

Letter from Mr. R.A. Butler

India Office.
Whitehall. 1937.   8th.March

To: Lady Gowan.

Dear Lady Gowan,

Many thanks for sending me the Annual Report of the Central College for Women. I do think you are achieving something and I congratulate you on your work. I was much interested to hear that a small sum had been handed over by the trustees of my parents' farewell fund and that there may be a scholarship in my father's name. I am sure he will appreciate this.

May I say how glad we were to read from the Times Correspondent today that Sir Hyde has given a very suitable lead on the proper attitude for a Governor to adopt, in face of a Congress majority, on being asked what his attitude would be if they take office. This has been well reported here and has made a very favourable impression. I must congratulate him too on this lead.

I often miss the C.P. and wish we could borrow a little of your sun. After continuous rain we have now cold winds and snow but remain as cheerful as can be expected.

This letter should reach you at the beginning of Provincial Autonomy and this is to wish you both well. I feel sure that the future will have few surprises for you and that you will be more than ready to cope with it.

Yours sincerely,
sg. R.A. Butler.

Copy of The Times' article on the 'Buldana Speech'
mentioned in Mr R. A. Butler's letter.

The Times.   March 8th. 1937.

NOVEL PROBLEMS IN INDIA. CONGRESS & THE GOVERNORS.

From our Own Correspondent. Delhi. March 7th

Unusual political developments have everywhere been
unfolding in India since the Provincial elections and the British
authorities and the Congress Party are alike facing novel
problems.

The definite inclination in the Congress Party to accept office
in those Provinces where it has majorities is being accompanied
by obvious manoeuvring by those who control the party
machine amid the centre and are anxious to keep it in the future
even in Provincial spheres.

Orders have been issued that Provincial Congress Ministers
must subject themselves to the instructions of the party
hierarchy, presumably with a view to dissipating any tendencies
which might arise to weaken the Nationalist front.

How far this policy will be effective remains to be seen. The
diversities of the Provinces today are likely to be emphasized
rather than lessened under the coming Provincial administration,
and it will be difficult for Congress leaders to uphold an all India
policy in matters of purely Provincial concern.

More serious is the proposal put forward by Mr. Gandhi that
some assurance should be forthcoming from Provincial

Governors that the new Act will not be worked to mitigate against popular authority by the invocation of the Governor's reserve powers. It is clear that no provincial Governor can renounce the powers invested in him by the Act for the purpose of reassuring Congress. This issue has already been met in a statesmanlike manner by Sir Hyde Gowan, Governor of the Central Provinces who has declared that the advice, energies and good offices of the Governor will always be at the disposal of Ministers, no matter to what political party they belong, provided that their object is the same as his – the good governance of the Province.

The Viceroy and Mr. Ghandi

There is much speculation about the possibility that Mr. Ghandi when he visits Delhi for the meeting of the All-India Congress Committee to consider the question of accepting office, will seek a meeting with the Viceroy. With the Government of India Act on the statute book, it is difficult to see now any constitutional question of importance could arise in any such interview. It is suggested in some sections of the Indian Press that Mr. Gandhi may wish to seek an assurance of the kind to which has already been suggested as an appropriate gesture on the part of the Provincial Governors, but it is obvious that even the Viceroy will be divesting himself of his statutory obligations in giving such an assurance, which would in effect change the policy contemplated under the Act and could be authorized only in London.

Many Congressmen are in a quandary at this stage. The acceptance of office appears to be the general desire among them, but it is not easy in view of their recent political history.

316

Moderate leaders are facing much hostility over this question from extremists who also hold that office must be accepted only to wreck the Constitution, and not to work it. This argument has been repudiated by Mr. Rajagopalachariar of Madras who has indicated that deadlocks should not be created lightly although they should not be avoided if they emerge naturally. That such Congress thinkers deserve encouragement in face of their political problems is admitted, but neither the Viceroy nor Governors can operate except within the confines of the Act, although assurances of the kind given by Sir Hyde Gowan may and will be repeated.

Reply from Sir Hyde to R. A. Butler

To: R.A. Butler.   India Office.
Whitehall.   31st. March 1937.

My dear Butler
        My wife has sent me your letter to read, and I am glad to know that what I said at Buldana was appreciated at home. The occasion happened just after the result of the elections was known, and it seemed to me that something had to be said. The regrettable part of it is that it has been of no avail; but the density of the official Congress brain passes belief.
        The more I think things over, the more I am convinced personally that the whole business has been a piece of deliberate hanky-panky on the part of the Congress high command. They were warned, as we know for a fact, that Governors could not constitutionally agree to any surrender of the duties and powers given them by the Act; and anyone who can read English can see that acceptance of the Delhi formula must involve such a surrender. Yet

the leaders managed to bamboozle the provincial delegates with a cloud of verbiage, and persuaded them that all was well, and that Governors would swallow the formula as a fish swallows the bait. Then, when the delegates found that the bait was not taken and asked for further instructions (it is amazing that none of them should have planned ahead, but that is the way in which Congress does things), the Big Three told them that they must stick to every letter of the Delhi formula. When Patel, who has always been supposed to be in favour of office acceptance, heard of the breakdown, he rubbed his hands in glee and said that he was the most relieved man in India. Can people who employ such tactics fool the electorate twice running? If we allow them to do so, we shall only have ourselves to blame for what follows.

Rao has risen to the occasion nobly, and has formed a Ministry for me. I wired to you the names yesterday. They will do well enough for four months, but as soon as we settle down we shall have to do a very great deal of hard thinking. The assembly will have to be summoned for August or September, and as it is unlikely that any large number of Congress wobblers will have broken away by then, we shall be up against the direct issue of a fresh election or Section 93.

Signed,
Sir Hyde Gowan

Friday March 5th

The speech (at Buldana) has been well received by the Press (including the T/I). Incidentally, the final result of the elections is – Congress 70, others 42. It now remains to see how long the very mixed Congress team will hold together. At present they can't agree about anything, except that Khare is to be their leader. Nehru has written to all provincial committees that they're not to give the Governor any answer until they get the word go from the A.I.C.C.. As far as I am concerned, they're not going to be asked until I am quite sure that they're ready to give an answer. I'm not going to have that little mountebank Khare saying that the Govr. sent for him, and he told him to keep quiet and wait till he was ready to come. As a matter of fact, Bannerji told me yesterday that he thought the local men wanted to be sent for, as they were quite ready to come and talk things over, whatever the Muscovite might say. I told him that I'd send for Kh. the moment that I could be assured that he would come – but not a second before. Now I'm awaiting developments.

Gandhi is one of those people who is always doing stupid things under the pretence of being very astute. He has proposed that Congress Ministers shall accept office on the condition that Governors shall undertake not to use their special powers. I suppose that he thought he'd put Governors in a dilemma. But even his own people had the wit to laugh at him, and point out that Governors could not possibly contract themselves out of their duties under the Act. They really are a priceless crowd. They had a meeting at Khare's, house, and Kedar tried to explain the G/I Act to them. But, as the Hit.'s reporter said, none of them knew anything about the Act, and all proved quite incapable of understanding what Kedar was talking about! And these are the people who damn the Act in heaps!!

Ajanta was delightful, both in its setting and in the beauty of the carving and the frescoes in the caves. Akhbar Hydaci insisted on us being the guests of the State, and they met us at Jalgaon, and did everything for us, even to giving us dinner in the saloon after we'd got back from Ajanta. (Two bottles of champagne appeared in the ice box!).

CHAPTER 10

Tuesday March 9th

A long cipher from H.E.. Rajagopalachari has approached Erskine and told him frankly that Congress wants to "save face" over accepting office, and will be able to do this if Governors give an undertaking not to use their special powers in the ordinary course of Govt. business. He wanted H.E to meet Ghandi, so that they could agree upon a formula. H.E. has replied (after consulting S/S) that it would be the greatest mistake on our part to take any step which would strengthen the position of the Central Congress machine vis à vis the provinces or help to extricate Congress from the difficulties in which this unwisdom has landed themselves. R. is therefore to be told that any guarantee, written or oral is impossible, but that E. in Madras will take the first opportunity to reiterate the spirit of sympathy with which he as Governor is willing to deal with any party which will take office. (I've done this already in my Buldana speech). The wire goes on: "All the information at my disposal shows that Congress are in an awkward position owing to pressure for office acceptance, the loss of face in which this will involve the Central Committee, and embarrassment of having to live up to their election promises; and that they are most anxious for any gesture on our part which will save their face and strengthen the position of the A.I.C.C.". Our first object is plainly to get the provincial committees to assert their independence, if only because we can't have the Muscovite dictating provincial policy from Allahabad; so we're going to sit tight. That's all to the good.

R.B. Pandit (a shaky M.B.) came to me yesterday and offered to act as intermediary between me and Khare, who is his family doctor. Kh. is at the Assembly in Delhi, but I told P. straight out that, while I had no intention of making any move myself till the A.I.C.C. has found, and made up, its mind, I was quite willing to see Kh. as soon as he let me know he'd like to be sent for. Funny devils they are! He had so obviously been sent by Kh. to find out how the land lay. An Indian when he starts to intrigue always reminds me of a mole – subterranean but obvious,

Thursday, March 11th

H.E. wired to me the other day, asking my advice as to who should receive a "dormant commission" to act as Governor in an emergency due to my being incapacitated – a thorny question which no-one at home could solve when the Act was being framed. He suggested an official from another province, as the S/S boggles at a local official. I told him that I thought the objection was unnecessary, and that I recommended the Financial Commissioner or the Chief Justice. He stuck to the S/S's point about the former, and jibbed at the latter. Apparently I was the only Governor who stuck out for a local. H.E. suggested Bamford of the U.P. for the C.P. and as there is never any point in sticking to objections about non-essentials, I said "ji hán".

A wad of correspondence comes from the S/S about what we must introduce, and what we needn't, on the 1st April. We've managed the business very badly. At a time when I want all my mental faculties clear for dealing with the Congress, and forming a ministry and getting it going on a friendly footing – if possible! – I'm being worried by abstruse legal conundrums about power to make rules and what to do if no rules have been made. If we'd had any sense we'd have had complete sets of rules drafted, to come into force automatically on April 1st, with the proviso that the Ministers could consider them later at their leisure and press for any alterations which they wanted.

Friday March 12th

Held a meeting this morning of "prominent agriculturalists" to form a Livestock Improvement Association, which is the only way to keep the movement started by H.E. alive, but, Lordy! how difficult the "p.a." is to get moving! They never seemed to know their own minds. However

I got them at last to agree to something definite, chiefly by putting onto the Central Body a young spark who always had something different to propose.

The Hit. has a new name for me – "an enlightened satrap" – what we used to call an oxy-moron! Apparently my Buldana speech (March 1ˢᵗ) has been given a good deal of publicity, both here and at home, and the Times' Delhi correspondent has commented on it. I said nothing but what any Governor who intends to work the constitution liberally is bound to say. But it's amazing how much suspicion there is abroad. From some of the proceedings of our local lot one would think that the first thing I intend to do on April 1ˢᵗ is to override the Ministers on every single question which comes up. They must think I'm a fool! I've no intention of doing anything but let them have their own way on everything on which it is not essential that I should put my foot down.

Sunday March 14ᵗʰ

I've got Dr. Khare's goat all right. There have been a lot of threats from Congressmen, especially in Bilaspur, that they will "see" (vernacular for "take it out of") various Govt. officers as soon as the Congress takes office – the reason being, of course, that they cannot take Rao's victory in a sporting spirit. And, as was to be expected from the nature of the Indian, these threats were demoralising our officers. So we issued a circular on the lines of one issued by Madras some weeks ago, pointing out that such threats were idle, because the law gave them ample protection, and assuring them that I should certainly see that no one harmed them. Up gets Khare, and issues a statement to the Press, not scouting the idea that the circular was required, nor denying that Congress could possibly be up to such dirty tricks, but saying that Congress had every intention of holding an enquiry into the conduct of certain Govt. officers during the elections, asking if the Govr. proposed to veto this enquiry, and complaining that the circular was untimely, as it would put the Congress back up. If any justification for the circular was wanted, Khare's statement supplies it. Nothing can be clearer than that Congress intend to bully-rag any Bilaspur officer whom they think helped Rao. That little poof Mani of the Hit. also says that the circular was ill-timed – as if anything could be ill-timed that was calculated to put a stop to such cowardly threats and reassure officers who have only been doing their duty! It is not possible to expect that every officer down to the lowest was completely impartial, but on the whole they did their duty splendidly. But the longer one lives in this country, the more one realises how utterly foreign the sporting spirit is to it. The Statesman, I am glad to see, calls the circular "a sturdy declaration" and says it is sad to think that it should have been necessary. One thing is becoming clear. Hitherto, the Governor has been above controversy, and has been kept pretty well out of the personal criticism in the papers. Under the new constitution he is to be forced into the fiercest of the Limelight – that is to say if Congress takes office – and anything he does in pursuance of his duty under the Act will involve him at once in acute personal controversy. A most distasteful prospect! But it is by no means a foregone conclusion that Congress will take office. I was talking to Rao a day or two ago, and he said that there had been a sort of "straw" vote, and it had shown a slight majority against. Ghandi is frightened of losing Nehru from the movement as he sees he's the one dynamic personality in it. And Nehru is fanatically against office, and has already overborne the U.P. Committee which by districts had a two-to-one pro majority, but in the main meeting voted <u>con</u>, after an impassioned speech by Nehru. And then too, Congress in its acts is like Charles II. Its path has always been the path of un-wisdom. The odds are about even, so Rao says. If they vote <u>con</u> he is going to form an interim minority Ministry, which will function till August; after that we shall see how things develop. Our local P.C.C.'s report to the A.I.C.C. was one of the feeblest documents ever penned. The papers jeered at it, and it certainly gave one a great contempt of Congress mentality.

Monday March 22ⁿᵈ Pachmarhi.

Up here for a breather for a few days, after a three day visit to Betul where I had to make three speeches – all short ones, luckily. A pleasant quiet spot and they looked after us well.

Congress has at last produced a resolution – I can't say that it has yet made up its mind. It will accept office provided that the Chief Minister is able to <u>say publicly</u> that the Govr. will not use his special powers nor disregard "the advice of his Ministers <u>in regard to their constitutional activities</u>."

Now what the devil does that mean? Low in the T/I says it's splendid. Of course the Govr. won't interfere with his Ministers so long as they act constitutionally. The D.N. and the Hit., knowing their own countrymen, are not so ingenuous, and say the resolution merely makes confusion worse confounded. Gandhi, when asked what it meant, burst out "It's a thoroughly honest resolution, and means exactly what it says". "Yes", jibes the D.N., "and what does it say?" The matter can be put very simply. I have an extra special responsibility laid upon me to see that Berar gets "a reasonable share" of the joint provincial expenditure. At present it gets about 34%. Now supposing the Ministers advise me to give it 20% only. That advice would be perfectly constitutional. But am I to contract not to set it aside? Not a hope. Or supposing they advised me to cut down the grants of all Muslim schools by, say, a third? Again perfectly constitutional, but totally unacceptable, in view of my special responsibility for minorities. The resolution is said to have been drafted "by one of the acutest legal brains in India". If that's the best he can do, God help India!

Everything will depend, of course, on what Khare, the Congress No. 1, says when he comes to see me. I've had a long wire from H.E., saying that Congress – or rather, the pro-office party – are desperately anxious to accept office, as they rightly see that any other course would be suicidal. But at the same time, they want to "save face", and we are asked to help them to do so; if this can be done without committing ourselves is any way to surrendering the powers and duties entrusted to us by Parliament. I wrote to Khare today, asking him to come on the 26th, when I get back to Nagpur. It will be very interesting to hear what he says as to the real meaning of the resolution. There is one thing quite certain. I shall neither let him think, nor give him an excuse to tell other people, that I intend to mortgage my "discretion" and my "individual judgment". To give any loop-hole for incorrect statements on that subject would be fatal.

One result of the Delhi Convention is that Nehru is as sick as mud, and has hinted that some day he may resign the Congress Presidentship, adding characteristically that there is no chance of that happening in the immediate future. If we can get Congress well settled down into office it will not be long before the left wing splits off from the right.

Tues March 23rd

Definite instructions from H.E. (a) clear "No" to any request for assurances touching the position re: statutory powers. (b) Declaration of intention to be a truly constitutional Governor. (c) Broad hint that if the Congress suggests in public that I have given any assurances, I will issue a démenti.

In view of the likelihood that if the Congress takes office it will ban Pach., there is a bitter flavour about a case with which I have just been dealing, i.e. the control of the Plateau, fighting the Military Landgrabbers. The matter seems likely to become of academic interest only.

Thursday March 25th

News of developments. In the U.P., Bihar, and Orissa the Govrs. have all seen the Congress leaders, and it's exactly as we thought. They do want a definite assurance from us that we will, by a sort of gentleman's agreement, put the Act aside – thus showing once more what little sense of reality they have. They seem to have been in a mood of bland and child-like make-believe at the Delhi Convention, playing with a wispy little veil of words without being able to realise that the first cold breath of reality would send it fluttering away like dead leaves. Of course they've had the usual answer, and are now all of a flutter. "Conversation inconclusive, and to be continued."

Nagpur. March 26th Friday

Khare duly came to see me this morning, clad in the usual nondescript garb that these people affect, and trailing his coat by wearing sandals and not taking them off. Naturally I took no notice – and at any rate he was clean. On his car was the Congress flag, which Malcolm and Dick were itching to dye blue in the inkpot while he was with me; and in it were three men whom Dick described as "toughs", secretaries of local Congress bodies. As a matter of fact Kh. was very polite and friendly, and we had a long talk for an hour and three quarters. He was evidently quite prepared for my point-of-view, and made practically no attempt to combat it. It struck me forcibly that (a) he was very anxious to accept office and (b) he knew perfectly well how hopeless the Congress formula was as a practical proposition. But the amazing thing is that these people have made no effort to look ahead. They've all got their instructions from what they call their "higher command", and the H.C. has apparently given them no sort of idea as to what to do in the almost certain event of assurances being refused; Kh. said that he would not dare to take the responsibility of giving me a definite answer, and must go and see, not his bosses, but Gandhi! G. is at present in Madras, where they say that Rajagopalachariar is determined to take office at all costs, and G. has gone either to tackle him, or to devise yet another of his "honest-to-God" face-saving formulas. So we're going to have another meeting on Monday. And Thursday is April 1st. Running it pretty fine. But they must have made up their minds by Monday, one way or the other. I told Khare plainly before he went that there was only one issue, and that a very simple one – Does Congress accept the Act re: Governors' powers or does it not? They've got to take the hurdle, or refuse, and no formula will remove it from their path. But will people in this country ever learn to face squarely up to facts?

Later. Kh. has gone to Bombay, to see that grumpy old autocrat, Patel. I suppose he was told that he mustn't ignore his boss.

Sat. March 27th

R-r in Madras went to see Erskine unexpectedly yesterday, and told him that Gandhi would not agree to the formula which he (R-r) had devised, and that when he came to see Erskine formally today it would "more probably" be to refuse acceptance of office. So that's that. If the probability becomes a certainty, Congress will have once more demonstrated its eternal un-wisdom – the un-wisdom of Gandhi, the banya saint, who beneath his smiling exterior hides all the craftiness of his caste and an unbreakable determination to upset British rule.

Sunday March 28th

An eventful day. The P.S., A.D.C. and I spent most of yesterday decoding long wires form H.E. saying that negotiations were on the point of breaking down in various places, and suggesting the way in which we should make their failure public. Then, this morning Khare, who had been after all to see the stiff-necked autocrat Patel, and not to Madras, wrote and said that he could not take office, and there was no use for a further interview.

So that's settled! And whether I'm glad or not I do not know. At any rate we ought to have four month's peace – unless they insist on our holding an April session, which would be the height of un-wisdom – and after that it would be a rash man who would bet on the position of affairs in the C.P.. But we lose our great hope – that the responsibilities of office would tame Congress as they have always turned everyone who shouldered them. That is what, of course their leaders feared. Now it is war – á l'outrance.

Communiqué, dated the 28th March 1937, regarding the refusal of office by the Congress Party

On March 26th His Excellency the Governor gave an interview to Dr. Khare, as leader of the majority party in the Provincial Legislative Assembly, and invited him to assist him in forming a Ministry in accordance with the terms of section 51 (1) of the Government of India Act, 1935. Dr. Khare intimated to His Excellency that he could only accept the invitation on the condition that he received the assurance which had been laid down in the resolution passed by the All-India Congress Committee, and was thus able to state publicly that "the Governor will not use his special powers of interference or set aside the advice of the Ministers in regard to their constitutional activities".

In reply His Excellency called Dr. Khare's attention to section 54 of the Act and to Instruction VIII in the Instrument of Instructions issued to the Governor thereunder; and he explained that for legal and constitutional reasons it is not within his power to give any assurance or to enter into any convention affecting the use of the powers entrusted to him by Parliament. On a recent public occasion His Excellency had given an assurance in unmistakable terms as to the spirit in which he intended to use those powers, and had declared that whatever Ministry was in power could rely upon receiving from him, as from one who stood apart from parties, all the help, sympathy and co-operation for which it asked. Further than that he had no power to go.

Dr. Khare then said that he quite understood His Excellency's point of view, but that he must consult with others before he gave a definite answer. His Excellency said that he was most anxious that the Congress, as the majority party in the Assembly, should agree to form a Ministry, and a further interview was arranged for March the 29th. The interview was conducted in the friendliest spirit, and both parties endeavoured to understand and appreciate the point of view of the other.

Today March 28th, His Excellency received a letter from Dr. Khare, in which he stated that as His Excellency was unable to give the assurance for which he was asked, he regretted that he could not take the responsibility of forming a Ministry, and he therefore saw no object in having any further interview.

His Excellency deeply regrets the turn which matters have taken, but it has been beyond his power to avoid it. The provisions of the Act with regard to the powers of the Governor are mandatory, and the issue has been a simple one – Does Congress accept those provisions or does it not? The Delhi resolution, if put into plain words, means that it does not; for there are many "constitutional activities", especially those affecting Berar and the minority communities, with which the Governor might be bound to interfere, and the obligations imposed upon him in these matters are of such a nature that he could not relieve himself of them, even if he desired to do so. One single example should suffice to make the position plain to everyone. If a future Ministry determined to cut down the amount of expenditure from the common purse in Berar to a figure which Berar opinion considered unreasonable, the proposal would be perfectly "constitutional"; but His Excellency, if he agreed with the opinion, would be bound to use the special power given him by section 52 (2) of the Act.

It is needless to stress the fact that a readiness to accept office upon a condition which is definitely impossible is not an acceptance, but a refusal, and His Excellency wishes to make it clear beyond any question that the responsibility for the regrettable decision which has been reached must rest solely and entirely upon the shoulders of those who adhered to the condition. As he has declared publicly, any government which takes power under the Act, now or in the future, can rely on his fullest help and support within the four corners of the Act; but there can be no question of any understanding in regard to the express provisions of that document, nor of any attempt to restrict or limit the obligations which are imposed upon the Governor under its terms.

Diary continues:

Monday March 29th

As soon as I'd heard from Khare yesterday I sent for Rao, and he undertook to form a Ministry. He said various people had already been trying to get at him because of the likelihood of a Congress refusal, but he had refused to make any move while negotiations were still going on. But he'd start wiring, and let me have names in two days. He was very adverse from the idea of having an April meeting, at which there would almost certainly be a vote of "no confidence". I discussed this matter in a letter to H.E. some days ago, and he said that the S/S thought that such a vote might be ignored. It's a funny idea, to face a radically unconstitutional position like that, when it can be avoided by the simple expedient of not summoning the assembly until August. The Act merely requires that it must be summoned within six months. So I've wired to H.E., begging him not to force me to call a meeting 'till August. I'm sure Rao will throw his hand in if he does. By August anything may have happened. The provincial Congressites may have broken away from the control of the Central junta; Rao may have gained some of their pseudo-followers to himself; or the A.I.C.C. may have come to its senses. But Congress are like the Bourbons; they forget nothing and learn nothing.

Of one thing I am certain. The first thing we've got to do is to let it be known in every village and hamlet in the land that Congress have let their voters down, and have refused to make any attempt to implement the promises which they broadcasted during the election.

A letter from Rab Butler to Edna says. "May I say how glad we were to read from the Times correspondent that Sir Hyde has given such a suitable lead on the proper attitude for a Governor to adopt, in face of a Congress majority .... This has been well reported here and has made a very favourable impression". Wow, Wow! It always tickles me to how one can slave at a thing, and get it just what one wants it to be, and somehow it just flops. Then one dashes off something else, without any particular thought, and every one exclaims "O wonderful!" I wrote that speech – or rather dictated it – off-hand within an hour or so of getting the address in which it was a reply; the reason being that they'd left me only just time to get the thing printed.

A letter from N.J., who is acting as our local member in the Assembly says – "The G/I are usually in a minority as some of their supporters have gone over to the other side. This is partly due to the mistaken tactics of the Front Bench, which have consolidated the opposition." Grigg is the man. He may be a clever financier but he's got the tact of a rogue elephant, and every session the position of Govt. in the Assembly has grown worse. We managed our Local Council – except when they went daft just before the elections – much better than the G/I have managed the Assembly.

Tuesday March 30ᵗʰ

A wire from H.E. saying that he has told the S/S that Governors should be let alone to summon their local legislatures when they and their Ministers think right. So that's one step forward on the right road, as the S/S can hardly refuse. Rao is relieved and so am I.

Thinking over the way in which the situation has developed, one simply cannot avoid the conclusion that Congress H.Q. are a set of dirty rogues. They bamboozled the pro-office section into agreeing to a formula which the latter thought that all Governors would swallow without difficulty, but which the H.Q., with a man like B. Desai to advise them, simply must have known was legally and constitutionally impossible of acceptance. They concealed it in some meaningless verbiage about it being only necessary for the local leaders to be satisfied in their own minds. And when the poor locals (? yokels) found that the formula didn't work and came running to ask Mother what to do next, they rubbed their hands in glee and said – "Insist on Governors renouncing their powers or refuse office". If anybody ever had cause to wail, "Nous sommes trahis", it's the pro-office party in Congress. Below is the resolution, with a comment showing the futile playing with words which went on, and "My Hat, Ma" Gandhi as commentator. It's the utterance of either a fool or a knave – a fool, if G. didn't see how utterly he has misrepresented the constitutional position; a knave if he did.

Note: Three cuttings from a newspaper are stuck into the diary at this point.

"ON THE PENDING QUESTION OF OFFICE
ACCEPTANCE AND IN PURSUANCE OF THE
POLICY SUMMED UP IN THE FOREGOING
PARAGRAPHS THE ALL-INDIA CONGRESS
COMMITTEE AUTHORISES AND PERMITS
ACCEPTANCE OF OFFICES IN PROVINCES
WHERE THE CONGRESS COMMANDED A MAJORITY
IN THE LEGISLATURE PROVIDED THAT
MINISTERSHIPS SHALL NOT BE ACCEPTED
UNLESS THE LEADER OF THE CONGRESS
PARTY IN THE LEGISLATURE IS SATISFIED
AND IS ABLE TO STATE PUBLICITY THAT
THE GOVERNOR WILL NOT USE HIS SPECIAL
POWERS OF INTERFERENCE OR SET ASIDE THE
ADVICE OF THE MINISTERS IN REGARD TO
THEIR CONSTITUTIONAL ACTIVITIES."

It will be seen that the words
'that so long as he and his Cabinet
act within the Constitution' have
been knocked out of the original
resolution and the words 'in regard
to their Constitutional activities'
added at the end. It will also be
noted that while the original
resolution speaks of 'Ministerial
offices,' the amended one speaks
merely of 'offices'.

(The change makes not the slightest
difference to the meaning. H.G.)

DOWNRIGHT HONEST RESOLUTION.

REPLY TO A QUESTION WHETHER THERE WAS ANY SUBTLE INTENTION TO USE THE IN RESOLUTION IN SUCH A WAY AS VIRTUALLY TO MAKE OFFICE ACCEPTANCE IMPOSSIBLE MAHATMA GANDHI REPLIED AT ONCE ANIMATEDLY AND WITH EMPHASIS, "THE RESOLUTION IS A DOWNRIGHT HONEST RESOLUTION WITHOUT SLIGHTEST MENTAL RESERVATION, BUT IT MUST BE READ AS INDIVISIBLE WHOLE. IF THE GOVERNORS WANT CONGRESSMEN TO TAKE OFFICE,

I SEE NOTHING IN THE RESOLUTION TO MAKE IT EVEN AWKWARD FOR THEM TO GIVE FULLEST SATISFACTION TO THE CONGRESS LEADERS IN THEIR RESPECTIVE PROVINCES. THE GOVERNORS HAVE DISCRETION, AND THE RESOLUTION HAS ASKED FOR NOTHING. ANY LEADER SUMMONED BY THE GOVERNOR IN TERMS OF THE ACT TO FORM HIS CABINET WILL NATURALLY USE THE CONGRESS RESOLUTION BY WAY OF ILLUSTRATION, AND HE WILL ASK FOR AN ASSURANCE IN THE CASES COVERED BY THE RESOLUTION.

The cat came out of the bag, of course, as soon as negotiations had broken down. With the peculiar facility of the Indian for shutting his ears to anything which the other side has said, Nehru proclaimed sourly that it just showed how rotten the new constitution is when Governors can't sign it away. Patel in Bombay rubbed his hands in glee, and said he'd never felt so relieved in his life! What better proof could there be of the fact that the negotiations were never intended by the Congress H.Q. to be successful. The thing that I should like to know is what part the banyas – Birla and his crowd – played in the breakdown. Did they fear expropriatory measures from Congress Ministries? There's little to choose between a Bombay banya or a Calcutta Marwari and a Levantine Jew.

Wednesday March 31st

Over the first hurdle safely, though goodness knows how many more there are on the course! Rao came to me at 5 p.m. yesterday and told me that he would form a Ministry consisting of himself, Khaparde, Rizvi, and Dharm Rao, the Raj Gond Zamindar of Ahiri, the biggest estate in the province. That gets two minority communities a place each and, and will do very well. Salaries as at present (2,250/- each) with 3,000/- for the C.M.. I've wired to H.E. and the S/S, but the communiqué will not issue till noon today, as Rao wants to issue a statement at the same time. That moribund rag the D.N. went demented – flaring headlines all over the place – "Frantic efforts of Governor to find Ministers" – "A.B. refuses". "C.D. refuses" – with a bitter attack on any one who was so false to the national cause as to accept a Ministry. That sort of behaviour is infinitely more pernicious than the hackneyed "seditious speech". It would be amusing to take security of 10,000/- from Joshi, Naidu, Mehta & Co. They seem to have no control over their editor.

Gandhi has issued a statement which for sheer mealy-mouthed fatuity beats anything that even he has done before. This is a sample: "The Governors have discretionary powers surely there was nothing extra-constitutional in their saying that they would not exercise their discretion against Ministers carrying on constitutional activities." One can see the old banya's head wagging as he mouthed it. And again:"The question may be put in another way. Should Governors be courteous to the Ministers or discourteous?" And so on and so forth. Not one single word in answer to the plain statement that Governors have no legal power to give the assurances asked for, and that that ends the matter. Just like Gandhi.

Thursday April 1st

All Fools' Day. I wonder! I held my last meeting of the old government yesterday, and said a few words of thanks to them. At any rate we've had three years of peace, without Ministerial crises. I never thought that the Brahmin – non-Brahmin alliance would last so long. At 9.a.m. the new Ministry turned up, and I swore them in, without any pomp or ceremony, just the four and three of the Secretaries who were there on business, I refused to make any sort of tamáshá over the coming of a new order which had been so universally proclaimed to be unwelcome, and by people not one in ten thousand of whom knew anything about its nature. The refusal of Indians, Congress and Liberal alike, to make themselves really acquainted with the contents of the new constitution is a lasting disgrace to the nation. And of course their hatred of the safeguards is inspired simply by the fact that they prevent the politicians doing the one thing that every Oriental thinks it right and proper to do – twist the tails of Government servants, minorities, and everyone else delivered into their power. Suggestions for action openly made in the newspapers show that only too clearly.

Rao took the oaths in a low, almost broken voice. He feels very keenly the attacks which have been made on him in the local Press, which is sick as mud because he has prevented the constitution breaking down – or rather becoming an autocracy – at the start. But every other Province is producing men who are doing the same as he, so there is hope yet that some decency and loyalty survives. The others were quite cheerful about it. Afterwards we had the first meeting of the new Cabinet, and got through all the necessary business for setting the new machinery going – Business Rules, rules for the custody of public money, constitution of a Revenue Appellate authority, appointment of an Advocate General, & so on. In one way, the turn which affairs have taken has been a blessing in disguise. All these matters had been discussed and drafts drawn up by the old government, so we simply ratified our own provisional conclusions. I am willing to bet that there's some sickness in the Congress camp over losing the Advocate-Generalship. A message in the papers from Delhi today makes it clear that Congressmen are beginning to rub sore heads, and realise that they've been befooled by their leaders. Congress are like the Bourbons – they forget nothing, and they learn nothing.

(I hope I haven't said that before! It's been on my mind for some time, and I stuck the jibe in a letter to H.E. a few days ago.)

It's been amazing weather – cloudy & showers & rain, with the lawn drenched in dew in the mornings. On Monday the maximum was 89° (F) against a normal 101°. We've all been blessing it.

Pachmarhi. April 6th

It's going to be a toss-up which way the appointment of the minority Ministry is going to turn out – like everything else in this country. A report today says that whereas Congress was getting cursed for refusing office, the new Ministry has caused a revulsion of feeling. It has certainly been damned heartily in the papers – though Venkatraman of the D.N. openly told McNaughton (D.C. Nagpur) that he was doing it to attract readers, the D.N. being on the verge of bankruptcy. So much for honest criticism in this country! The truth, I suspect, is that although certain people disliked the idea of Congress refusing office, they also dislike still more the idea of Congress having been done in the eye through Rao's acceptance. They'd have loved nothing better than to see the Constitution break down at the start, and the Governors taking the whole show over. Chagrin and thwarted malice are writ large over the articles which have appeared, though I will say that there have been no personal attacks on the Governors themselves. The only thing to do is to sit tight and see how things develop.

The G/I have just proposed that appointments made by the Governor to his personal staff (M.S and A.D.C.) should be made in his "individual judgement". I wrote to Craik d.o. and told him that it was intolerable that Ministers should have any say in the appointment of the Govr.'s personal entourage, and most unwise that he should be put in the position of having to differ from them in the matter. It is certain that Ministers would press for an Indian M.S. – which means that we should never be able to talk freely at table. I can't understand how such a proposal ever came to be made, remembering the excessive care which they have taken to shield the Governor from interference in all that pertains to "G.H." – the Governor's private and semi-official life.

Wednesday April 7th

A report from the C.I. Bureau confirms exactly what I said (30th March) that the Congress H.Q. never intended that office should be accepted. "It is now clear that Gandhi has all along been determined to defeat the office acceptance drift. He has deceived some and convinced others ………. It is impossible to believe that the able legal brains which helped Gandhi in drafting his formula can have seriously expected that Governors could be induced to castrate the Act in the way that they have actually been asked to do …..Much of the attitude of the Press and of the talk of leading Congressmen has almost certainly been part of the deliberate plan to endeavour to put Governors in the wrong in the public eye…….. Nehru is openly exultant." What a dirty lot of rogues they are!

Collins sends me a gloomy report, saying that moderate opinion is hardening to the side of Congress, because the new Ministry is said to be "unconstitutional". It is just the sort of attitude you might expect an Indian to take up – to damn the constitution in one breath and try to break it by refusing office, and in the next to make the welkin ring with appeals to the very constitution he has rejected because he finds his pretty design thwarted for the time being. C. says that if there were a fresh election now, Congress would have a bigger majority than ever. Well, there isn't going to be a fresh election yet, and it's much too early to get excited. We shall see.

Friday April 9th

Collins came and saw me yesterday, and gave a much more cheerful account of things. Rao, it appears, was in the depths when C. had talked to him first, but at a subsequent interview was beginning to pluck up heart again, and said that he had already secured one or two extra followers. He is very easily depressed. They had a meeting in Nagpur to condemn the Rao Ministry and demand an early session of Council, but it struck me that they weren't as excited as they might have been. Kedar read a letter from Paranjpe (Hindu Mahasabha), whom Khare defeated in the Nagpur election, saying that the outcry against the minority Ministry was all fiddle-dedee. Kedar was as bombastic and silly as ever. Sharif was there, because he detests Rao. And of all people, Moro Joshi was the "patron" of the gathering, supported by his barrister son. Reason? Because the son hasn't got the appointment of Asst. Advocate General, for which Moro has been touting for the past year. Such are politics in the C.P. – all a matter of jobs and personalities. Sharif, by the way said that I personally was sympathetic to the aspirations of the people. So I am; but I wish to goodness that they'd do more to deserve it!

Hallett in Bihar is getting on to the publicity tack, and I'm sure he's right. I'm going to tackle it as soon as Govt. gets up here. We ought to placard every village with large notices – "Ghandi has betrayed you".

At the end of the old regime I wrote to Rao and the Ministers to thank them & had very nice letters back from them all. R. says: "A line to thank you for your kindly letter of appreciation which, believe me I value very highly. You are most generous. You play the game and lead the team without "panache". I'm most grateful to you". So in one way at any rate the old order passed away smilingly. I see that Moro Joshi said at the meeting that he had been asked by some as to why H.E. did not invite him to form the Ministry. "My reply" he said "is that H.E. is well aware that I am still sane". As "The Rasher" (the Rev. Dr. H.D.R. Rashdall, my tutor at New College) used to say to my wilder flights of fancy, with a Homeric cackle, "Isn't that rather a large assumption?"

Saturday April 10th

If further proof were wanted of the fact that there has been a ramp, what more could one ask for than this? An intercepted letter of 2.4.37 from Nehru to Gandhi says (N. is sick) – "Lying in bed I read the statement you have issued about the A.I.C.C. resolution. Being the author of the last part of the resolution, you are obviously the best person to explain it. And yet the explanations you now give seemed to me to be quite new; at no time during our talks had it struck me that way. It all resolves itself into courtesy and discourtesy. Our chief grievance is that Samuel Hoare's promise has not been kept. We are going to work the Constitution for what it is worth." Now I had imagined that these men (?) were vital conflicts and that we had laid stress on a different policy all this past year. It is not a question of who is right and who is wrong but of knowing where we are.

"I read your statement with a sense of shock and realised how very different was our outlook in such matters. I feel I must send you these lines from my sick-bed. They may not be very coherent but they will give you an insight into my mind."

So there we are, with the cat out of the bag, and Nehru finding that Gandhi has double-crossed him, and has issued an explanation of the formula which he'd never mentioned to N.. A pretty pair they are. There is a bitter satisfaction in finding one's judgment of the Indian character justified. I said – off my own bat – that Moro Joshi had led the meeting on the 6th through pique. Today comes a report from the C.I.O.. "It is believed in well-informed circles that the former's (M.J.'s) hostile attitude is due to the failure of his efforts to secure the appointment of Asst. Adv. General for his son." Sharif apparently hopes to get a place in the Ministry, if there is a compromise and Congress takes office. I'd take long odds against it, from what Khare said.

Wednesday April 14th

Bannerji (Governor's Secretary) just up from Nagpur, doesn't think that the situation has developed in any way, though he's heard privately from Bihar that Congress expect to be able to take office there. Khare wrote to me today asking that if I didn't intend to summon a meeting of the Congress and other members; and would I lend him the Assembly Hall for the purpose? Could anyone but a Hindu make such a deliciously naive request? "I intend to call a meeting to defy the Constitution and the Government, and please may I have the Government Hall to hold it in?" The letter appears to be an ultimatum, as a reply is demanded in four days! The answer to all parts is, of course, "Rats", but I shall wait till I see Rao tomorrow before sending it. Also a letter from Hallett, saying that he has no intention of summoning a meeting in Bihar. And one from H.E. about publicity, a ticklish business, but of vital importance. The difficulties are (a) To what extent can the Government forsake its usual attitude of neutrality? (b) To what extent can the Govr. carry on a publicity campaign as distinct from the Government? I must talk to Rao to clear the air.

I am much oppressed with the idea that if things come to the worst and I have to use §93, I may have to play the part of dictator in the province which I have helped in some small measure to grow from autocracy to responsible government. If I do have to, I shall seriously consider my position.

Thurs April 15th

I had a cable last night saying that Mother was dead. Father, Mother and one of two brothers gone in 20 months, and I've not been there to pay the last tributes to any of them. People may scoff at the "White Man's Burden", but it's a very real one sometimes.

I had a letter from Khare yesterday, asking me to summon the Assembly, and saying that if I don't he proposes to do (so), and may he have the Assembly Hall for the purpose? Could anyone but a Hindu make such a deliciously naïve request? "I intend to call a meeting to defy the Government and please may I have the Government Hall to hold it in?" The letter also contains an offensive remark about the British government, never observing parliamentary forms, and finishes up with a demand for an answer within four days. Congress has so much riff-raff among its members that it can never hope to learn good manners. I intend to ignore the contents of the letter – including the time limit! – and merely to reply that I don't intend to call a meeting now, because it would precipitate a crisis, and I want everyone to have ample time for reflection before they get committed to a course which they may regret later. That gives them their answer, and will not add any fuel to the controversy.

Friday April 16th

Rao came and saw me yesterday, but had no developments to tell me of, and the situation remains much the same – Gandhi firing off statements at the rate of one a day, Lothian, Shastri, Sapur and God knows who else letting off their own little muskets indiscriminately. Meanwhile if each Governor were left to deal with his own Congress leader – or rather if each C.L. had a free hand to deal with his own Governor – we'd have Congress Ministries functioning in the six provinces tomorrow. Rao tells me that the C.P. are going to follow the tactics of the U.P., which is unfortunate, as under Nehru's influence the U.P. is the least pro-office province of the six. They will probably collect the members of the Assembly and hold a dummy meeting, electing a Speaker and so on, and passing dummy laws. But that's a futile game that's been tried before and has failed, and won't amuse them for very long.

Rao says he sees no point in imitating Bombay and framing a policy and pretending to be a full-blooded Ministry. I am inclined to think that he is right. We don't need any petty measures of reform here, and the big measures, such as reorganising our antiquated land revenue system, need a Ministry with a big majority if they are to be tackled. Anyhow I can do nothing but let Rao follow the course he thinks best.

He told me an amazing story, to the effect that Erskine, whose capacity to handle the situation in Madras he gravely misdoubts, had a private interview with R— C— "at the end of February", and left R— C—with the clear impression that Governors would have no difficulty in accepting the Delhi condition. Hence all the subsequent trouble.

Now I know that an interview did take place on March 3rd, that E. sent an account of it to H.E., and that on the 8th H.E., without saying what E. had proposed, wired him instructions from the S/S that Governors could have nothing to do with formulas; further, that later on R——C— came back to Erskine and tried to get him to accept another formula (which looks as if he and E. thought that a formula was possible); and finally that H.E. wired to me telling me to say nothing about this last bit of news, as he was "most anxious to discount any notion that any question of a formula in any degree establishing convention or modifying Govr.'s discretion arises". I wonder if Erskine went and sold the fort before he realised what he was doing.

Sunday April 25th

Ewart, The director of the Central Bureau, came and spent a few days with us last week. He tells me that the G/I have got a drastic Ordinance in draft – a combination of our C.D. one with the Palestine orders, all ready in case we have to use Sec. 93.

Gandhi has been issuing more statements, and has made it still more probable that he's going potty. Honestly, after reading his latest statement yesterday I hadn't the vaguest notion what he wants, or what his terms are for office acceptance. At one moment he says one thing, at another something quite different. He's like a cuttle fish, that squirts ink so as to conceal its movements, and the only thing you can say about his next move is that it's sure to be something that will make this into a worse mess than ever.

Strange as it may seem, it appears to be an established fact that the appointment of minority ministries took the Congress by surprise. Hence the howl of baffled wrath with which they were greeted. Apparently Congress thought that we should have to use Sec.93 at once, and that they would be able to caper about, like an Indian hockey team does when it has won, and shriek that the Constitution had broken down at the very start. Rao has changed his mind as to a programme, and the Ministers are now working one out. Most of the items consist of things which we've wanted to do for years, but have had no money for; and the last item is pathetic in its brevity – "Ways and Means – To devise methods of financing the above schemes." Aye! There's the rub."

H.E. has been writing to me about publicity, on the need for which he is somewhat insistent. I have had to tell him what the experience of the N.C.O. days taught us – that as a publicity agency Govt. is slow, unimaginative, & hampered by the fact that it can't sling mud as the other man can and that it can only give a small part of its attention to a job that the other man is giving his whole mind to. When Govt. starts issuing propaganda leaflets it becomes an Aunt Sally – every leaflet is an additional target for the enemy and Govt. officers have neither the time nor the inclination to pick the missiles up and throw them back.

Monday April 26th

The Statesman in the first of its 'Occasional Notes' says that my utterances have been "uniformly helpful"! We seem to be in the limelight! But it goes on to say that it would be "a grievous mistake" to delay too long in summoning the Assembly. Quite – but no period is to my mind too long if it allows Congress to make up its mind up the right way. The 'W.C.' meets today (at Allahabad, because Nehru is too sick to come to Wardha), and Waterfall thinks they must be going to change their tune, otherwise why should they meet? The Times is reported as saying that it is up to Govt. to make a move now. I don't think that's right, though we should not let any sense of prestige stand in our way, if we see a chance of moving profitably.

The problem is now perfectly simple –

A. Governors cannot swear away the responsibilities put upon them by parliament.

B. On the other hand they have made it as clear as daylight that in Sammy Hoare's words "they will not ordinarily use these powers".

C. Congress has the additional safeguard that a Governor dare not risk the resignation of his Ministers except on a vital issue, on which he is prepared to face public opinion.

D. Is Congress prepared to accept office on these terms, without any more shilly-shallying or formula-making, or is it not? If it is, well and good – pax vobiscum. If it is not, then it's war, and the sooner we get to work the better. "Twice blest is he who gets his blow in first".

If I were given my own way, I would abandon all but three of my S.R.s. Peace and tranquillity and the rights of Indian States, are plainly essential, and so is the protection of the Imperial Services appointed by the S/S, who have a right to look beyond the provincial government. But I would give the P.G. complete control over all the Services appointed by it, and if it chooses to make a mess of them – well sooner or later the Indians have got to learn of the dangers of self-rule. In the C.P.at any rate the "excluded area" business is a first-class mistake. It antagonised and offended liberal thought without the slightest need. And as for minorities, separate electorates should stay, but later that they should fend for themselves, if democracy has any meaning. I would retain the absolute minimum of protection against trade discrimination, that being not only just, seeing how we have developed the country, but also the right of paramount power. In the C.P, too Berar must have its special clause. But with safeguards limited in general to peace and order, the Imperial Services, rights of Indian States, and the minimum protection of British trade, we should be in a far stronger position vis à vis the world than we are now, with nothing lost that we need retain.

Damn all Die-Hards say I! They've been as blind and as futile in the case of India as they were in Egypt and in Ireland.

In a leading article called "Gandhiji queers the pitch again", the Hit. says – "We can understand the objections of open and undisguised wreckers like Mr. Nehru, but we confess we are unable to place the Mahatma. Is he a wrecker or a co-operator? We confess we are unable to answer the question in view of the nature of the plethora of statements that he has been issuing lately." Exactly.

Friday April 30th

The W.C. has issued just the sort of resolution I expected. It ends up – "This Committee has grave objection to Ministers having to submit to interference by the Governors with the alternative of themselves having to resign their office instead of the Governors taking the responsibility of dismissing them." The attitude is typical – "We object to any interference, and at the same time we object to having to make our own minds up or take any responsibility." The resolution is said to be a compromise between the Right and Left Wings. Whatever it is, it gets us nowhere, because it means the abrogation of safeguards. The sole method which a Governor is to have of stopping, say, a piece of injustice to a public servant is by dismissing the Ministry and ordering a fresh election! Utterly impracticable. The truth is, as Rao says, that Congress is behaving like the (wo)man who "lingered shivering on the brink, And fear to launch away". She wants to accept office, but funks it. To me she seems to be behaving like a coquettish old spinster who gets her first proposal at the age of 40.

There is no doubt that under the new dispensation a Governor's job is going to be a nasty one. He's to be a mixture between a puppet, an Aunt Sally, and a somewhat senile Assistant Commissioner. In all ordinary administrative matters, a puppet; in a case like the present impasse, the target of attack from all sides, a position into which he has been forced without any fault of his own; and in all matters connected with his S.R.'s and discretionary powers, a mere tool of the S/S and the G.G.. I've just had orders down according to which I've got to send both of them every fortnight a full account of everything that anyone has been doing, saying or thinking in the Province. I'm thinking very seriously of throwing my hand in next March, by which time I shall have completed 35 years' service, and can justly say that I've done my bit.

Wed. May 5th

Khare has issued notices for a meeting of his mock parliament, couched in the usual Congress style, and with the usual Congress disregard for veracity. He puts the whole blame for the failure of Congress to take office onto me – a flagrantly dishonest statement. It remains to be seen what sort of response he gets. I shall have no hesitation in taking action against anything that goes over the mark. M.G.Chitravis (the Rabbit) is to be president of the Reception Committee. Shades of old Sir Gangadhar! He must be turning in his grave at the doings of his degenerate son – only he was cremated!

Sat. May 8th

Rao showed me yesterday the reply he is sending to Khare's invitation to the meeting – a dignified and restrained rebuke, which will have as much effect on Khare and his ill-mannered crowd as an Early Christian's appeal did on the Roman rabble.

I've just had a very interesting report of the W.C.'s meeting at Allahabad. First, the Right-Wingers (Desai, R.C., Rajendra Prashad, Khare and others) said they hoped Govt. would make a move which would enable Congress to accept office, and were averse from any decision which would make the position worse. But – just to show how blind they are – they would not hear of any toning down of the impossible Delhi resolution. Then Nehru voiced the Left-Wing ideas, and said they ought to call meetings of the Assembly members and set up parallel Govts. (as Khare is doing).

Then Gandhi took complete charge of the show. He stopped the budding quarrel by brusquely silencing both parties – incidentally telling Nehru that his proposals would cause a clash with Govt. before he was ready for it. (Curious that Kh. should nevertheless be calling his meeting!) He then unfolded his own plan, reluctantly, as the only means of stopping discussion. The plan is that all activities are now to be directed to preparations for a renewal of C.D.. Gandhi is to decide the time and method, and has agreed to see the movement through, though operating through the President, A.I.C.C., but is insistent that there shall be no premature clash. It is to be started piecemeal in selected areas.

To show how foggy the situation is, the report goes on – "In spite of the fact that Gandhi stated that there was now a complete breach with Govt., I have a strong impression, on my information, that he still hopes that Congress will take office. Underlying all his talk of avoiding an immediate clash is the desire to use a comparatively short term of office for weakening the administrative machine and the weapons in the hands of Governors."

I have just had a talk with Rao, and he now thinks we should use Sec. 93 in July, without summoning the Assembly at all. "Don't", he says, "give them the chance of passing wild-cat Acts and resolutions, and then going to the country and saying they had done what they could, but the Govr. had vetoed it all. And don't give them a chance of making attacks on the Governor, and weakening his authority, which is vital for the success of the Act." Sound advice, and I've written to H.E. and passed it on. Gandhi has just issued a statement to the Press that nothing was discussed at Allahabad except the terms of the resolution. Little liar! I wish he hadn't stuck himself down in Wardha. His host, J.Bazaz, has brought a libel case against a paper which accused him of "swallowing" Congress funds – and he daren't go on with the case. What a crew they are!

Wed. May 12th

I have just had a wire from Nagpur saying that Khare's mock Parliament was a frost, as I rather thought it might be. Only 51 turned up – 47 Congress, the Rabbit, and three Mahommedans led by Yusuf Sharif. There were hardly 100 spectators, and at the "Convention" in the evening the audience was only 400. That's very satisfactory, and I can't help feeling that it shows what a false position Congress has put itself into, and how people realise it. Khare is flogging a dead horse in trying to work up indignation over the refusal to summon the Assembly. Incidentally, Hemeon gave me a jab yesterday by telling me that I was bound to summon the Assembly in July or August, because §62(3) is mandatory and neither 62(2) nor 93 get over it. So that's that. I wish I hadn't been so hasty in telling H.E. that we wouldn't have a meeting – but that's me. I'm always doing things without taking long enough time to think them over. Rao misled me this time.

W.G. Joshi, the "Lion" (quotha) of Berar, wrote a letter the other day which is an amazing giveaway of what goes on behind the scenes in Congress. (It's a private letter to a Congr. Socialist.) It's full of – "Don't trust A, because he's B's man". "You must appoint C, so as to bring D in". "E is trying to get hold of F, and if he does G will join H". And so on – a sorry tale of intrigue, back-biting and place-hunting. And these are our "selfless patriots" who refuse to take more than 500/- a month. The refusal is wise – there isn't one of them that's worth more.

Friday May 14th

Further reports about the Convention confirm the first one. The public seems to have thought the whole show a waste of time, trouble, and money, and though the Rabbit tried to buy favour by giving a large dinner, even that didn't fill. There was one delightful touch. In his "democratic" Assembly the Speaker and Dy. Speaker were <u>nominated</u> by Khare!! It's almost unbelievable, especially seeing that one of the published objects of the meeting was to "elect" officers according to the Law. Rao says that they knew there'd be a squabble if the matter was left open to election, so they told Khare to nominate in order to save their faces.

I came across the following in Gunther's "Inside Europe" this morning – "Anyone who tries to hoodwink the British suffers for it – in the long run". I should like to quote that to Gandhi.

Sat. May 15th

Edna left for England yesterday, and I've now got 5½ months on my own. We have quite settled that we will not have another separation, but that I will go home with her next spring – unless something very untoward happens to stop me. One lives and works now in <u>unpleasant</u> surroundings, in the midst of suspicion, hostility, unreasonableness, childishness. One has the right to say that after 35 years in the country, and in one's 60th year, release is due. By the pomp and vanity of my office I set little store. Most of it seems to me to be rather silly, and made necessary solely by the Indian love of tamáshá; and all of it is tedious. As the Stevedore sang: "It ain't so much the honour and the glory as the pay"! And even that's no great attraction when you think what salaries business men get.

Note (JHBG):

The reference is to a negro melody that a family friend, Capt. Paterson, used to sing to us over the camp fires at night out in the plains, accompanied by his banjo, to a simple melody in a minor key.

"Here we go , two Laktawava niggers,
Walking down the Broadway showing off our figures,

★ ★ ★ ★ ★ ★ ★ ★ ★ ★

For we represent the Laktawava Gang
We go to work before de break of day,
It ain't so much de honour and de glory as the pay,
Scooping out 'de, barges as dey come along de quai,
For we represent de Laktawava Gang.
Aunt Dinah makes de batter puddin';
My word, and don't she make a good 'un;
Our appetites are hearty an' Ah don' see why de shouldn'
For we represent de Laktawava Gang.
— Chorus — etc."

Diary continues

Wed May 19th

A letter from Emerson in the Punjab, to whom I wrote to congratulate him on a "G", says that two days ago he had written to Haig, putting the chances of Congress accepting office at 2 to 1 against, but since then he had seen signs of a change, & was now laying 2 to 1 on! I must have missed something. I should have said personally that the odds had lengthened considerably. He ends – "But if Congress are out for trouble, it will be necessary to deal with it when the Time comes, swiftly and sternly all over India. The Viceroy will do it at night". That's the spirit.

Friday May 21st

Rao has just produced his programme, with an excellent preamble, in which he reproduces what I've been telling them all, that the money market is a far more potent safeguard than any special powers of the Governor, and that the Ministry refuses therefore to have anything to do with wild-cat schemes like cutting the land revenue down. He points out boldly that our assessments are the lightest in India. Similarly he shies right off prohibition, which he says is utterly impracticable in the C.P. – as anyone but a purblind politician knows. It will be very interesting to see what reception the programme gets. It includes a tax on agricultural incomes, and an increase in the takoli of the zamindars, both measures that ought to have been introduced years ago, but that the old government could never have hoped to get through the Council.

Tues May 25th

I've just answered a long letter from the Viceroy – or rather two, one addressed to all governors, & one to me personally. The latter was (a) to beg Rao not to resign before the meeting of the Assembly, which he has agreed not to do, because it would leave me to face the Assembly without a Ministry; and (b) to ask what I thought about a suggestion which has been made that, as the Govr. onto whose Province Gandhi has fastened himself, I should send for him and try to get him to agree to office acceptance. A hopeless idea. G. doesn't mean to allow office acceptance, and nothing that I could say would have the slightest effect on him. I would probably get a rebuff from his hangers-on, and if I didn't I would either be told to apply to Nehru, not G. or else he would come and talk sweet nothings to me. Fortunately H.E. didn't seem at all enamoured of the scheme himself, so I had no fear about telling him my view. People at home show signs of getting impatient and asking for an early summoning of Assemblies. A fatal error to do anything of the sort until the monsoon has set in well. They are also talking a lot of twaddle about "direct contact" with the Congress and "the mollifying effect of personal contacts". Fancy me having direct contacts with people like Khare and D.P. Misra, sworn enemies of the British Govt., who lose no opportunity of vilifying it & its officers. I said I was in touch with all their sayings and doings, but that direct contact was out of the question. H.E. also had things to say about a Govr. consulting his C.M., which he thinks ought to be done with great caution, so that the Governor may preserve his extra-party attitude. I can't see it. The Ministry are the Governor's advisors under the constitution & the point of view that I put forward in reply was that he has the right to ask for their advice, formally or informally according to circumstances, on all occasions. I do wish they'd let us alone over that sort of thing. I do not need anyone to tell me how to treat my Ministry.

Wednesday May 26th

I've just had a letter from McClenaghan (D.C. Nagpur.) which may mean nothing, and on the other hand may mean a great deal – a complex change of front on the part of Congress. Khare came to his office to file a nomination paper for a candidate for the Central Assembly, and stayed behind, obviously on purpose, and started talking about things in general. He said frankly that he was in favour of office acceptance, that Gandhi had told him that he was keener seeing the constitution worked than his friends realised, and that if the Viceroy let it be known that he would give G. an interview, he (Kh.) believed that G. would ask for one. This letter coincided with one from the V. in which he said that he had decided not to invite G. off his own bat. It's a curious business. Is G. genuine, or is this another move in his game? I've sent a copy of the letter to H.E., and said that if H.E. decides that he will say "yes" to a request from G., I will get that fact conveyed to G. If I get no response, no harm will have been done. But if the bell rings, then we shall be headed for peace – for a time at any rate.

Saturday May 29th

A telegram from H.E., giving what may be a clue to the above. R—C— in Madras has been to see Erskine – no, has written to say that he'd like to see him – and E. has reason to believe that R. will tell him he's ready to accept office, if a compromise can arrived at on the absurd dismissal vs. resignation issue. (How they haggle to the end!) H.E. says quite rightly he's not going to have any nonsense over the matter. It's merely a silly red herring that Gandhi drew across the trail for tactical reasons. Erskine is to see R—C—, and make him see reason. But it looks very much as if the local men are getting out of hand, and Gandhi is beginning to realise that he can't keep them back from office and is trimming his sails accordingly. If that is so, it will (be) an ample justification of the policy which I have advocated from the start – that we should go on our way normally, doing nothing (such as summoning the Assembly) which would precipitate a crisis. We shall see. I think the production of the Ministerial programmes has shaken Congress up, because they contain a number of items which Congress simply daren't oppose!

Tuesday June 1st

Really there is no end to the things against which one has to contend in this country. An election petition was filed against Rao – in the very last permissible hour, in the true Indian fashion. Under the rules I have power in my "individual judgment" to reject it summarily if it is not concise and does not contain statements of material fact. But nothing could be clearer than the fact that in the peculiar circumstances of the case I cannot use this power to shield one of my Ministers unless the petition is found to be grossly defective. The truth is that it is tolerably well drafted, and attached to it are 20 pages of details of alleged offences; and it never even entered my head, or Hemeon's (L.R.) either, that I could reject the petition. What happens. I ask the Ministry advice. Rao sends it down for our new Advocate-General's opinion. The A.G., in a note which reeks of petty-fogging lawyerism, "humbly advises" me to reject the petition. And when I send for the Ministers (minus Rao) to talk the case over with them, they back the A.G. up, Khaparde mildly, Rizvi mulishly. Then I'm afraid I went off the deep end – to the extent of speaking with complete frankness – and pointed out to them that if I were to pass an order in consonance with their advice we should be accused from Simla to Comorin of deliberately burking the case to shield a colleague. If the petition were obviously bad it would be difficult and inadvisable for us to reject; in the circumstances it would be an act of falsehood to our public duty. Khaparde was shaken; Dharm Rao said nothing; Rizvi – I don't know. They went away, and said they'd record their advice in writing. Then I sent for Rao, and explained things to him. Once before, when he was Home Member and attacks were made on him in Council, he tried to get me to shield him by refusing to allow a resolution to be moved. And this time he talked about candidates "being entitled to protection". But I think I got him to see what a fatal mistake it would be to appear to burke the case. All of them, incidentally, quoted to me the report that the Congress Boss Gang had refused to sanction the petition – as if that made any difference! Any suggestion of that as an argument would be met by a flat denial of fact. Is there just one man among these people who can look at things in the simple, straight-forward way in which the white man is brought up?

H.E. doesn't think anything can be done about Gandhi – says he's been in touch with him through intermediaries like G.D.Birla and G. knows perfectly well that he can get an interview at any moment, if he wants it. H.E. has a most disarming way, when one differs from him, of saying that he greatly appreciates what one says, & that we really agree at bottom, only look at the matter from a slightly different angle. Vide March 25th for instance. He admits that each province must go its own way, & I must be allowed to treat my Ministers according to C.P.

methods. But he adds gently that the other five "Congress" Governors have all agreed with his more "rigid" ideas. It seems to me that they must be either ji-hán-wallas, or sundried. I cannot see how any Governor can brook any interference with his right to consult his Ministers as and when he pleases.

Wednesday June 2nd

A piece of luck! The Ministers insisted – quite moderately – on supporting the A.G., and represented that it would be a very bad thing to differ from him almost at the start. I admit that that argument shook me. I have had to protest before this about Khaparde ignoring legal opinion in L.S.G. cases; and in the future the Govr. will probably have to rely on the A.G.'s opinions in keeping Congress Ministers straight. That seems to me a consideration of first-class weight, and Waterfall and Bannerji both agreed with me. But I was saved at the last moment from having to make a decision by the fact that the petitioner withdrew his case! We had seen an intercepted letter of his, appealing wailingly for funds, and I imagine he must have failed to raise the wind. Anyhow he saved me from a very embarrassing decision, and incidentally made Govt. a present of 1000/-, his deposit.

Friday, June 4th

Rao says that Agrihotri withdrew his case because he was afraid of an action for libel. I don't understand; I thought such proceedings were privileged. R. annoys me sometimes. He is too fond of talking about "undulatory" policy, and preaching consistency – that being the last virtue of an Indian politician. Because we let go certain people who had been talking hot air during the elections, he doesn't want to prosecute anyone now. There's to be a meeting of the provincial Congress Committee at Pipariya on the 10th – to be followed possibly by a march on Pachmarhi – and with Rizvi's help I got him to agree to a postponement of orders till after that date. Rao's difficulty is that he is apt to hang ideas on to long words, as to the meaning of which he is sometimes not very clear. Some of his phrases leave me completely puzzled. Gandhi has issued another of his statements, rambling as usual, and full of the whine of the banya. It is beyond me how anybody takes any serious notice of what he says. "Congress has made all the concessions. It is time for Govt. to make some now." – Congress having made impossible demands to start with, and its "concessions" consisting of retreat from part of those demands. "The difference between us (dismissal vs. resignation) is a trifle. Why not give that trifle to Congress?" Can't you hear the whine? And still no answer to the plain, blunt question – Are Governors to be allowed to use their powers when necessary, or are they not? R—C- has just been to see G., who is having a holiday at the sea, and I shrewdly suspect he has been threatening revolt. And quite right. Revolt from the paralysing hand of the Congress Central executive is the only chance for the healthy political life of the country.

Tuesday June 8th

I have just read Baldwin's political swan-song, his "Call to Youth" speech. It's a long time since I've read anything so fine. No frills, just virile, moving Anglo-Saxon spoken straight from the heart. I'd have given anything to hear it.

In writing my fortnightly to H.E. yesterday I told him about the election petition. It's good for him and the S/S to know what sort of things one has to deal with. Rao is not very hopeful about the chances of a Congress break-up, though we have definite information that the Mahakoshal group dislikes Khare's autocratic ways, and is plotting his downfall. They're holding a conference tomorrow at Pipariya to which they haven't invited him. I have never, of course, been able to understand – except on the general ground of the "ultá pultá desh" – how a little jack-an-apes like Khare could be given the leadership of a provincial party.

Sunday June 13th

The Pipariya Conference did an awful lot of talking, but most of it pretty temperate. The truth is that these people have no real grievances at present. Rents are the lightest in India – probably in the civilised world. They know perfectly well that we do everything we can for them, consistently with financial possibilities. And they also know perfectly well – it keeps cropping up in speeches – that the G/I Act transfers all the real power to the people. Thus D.K.Mehta – "The 1935 Act despite its faults has allowed that India should have government of the people by the people, and that it should no longer be in the hands of a handful of people in England." (Then why not accept office, and bring govt. o.t.p. for t.p. into being?) You can't make a revolution without some very real grievance to provide it with a mainspring – and they haven't one. D. P. Misra said – "Resorting to satyagraha is out of the question, because it had in the past always followed some cause, whereas there was none at present." The question of malguzars produced a split; but there were no signs of the anti-Khare business. Possibly they had been warned off by Vallabhai Patel, who is adjudicating on the quarrel. The suggested march on Pachmarhi came to nothing – was scarcely mentioned.

Tuesday June 15th

Khare has sent me a packet of pink papers, each signed by an M.L.A. and expressing no confidence in the Ministry. "Cui bono?" As if everyone didn't know it! But they do love wasting their time in these futilities. I must talk to Rao about a reply.

We're getting onto preparations for §93. What we think of doing is to have a second Financial Commr., and he and Burton will run all the depts. except those which are directly under me. B. and Waterfall think it can be done with ease. They say no Minister has more than 2 hrs. work a day, except such as he chooses to make for himself.

Wednesday June 16th

I dislike the Indian when he's got a down on a man. He's utterly unscrupulous. Khaparde has a down on Logan, and wanted to blackguard him in his confl. report – a continuation of the Naidu business that I think I wrote about. The reason turned out to be that Logan had not called on Kh.! And because of that he was ready to believe anything that was said against him, though Naidu's stories had been proved false.

The Viceroy is going to make a statement at last. But I'm afraid from a wire I got this morning that it's going to be a long one – a pity. There's nothing in the situation that can't be said in a few sentences, & long sentences merely confuse people. Moreover it's going to be a "Vice-regal pronouncement" – too pontifical altogether.

Rao says I should take Khare's letter as an indication that the majority now wish to accept office, ask if that is so, and say that I'll see Kh. when he likes. A good move, I think. At any rate it opens the door (not that it has ever been anything but open) and if Kh, chooses to shut it, it's his look-out and not mine. On the other hand, if he really is wanting to walk in, here's his chance.

Sunday 20th
The Result!

THE DAILY NEWS

NAGPUR, JUNE 19, 1937

THE GOVERNOR'S GESTURE

H. E. Sir Hyde Gowan has cut the Gordian knot instead of wasting further time in an ingenious attempt to untie it. Replying to the communication of Dr. Khare conveying want of confidence in the interim Ministry, the Secretary to the Governor has explained the circumstances under which the present Ministry was formed. "The fact that the Ministry's supporters formed a minority in the Assembly was known to every one from the start" proceeds the letter, "and the sending of this resolution so long after the formation of the Ministry appears to his Excellency to suggest that as a result of its reflection the majority party now desires the Ministry to demit office in its favour." * * * * * * * His Excellency's conclusion that the majority party in our province desires the interim Ministry to demit office in favour of the Congress is right.

The most important part of the letter from the Secretary to the Governor to Dr. Khare is where it says that his Excellency "will be ready at any time to give you a personal interview on the subject of your acceptance of office." One of the minor points which appeared to worry both the Government and the Congress was how to bring about a meeting between the Governors and Congress leaders. Both sides stood on prestige and it was thought that the summoning of the legislatures would provide an opportunity for this purpose. But Sir Hyde Gowan has laid the ghost of so-called prestige and, in a courageous manner which is worthy of all praise, has invited the Congress leader to meet him. Incidentally, His Excellency has set an example to the other Governors. The Congress believes in uniformity of action and if the dead-lock is solved in one province, it will be solved everywhere. It is now for Dr. Khare to accept the constitutional challenge of the Governor and accept the responsibility of office. We realise that Dr. Khare is not free to act as he would wish but fortunately Mahatma Gandhi, who is keen on ending the dead-lock, is in our province and he can give the necessary guidance to Dr. Khare.

* * * * * * * * * The next step in our province must be taken by the Congress leader. If the dead-lock continues any longer it will be the Congress that will be solely responsible for it. H. E. the Governor has made a fine gesture of co-operation and it is for Dr. Khare to act.

Sunday 20ᵗʰ continued

Most of that is tommy-rot. The letter was merely a move – though I think a fairly astute one – to force the Congress to come off the fence and make its mind up. As someone said of Ramsay Macdonald, it has sat so long on the fence that the iron has entered into its soul! The moment is opportune, because (a) Khare is going to see Gandhi today, and (b) H.E. is issuing on Tuesday a Message to India, which puts the whole position very clearly, and Congress will now have no excuse for a refusal. A "No" now will be a clear act of Leftism, and we shall have to take action accordingly.

The monsoon broke with a bang on Friday, and yesterday night we had an appalling storm – 3¼" in 3 hours. Once I thought the house had been struck. It's pleasant to think that, bar accidents, I haven't got another hot weather to do. Pach., with its maxima of 100° and its minima of 80°, is merely a refuge from the worst of the heat, and 35 years of it is enough.

Later. Khare has replied in a typical letter. Starting with a defiant assertion that his letter to me was intended to show the solidarity of the Congress party and to "nail to the counter" the lying propaganda that it was falling apart, he proceeds to parody my letter, and ask if he may now assume that Governors are ready to give assurances. I shall probably ignore the letter – Rao says that my letter has very much strengthened my position. The curious thing is that this answer has been sent without Kh. going to Wardha. I do not believe that these people mean to accept office.

I have just been asked to become a Knight of Grace of the Order of St. John – a compliment, but an expensive one!

A SOFT QUESTION AND A HARD KNOCK

HIS EXCELLENCY SIR HYDE Gowan was responsible for a pleasant surprise when he instructed his Secretary to write to Dr. Khare suggesting that the latter should see him if his party had decided in favour of acceptance of office. The invitation was the sequel to the resolution of no-confidence against the Ministry which had been forwarded to the Governor by Dr. Khare. The language in which His Excellency has extended the invitation for an interview is definitely friendly.

* * * * * The position taken up by the Governor from the constitutional point of view, is logical, as a motion of no-confidence in a parliamentary democracy connotes the desire of the Opposition to be the alternative government. A soft question like the one put by the Governor to the leader of the Congress party has been met by a rebuff which in its unceremonious character is hardly worthy of the Congress. Dr. Khare seems to have imagined that the letter was an attempt on the part of the Governor to pull his leg. * * * * *

* * * We think Dr. Khare missed a valuable opportunity to solve the present deadlock when he thus abruptly banged the door against negotiations * * * *

* * We are sorry that Dr. Khare in a fit of thoughtless haste refused to shake the friendly hand extended by the Governor. * * * *

* * * * * Whether or not the strings of provincial politics continue to remain in the hands of one individual, the answer given by Dr. Khare to the Governor was most unfortunate. It does not matter who writes or inspires a letter as long as its terms are honourable and its end is constructive and not mischievous. There can be no doubt at all that local Congressmen are hankering after office. Some of them are terribly disappointed at the prospect of office acceptance receding as a consequence of Mr Nehru's angry thunders in Calcutta and Chittagong. When the heart of the local Congress is set on office acceptance, there is no point in putting on a brave show about assurances. The only answer to the Governor's letter should have been the purchase of a railway ticket by Dr. Khare for Wardha. Wardha would have given a more conciliatory answer to the question put by His Excellency Sir Hyde Gowan,

Monday June 21st

See the Hit. on the subject of Kh.'s answer.

As I said to H.E., commenting on the incident, how can one be expected to maintain "direct contact" with people like this. The only possible form of d.c. would be a straight left to the mark!

Wed June 23rd

The Statesman approves.

We decided to ignore Kh.'s letter. Rao says that Congressmen themselves disapprove of Kh.'s answer, and that he has done himself a lot of harm.

H.E.'s message to India appeared this morning. It might have been shortened with advantage; but it's very clear and tells Congress exactly where they get off – or get on! After this these can be no excuse for misunderstandings. The W.C. is meeting on the 5th, and then at last they must come to a decision.

COURTEOUSLY and with quiet emphasis on the essential the Governor of the Central Provinces has dealt with the resolution of no-confidence in the present Ministers that several members of the Assembly have put in. The resolution, he suggests in a letter to the leader of the Congress party in the province, shows that after reflection the majority party now desires the present Ministry, based on minority groups. to demit office in its favour. If so, the Governor announces himself to be ready at any time to give Dr. Khare a personal interview on the subject of his acceptance of office. The door is not bolted nor banged nor shut. It is now Dr. Khare's turn to answer. The Governor of the Central Provinces is as far as is known the first Governor to reopen the negotiations with the Congress leaders. We wish both sides all success, and feel sure that they will earnestly seek agreement.

Supposing that they refuse office, I believe there's just a chance that Rao may obtain a majority. Anyhow I'm not going to resign myself to §93 until I'm quite sure that the Minority Ministry cannot by any possibility carry on. We shall meet on the 7th to decide finally.

"The rain it raineth every day". And the mushrooms are growing. We had our first dish this morning, mostly the gift of the Hemeons. It is very pleasing when people show they appreciate one's hospitality by little things like that.

Friday June 25th

English as she is spoke – "If Congress again funks taking office, it will find itself in the devil of a soup."! – my hon. Colleague, "Dr." Rao. About as good as – "We cannot get more savings even by cheesing and paring". Deshmukh, F.S.

These present trials seem to be upsetting everybody. Waterfall, usually the most level-headed of people, came to me specially this morning to complain about a note which Rao had written criticising him. The case was one of discipline. A young Indian had been told by his Commr. that he ought to call on a certain officer. He, full of his own importance, & appealed to the L.G.. Rao (as H.M.H. before 1.4.37) had backed him; but recognising that it was a Service matter had very fairly left it to Burton and me to decide, and we had told the lad quite mildly that he must obey orders. Now he appeals to the S/S, and Rao as Chief Minister calls attention to his note as H.M.H. & says he still holds to the same view. Without consulting me as he should have done (the case coming under my special responsibilities), W. puts up a draft repeating the G. in C.'s views, & ignoring H.C.M.'s; and then is surprised when the H.C.M. tells him, plainly but politely, that it is not the business of Secs. to behave as though the late constitution was still in being. (And W. had made his case worse by including in the draft a para. about a point which Rao had said specifically need not be mentioned.) It took me two hours to convince him that he'd not marched with the times & that Rao was right – also that he'd overlooked the fact that there was a strong racial element in the case & it behoved him to be doubly careful and walk warily.

Wed June 30th

According to a leader in the D.N., which is very caustic on the subject, someone has been writing to the papers from Pach. and from Chanda

(H.M.A.'s district), suggesting that there should be a coalition ministry, including Rao and Dharm Rao. "Why not" says Chanda, "close up their ranks by winning over these Ministers and bang the door in the face of the Governor?" The suggestion is that Dharm Rao is responsible for the letters at Rao's instigation. Considering all Rao has been saying about the Congress, I do not believe the latter half – nor the former, because D.R. is not the type. But one never knows. And, of course, even with Rao one can never forget his early days in Bilaspur, and he has recently shown an increasing bitterness towards European – witness his difficulties with the C.J. and his remarks about Greenfield and Waterfall. Valuable as his work has been in many ways, and sound as many of his views are, I never feel quite sure of him. The Chanda man says – "He is really an ace in politics whose war strikes terror into the heart of the stoutest civilian. Practically, he alone ruled the Province with justice and fairness during the past 5 years." The D.N. remarks – "What a compliment to Sir H.G.!" I'm afraid it doesn't realise that Sir H.G. has long ceased to set any value on any judgement of any inhabitant of this country. But every day he lives, he dislikes more & more the position into which Governors have been forced under the new constitution. They should have installed a completely new set.

I view with great misgiving the recent happenings in Spain, where Germany and Italy have withdrawn from the Naval arrangement. As usual, our F.O. seems to pile up for us enemies by its blundering tactics – Italy for the sake of "that foul race the Abyssinians" as a British Cabinet Minister once described them to Christopher; and now Germany for the sake of the Spanish Reds, who are, I suppose, the worst set of scallywags and cut-throats to be found in Europe. I simply cannot conceive how anyone except a Glasgow M.P. can wish them to win. And it's pretty clear that they're not and that as usual we shall have burnt our fingers for nothing.

CHAPTER 11

1937
JULY - DECEMBER

Friday July 2nd 1937

A surprise. Yesterday morning H.E. wired that Erskine's interview with R.C. had been very disappointing. It seemed to consist of still more of futile wrangle about conditions and formulas, and to be definitely discouraging in fact to pretty well put the lid on office acceptance. Then in the afternoon I got a note from Rao, saying that the reception of the message in Nagpur had been most favourable; that all the Congress leaders wanted to accept office; that the Bosses thought the same way and Nehru would give in; and that Khare "might" call on me about the 20th. That's a very different tune. But Khare will have to ask for his interview, and I'll believe in his coming when I see him in the doorway.

This is the sort of people we have to deal with. Misra (D.P.) is going to be run in criminally for abducting a minor Mahommedan girl, and Govind Das will probably join him in the dock, as the girl is said to have been kept in his house for a time. "An unsavoury pair", as I told the S/S a short time ago. And these are the leaders of Indian political life. At the time of the C.D. movement Monty told me it was notorious that G.D. and M. were homosexuals, & he chuckled over having them sent to separate jails, and the howl they raised.

Nagpur. Wednesday July 7th

Wardha is in full session over office acceptance, and the talking is endless. Yesterday I received a report containing the information from 3 different sources. One said that Nehru would give in, and office would be accepted; the second that Gandhi was drafting a formula which would satisfy everyone, on the lines of Government undertaking not to interfere with the Congress Programme (hopeless, of course); and the third that Ministers would have to give an assurance that they would reduce land revenue by 50%, abolish Excise, and wreck the Constitution. Another lamentable exhibition of divided counsel and indecision. As Rao says, the W.C.'s sole object is to preserve the unity of the party at whatever cost – a unity the precariousness of which is a byword in all political circles.

Rao laughs at the notion of his having inspired the idea of the "coalition Ministry". The letters were the work of one Pundlik, a tame pleader who acts as Dharm Rao's jackal, and writes this sort of stuff in order to keep in D.R.'s good graces. The country abounds with men of that type – hangers-on and lick-spittles.

Fawcus, late D.P.I. of Bihar and first President of our P.S.C. is staying with me. I think we've got a good man for the job. He told me with glee that Khaparde's first suggestion to him was that all applications should come before the Commission with the recommendation of the Local Govt. on them. In other words, instead of the L.G. taking the people recommended to it by the P.S.C., the P.S.C. should take the people recommended by the L.G.! A typical example of the working of an M.B.'s brain, that involuted organ.

Thursday July 8th

A decision at last! Late yesterday evening the W.C. issued a resolution which, boiled down, simply means that Congress will accept office unconditionally. The resolution starts by saying that the S/S's, and H.H.'s statements fall short of the Congress demands, and that the relationship between England and India is not a partnership but one of exploiter and exploited (the true Communist tang). It goes on to say that as it won't be easy for the Governors to use their special powers, and as everyone is clamouring for office, it may be accepted. But it must be utilised for the avowed purposes of Congress "combating" the Act ("wrecking" was suggested, I hear, but rejected) and carrying out the constructive programme laid down. And they've woken up at last to the fact that it was time they did something, and have said that they see danger in waiting to refer the matter to the A.I.C.C.. Round 1 definitely to us. Stripped of verbiage, the resolution gives local leaders "carte blanche" which they should have been given in March.

Rao came to see me this morning and asked me what my reaction was, and whether I wished him to resign at once. He seemed willing to do so, and said that Congress ought to have as long as possible to deal with the budget. He had not consulted his colleagues, however, and I told him (i) that I felt no obligation for precipitancy, in view of the way in which Khare had treated my overture of last month, and (ii) that I would like him to consult his colleagues, and let me know whether they wished to resign at once, or to await the meeting of the Assembly, which we decided yesterday should be on the 30th. Personally I prefer the latter course, but I can quite understand his preferring not to face a no-confidence motion.

EXTRACT FROM THE DAILY NEWS OF NAGPUR 10th. July, 1937.

DEADLOCK ENDS

His Excellency Sir Hyde Gowan deserves to be congratulated on his promptness in inviting the leader of the Congress Party to form a ministry. We are also glad that our interim ministers have tendered their resignations. Dr. Khare had a long interview with His Excellency this morning and undertook the formation of the Ministry. It has been decided that the Congress Ministry should be composed of seven members, including a Moslem. We welcome the decision to include a Moslem in the Cabinet but we do not think that a small province like ours needs seven Ministers. There is not work enough even for four Ministers and an unwieldy Cabinet, as Britain's experience has shown, leads to dilatoriness and delay. We realise that the Congress Ministers will vote themselves reduced salaries but this does not justify almost cent per cent increase in the numerical strength of the Ministry. We thought yesterday that Madras would steal a march over us but ours is the first province in India to end the deadlock. A new chapter alike in the history of the province and the Congress is opening and let us hope that it will be filled with events which will redound to the credit of everyone concerned in the great adventure. Our hearty congratulations to Dr. Khare and his Cabinet colleagues.

[The Daily News (Nagpur), 10th July 1937.]

Sunday July 11th.

Matters have come to a head quickly. Rao told me on Friday that they wanted to resign at once, and that he knew Khare was ready to be sent for. So I wrote to Kh., and he came and saw me yesterday, all smiles and pleasantness. He said just what he might have said in March, that he would form a Ministry. No word of assurances. He wanted seven Ministers, because, as he said, he'd got to satisfy three provinces, (Mahakoshal, Maharashtra and Berar) and the Mahommedans; also he wanted to give as many people administrative experience as possible. That sort of matter has got to find its own level, so I raised no objection. The seven are to be Khare, Shukla, Mehta Gole, R.M. Deshmukh and that nasty little man D.P. Misra, who has just narrowly escaped a prosecution for abducting a minor. The Mahommedan will probably be Sharif, who seems to have ratted definitely. Bar Misra, it isn't too bad a team, and Deshmukh and Sharif both know the ropes. They're to take office on Wednesday. There is an interesting comment on the accusation levelled against us, that our administration is top-heavy. Under Sec. 93 I should have run the province on 2 Financial Commrs. minus my Governor's Sec. – cost Rs. 7,000/- less 2,000/- equals 5,000/- p.m. Congress are going to run it on 7 Ministers on Rs. 1,100/- each, equals Rs. 7,700/- ! And after persistently attacking Govt. for giving allowances to its servants, the first thing it does is (a) vote itself 600/- p.m. a head for "house and motor"! More than double what we should have given for the purpose. What a land of make-believe it is!

Tuesday July 13th

The last meeting of the Minority Ministry, held while the heavens wept copiously. They've done well. As H.E. said in a private letter, amongst ourselves we may acknowledge that it's a complete win for us. And the way things have turned out is all to the good. We have got the new machine running smoothly, we know the feel of the controls, and it's going to be much harder for the wild men to upset it than it would have been in April. They, on the other hand, have been scrapping among themselves, and are desperately afraid of falling to pieces, and therefore more likely to behave themselves.

Thursday July 15th

I swore the new Ministry in yesterday. Sharif was in khaddar from head to foot. I should have loved to congratulate him on the speed of his tailor! They grinned affably, and shook hands. (Misra looks an awful little worm.) It is said that Gandhi has told them to be good boys for three years. We shall see.

Saturday July 17th

The first sign of the cloven hoof. Misra (L.S.G.) has sent for some nominations for local bodies that the late Ministry made, because he wants to reconsider them. I have asked if I have power to allow them to be reconsidered, as the orders have already left the Sectt.. Sharif came and saw me this morning, and I did congratulate him on his tailor. He laughed, and said he was turning out a suit a day. I gather from him that Congress are going to run straight as regards finance, and are examining the possibilities of a surcharge on agricultural incomes and a tax on sales – both sound propositions. I told Sh. that the province could never say it was making proper use of its resources unless it introduced a tobacco tax. He talked the usual twaddle about taxing the only luxury of the poor, till I showed him that it wouldn't make the slightest difference to the smoker – or nothing that he could notice.

I am told that they are thinking of asking that meetings of Govt. should be held in the Sectt., so as to lower my prestige in the eyes of people in general, and of Govt. servants in particular – a typically Indian trick. Is it surprising that one gets pretty sick of dealing with such people? Also that there are going to be four Council Secs. on 300/- each, purely in order to make jobs. The Congress Ministry will now be definitely more expensive than its predecessor. So much for Congress economies. They're all "an eyewash", as Indian editors say.

A cable from the S/S conveying the thanks of the Cabinet to H.E. and the Governors for the way the "most delicate" situation has been handled. Also a letter from Rab Butler, very appreciative.

Note:

At this point, having achieved his major objective, Sir Hyde decided to start his resignation process and wrote to The Viceroy, Lord Linlithgow

Copy of letter from Sir Hyde tendering his resignation.

```
To: Lord Linlithgow
17th July 1937
Viceroy's Camp.
India


Dear Lord Linlithgow,


Now that the crisis is over, and matters may be
expected, barring accidents, to run a normal course
for the next few months, I am writing to make a
request which has been forming in my mind for some
time.  In the usual way my term of office expires in
Sept. '38; but unless Your Excellency sees serious
objection, what I should like to do would be to go
at the end of April; that is about 4 or 5 months
prematurely.  I have several reasons for this desire,
but need only trouble you with two.  The first is of
```

a public nature. In April next I shall be near my 60th birthday, and shall have served for 35½ years in a province which has no real hill station. (You may remember that Kipling once called the C.P. "a place where they ride in bullock-carts and call Pachmarhi a hill-station"). This is the day of the younger men, and I feel that by the end of the cold weather it will be quite time for me to hand over my charge to someone not quite so long in the tooth.

These changes of constitution, inevitable and proper as they are, involve a "tour de force" to one's whole outlook, and I confess to finding this last one - the third I have been through — somewhat tiring. And then again my wife and I have had six deaths in our immediate family circles during the past two years. One carries on, but they rather take the heart out of one.

The second reason is of a private nature. Owing to the demands of our family, my wife has had to spend a great deal of her time in England and for the past 22 years our life has been a continual series of separations. We are tired of them, and I don't want any more. On the other hand, I do not want her to stay out beyond April, as she gets knocked up by the heat, and, like all of us, feels it more every year. The only solution is that we should go home before it gets really hot.

I have written now, so as to give plenty of time for the choice of my successor, who will presumably want preliminary leave and also because for private reasons it would be of great advantage to me to make my own plans as far ahead as possible. I should be very grateful if you would let me know whether you see any objection to my proposal. After 35½ years I

```
don't think I can fairly be accused of "not staying
the course"!

Yours sincerely,
sg. H.G.
```

Tuesday July 20th

I gave out 225 Coronation medals this morning, all placed fairly on the breast, with a handshake to follow. Julius said it would take at least an hour. It took 18 minutes! Staff work good, just like a machine!

Gole is starting to interfere with land revenue collections in Berar, a dangerous precedent. Fortunately there is little at stake in the present case, but I've told F.D. to keep an eye open for further developments.

Wednesday July 21st

Khare made tentative enquiries from Bannerji as to intercourse between me and the Ministers. He seemed afraid that if the Ministers came and called on me I might embarrass them by asking them to some social function, when they would have to refuse. He need have had no such fear. The Faizpur resolution is on the paper, and until it is deleted I have not the slightest intention of making any move towards social intercourse. I told B. that I would gladly see any of the Ministers who liked to come and see me in my office, and that I should certainly not embarrass them as above. Kh. came and saw me today, and discussed matters in general. He wants, of course, to release political prisoners and refund forfeited securities. We are to discuss the matter on Saturday. The Ministry are evidently not finding matters easy. They don't want the budget session till Sept.

Khare has come up against another of my special responsibilities by objecting to the confirmation of the Director, Veterinary Services, an I.V.S. officer whom we are bound to confirm unless there is good reason to the contrary. But I think it means that it's merely because he misunderstands the position, which I am explaining to him.

Thursday July 22nd

Sorabji Mehta told me this morning that the D.N. will probably demise in a day or two. No loss. He told me the strange tale that Rao gave him a cheque for Rs. 5,000/- to help keep the paper going, but he can't get it cashed! And another – the Cawnpore Chemicals people bought the old Kampti Distillery and wanted to start a branch, with a capital of 5 lakhs, of which 1½ lakhs were to be raised locally. Sorabji and a few others put up 80,000/- but people like the Chitravises, Ghatate, Buti and others who are rolling in money would not do a thing to help. As I've told them often, there would be quite a lot of employment for their sons if the local holders of the money-bags would use their money, instead of burying it or doing sahukari only.

Sharif is taking to interfering with the law. Yesterday he let off a murderer, simply because the motive was unknown – let him off hanging, that is. Today he has let off another ruffian who has only served half his sentence for hitting another man over the head in a temper.

Friday July 2rd

Mehta and Shukla both came to see me this morning, and talked about their depts.. Shukla has a scheme for making primary education pay for itself by making every malguzar put aside 20 acres for the maintenance of the schoolmaster. All right, so long as you don't remit the land revenue on the land! Mehta is a sound man, and will probably look after the F.D all right. Shukla has taken to flying the Congress flag outside his house, but we can't object to that. Flying it on Govt. public buildings is to be stopped at once.

Monday July 26th

The Council met on Sat. and decided to release the few political prisoners we have. I could not possibly hold that any of them constituted a menace to the peace of the province. A more difficult matter was the refund of securities forfeited from newspapers, as one – the Maharashtra's – had been forfeited for a series of scurrilous articles against the Nizam's Govt.. But I wired to the Resident, and he has replied that he's no objection. Misra turned up 10 minutes late. I took no notice, but ignored him, and when he tried to butt into the discussion he "failed to get the Speaker's eye", and no one else seemed anxious to hear him either. The Oriental usually runs true to form in these matters. Lateness on such an occasion is intended to show one's superiority.

"The rain it raineth every day", and unless we're lucky we shall have another cotton crop spoilt. Gole (H.M.R.) tells me that the Akola Central Bank, of which he is Chairman, could make no profit last year out of cultivating lands which it had taken over for debt, although it put experts on the job.

Reply from H.E. the Viceroy to Sir Hyde's request for Resignation

Viceroy's Camp.   26th. July 1937
India.

My dear Hyde Gowan,

I need not say how very sorry I was to get your letter telling me that you were anxious to hand over early next spring. I would like, if I may, to wait for a few days longer before I send you a definite answer; but if I ask you for this further time in which to think over the situation, you will not for a moment imagine that I do not fully realise the reasons for which you are anxious to go home, or the force of the arguments which you advance.

Yours sincerely,
Linlithgow.

Wednesday July 28th

Khare and Sharif came and saw me yesterday. First they asked for my views on the release of the two men who were convicted for murder in the communal riots of 1927. I told them that no S.R. of mine was involved, and that they must take all the responsibility. (I learnt afterwards that they had had a disagreement about the release.) I went on to tell them that these two men were common, cold-blooded murderers who could not say that they had done the deed in the heat of passion, and that they (the Ministers) would be very ill-advised to start tampering with the law.

Then Sharif wanted to know whether he should go and see the C.J., or the C.J. him, when they had a case to discuss. Easy. The C.J. is senior to the Ministers in the W.P.. Sharif said "someone had told him" that the W.P. only governed social matters! Easy again. From the way he grinned it was plainly a try-on.

Next they asked about Hon. Mags., the appointment of whom they said, of course, had been a scandal under Rao's regime. I told them that that was a matter for which they were entirely responsible.

Then came the main thing. "Would it be possible to have a flag salutation in the Assembly Hall compound on the 30th (opening day)? It would only be a very little ceremony – with a very little flag – and in the very farthest corner of the compound"!! Anyone who knows the East can imagine the way the request was made. I pointed to the flagstaff on the lawn outside my office, and said that "public buildings" included their compounds, were Government property and that no flag but a Union Jack could be flown on, or in the precincts of, a public building belonging to Govt.. They were quite nice about it, and said they did not wish to press the matter.

H.E has sent us, to be delivered by hand, a personal letter to be delivered to Gandhi, so he evidently intends to see him.

Thurs July 29th

More about flags. Shukla ordered Kochar (E.E.) to build him a lordly flag-post in his compound. K. said "Get the money from the Governor". The Commr. sent the case to me, asking what he should do. I sent for Shukla, and explained to him that only certain persons were permitted to fly flags – vide orders of the G/I – and only such persons could have flag-poles built for them at the public expense. Check. I also pointed out to him how very undesirable it was that this delicate flag question should be raised on a single individual without the general consent and approval of the Ministry. Mate. He said he didn't wish to press the proposal, and if the Ministers wanted to take the question up they would do so as a whole and after due deliberation.

Sharif has let another murderer off hanging; a young Mahommedan who hacked his wife to death. S. said he suspected her of unfaithfulness, though the High Court had definitely rejected that plea. On the other hand Gole has refused to be hustled over remissions of revenue, and before there is any general lowering they are going to appoint a Committee to examine the whole matter.

Friday July 30th

The local Congressmen met yesterday, and heard Patel's ukase that (i) The Ministers allowances are to be reduced from 600/- to 250/-. (ii) The Speaker is to get nothing outside his 500/- pay, & the Dy. Speaker

4. It may be useful to summarise briefly the development in the attitude of Congress in the last year. Its election manifesto was issued in August 1936. This stated the necessity of independence from British control as the pre-requisite for national regeneration: affirmed opposition to India's participation in war dictated by British Imperialists: defined the purpose of sending Congressmen to the legislatures as the combating and ending of the new Constitution: and declared that in the legislatures and outside they would seek to strengthen the people and develop the conditions essential for freedom. The detailed programme included the abolition of all "repressive" legislation, the release of "political" prisoners, reform of land tenure, relief of indebtedness, great improvements in the lot of industrial labour, civic equality for the humblest communities, and sweeping reforms in prison administration. Also absolute hostility to the introduction of Federation was affirmed.

At the annual session at Faizpur in December the determination to combat and end the new Constitution was reaffirmed: the election manifesto was endorsed and Congressmen exhorted to demand, inside and outside the legislatures, the summoning of a "Constituent Assembly" for the framing of an acceptable constitution.

In February of this year, immediately after the general election, the aims of Congress were repeated at a meeting of the Working Committee: and stress was laid on the necessity for contact and discipline in the organisation from the villages upwards. Then followed the All-India Congress Committee meeting at Delhi, which on the 18th March passed the notorious resolution permitting the acceptance of office in Provinces where the Congress commands a majority, provided each leader was satisfied and could state publicly that the *Governor would not use his special powers of interference or set aside the advice of Ministers in regard to constitutional activities.*

Immediately after, a "Convention" of provincial legislators and others met and a solemn oath was taken to work for the independence of India and the furtherance of Congress aims.

At Allahabad towards the end of April the Working Committee approved the refusal of office that had followed on the Delhi decision. Though its resolution proceeded to explain what that decision did and did not mean, the result was to leave its terms unchanged. The next development was the Wardha *volte face* of July 7th. Lest however that should be interpreted as an acceptance of the Constitution, the resolution referred to the relation of Britain and India as that of "exploiter and exploited": and explicitly affirmed that office was to be accepted for the purpose of combating the Act, and prosecuting the programme of the election manifesto.

5. No audible voice has been raised for the summoning of the full All-India Congress Committee to endorse the Working Committee's decision. It has been acclaimed by all sections of Congress except the extreme left. In accordance with it the minority Ministries in the six Provinces in which Congress are in a majority in the legislatures are vanishing from the scene and Ministries are being formed by the Congress leaders. The public spirit shown by those who formed the minority Ministries, the good work done by them, and the value of this interlude for the emergence of wiser counsels are recognised by sober opinion. But the professed determination of the new Ministries to combat the Constitution; the difficulty of conversion in a moment, from long and determined intransigence, to the exercise of authority; the impracticability of some of the election promises; the possibility of left wing pressure; the retention of control at the Congress Centre over the actions of each provincial Ministry – these are disturbing circumstances which have to be set against the undoubted gain of the moment in hope and good-will.

no pay. (iii) members are to get no pay only d.a. of 7/8 as now, & t.a. according to class actually travelled. There was such a lot of squabbling that they did not get to what some of them intended to do – propose a vote of no-confidence in Khare as leader.

This month's "appreciation" which we send to the Dominions contains an interesting summary of Congress' attitude.

Friday July 30th

The various assemblies are being opened to the accompaniment of processions, crowded galleries, singing of "Bande Mataram" and flag salutations – in fact all the usual signs of rejoicing – which bear eloquent testimony to the value of the new constitution, and the realization by the people of the power which it confers. People don't make such a Hallelujah Chorus over something which is valueless.

Further Reply from H.E. the Viceroy to Sir Hyde's request for resignation.

Camp Shillong.
28th July 1937.

My dear Hyde Gowan,

I wrote to you a couple of days ago to say that I was turning over in my mind your request to be allowed to retire in the spring of next year and that I would write to you again in the very near future regarding it.

2. Now this is a matter on which as you know I shall not feel justified in pressing you beyond a point, and as I mentioned in my previous letter, I fully appreciate the force of the considerations which have led you to your present conclusion. If therefore after reading what I have to say in this letter you remain clear and definite in your own mind

that you would not be justified in staying on for even a short further period, I will of course be guided by you and will not press you to do so. But the proposal I would like to put to you is one which would I think to some extent meet the points which you raise, and which certainly, if you find yourself able to accept it, would be a source of very keen satisfaction to me as well as to the Secretary of State, and would leave me with a feeling of entire confidence as to the manner in which the affairs of the Central Provinces would be conducted over a period which is likely in many ways to be one of great importance. Briefly what I would like to suggest is that you should resign as you suggest early next spring or summer, that you should then proceed on leave without pay for four months or thereabouts, a substitute appointment being made in your place during the period of absence, and that at the end of your leave you should again be reappointed for say two years. The simplest thing would of course be merely to extend your period; but were we to do so, you would not become eligible for further leave, and as it is quite clear that it is of real importance to you to be able to go home in the fairly near future, the suggestion which I have made is I think the most satisfactory way of combining the two objects of giving you your leave and of making it, I would hope, easier for you to accept a further period of service. I do not see any reason why we should not in the event of your feeling able to accept this offer make it clear at the time that you had been good enough to indicate your readiness to serve for a further brief period as Governor of the Central Provinces, but that equally you had made it clear that you would not be prepared to retain that post

```
for more than two years at the outside.
     3.Let me repeat that I have no desire in any
way to tie your hands or to bring improper pressure
to bear upon you.  But I hope very much in to
interests of the public service that you may feel
able to consider an arrangement such as that I now
suggest.

Yours sincerely
Linlithgow
```

Note by TJG. Looking back from 2014 this seems a little ungenerous in that Sir Hyde was offered unpaid leave after nearly 36 years' service and then a further 2 years' service in India without any mention of any extra leave entitlement. However, Sir Hyde took it as a considerable vote of confidence and his thoughts are below in Monday August 2nd.

Saturday July 31st

The opening of our Assembly yesterday was a dreadful show. There was a large crowd, which swarmed in to the galleries, packing them tight, and even bursting into the Hall. There was so much noise that the taking of the oath by the members would scarcely be heard. The ex-Ministers were hissed and boo-ed in the most disgraceful way, and the temporary speaker – fat old Hifizat Ali – made no move to protect them until Rizvi got up and made a dignified protest, whereupon Khare did the same and H.A. at last said he'd clear the galleries if the noise did not stop. A bad omen for the new regime. I had an example of how people's estimates of crowds vary. Bannerji, in a somewhat shaky voice told me over the phone that there were a crowd of 7,000 in and around the building, adding that they were quite good tempered and cheerful. Hemeon (L.R.), an Irishman, told me as a great joke that there were 10,000 there & they'd been swarming all about his room and offices.

In the evening I was golfing with a real Scot, Moir of the Allahabad Bank who lives just opposite the Hall, & had watched all the proceedings. "Well", he said "that show this afternoon was a pretty good flop. A procession 100 yds. long led by a man on a tat, and they didn't seem to know how to cheer. About 300 people inside the railings and 600 in the road." He couldn't, of course, see the crush inside but I gather that his estimate was not far wrong.

Sharif has refused to prosecute U.N. Thakur, Congress M.L.A., who, as Sec. of an Agrl. Assoc., used its funds for his own purposes for years, in spite of repeated requests to deposit them – the regular "main bis dafe bolá," business – and only did so (in instalments) when threatened directly with prosecution. Sharif's reasons – i. the money has been refunded. ii. the case has been hanging on too long. Something in that.

Monday August 2nd

They gave a "civic reception" to the Ministers in the Town Hall yesterday, "seating in Indian style", and asked various Govt. Officers, who appealed to me to know what to do. I said – "Do as you've always done. It's not an official invitation, and you can go or not, as you like. But if you want to go, find out first that you haven't got to sit on the floor." (As a matter of fact, they were given seats in the gallery.) It was an awful show – pandemonium, and McClenaghan (D.C.) said he thought some of the Ministers had been hurt. The scrum was so bad that they had to present the address in the compound outside, as the Hall was in hopeless confusion.

I have had a letter from H.E couched in the kindest terms, asking me if I would like to take 4 months rest next year & be reappointed for two years! "The proposal I would like to put to you is one .... which certainly if you find yourself able to accept it, would be a source of very keen satisfaction to me as well as to the S/S & leave me with a feeling of entire confidence as to the manner in which the affairs of the

C.P. would be conducted over a period which is likely in many ways to be one of great importance.......I hope very much in the interests of public service that you may be able to consider this arrangement.". And I have been brought up to believe that if a thing is asked of you "in the interests of the public service" you must do it without question. But it would break E.'s heart, and the V. also says – "I have no desire to tie your hands or to bring improper pressure to bear on you." Anyhow I must tell her before deciding finally, & get her to cable. At any rate I think I can feel that I haven't been a failure – I must add "as yet" because in these days one walks among pitfalls.

Wednesday August 4th

I wrote to E. and also to H.E. to tell him how grateful I am.

Yesterday had a long talk with Khare, who was pleasant as usual. There is dirty work going on over the Directorship of the Veterinary Service. Under the rules the appointment must go to Garewal, an I.V.S. officer, who is acting in it at present. But a provincial man who officiated in an emergency vacancy has been intriguing for the post and promising Congress that he will take less pay if he is given it. I shall stick to my guns, of course, and Khare showed pretty clearly that he did not intend to make a case of it.

A much more difficult situation is going to arise over the Bilaspur election. Kedar – "Bombastes Furioso" – brought an adjournment motion in the Assembly, and Khare promised to "enquire" into the way Govt. officers behaved. The Ministry has not decided what to do yet; but I warned Khare that the Services would look on the appointment of any Committee as an unsporting act of bullying. I also pointed out that Bhulabhai Desai had put the egregious enquiry which Kedar held after the election into the w.p.b.; that Agrihotri had filed his election petition at the 59th minute of the 11th hour (here Kh. interjected that he had written to A. and told him not to file it!); and that he then withdrew it because Congress wouldn't back him and refused to face the tribunal. This is likely to be a serious matter, but I cannot make up my mind in any way till I see what they propose. I'm pretty certain that Kh. isn't at all keen on an enquiry himself. Finally I asked Kh. if it was true, as had been reported to me, that Congress had ordered complaints against Govt. servants to be sent direct to the Ministry, and was setting enquiries on foot through its own agents about Hon. Mags., Public Prosecutors, and members of the Debt Conciliation Boards. He denied the lot, and said that all that had been done was to tell people to lay complaints before the Congress "Public Grievances Board", because they were often afraid to complain to officials. These complaints were to be investigated in the ordinary way. That's all to the good. The setting up of a parallel system is public danger No. 1.

Letter from Sir Hyde

```
Governor' Camp. Central Provinces.
4th. August 1937.
To:- H.E. the Viceroy.
```

Dear Lord Linlithgow,

I need hardly say how deeply grateful I am to Your Excellency and the Secretary of State for the offer which is conveyed to me in your letter of July 28th and how greatly I appreciate the terms in which it has been conveyed. Whatever my decision with regard to it may be, it will always be a great comfort to me to know that I have justified to some extent at any rate the trust which has been placed in me. You will understand that in a matter of this nature I must consult my wife before making up my own mind in any way, as her future happiness is very much involved in my decision. I am writing to her

by this Air Mail and asking her to cable her answer
according to a prearranged code. I hope to be able
to give Your Excellency a definite reply before the
middle of the month.

With renewed gratitude,
I am yours sincerely,
sg H.G.

Letter from the Viceroy.

7th August 1937.

My dear Hyde Gowan,
Many thanks for your secret and personal letter of
4th August. Let me say how very much I hope that your
decision in the light of Lady Gowan's views may be
favourable.

Yours sincerely,
sg. Linlithgow

Sunday August 8th

A meeting of the Council yesterday, very friendly. The Ministers asked
for time before coming to a decision about Garewal's fitness for
confirmation, and I had no option but to give them three months. It's
plain that they don't like Garewal personally. Nor do I, and we only
took him because we could get no one else.

Then we discussed a letter from H.E. about Ministers holding
directorships. They said they had discussed the matter already among
themselves, and I was glad to see that they are at any rate starting out to
be strict. Gole had refused the directorship of a Bombay bank, and

Khare had shut his practice down. This time the whole lot of them were punctual to the tick. I hope Misra has learnt his lesson.

I had a pleasant surprise in the post — a book called "North to the Orient", by Ann Lindbergh, and autographed by them both. Little remembrances like that, and the meeting with such people, are the really nice parts of my job.

The C. in C. was passing through and had to spend 2 hours in Nagpur Station, so we asked him and his staff to come and have tea with us and go for a walk, to break the monotony of the journey. He had had a dreadful crawl on the Vizianagram line, and was fed up with the train, and I think was really grateful for our thought. He's a very gaunt man & looks anything but fit, but he was very interesting and easy to talk to, in spite of the fact that I couldn't talk horse to him! In the evening we had a dinner and went to see "Romeo and Juliet" the first Shakespeare I've seen on the films. It was very good, the only jar being Norma Shearer's accent, which was shown up by the pleasant English voices of the rest of the company, especially Leslie Howard's. But she acted very well. It was delicious to hear some of the old lines again after not having read the play for many years.
"Would that I were a glove upon that hand"

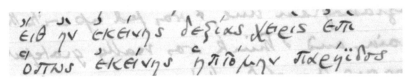

(I forget how the accents go). Pity one doesn't read more Shakespeare & the bible instead of this modern trash.

Wednesday August 11th

Ministers have come out into the open about honours, and the C.M. has written a minute saying they do not wish to be associated with the grant of them. Thank goodness. It would be a dreadful business if 7 Ministers were to submit recommendations, and the Commrs. and I can do quite well on our own.

Shukla has raised a difficult question. He is organising a fortnight's tour in the North, his object being to oust (i) Misra (ii) Khare, so I am told. He asked Owen (D.P.J.) to tell D.C.s to arrange his local programmes in consultation with the local Congress Secs.. D.C.s have never had to arrange Ministers' programmes before, and the first question is whether they should be made to, with 7 Ministers in the offing. The second question is – can they be told to work "in consultation with" a party organisation? I told Owen to refer Shukla to the Ch. S. and the Ch. S. to refer him to the C.M., who is in charge of general administration. If the C.M. passes the proposal, I shall them have to take the matter up as a Service question. Pitfalls seem to arrive almost daily.

When the new Ministry took office the first Special Branch report said – "There is nothing to report". The S.B had closed down on all its information, I said this would never do, and told Smyth (I.G) to make his D.I.G.s go round and <u>tell</u> their D.S.P.s without any circularising that they were to report exactly as before, but from a different angle. They must report what is actually said and done, but leave out all colouring-matter about seditiousness, anti-Govt. intent & so on. We at the top can supply all that. Reports are now normal, and so far the Ministers have said nothing. If they do, I shall have to say I must know what is going on; and I shall also point out to them that the day will almost certainly come when they themselves will be very glad to have these reports. I told H.E. & he says he agrees.

Cable from Lady Gowan, at Newby Bridge.

14th. August 1937

To: Sir Hyde. Governor C.P. Governor's Camp.

ADVISE REFUSAL BUT WILLING SUPPORT
WHATEVER YOU DECIDE.

EDNA.

Letter from Sir Hyde

To: The Viceroy   16th August 1937

Dear Lord Linlithgow,

I have now had a cablegram from my wife about the offer conveyed in Your Excellency's letter of July 28th. As I expected, she does not encourage me to accept it, though she says loyally that she will support any decision which I may make.

2. I must, therefore, make the decision for myself, and I am afraid that, greatly though I appreciate the offer my answer must be in the negative. When I first wrote to you, I told you that there were other reasons besides the two which I gave why I wished to go home in the spring. The chief of these is that my appointment as Governor involved my wife in a considerable sacrifice. She is devoted to her children and grandchildren, and when I was appointed Revenue Member in 1932 we looked forward to retiring in 1935, when we expected the new Constitution to start working. Since my appointment she has done her duty as the Governor's wife nobly,

as I think everyone will tell you. She has spent more than half of each year with me, and has devoted the whole of her working hours while out here to promoting various public schemes. But she is practically the same age as I am, and I simply cannot ask her to postpone any longer the retirement to which she has been looking forward, and which has already been postponed once, unless there are very strong public reasons for doing so.

3. As for that, I have thought over the matter earnestly and I honestly think that in asking to be allowed to go next spring I am doing what is right. I know that by the time I am 60 I shall have done my best work, and that if I were to stay on after that I should deteriorate, as I have seen other men do, both physically and mentally; and I cannot abide the thought. I want to go before I am past my best, and before men start saying of me:- "H.E. isn't what he was." Only recently I have had an example of what happens to men who stay too long in this country, in the death of my oldest friend in India, the late Bishop of Nagpur. It was not his death which was tragic so much as the mental and physical failing which preceded it, and which might have been avoided if he had left the country at the proper time, as I myself advised him to do.

4. And so, Your Excellency, although I am very grateful both to you and to the Secretary of State for the honour which you have done me in offering me an extension, I feel I must refuse it, and that I must abide by the request which I made in my original letter to you. I should like to thank you at the same time for the great consideration which you have shown me.

Yours sincerely,
sg. H.G.

Saturday August 14th

Khare and Misra both came to see me yesterday. Misra is a dreadful little worm, who speaks in a low husky voice that one can scarcely hear. He hadn't much to say, except that he was afraid I was prejudiced against him, and that he hoped I'd cut that out and give him a fair start. These Congress Ministers are amazing – they roar like any sucking-dove! Khare was more interesting. First of all he produced a draft of an appeal to the Services to make a voluntary cut in its pay, about which I told him I must consult the Viceroy. Incidentally I pointed out to him that to base an appeal which at the most would produce 12 to 14 lakhs on the poverty of the Indian masses was like asking for private subscriptions to finance a war. Then he asked me what I thought about making all officers with more than 25 years' service retire. It was easy to point out how uneconomical such a proposal is in any true sense of the term. Finally he asked me if I'd accept a present of khaddar, to which I said "With pleasure". Up it came this morning, a piece of heather mixture cotton and one of yellow Bengali silk. They look rather nice; but if one feels penitential and in need of sackcloth to wear, I can think of no better substitute. Possibly the dhobi may soften them. With them came a note, asking me to accept them, "in token of a new friendship". We are getting on, aren't we? I replied with cordial thanks, hoping that the gift would be "an omen of peace, goodwill and mutual trust". Wow, wow!

Monday August 16th

E. cabled yesterday, saying she advised refusal of the proposed extension, but would fall in with any decision I made. Great hearted lady! She'd spend the rest of her life in this country if she thought it her duty to. But I'm not going to make such a call upon her. I'm frankly tired of the country myself, & seeing all I have helped to build being pulled down. And I do not believe that anyone should stay on in this country after 60. As for the pomp and circumstance; I've had enough of it; and the little extra I should save financially isn't worth the loss of precious days in England. So I shall refuse.

The S/S and H.E. have set their foot down firmly on the proposal for the pay-cut. I wonder if that means trouble. The difficulty is that everyone knows that provincial and subordinate rates to be too high.

Thursday August 19th

Bannerji tells me that the Ministry are beginning to want to be asked to dinner. I said that if the want took definite shape, I would ask them without hesitation. H.E. rightly regards the establishment of personal contacts as of very great importance. Really one couldn't tell the difference between this Ministry and their predecessors, if it wasn't for their Gandhi caps and rather ramshackle clothes. At a meeting of the Council yesterday we started off with the budget – balanced and containing nothing new except a small extension of the no-liquor area, and a small provision for reducing excessive rents and revenue. Then the cold weather postings, about which they showed no sign of disagreement, but asked for a week to consider them. Then various ordinary cases, in one of which they insisted on backing stoutly our old policy of running the Forest Dept. for ourselves, without any vamps from Simla. They fell foul of the Viceroy's order that I am not to consult them (except informally) on the appointment of Judges to the High Court, and pressed for the setting up of a convention – but quite nicely, and they were satisfied when I promised to represent their view.

I had a little difficulty with Misra, who wanted to cut out a post of European Civil Surgeon. But I pointed out that the S/S was very unlikely to agree to any change & he didn't seem to be getting much sympathy. They agreed to a proposal of mine which avoided associating Congress officially with D.C.s in arranging Ministers' programmes on tour. Then came the adjournment motion for the Bilaspur enquiry & to my relief all that they pressed for was the appointment of a responsible officer of Govt. to enquire into the allegations actually made in the

Assembly. That I can't refuse though I must write to H.E. first. Finally came the cut in pay, and I had to tell them that the S/S had vetoed an appeal to individuals. They took it much better than I thought they would, and fortunately I was able to say that the question of an appeal to Service Associations had not been decided. There were no signs of a desire to force a crisis. If we could only get the provincial Ministries to break away from the hide-bound caucus of cranks at Wardha, half our task would be done. Gandhi has insisted on prohibition in three years in spite of great opposition, and when they come to working out the details of the scheme they may summon up their courage to rebel.

Friday August 20th

Manekji Dadabhoy, who came and saw me yesterday, told me that he was worried about Rao's future, now that he is out of office. He said that a man like him has very little chance of saving, because he actually has to pay salaries to his supporters – 25/-, 50/-, and 75/- p.m, according to their value! It shows what stuff politics are made of in this country. And of course Rao's election must have cost him goodness knows what. What a lot he'd have saved himself and everyone if he'd just stood quietly for the University seat, which he had in his pocket!

Geoffrey Burton has got to go home, a year's leave, which means that Roughton will act for him when he comes out in October. I've now got to think whom I shall recommend as my successor. Not R. at any price. Possibly B.; but I wonder if he's big enough. He's a terrible niggler.

Wed Aug 25th

H.E has accepted my wish to retire in April "with great regret", and has asked me to come up to Simla for a couple of days at the beginning of next month to discuss the affairs of the province & my successor. Every day I spend in this filthy climate, slopping round the expanse of mud and stone and coarse tufts of grass that we call a golf links, I wish I was in England. And no-one can say at the age of 60 I have no right to retire. I'm going to Jubb. at the beginning of next week, and shall go to Simla from there – a beastly nuisance as it means four nights in the train for 48 hours in the damp mists of Simla.

Letter from The Viceroy.

Viceregal Lodge. Simla.   19ᵗʰ/21ˢᵗ August 1937
To. Sir Hyde Gowan

My dear Hyde Gowan,

Many thanks for your secret and personal letter of 16ᵗʰ August. I need not say how greatly I regret your decision, but I fully accept the weight of the considerations which have led you to it. I shall communicate it to the Secretary of State who will, I know, regret it as much as I do.

    2. It would give me great pleasure if you found yourself able to pay me a short visit at the beginning of September. Would it, for instance, suit you to arrive here on the morning of Wednesday 8ᵗʰ September and to go away again on the evening of Friday 10ᵗʰ? If so, I need not say how delighted my wife and I would be to see you. There are many things I should welcome the opportunity of discussing with you in connection with your Province, and the matter of your own succession must, of course, be one of immediate importance.

Yours sincerely
sg. Linlithgow.

His Excellency Sir Hyde Gowan
K.C.S.I C.I.E.
Governor of the Central Provinces and Berar

Wednesday August 25th

I had a long talk with Khare yesterday. District Officers are getting very cross at the way they are treated by Ministers on tour. There is no intentional discourtesy, but Ministers go and stay in some squalid house in the middle of the basti, and then expect Europeans and decent Indian officers to call on them there, surrounded by National Scouts and the riff-raff that these people always attach to themselves. Khare was very decent about it, and said that it was partly due to Ministers' inexperience and partly to the enthusiasm of their supporters, that he quite realised that any be-izzating of the District Officers could not be allowed, and that he would talk to his colleagues and see it put right. I asked him about Pach., and he said the second season was definitely off, but that he himself hadn't spent a hot weather in Nagpur for 10 years, and he hoped none of his colleagues would want to stay here then. He then went on to say that he wanted to get Logan back to Nagpur, and to put him in charge of the scheme for a Medical College. Logan was the victim of a dirty intrigue by Naidu, to which somehow Khaparde seems to have been a party, and was made to go on leave while C.S. Nagpur, and sent to Amraoti on return. Now he has applied to go back to Military duty. He's a good man, and I nearly came to blows with the late Ministry over his case, but was powerless to do more than get him out of their way, to save him from persecution.

The unsavoury characters that one has to reckon with in this job seem endless. Bannerji told me yesterday that Brijlal Bizani – "the Hon. Mr.", member of the Council of State for Berar – goes everywhere with two Brahmin sisters named Oke (they married two brothers of that name). They say they're his secretaries, but everyone knows that they're his mistresses; and Bannerji quoted Gole (H.M.R.), who comes from the same town, as his authority.

Thurs Aug 26th

A meeting of the Council yesterday. I told them that the cut in pay was to be barred, and that the idea of appealing to associations was held to be as unfair as the appeal to individuals . They took it very well but asked somewhat pointedly whether they would be allowed to issue the appeal as individuals, and not as Ministers! I had to explain to them that in official matters they could only act as Ministers.

I then had to tackle Sharif, who had given out to the newspapers that he was releasing seven prisoners of the 1927 communal riots. The other Ministers rather jumped down his throat, I thought, and said that they wanted to see the case, & that meanwhile the news of their release must be contradicted. A short time ago Khare told the Newspapers that he was removing the ban on certain proscribed books. Unfortunately the ban had been imposed by Bo. and not by us. Kh. wanted to write and ask them to remove it quickly, as we had promised that it would be removed, & I had to point out that we couldn't lay ourselves so obviously open to a snub. These are all growing-pains, and they'll learn all right. The danger that I foresee is that these 500-rupee-wallahs are going to be too much at the mercy of their followers. They haven't the money to buy authority, as the old Ministers did.

Jubb. Thursday September 3rd

A change from Nagpur in the rains is very pleasant, and I wanted to see how the alterations to the Circuit House, which has now become G.H. were getting on. I'm having proper sanitation put in, and now Pach. G.H. will be the only house which still sticks to the horrible methods of the country. The water problem is the difficulty here.

Khare has gone back on his decision to appoint a Commr. to hold the Bilaspur enquiry, & now wants Subhedar, ex A.J.C. whom we refused to make a High Court Judge, & who therefore has a grudge against Rao with a serviceman and a Lawyer "to help him" – in other words a non-official committee. He also wants the C.I.D. to take the case up. I've told him I'll discuss the case with him when I get back.

Another move I dislike comes from Sharif, who wants to reform the whole machinery of Govt. – A.G. Govt Pleader, & all P.P.s! Abolish the lot & appoint new ones on the Congress scale of salaries. I've said "hands off the A.G. & put his case up separately. It is simply a case of American political methods, but is going to be a difficult one to handle.

The cat out of the bag with regard to prohibition. Gole has told the F.D. that the liquor revenue is to go, and that while it lasts it is to be spent on village uplift etc.. I have pointed out to Ministers that the last effort was a failure, but nothing that one can say will make an Indian obey reason when he's dug his toes in, and I have no hope they'll listen. A Mulish race.

Simla Tues Sept 7th

We got here yesterday morning, after a train journey up the Ganges valley which is the dullest I've ever known – dead flat country, without a hillock to relieve it. But I was much struck with the cultivation. No weeds, no half-cleaned fields with bushes and patches of grass in the middle. The crops look twice the size of ours at this stage, & far better tended. I've had two long talks with H.E. about this and that. To my astonishment, there seems some difficulty about my successor. I can't recommend Geoffrey B.. Gordon being out of the question because of his membership of the P.S.C.. I asked him his opinion and he said without any hesitation – "Honestly, he doesn't carry enough guns" – which fitted in exactly with my own opinion. That means a G/I man and H.E. says they're very short of good men at the moment. I gather from Laithwaite, his P.S., that he was somewhat surprised at my appearance of physical well-being. I told L. that had had nothing to do with my not wanting to stay on. It's a matter of the mind. I've had enough of it all, and I'm sick to the heart of living in the midst of unpleasantnesses. H.E. didn't press me in any way. He said "I see you have made up your mind, & that is enough for me." He struck me as having that admirable combination – a man who had a very pronounced mind of his own, & at the same time allows other people to have theirs, and doesn't try to force his upon him. In fact I was much struck with him. He is very easy to talk to; takes a thoroughly practical, common sense view of everything, infused with a distinct sense of humour, and is unquestionably strong. I liked her too – one of the biggest women I've ever seen with a fine pair of shoulders. I had a talk with her last night after dinner before she went to a ball, and she seemed bent on being nice.

But Simla, as a place to live in, seems to me more detestable than ever.

Nagpur Friday Sept 10th

Back again after two nights & a day in the train.

On Tuesday there was a large dinner in my honour, 73 guests, and before dinner H.E. invested me with the trappings of a "Knight of Grace of the Most Venerable Order of St. John of Jerusalem" – sounds a lot for putting Sleeman up and saying "Ji hán" to Wilson's plans for putting up an ambulance show! The real reason, I think, was that at Sleemanabad, 40 miles from Jubb. which was his grandfather's H.Q. against the thugs, they organised a guest reception, which pleased him immensely. They showed him a sacred fire which had been kept burning since his g.f. left. The malicious say, of course, that it had only been lit the day before. I don't know the truth. I met various old friends at the dinner, and altogether enjoyed it. I saw H.E again next morning before we went, and talked about the admittedly excessive pay of the higher grades in the Provincial and subordinate services. If we agree to their being lowered, it will open up a gap below the Imperial Services. Can we refuse to agree solely on that ground? I said "No". You can't refuse to right a wrong merely in order to protect vested interests. The latter must stand by themselves. It struck me that H.E. thought the same, though he didn't commit himself.

Wednesday September 15th

I forgot to mention that I met Lord Brabourne, Governor of Bombay, at Vice-regal Lodge on 6th. I had met him before I came out, at a dinner in London given by Sir Acbar Hydari. He is a charming man, and everyone in Bo. says how they'll miss him when he goes to Bengal. He told me he didn't want to go there in the least but it had been put to him in such a way by the S/S that, having his career in front of him, he couldn't very well refuse. We found out that we had both been going through the same experiences lately, & had both reacted in the same way to them, & had the same ideas about the crowd we've got to deal with.

If the Hindu has one characteristic, it is that the saying – "Spoken word plighteth troth", has no meaning for him. Khare is now being got at by his followers – some of them – not to come and dine with me on the 20th. At Bannerji's suggestion, I have written to him putting the party as a chance to talk over things we haven't time to talk about while the Assembly is sitting – silly camouflage, but just the sort of thing that attracts an Indian. At the same time I've given Bannerji clearly to understand that the Ministers confer no favour on me by coming to dine, and that if they have scruples about coming, they can d——d well stay away for all I care. I'm asking them solely from a sense of duty. Some of them don't even know how to use a knife and fork, and they'll probably belch and spit on my carpets. The trouble is the Marwari element among Congress followers. Shukla is hoping to detach them from Khare, and then oust Kh. from the P.M.'ship. And they in return are shoving Shukla to the left.

Friday September 17th

E. in her last letter, talking about Geoffrey B. said exactly what Eyre said about his not being a big enough man to be Governor. So I am more than ever fortified in my opinion.

Bannerji surprised me yesterday. He's had a volume of my speeches up to 31.3.37 prepared, and I said, "Why not wait till I go?", to which he replied that Govt. officers wanted them to refer to, and that he himself had already made his own private compilation. I seem to be in danger of becoming an authority!

Saturday September 18th

The Ministers have been havering to the last about coming to dinner, but it seems settled now. They referred the matter to Gandhi, and he, like a sport, said that as they'd accepted, they must come – the first really sensible thing he's said for a long time.

Chote Lal Verma, who rose from a post of 50/- to be a D.C., told me that he didn't know what to do with his pay. How can one oppose the demand for cuts with any conviction, when one knows that the higher posts in the provl. and subordinate services are grossly overpaid according to existing Indian standards?

Two things, one good, and one bad, have happened in the Assembly. In Assam they cut the establishments of Commrs. Here a motion for that purpose was withdrawn. Lucky, because, as I warned the Ministers, I should have had to use my special powers to restore the money. A Govt. servant's first right is the right to serve, and he can't do that unless he has his establishment. The bad thing is a ruling of the Speaker's – a typical piece of Hindu craftiness. The Act says that proceedings in the Assembly must be conducted in English, unless a member is insufficiently acquainted with that language, in which case he can speak in the vernacular. The Speaker has ruled that if a member starts speaking in the vernacular, he (the H.S.) assumes that he can't express his thoughts sufficiently well in English. The result has been that proceedings have degenerated into a sort of polyglot affair, which can't be reported properly, because there is no vernacular shorthand. Even the newspapers, while admitting that the ruling is "clever" – "chálák" is the word they should use – say that it is a bad one. As an interpretation of the Act it is, of course, beneath contempt. It's the sort of thing that makes the Englishman despise the Indian character. The same man is the man who eats with his fingers, and yet specially asked that he might be included in the dinner to the Ministers, though he is unable to conform to the manners of his host's house.

Tuesday September 21st

The dinner last night was a great success, I think. We sat at 5 tables of 8, the ministers being distributed and there seemed to be plenty of chat going on all the time. I had Khare and Mehta at my table. We gave the H.M.'s special food, in special dishes, and Mrs. Bannerji ran all that part of the dinner. Afterwards I talked to all the Ministers and the Speaker in turn. The only hitch was when Crawley A.D.C. who is not one of nature's bright stars, brought Shukla up first to me instead of Khare. Seeing that Sh. is intriguing might and main to oust Khare it was hardly a tactful thing to do! C. is one of those wooden headed, obstinate youths who get an idea fixed in their heads – in this case that as Khare had been at my table I should not want to talk to him – and follow that ignoring later orders. I had told him definitely to bring up every Minister. They were all very pleasant to talk to, and appear to me to be honestly doing their best to run the show properly, and keep the hotheads of their left wing in order.

Things are looking pretty grim in Europe. It's difficult to see what Italy is playing at, but I cannot believe that with Abyssinia only half pacified she intends to provoke us into war. The Viceroy seemed to think that it was a case of units of a new navy, away from their base getting out of hand and trying to see how far they can go. It is curious that since the Nyon Conference was summoned attacks on merchantmen have ceased. The thing that sickens me is that Englishmen should be forced into opposition and possibly conflict with the two men who, by reducing chaos to order in their respective countries, are largely responsible for such peace as exists in Europe at the moment. Say what you like about the two dictators, they've made orderly, self-respecting nations out of which might have been seething Communist stews. And Franco is in a fair way to making a third. And Pretty Boy Eden & his band of footling idealists have succeeded in antagonising every one of them, & tacking us on to these disorderly Frenchmen and murdering Russians. It is my firm opinion that our foreign policy of the last three years has been beneath the contempt of any man who isn't a mawkish muddle headed dreamer. They talk about "British ideals" when they refuse to recognise the Italian conquest of Abyssinia. From Britishers whose forbears conquered native peoples in most quarters of the globe, the hypocrisy of the thing is almost sickening. And anyhow what on earth is the use of not recognising facts, whether we like them or not. The way we've antagonised Italy & endangered our Mediterranean route is costing us millions of pounds in rearmament.

Sat Sept 25th

A letter from Phil Green, a very old friend writing from Hazlemere. "I find your name is much revered here for the fine way in which you spoke out to Congress, and gave the lead to all the other Governors. You know, I'm so used to the feeling that you always do speak out without fear or favour that it needs a jolt from outsiders to make me realise that it's a somewhat unusual virtue". I suppose one of these young things would say "Coo!" to that. One oughtn't to laugh, I suppose, at the idea of being revered in Hazlemere, but somehow it tickles me. Anyhow it's very nice of them.

We had a meeting of Govt. this morning – nothing very interesting except that the ministers announced their intention of coming up to Jubb. in November. Khare had a dig at Shukla. "I shall do my Northern tour then" – alluding to S.'s tour when he tried to get the whole of Mahakoshal to support him in his intrigue for the P.M.'ship. I'm glad to say that Khare shows no intention of throwing his hand in, as he was said to be going to do.

Sunday October 10th Pachmarhi.

I came here on the 28th, as I was fed up with the fetid atmosphere of Nagpur, and felt I must get away from the Ministers and have a little peace. Also because it's my last Lansdown Golf Week – rather shorn of its glory by the absence of the civilians, but still very pleasant. My garden is a joy – dahlias, roses, gladioli, tucenia, alamanders, red and blue salvias and even honeysuckle. Unfortunately the course is awful. Why will people try to be too clever? They said that they'd make "the rough" like an English course; so they forbade all grazing. The result – "the rough" is like a hayfield in June, and owing to the heavy monsoon they completely lost control of the fairway, which is like a lawn that hasn't ben mown for a month. We've hacked our way round till we've tired of it. I've a delightful house party – The Grigsons, Tuckers & Mildred Mackenzie-Mair (ex- Moberly). Various others have floated in and out – General Nicholson & the Coxes.

In the midst of this peace – not a sound at the moment except the roller on the tennis courts and a man clipping a hedge – I've been able to look at things from the outside. On the whole they're going as well as can be expected. The Ministers are slowly putting a stop to the abuse of Govt. servants, and the latter are getting less jumpy. The difficulty is that the Ministry itself is full of dissensions, and cannot act with determination. Also, the Congress tail has an unpleasant habit of wagging the dog, and when the sober members like Mehta and Gole tell the party that they can't go playing ducks and drakes with the revenue, the latter insist on electioneering promises being implemented. Just what I warned them of in my last address to the old Council their sins are coming home to roost. Misra is the snake that I've got to keep an eye on. A month ago an article appeared in the Hit., saying he was going to make D.C.s and D.S.P.s the servants of local bodies, which were going to be given charge of various branches of the administration. (Imagine extending the powers of such dreadful organisms as our local bodies!) I asked about this, and was assured he had no such idea. What he was after was to make the D.C. more or less the master of the District Council (H'm.) – like the official Municipal Commissioners of Bombay and Calcutta. Quite recently I've seen letters written to Nehru and Bose, which independently confirm the newspaper report. Of course I shall have to stamp on the first sign of such a plan being hatched, and it's lucky I've been forewarned.

The other day – the 6th – I received a note saying that Khare wanted a meeting of Govt. on the 11th and Bannerji said he felt I ought to attend as the subjects to be discussed were "very important". When I looked at the files I found that not one of the serious ones had even reached the stage of discussion of policy, so I gently rode Kh. off any Council discussion of them before they were ripe. (Monty always used to stress the futility of Cabinet discussions of matters which had not been reduced to the state of concrete proposals for orders.) A note has just come shows that these have been cut out of the agenda. But they show which way the Ministerial minds are working – reduction of districts and tahsils, abolition of Cl. 1 Services, a 500/- salary limit, retirement after 25 years' service, recruits to sign on without any guarantee of stability of service. Every one of those propositions is hopelessly unsound and uneconomic, but no Indian ever yet took the long view in such matters – or so one is tempted to say when feeling petulant!

Two compliments, which I record because such things bring a gleam of pleasure into a rather dour & drab existence, & not because I'm getting my head turned. Talking of my dinner to the Ministers, H.E. says "I congratulate you most warmly on the step forward which you have made", and when I told E. that they were having a volume of my speeches prepared by request, she said "I've always told you that they were good. Sound sense expressed in beautiful English". As I've said before, I think, the one thing I'm thankful for in this job is my classical education.

Wed Oct 13th

I made my last speech at the Lansdown G.C. prize meeting last night – rather a sad occasion, as I've been a member for 32 years, and have won the Gold Medal twice. I therefore made a purely frivolous speech, recalling various amusing anecdotes of the links. The Brigadier said afterwards he was sure I'd be here for another meeting. I said I'd definitely refused an extension, & there wasn't a hope of it. Everson, I see, is getting one, but he's much younger than I am.

Bannerji says that at a meeting of the Council on the 11th they argued for three quarters of an hour about Standing committees, and "the discussion generated a slight heat", though he couldn't quite make out what it was all about. They always start quarrelling when my back is turned.

Sunday October 24th Jubbulpore.

I came here on 17th, very sorry to leave Pachmarhi, which was at its best. But here I am in telephonic touch with Nagpur and can get back there rapidly, if needed. Nothing of any interest to record till yesterday, when Khare came specially to Nagpur to bring me the case of the Advocate General. The A.G. (Puranik) has been acting in the High Court in a leave vacancy, & Sharif, who is a regular sea-lawyer, thinks that on his reversion he has to be "reappointed" as A.G. & thinks that the Ministry can therefore ask me to put their man in instead. They first wanted to propose Kedar – Holy Smoke! He was the man who wrote an open letter to me asking me to do something in connection with the Revenue member which was unconstitutional. There are few people I trust less in the province than K. & I let this be known "sub rosa". The result was that when Khare came to me he said they wanted to make my way easy by proposing someone who would be acceptable to me, & they suggested Golwalkar of Jubb. who is a no–party man. That was a pleasant gesture, but of course useless. Puranik has the post, and I can't turn him out unless he is proved inefficient. Sharif tried to do this by citing two cases in which Puranik's office had let him down by not asking for warrants against two accused, who promptly absconded. But if that was the worst that could be said about P. there was evidently no ground to kick him out & I had to tell the Ministers so.

What humbug this 500/- limit is! Sharif gave it as his first reason for proposing a change of A.G. – economy, wrapped in the usual cant about poverty. Subsequently I heard that if I had agreed to the scheme at the start they would have allowed the A.G. to receive fees per case, which would probably have brought him in more that his present pay. It's all what the Hit. would call "an eyewash".

At the end of the interview Khare asked if I'd seen a report in the T/I about quarrels in the Ministry & his desire to resign. I said "Yes"; he said "don't believe a word of it"; I said "I didn't". It was obvious kite-flying by one of Shukla's men but I was relieved to hear it from Kh. himself. I don't want to have the Walsey as P.M.

The other day these Wobbly Bobs first decided not to prosecute an M.L.A. (Congress, of course) for an admitted case of misappropriation of public funds extending over a period of years. When I asked if there was one law for the Assembly and another for the rest of the community they decided to prosecute. Then political strings started on the pull, and they changed their minds once more. At the same time they refused to withdraw a prosecution for theft of electric current against a political opponent, not an M.L.A. I have asked that the case be taken in Council, and have pointed out that it is for them to enforce whatever standard of public morality they desire – leaving them to infer that I don't think much of their present ideas on the subject. And these are the people who are starting on a campaign against "corruption" among public servants, and accuse the late Govt. of being largely to blame for its existence. Is there any honesty of thought in this country?

Wednesday October 27th

Edna has arrived & I hope sincerely that we are now at the end of these annual separations I'm sick of them. It is a great comfort to have her with me again, as she is inspiring and heartening. The Ministers have returned to the charge about the A.G. in a long rambling note which says nothing more than that they have no confidence in him. Of reasons therefore there is not a trace. At the end they say that if I retain him they won't consult him – cutting off the Ministerial nose to spite the Ministerial face. The threat is the work of Misra. I've written to H.E. to tell him all about it, but I have no intention of changing my mind unless I am ordered to.

Misra has produced a pamphlet letting the cat out of the bag with regard to his scheme of local self-govt. (Oct. 10th) The little liar wants to do exactly what I thought – put all the District Officers under the thumb of local bodies. As our l.b's are about the most dilatory, corrupt, inefficient, faction-ridden, self-seeking, unpublic-spirited bodies of men on the face of the globe, the scheme is fortunately so ridiculous that it will probably be killed by laughter. If it isn't, we shall have to kybosh it by a flat negative.

Friday October 29th

The time is coming when I've got to have a show-down with M. I've just seen a letter which he's written to a prominent Congressman in Bilaspur, containing most improper threats against the D.C. about the election enquiry. And it isn't even his portfolio. He's at the back of every difficulty and dirty piece of work that's been going on since the Congress took office. I've also got to have a show-down with Shukla over his Turiya speech, when he talked such drivel about the "martyrs of 1930" – 4,000 men attacking a small body of 20 police and forest guards. Martyrs, forsooth! Such canting hypocrisy makes one sick. H.E. said that in England a Minister who talked like that would be put heavily on the mat by the P.M.. Things are rather different out here, where a resignation of a Minister might cause a landslide in the 7 Congress provinces. But Shukla's offense is so flagrant that he could not demand any sympathy from decent public opinion.

Speech at the Annual Prize-giving of the Forest School at Balaghat on Thursday, the 4th November 1937

Mr. Cox, and Students of the Balaghat Forest School,—My wife and I thank you all most sincerely for the invitation which you have given us to attend your annual prize-giving and for the cordial welcome which you have extended to us today. When Mr. Bell suggested to me some months ago that I should pay this visit, and told me that my doing so would be a great encouragement to the school, I agreed without any hesitation, and I did so for a very particular reason — a reason which is founded partly on the experience of 35 years of service in this country, and partly on the lessons which those who run may read in the recent history of certain other countries.

The forests of this country, and the forests with which so large an area of this province is covered, are a priceless heritage — a heritage which it takes years, generations, centuries even, to bring to maturity, but which can be destroyed almost in a night. No one who has read the history of the recent droughts in America, or such books as Professor Huxley's "Africa View" can fail to picture the appalling disasters to humanity which may result from forest denudation, or to realise that a people which gives in weakly to the clamour for such measures as free grazing and the relaxation of forest control barters its heritage for a mess of pottage. You who are the students of this school will go forth to be the guardians of that heritage. It will be yours to see that the trust which is placed in you is fulfilled; that, while everything is done to see that the people of the villages have the proper use of the forests, nothing is done which may damage them permanently or decrease their capital value.

And in the performance of that task I would ask you to remember one thing. Power will be put into your hands, and the temptation will come to you to abuse that power. That temptation you must resist at all costs; for there is nothing that will bring greater credit to your department than the knowledge that its officers, from the highest to the very lowest, are as anxious to see that the people have the right use of their privileges as they are vigilant to protect the property of the State.

My advice to you then is: go forth and endeavour to practice in your daily life the principles which the Chief Conservator has just laid down so ably for your observance and the lessons which are taught to you during your year at this school. And may God speed you in your task!

Friday Nov 5th

Just back from a very pleasant three-day visit to Balaghat, where I had promised to go to the Forest School prize-giving in order to give the school a fillip. Then the C.P. M.O. Co. asked me to go and see the Ukwa Ropeway, which was just nearing completion – a most interesting show.

The ore is brought down 1000 ft, 17 miles as the crow flies, on three endless ropes, one from Ukwa to the 1st station where there is a break and a slight change in direction; one from the 1st to the 2nd station, where there is ditto and ditto; and one from the 2nd to the railway siding in the plains. The transfer of buckets at the two intermediate stations is automatic. The jál forest was lovely, and I haven't seen a prettier road in the province. They gave us an excellent champagne lunch, including oysters which we all ate in fear and trembling. But no-one was ill. And there were champagne cocktails when we arrived. It always seems to me that that sort of hospitality is a mistake. As in all things, the good is that which is fitting.

And after all that clambering about dumps and machine-houses on a warm morning in early November what I want is a gin and ginger-ale and something which doesn't keep me wondering for 24 hours whether I am going to be ill! However, it was all a very jolly show.

There was a Dt. Council address & the inevitable "tee-partee", but the latter was relieved by tennis, boy-scouts and fireworks. Various people had gathered for the occasion, and altogether we enjoyed ourselves thoroughly.

Tuesday Nov. 9th

I had long talks with Khare and Misra yesterday. I told Kh. that he'd got to rope Shukla in, and he said he disapproved entirely of the way Sh. had been behaving, and would deal with him himself. I also had to tell Kh. he'd got no business to smoke a cigarette while taking a police parade, as he had done at Bilaspur, and he admitted he had been wrong, and said that it was due to absent-mindedness! He's a reasonable little man, and genuinely anxious, I think, to make things go smoothly. I gathered from him that the A.I.C.C. have come to realize that it would be very bad tactics for them to try and wreck the Federation, when the time comes for its introduction. But they dislike it intensely, because they say that our

Machiavellian statesmen have introduced the reactionary nominated members from the States as a substitute for the official and nominated blocs in the Assembly. I pointed out to him that the people he'd got to blame were the Br. Indian delegates to the first R.T.C.. It's very difficult to discover anything for which an Indian is willing to take the blame himself, instead of laying it on someone else's shoulders.

Take, for instance, Misra, who came and saw me after Kh.. His pamphlet lays the blame for the failure of L.S.G. on the Montford reforms – the most utter rubbish I have ever heard. I told him straight what the real reason was (vide October 27ᵗʰ) and asked him a question. Suppose the head of one dept. of a firm say, the sales dept. makes a complete hash of his job. And suppose the directors say – "Poor man, his job isn't big or interesting enough for him. We'll give him the management of the whole business, and then he'll be quite a different person". What would the shareholders say? He could give me no answer – in fact he seemed unable to put up any sort of defence of his scheme. All he was anxious to do was to show me that he had not intended to short-circuit his colleagues or me by having his scheme printed & privately circulated. His apologies were profuse, and when I told him that, so long as he understood the need for not queering my pitch by premature publicity, I'd like to drop that part of the question, he didn't seem to have anything more to say. Of reasoned defence of his scheme I could elicit no word. Bannerji tells me that he's intriguing to be P.M. I really think that if the Congress put him up I'd send my papers in at once rather than argue. He makes me shudder.

Sunday November 14ᵗʰ

The task of keeping this diary up is getting slightly wearisome, the reason being that I have to make so many records and reports of my doings officially that is hard work putting it all down a second time! I had a difficult meeting with the Ministers on Wednesday, when I had to tell them that I could not budge from my standpoint about the A.G., to pass orders on the Bilaspur enquiry case, and to get them to see reason about the conduct of officers at their (the Mins.') visits and about not publishing schemes which affected my special responsibilities beforehand, until they had let me see them. They were quite calm over the A.G.. I believe they'll try to make Puranik resign; but when a half hint was given that I should ask him to do so, I told them plainly that I didn't play the game like that, and that I could make no move. I was relieved that they made no more trouble over Bilaspur. At any rate we have a strong tribunal, which won't come to any silly conclusions. Over officers attending party functions I said that now that we all know each other's views we could leave the matter to the good sense of both parties. I refused to be drawn by two provocative notes which came from Misra and Shukla, and I kept them from giving tongue. Finally I pointed out how embarrassing it was for me when schemes affecting the whole government of the province were broadcasted without my having any formal knowledge of them. They agreed that I must have the same right of being consulted in such cases as they had, before their colleagues committed the Govt. to any schemes.

There were two comments on the meeting. E. (Edna) asked J. (Julius Caesar, A.D.C.) whether it had sounded stormy, and J. replied that to judge from the laughter a musical comedy might have been going on! And Misra and Gole remarked to Bannerji: "H.E. scored over us all along the line today." My reply to him was – "There's no question of 'scoring'. I simply pointed out to them what I held to be right, insisted on its being followed in the cases in which I had the last word, and left it to them to do so in the others." But these people never can take an objective view of anything. What matters at a meeting, in their view, is not whether we've got through some good, work, but whether I've scored off them, or they off me. So far I cannot find that they've worked out a single scheme that's any use to anybody.

Wednesday November 17th

Spent a day in letter-writing yesterday. First to Khare. At the end of the last meeting of Govt. I asked him to let me know if his party would like me to address the Assembly, and if so, if there were any particular points he would like me to talk about. An Indian is adept at the art of misunderstanding one, and Khare's reply (by letter) was that as there were no points they could think of, I need not address them. I wrote back at once, saying that it was more or less my duty to give an address, and asking him for a categorical statement as to whether his party would attend it I did. Today he writes to say that he thinks his party ought to attend, but as everyone knows they have not done so in the Central Assembly hitherto, and he cannot give a guarantee off-hand. He thinks therefore that I had better postpone my address. And he adds: "The situation is which we both have to work is somewhat difficult", I shall write and say I quite understand, and postpone the matter till the budget session.

Then to H.E. about Misra's scheme, which I fear I didn't treat very seriously. I cannot imagine that anyone will. Stent says that one or two non-officials with whom he has discussed it call it wildly impracticable. I have suggested to H.E. that if Misra pursues it the best thing to do will be to veto it straight away.

Finally to Lady L.! She is starting an Anti-Tuberculosis Association, an excellent idea – in ordinary times – BUT – this will be the 5th major appeal in four years; the 4th (King George V Memorial Fund) has gone anything but well; the province has not had a normal crop of cotton or wheat for over ten years; landlords are finding it difficult to collect their rents; and the Tuberculosis mortality is 0.39 per mill, against a general death rate of 34.39. You can't whack up much excitement over that! Having no axe to grind, I've told Lady L. exactly how things stand, and warned her that she may expect a flop, though of course I've said that I will do all I can to help her. But I do think that she ought to have consulted Governors as to prospects before even starting to frame a scheme. The appeal is to be called a Coronation appeal, so as to get a royal connection. That, of course, is pure "tour de force". I have never yet heard of the Coronation being made the ground for an appeal.

Nagpur Sunday Dec 5ᵗʰ

I really have been too busy to keep this going, not that anything really interesting has happened, except that Misra has started an intrigue, owing to his scheme being turned down, and various Congress M.L.A.s will not attend the Assembly if I address it. But Khare says it will be all right at the Feb. session because he has a letter from Patel which definitely disapproves of such tactics. Misra he says is merely making a demonstration. Rudeness of that sort hurts no one but those who are guilty of it, and personally I don't care two hoots. Governors' addresses, for one thing, seem to me to be out of place in the new order of things. But lordy! how sick I am of having to deal with such petty minded, unpleasant people! Thank goodness not all of them are like that, witness the following from The Hit.

I wish I could be sure that Congress will not go off the track.

The Voyage of Reform

At Balaghat last week, His Excellency the Governor made a few interesting observations about the "good ship Reform" couched in the telling manner and picturesque phrase, characteristic of his utterances. He spoke about the storms that the ship had to encounter in the first four months of the voyage and the criticism of those in charge of the ship for what they had done, oblique references to the unhappy days of the interim Ministry There was an observation about the storms that might gather and his hope that the ship would have a peaceful voyage to its journey's end. His Excellency need have no fears of the ship running into fog and storm during the remaining period of his tenure of office as the Congress is not likely to go off the ministerial track. For his part, we are sure, His Excellency will guide the ship that has been entrusted to his care, off the breakers. Those who know His Excellency can easily testify to his refreshing candour and immense adaptability, and we are glad to find that these qualities have found appreciation in the only circles that count at present, namely, Congress circles.

I suppose one always likes finding someone who agrees with one's own views, but here's a cutting from the Sphere of Nov 13ᵗʰ that I might have written myself.

SIR A. WAUCHOPE — A NOTE ON RESIGNATION.—

Whenever a public man resigns the public must try to discover some reason of a sensational kind to account for the fact. The simple truth is not enough. And the simple truth is that public men (especially in these days of intolerable stress) wear out like razor blades and must be replaced. When responsibility has worn one out and blunted his edges, another must take his place in the socket, and the more those edges are worn, the higher is the honour due to the old blade for hard work and good service. And this simile essentially fits Sir A. Wauchope and his last post of honour and responsibility. It is a thousand pities that Englishmen indulge in this silly inquisitiveness and for ever keep alive the fiction that to resign is to be convicted of incompetence. Why? Because public men to-day ought to be *encouraged* to resign much more freely than (alas!) they are. There ought to be spare parts available and fit to replace worn parts in every great office of State and administration, political, industrial, and religious. Only the wise and tiny minority know when they are worn out and past their best service. Lord Baldwin is a case in point. If only our statesmen, administrators, industrial leaders, church leaders, and school-masters possessed that last and greatest grain of wisdom, the Empire would be far better governed and run than it is. Of all our leaders there is only one who cannot be replaced and must not break under the strain of modern life, only one whose resignation clearly implies failure.

Judging from the recent clear-out in the War Council, other people seem to be coming round to the same views.

The Anti-Tuberculosis Scheme is being pushed through, needless to say. I have every sympathy with it, especially after the tragedy of George's death. But there is no getting over the fact that it is unlikely to raise any great enthusiasm in the C.P. and on the other hand there are so many things for which money is urgently wanted – a new Elgin Hospital at Jubb., a building for the Women's College, The King George Memorial fund, which is to build an Eye Hospital & so on. After all that Lady W. did, I suppose that Lady L. feels she must do something.

Speech at the laying of the Foundation Stone of the Laxminarayan Technical Institute, Nagpur, on Wednesday, the 8th December 1937

Mr. Vice-Chancellor, Students of the Nagpur University, Ladies and Gentlemen,—A Wise man once said: "Unless its young men dream dreams, a nation must surely perish." In the early years of this century there was a young man in this province who dreamt a dream. Born in a rigidly orthodox but very poor Brahmin family deprived of his father while still a boy, rejected by the examiners when he tried to matriculate, without fortune or influential friends, the future might well have seemed to him a prospect of gloom. But those who can see visions appear to have within themselves an inner light with which to lighten such darkness, and this youth had a vision that fame and fortune could be won for himself by leaving the beaten track, by educating himself for his chosen task, and by forcing his way to success through sheer grit and power of will. And when that dream had come true, when by his own unaided efforts he had won for himself not only a large fortune but also a leading place in the political as well as the industrial life of the province, in middle age yet another vision came to him. He dreamt that if the wealth which the province had yielded to him were given back to its youth, were used to enable its young men to break away from the old traditional lines, even as he had done, they might be able to carve out for the province that future of industrial development which he saw to be essential to its progress. Today the first step will be taken to give concrete shape to that vision. And as we see it taken, the thought which will be uppermost in the heart of each one of us will surely be that we should pay a silent tribute of thanks to the memory of our great benefactor.

And here I must pause for a minute, so that we may give our thanks also to those who have helped to bring his scheme to fruition. As the Vice-Chancellor has explained to you, the task of doing so has been beset with difficulties, and that they have been overcome at last is almost entirely due to three men—to Sir Hari Singh Gour, your Vice-Chancellor, who gave his services free of charge in obtaining probate of our benefactor's Will, and to Mr. P.S.Kotwal and the late Diwan Bahadur V. M.

Kelkar, who acted jointly with him as administrators *pendente lite*. These three were subsequently appointed by the University to be members of the Bequest Committee, and the ability and devotion which they have shown in administering the bequest has earned them the warm and undying gratitude of all those who are interested in the affairs of the University. I may mention that it was entirely owing to Sir Hari Singh's financial acumen that an investment of 11 lakhs was made which is now worth 18 lakhs, thus adding a clear 7 lakhs to the fund.

I feel that I cannot leave this, part of my subject without calling attention once again to a matter about which I have spoken on more than one occasion in the past. It is of no use to train our young men to industrialism unless, when they have completed their training, capital will be ready to back them up in their future work. There is in this province plenty of money available for employment, but too little readiness to employ it for any purpose except that of fastening the chains of debt upon the peasantry. To those who own it I would appeal with all the earnestness which I can command that they should show themselves alive to the real needs of the province; for then, and then only, will our benefactor's dream come wholly true.

And when the building that will rise upon this ground is finished, and work starts within its walls, what shall we say to you who will come here – to the young men who will be setting forth on their careers with the aid of a princely bequest? Let us say just two things. For the first you shall go with me to some words which the late Prime Minister of England once used in speaking of a great Englishman. "His ashes," he said, "are in the north, in his beloved Northumbria; his soul is with his Maker; and his spirit will abide in our hearts for ever." The founder of this Institute was a man who led a simple and godly life, a life of devotion to study and to his work, both public and private. Surely no better spirit could be breathed into the hearts of his *alumni* than that which inspired his own life. And the second is contained in the words with which I began this speech— "Dream, even as your founder dreamt. Dream of what you can do for yourselves, your fellowmen, and your country. For unless you who are its young men do so, your country must surely die." I can pay no better tribute to the new spirit which is abroad in the land today than by saying that I have no fear as to the response which you will make. And as you dream and as you work, I would have you repeat to yourselves a quaint old verse written by an Elizabethan poet, Thomas Dekker, which every man should know by heart:—

"Art thou poor, yet hast thou golden slumbers?
O sweet content!
Art thou rich, yet is thy mind perplexed?
O punishment!
Dost thou laugh to see how fools are vexed
To add to golden numbers golden numbers?
O sweet, 0 sweet content!
Work apace, apace, apace,
Honest labour wears a lovely face."

Thurs Dec 9th

An orgy of foundation stone laying. Yesterday I laid the stone of the Laxminarayan Technological Institute in the morning, and of that of the Pavilion for the new University Playing Fields in the afternoon. After the morning show Inglis, the "Times" correspondent in India, who is staying with us, said "that's the first time I've heard a Governor make a literary speech"!! Rather a nice compliment, though there was nothing very literary about the speech except a quotation from Dekker – the "Workapace" poem.

This morning I laid the stone of the Law Coll. There was a typical contretemps about this. The University seems to be composed of a number of bodies, each with power to interfere with the other. Led by Gour, the Vice-chancellor, who wanted to have all these stones laid before the end of the year (with his name on each!), when he goes out of office, the Executive council decided to devote most of the U.'s cash balance to building a Law Coll. which is an obvious necessity. Piqued at not being consulted, some other body vetoed this decision at the very last moment, and yesterday was spent in joint sittings and heated and acrimonious discussions before they decided finally that the project must go on. There is nothing in this land on which one can depend as final and stable.

Sunday Dec 12th

Convocation yesterday, & they made me, much to my surprise, an L.L.D. – an honour which they gave to neither of my predecessors. Personally I see no reason whatever why the Chancellor, who is ex officio at present should get an L.L.D., but they seem to have been moved by the fact that I put my foot down about giving the U. land for institutions above, when certain people were sure that they knew better what the U. wanted than the U. did itself. The usual endless arguing was going on, & I told them to stop talking and get something done. Also the pandits seemed to have liked my speeches. The amusing thing is that I share the distinction with Gandhi, and that whereas his "honoris causa" was voted unanimously, there was a small section, led by a disgruntled Congress pleader, who objected to mine, an objection which the Hit. condemned as "unfortunate". I had a very cordial reception from the students, and the Sec. of the Union took the trouble to write and congratulate me.

Tues Dec 14th

My successor's name is indeed a surprise – Wylie, a Political aged 46. But he's a very fine record, including being P.M. of Alwar after the troubles, and from what H.E. tells me he should do very well. He will be junior to Roughton, Burton, Binney and Stent, but I am sure the choice is a good one. Administrative experience and ability is of secondary importance in a Governor now. What is wanted is the ability to deal with men and situations, tact, infinite patience, humanity and sympathy. The old promoted-bureaucrat Governor is out of the picture now; Wylie wants leave till the end of May, which is disturbing my plans, but of course I must help him to take as much as he wants. I know how all too short my preliminary leave was.

Life is drab at present. I've bust a tendon or something in my leg, and can't take any proper exercise, and that always gives me the pip. But it's good for one for one to go through a bit of pain – teaches one to appreciate one's blessings.

(Note (TJG): What he did not know was that the pain, that he thought was merely a bust tendon, was, in fact, the first signs of cancer of the liver, probably caused by a certain mould that flourishes in the tropics and which is now known to be carcinogenic, of which he was to die within four months.)

Saturday December 18th

I had a curious show on Wed. when I opened the Session of the Indian Philosophical Congress. Being quite unable to discuss philosophic doctrines now, I thought the only thing to do was to talk about my adventures in Greats, when I shocked the Dons by only getting a Second. (Curiously enough the senior Winchester Scholar of my year – I was the senior Open – ended up also with a Second and later became H.M. of Sedbergh. So it doesn't look as if Firsts were essential to success!) Having done so, I then told them about the great men of my day – Sfoo, Raasher and Jobags – and said philosophy had made me what I was! They seemed to like it, especially as the other two speakers, Gour and Ranade, were abysmally dull. There is a certain brand of Maratha which simply cannot speak clearly. Every word is gabbled out at top speed. And I think Ranade was the worst I've ever listened to. Below is the Hit. on my speech.

I am in no danger of getting swelled headed! But it is pleasant to feel that one can give people pleasure by talking to them. I am glad to say that the opposition in the Assembly, led by Khaparde and Rizvi, is really waking up. It succeeded in getting the passing of the Prohibition Bill postponed, so as to allow members time for consideration; and it put up a stout fight over the Committee of Enquiries Bill. Meanwhile the Ministry are doing nothing so far as I can see, to solve their problem. Internal dissensions and petty personal cases seem to occupy their attention. This morning the D.N. attacks them because they have spent five months with nothing constructive to show for it. Well, the day of reckoning cannot be postponed indefinitely, and when budget time comes I think they'll get a shock.

Friday December 24th

A Gilbertian country! Khare has made a solemn proposal that Govt. – which consists of the Governor and 7 Ministers who have sworn allegiance to the Crown – should declare a public holiday on Jan. 26th, Independence Day, to celebrate the future day when India will have thrown off the British yoke. His note ends up with a typical Indian touch – "There should be no objection to granting this trifling wish." "Trifling", forsooth! In any other country it would be called a piece of gross impertinence.

In another matter Khare was reassuring. He swore to me that he

His Excellency's Address

H. E. Sir Hyde Gowan's address to the Indian Philosophical Congress is once again a felicitous example of his enviable capacity to clothe his ideas in language which is at once beautiful, clear and logical, 'stripped of all meretricious adornment and directed solely towards the furtherance of the argument'. How delightful is the description of his years in Oxford—'years of somewhat puzzled wondering in the realms of pure thought'. A few picturesque phrases bring to life the 'scholars of no mean repute' under whom 'the somewhat practical minded young man with a liking for good fresh air and for the things that can be done in it' imbibed 'the seeds of universal wisdom which would later spring up and bear fruit'. The study of philosophy in India is not seldom considered to unfit a man for the hard realities of life. His Excellency's speech, apart from its autobiographical interest is of great significance as a true evaluation of the place which the study of philosophy occupies in the modern world of strife and stress.

had not dropped the taxation of malguzars, but intended to carry it through. We shall see. He and Misra have been talking a lot of dishonest humbug about the Ministry being unable to do anything because of the imperfections of the Act. But the elections to the next session of the Congress are just coming on, and they've all got to talk big at present.

CHAPTER 12

1938
JANUARY - FEBRUARY

Sunday January 2nd 1938.

Just finished my last Xmas camp in India. It was a very jolly camp – The Gordons, Chittey, Jolleyes and Michael Sullivan besides us five. Julius got a tiger, and we got about 150 head of small game. It was all marred for me by two crocked legs, & tummy trouble due to lack of exercise. Luckily I was able to do the duck shooting. The camp was at Rukha, on the main road to Seoni. Things are so uncertain these days that I dare not go off into the real jungle where E. would have liked to be.

Lady L. has sent E. 500/- for her Women's College, which is very good of her. She also sent me a very cordial letter about the Tuberculosis Fund. H.E. wants me to kill Khare's Independence Day stunt with gentle ridicule. I'm afraid it won't work. But he agrees that in the last resort there must be a flat "no".

The S/S is being completely die-hard over the pay of Govt. servants already in Service, and I'm sure he's wrong. He says he's considered very carefully the view which I myself put before H.E. in Simla – that in many case the present scale of salaries is economically indefensible. But he thinks that the sense of security must be safeguarded at all costs. He fears evidently that any cutting might eventually produce a landslide which would involve the Imperial Services too. I doubt it; but anyway that would be better than keeping this festering sore going. Every ill from which the country suffers is referred eventually to its poverty, caused by the "fat salaries" of Govt. servants; and the latter will never fill their proper role as long as the thought of them fills the mind of the non-official with envy, hatred and malice from Sunrise to Sunset.

Khare has had a knock. He has only come out third in the Congress elections, the top two being two scallywags, Punamchand Ranka and "General" Awair, the hero of the Flag and Arms Act satyagrahas. The latter is almost a lunatic, and yet they say he has a very good chance of being the next president of the Nagpur M.C.. Heaven help us! The people whom our provincials delight to honour fill one with amazement, mingled in many cases with loathing and contempt.

I gather that Khare has also been making himself unpopular by two speeches he made at the Women's Conference, which were criticized as tasteless and unsympathetic. I'm afraid he's one of these people who ought never to make a speech or write a letter if he is to get on. He has the gift of putting people's backs up every time he does either. It affects me closely because at the moment Khare's fall could only increase my difficulties.

Monday January 3rd 1938.

We dined with the Stents last night, and I had some amusing gossip from Pam about the Women's Conference. Mrs. Pandit (Nehru's sister), who was brought up in England, stayed with the Khares, and was horrified – a cot to sleep on, a common latrine, dreadful food, and a

424

hostess who spoke no language except Mahrathi. She was amazed to see Pam sitting in a group with Shukla, Mina, and Mehta, and was altogether struck with the friendliness which exists here between officials and others. I gather that the Congress women from other provinces are very angry with the wives of I.C.S. officers here, whom they accuse of being false to the national cause. Khare seems to have made himself thoroughly unpopular. He was badgered into making a speech on the first day, and spoke in a coarse vein and in bad taste. (That was Shukla's opinion!) The next day he presided, and offended everyone by scoffing at religion, and pointing out how no nation ever lived up to its religion, and so what was the good of it? The only religion was doing things, and not talking and praying. Altogether Khare's stock is slumping, and the net result of the Conference is that delicately nurtured people like Maharani Amrit Kuar, the president, and Mrs. Pandit have gone away with awful ideas as to the jungliness of our locals. A very good thing. People who behave as the people here have behaved towards every scheme for civilising the place – Kanhan water scheme, Improvement Trust scheme, Mayo Hospital scheme and so on – and who are quite willing to ruin the finances of the province for a silly stunt like Prohibition, are nothing but junglis. So is Gandhi, if it comes to that.

I gave the editors of the Hit. and the D.N. copies of my "Speeches" the other day. On the next page is the D.N.'s effort.

The Daily News
29-12-1937

ILY NEWS

Speeches of H. E. Sir Hyde Gowan

The Daily News - 19.12.1937

The quotation at the end is a crib from a brief introduction which I put in, saying that I could only hope that the reader would say that according to C.J.F. I must be a damned bad speaker! The description of the flag satyagraha is quite good.

Speeches of His Excellency Sir Hyde Gowan—Vol. I. 16th September 1933—31st March 1937.

It was on a grilling Nagpur May afternoon in 1923 that I first saw Mr. Hyde Gowan (now H. E. Sir Hyde Gowan). A large crowd had collected at the cross-roads near the Bansilal building in the Civil Station to watch the Congress flag procession march beyond the prohibited area and disobey an official order. About half-a-dozen 'Satyagrahis' constituted the procession every day and as soon as they advanced near the prohibited spot an E.A.C. used to declare that they were arrested. The crowd gradually melted away after shouting some slogans. Mr. Gowan, Deputy Commissioner, and Mr. D. A. Smyth an Irishman with a strong sense of humour who was D.S.P. directed the whole operations. The flag procession usually came at about 4 o'clock in the afternoon but if it was delayed Mr. Gowan would get impatient for he insisted on having his tennis every evening. He would tell Mr. Smyth: 'you see to it. I will go and have my tennis.' Although Mr. Gowan was reputed at that time to be bureaucratic and somewhat short-tempered, his sense of sportsmanship always asserted itself There was a story at that time that Mrs. Subhadra Kumari Chouhan (now M.L.A.) who was the Joan of Arc of the movement, flung herself into the arms of Mr. Gowan one day and pleaded that she should be arrested! The story was never contradicted. Although hundreds of people were sent to jail Mr. Gowan discharged his unpleasant task without malice. Many people must have seen Sir Hyde Gowan playing golf, walking along half the length of the Civil Station pursuing a ball. Those who have attended the University Sports function would have seen Sir Hyde on his legs for hours mixing freely with students and professors. These incidents are mentioned here to show that the love of sportsmanship has always been strong in him. There must be many people in our province who have seen Sir Hyde Gowan's hand-writing. His predecessor in office, Sir Montagu Butler used to write a nervous hand with scratchings and erasings. But Sir Hyde writes a clean, round hand. Every little thing he does is spick

and span. There is a theory that it is only a clear mind that can write a clean hand and tidiness is only a reflection of mental orderliness. The speeches of H.E. Dr. Sir Hyde Gowan (Vol I), which are brought together in a well-printed and beautifully bound book reflect the two characteristics mentioned above namely, sportsmanship and clear-headedness. Opening with his address to the C. P. Legislative Council on the 18th Jan. 1934 the first volume closes with the Preface which His Excellency wrote to the Letters Patent and the Instrument of Instructions published on the 1st April 1937. It also contains the communique drafted by him on the 28th March 1937 regarding the refusal of office by the Congress Party. Inside these 120 pages we get together what may be called a gubernatorial survey of the events of the closing years of the Darch'e era. Every one of these speeches has appeared in the 'Daily News' at the time they were delivered but they repay perusal a second time. An unusual number of speeches has been delivered by Sir Hyde Gowan at educational institutions. In his famous Buldana speech which attracted all India attention, His Excellency gave an assurance that his special powers would only be used in the case of grave necessity while his energies, his advice and his good offices would always be at the disposal of his Ministers. No one who has been keeping in touch with the events in our province, after the Congress accepted office will deny that Sir Hyde has been true to his word and that he is playing the game. His speeches reflect the man—frank, straight, clear-headed and friendly. There is no beating about the bush and no intellectual snobbery. Above all, they sparkle literary grace. Few who were acquainted with the over-strict Chief Secretary, who frightened many clerks out of their wits but ruined none, would have predicted that in a few years, he would mellow into a broad-visioned administrator. But the thing has happened. It was in a moment of political vexation that Charles James Fox said: 'If a speech reads well it must be a damned bad speech'. The speeches of H.E. Sir Hyde Gowan read well and we can say—pace James Fox—that he is a damned good speaker.
                                V. S. V.

NAGPUR, JANUARY, 5, 1938

SPEECHES OF SIR HYDE GOWAN

IT WAS A HAPPY IDEA OF the friends of His Excellency Sir Hyde Gowan that they should have persuaded him much against his will to publish the first volume of his speeches. The volume un-under review covers the speeches that His Excellency delivered before the inauguration of the constitution. Dealing as they do with the problems of a semi-bu-reaucratic regime, the speeches have in them the usual guberna-torial finality of utterance, but they are singularly free from the patronage and sneering sympathy characteristic of Governors' ora-tions. Those who know his His Excellency, Sir Hyde Gowan will with willingness testify that in his frankness, he is appalling, to use of one of Mr Baldwin's charac-teristic words ; in his desire to have a square deal between man and man, he is a crusader; in his anx-iety to serve the province which he has made his home for the past thirty-five years, he is as sincere as any of the old indigeneous resi-dents of the area. His speeches bear the impress of his eagerness to see the province which he has served attain the position and esteem that are her due. They have further a striking literary elegance which make them excel-lent reading. It must be said to the credit of His Excellency that in the literary grace and finish of his speeches, the swings and the swerves of his perorations,

he takes a very high rank among pro-consul orators. It is no exaggeration to say that he and Sir Malcolm Hailey alone among the Governors of India during the past fifteen years have made signal contributions to Anglo-Indian political literature by their ora-tions. The speeches of His Excel-lency are not mere shining words strung on a silken thread but thoughts based on a wide range of experience which deserve the serious attention of every well-wisher of the province, We want to quote just one excerpt from one of his speeches as an illustration of his brutal candour and striking sincerity. Speaking for the last time to the now defunct Montford Legislative Council, His Excellen-cy observed. "The concrete problem before you is this: instead of the present electorate of some 200,000 voters, you will have to deal with an electorate of over a million and a half. It is the sacred duty, the duty of everyone who styles him-self a leader of the people to edu-cate the new electorate aright, and upon the way in which you fulfil that duty the fate of the new structure will depend. As you go forth into your constituencies, two paths will lie before you; one will be broad and easy and the other straight and narrow. In the days of Rome's decline, the populace clamoured for *panem et circenses.* The Emperors gave them what they asked and Rome fell. You too if you wish can promise the new voters, their dole of food and amusement, remissions of taxation, boons of various kinds, the coming of that millenium which in your hearts you know is not attainable. That is the broad and easy path, the slippery path that leads to destruction. Or if you are so minded,you can go forth to educate, to teach every voter what are his duties as a citizen, to put before him no policy which is not com-pacted of sound finance, sound administration and equal justice to all men, and to ask to him to return to the House none

but those who will work for the good of the State. As one of your own countrymen said recently "On the quality of our representatives we shall be judged of the capacities to govern ourselves". Sounds like the voice from the class-room but how much we need it today and how much more we will need such advice in the years to come ? The first volume has whetted the ap-petite and we are looking forward to its companion volume making its appearance in the near future.

*Speeches of Sir Hyde Gowan Vol. I.

Wednesday January 5th

The announcement of my going in May was made yesterday, and I have been deeply touched by what has been said. Bannerji came to me in the usual course of the morning, and as he sat down he said: "Sir, I do not know what to say. I feel that I have been made an orphan." And Lady Dadabhoy rang my wife up and said she had been unable to sleep all night because of the thought of losing us. This morning Sorabji Mehta came to see me, and said he too had scarcely been able to sleep, because he should not know for the future where to go for advice and help. The Hit. and the D.N. are equally kind. The Hit says:

H. E. Sir Hyde Gowan

The communique announcing the impending resignation of His Excellency Sir Hyde Gowan on May 27 has come as a great surprise to the public. It was expected that His Excellency would stay in India till the completion of his term of office but evidently ill-health and domestic reasons have combined to hasten his departure from India. We are sorry that His Excellency should have decided to leave the province before the expiry of his term of office for he has endeared himself to those who have come into contact with them. To him goes the credit for the smooth working of the administrative machine in these difficult times. His handling of the Congress Ministry has won appreciation in high quarters and we are reliably informed that he was requested by the India Office to accept an extension of his term of office. But thirty-five years of service in India seem to have told on his health and he had to refuse an extension of his term. This is not the time for us to take a review of his term of office as Governor in the province but we take this opportunity of wishing His Excellency Sir Hyde Gowan many long years of useful and happy activity in his retirement.

And the D.N

H.E. Sir Hyde Gowan

There will be general regret in our province at the decision of H.E. Sir Hdye Gowan to retire four months before his normal term of five years. According to a communique published on another page, His Excellency has desired for domestic reasons, and the King Emperor has agreed, that his resignation should be accepted as from May, 27, 1938. Even the Congress Ministry, with whom Sir Hyde Gowan has been working in close and sympathetic cooperation, will be sorry at his decision at a time like this before sound and healthy conventions have been established under the new Constitution. The Ministry has yet to tackle big problems and it would have been a great advantage to have a Governor who knows the province, its people and problems so well as Sir Hyde Gowan does.

It's very nice of the D.N. to say that but I do not flatter myself that the Ministry cannot get on without me. I have already told them my mind on the main problems which confront them, & by the end of May we shall have established all the conventions that are needed. E. says that people tell her I shall be missed because I've been "a friend to everybody". Well, I've tried to be, and it is comforting to think that I've not been altogether a failure.

I record all this, not because of any pride, but from a deep thankfulness that I have been spared the humiliation of being a failure, as I might well have been, knowing myself and my queer temperament. But I have prayed every night that I might be given "patience, and wisdom, & strength, & gentleness, so that I might fulfil the great trust which has been placed in me". I am not a religious man, but I have a belief in the efficacy of prayer as inducing a state of mind.

The Hit. once more:

Reasons For Retirement

In our comments on the reasons which led to H. E. Sir Hyde Gowan to refuse an extension of his term of office, we observed that thirty-five years of service had told on his health. The deterioration in his health alone was not responsible for his refusal. His Excellency is said to be feeling that he should make way for younger men, a spirit which is in keeping with the best traditions of the services. It is characteristic of Englishmen that they are anxious as a race to give a chance to younger men. Such a feeling pervades the services and we have other instances of sacrifice of one's own personal interests on the part of the British Services. Sir Charles Deverell and his colleagues in the War Office willingly made way for younger men when Mr Hore-Belisha submitted his proposals for re-organisation.

The tribute to Englishmen is as refreshing as it is unusual now-a-days.

Not by any means so pleasant is a job that is falling on me to tackle. Gour came to me yesterday and told me that the Bar Association are to put in a formal representation to Govt. about the C.J.. It appears he loses his temper in Court, does no criminal work, & won't take the trouble to read a case. (The representation will presumably be confined to the temper.) Sharif told me exactly the same thing this afternoon.

What to do? The Executive Govt. can't interfere, and so far as I can see the only thing to do is for me as No. 1 in the province tell the C.J. what has been represented to me, and use my personal influence with him to get him to behave. A difficult and delicate talk, but I can't refuse to help. How on earth does a man expect to control his magistrates if he can't control himself? Rows in court have always resulted in censures; what is to happen when they occur in the C.J.'s Court?

Jan 14th Friday

Back from a shoot at Sarangach, where we got 224 birds the first day and 445 the second – not nearly as many for the big day as when I was there three years ago. It was good fun, though rather marred for me by acute rheumatism in both feet. The third day we ought to have shot geese but word came in that a bridge had been broken, & as I had to get back into the province we spent the day so far as I was concerned, in making arrangements for repairs and transport. They repaired it just before sundown, and we got the cars across. Sarangach did us very well, a party of 12 guns. But may I be delivered from marble baths! I've never known anything so cold and uncomfortable to sit in.

Tues 18th Jan

The budget came up today & at least on paper all is well. They've refused to do any borrowing, will cover a revenue deficit by economies, & will raise 29 lakhs by extra taxation. I shall believe the last item when I see the bills come up for my signature. The main tax is a surcharge on agricultural incomes, and the landlord interests, which are strong in the party councils, will fight it tooth and nail. But it's either that or a crash, because they've committed themselves to spending Excise revenue on rural uplift.

The move to Pach. has been saved. They won't have a formal move but everybody who wants is to be allowed to go, provided he goes at his own expense. There is no great hardship in that.

No further developments about the C.J.. The Ministers are to send me a note, & then I shall have, I suppose, to use my influence as No. 1 in the province to smooth matters over.

Monday Jan 24th

Tennyson's team have come and gone, but the visit was rather spoilt by the fact that the Tennysons didn't turn up, as her daughter was ill in America & she thought she might have to fly to England from Delhi, where they were. The cricket was poor; the Tourists won by 8 wickets, but their batting was feeble, and they were only saved by the fact that the C.P. batting was even worse.

I've just had a difficult case with Khare, who wanted to declare a holiday on Jan 26th, Independence Day – camouflaged, of course. What a Gilbertian country. At one time I didn't see how I could stop it; but Haig said that the precedent would react very badly in the U.P., and Lumley & Hallett had both told their P.M.s that they hated the idea, and the P.M.s had chucked it. So I told Kh. he had no supporters, & eventually he said he didn't want to make an issue of the matter, and withdrew in good order. The whole show was a stunt to improve his position, which has been sadly shaken lately. The Matrakoshal people – Misra & Shukla, who hated each other till recently, are now combining to down the M.B.s and make Misra P.M. – awful thought!

Friday Jan 28th

Back from a brief visit to the Fitzes at Indore, rather spoilt for me by the fact that ever since my attack of rheumatism I've had tummy trouble, which Allen puts down to gall-bladder. If it is I must try and stick it out till I get home, as I cannot endure the thought of an operation in that dreadful place the Mayo Hospital. The Maharaja was not there. He looks the image of his father. One of his palaces is the most "modern" thing you can imagine. It cost 24 lakhs – and I'd sooner live in a barn.

They say the M. grudged bitterly the money spent on the Yeshwantsagar Dam (26 lakhs) with its famous spillway. We saw it on the way out to a duck shoot. The latter was one of those shows where we'd have got four times the number of birds if we'd had double the number of guns. I was warned to take out at least 400 cartridges. I used 120, as the birds kept out of range to right and left, where there ought to have been guns, but weren't. The G/I do their Politicals well. The Residency and its garden are twice the size of G.H. Nagpur & my garden. We met a charming lot of people & were sorry to leave.

Wed Feb 2nd

Dined last night with the Dadabhoys, and of course old Manekji got up and made a speech without warning me. He was very kind, as usual, not to say flattering. After dinner he whispered confidentially in my ear that he was going to tell the Viceroy to give me a G.! I murmured that that was very nice of him but, I could not tell him that I did not care two hoots whether the V. listened or not. As no Governor of the C.P. has ever got a G. in the province, it's not in the least likely that he will anyhow.

Tues Feb 3rd

The budget came up yesterday. As I thought, they've abandoned all idea of a surcharge on land revenue or a tobacco tax, & have attacked those who can least resist them – a surcharge of 200/- flat on all incomes over 5000/-. I shall be interested to see what the G/I say about it. But at least they have balanced the budget, on paper, without borrowing, which is something to their credit.

I had a long talk with the C.J. the other day, and he says that Gour's conduct in misleading the Bench was so disgraceful that he won't apologise unless G. does first. Also that other incidents complained of were trivial, and that the matter is a domestic one, which he is quite willing & able to settle direct with the Bar. I told the Ministry that I thought it would be difficult for them to claim a locus standi, & suggested that they should ask me to tell the C.J. privately to square matters up. They're now thinking it over. Stone has a queer temper; but the Bar Association are also a queer lot, and Gour at their head is just about as trustworthy as Old Nick himself.

Monday Feb 7th

Cypher wire in yesterday, to say that the idea of a Coronation Durbar has been given up. That is what I advised. I think it would have been a great mistake, & would almost certainly have been a partial flop, besides being a terrible waste of money, quite out of keeping with the spirit of the time in this country.

Note (TJG)

This is the last entry in the diary which covers 873 handwritten pages (6 ins x 9 ins) in three loose-leaf volumes.

The last important matter to occur during Sir Hyde's tenure was that the official copy of the Treaty of Berar was sent to him from S/S signed by King George VI. Sir Hyde was too ill to do anything about it just then so put it in his private file for future consideration, which he was unfortunately unable to give. It was found by JHBG in the file. This must be one of the few official copies of a Treaty in private hands.

At the end of February there were two letters and a phone call to Delhi, and he told the Viceroy that he had been ordered immediately to go to Bombay to consult a specialist and that: "Bomford, as you know, has taken over under dormant commission."

Sir Hyde was taken to St George's Hospital Bombay at the end of February, and the specialist's immediate reaction, after seeing him on 1st March was to ring the P. & O. and book a berth on the first mail steamer for home. He sailed on 12th March on S.S. Rajputana. What Sir Hyde had thought to be a strained tendon and a touch of rheumatism turned out to be inoperable cancer of the liver with which he must have been living for some years.

He arrived at Tilbury on 25th March and went straight into the Royal Masonic Hospital, where he died early in the morning of the 1ˢᵗ April 1938.

May his soul rest in peace.

The Position of Berar

As this record started with a statement on the position of Berar, the following extract from The Times is appropriate to be included:

The Times. 4th. January 1938
CENTRAL PROVINCES & BERAR.
A NEW GOVERNOR.

The India Office issued the following announcement last night:-
Sir Hyde Gowan, K.C.S.I., C.I.E., I.C.S, whose term of office as Governor of the Central Provinces and Berar will normally expire in September 1938, having expressed his desire for domestic reasons, is to be relieved in the April of 1938. The King is graciously pleased to accept his resignation as from the 7th May 1938. His Majesty has been graciously pleased to approve the appointment of Mr.V.F.Wylie C.I.E., I.C.S., at present Resident, Jaipur, to be Governor of the Central Provinces and Berar with effect from the date of Sir Hyde's resignation. In accordance with Article 4 of the Berar Agreement this appointment has been made after consultation with H.E.H. the Nizam of Hyderabad and Berar.

THE NIZAM'S DOMINIONS.

The Central Provinces and Berar have been administered together as one charge since the beginning, of the century but this is the first official announcement in which the special position of Berar as a part of the dominions of the Nizam is formally recognized.

In the current India Office List, the Government is described simply as that of the Central Provinces. The full description becomes necessary now that, in accordance with the Berar Treaty of 1936 the Nizam has been consulted on the appointment. The Central Provinces are part of British India but Berar is to continue to be administered with them.

Note:

This is not absolutely accurate. The India Office List of 1933 and before gives, in the index: "Central Provinces & Berar." For the years 1934/5/6/7 it lists only: "Central Provinces", though Berar sent a member to the assembly during these years. The India Office List reverts to: "Central Provinces and Berar" for the year 1938.

Obituary from The Times

Saturday April 2nd 1938

SIR HYDE GOWAN
GOVERNORSHIP OF THE
CENTRAL PROVINCES

Sir Hyde Gowan, K.C.S.1., C.I.E., whose five years' term as Governor of the Central Provinces was substantially shortened on grounds of impaired health, died at a London hospital yesterday at the age of 59. Last week he arrived in a serious condition at Tilbury with Lady Gowan in the *Rajputana* from Bombay. There will be profound regret among his many friends and admirers in the Province which he governed for four-and-a-half years and far beyond its borders that cherished hopes of his recovery of health were not to be fulfilled and that he was not destined to enjoy a well-earned retirement.

Hyde Clarendon Gowan was one of a number of able men Australia has provided for the Indian Services. He was born at Sydney, N.S.W., on July 4, 1878, the son of the late Dr. Bowie Campbell Gowan. At Rugby he was Senior Classical Scholar and at New College, Oxford, Senior Open Scholar. He entered the Indian Civil Service and went to the Central Provinces at the close of 1902. Except for a few months in 1908, when he was officiating Under-Secretary to the Government of India in the Commerce and Industry Department, the whole of his service was in the Central Provinces, where he had good experience in both settlement and revenue district work. He was Under-Secretary to the Government there from 1904 to 1908, and was

Financial Secretary from 1918 to 1921, and again in 1925-26. A man of athletic tastes, he was a keen volunteer, and from 1920 to 1925 was lieutenant-colonel commanding the Nagpur Rifles, Indian Auxiliary Force. For this service he was given the V.D.

Gowan was Chief Secretary to Government from March 1927, and had the advantage of the guidance of so successful an administrator as Sir Montagu Butler. He served on two occasions as temporary Member of the Governor's Executive Council, and was confirmed in the appointment in the summer of 1932. When a year later Sir Montagu Butler resigned from his second term of Governorship to become Lieutenant-Governor of the Isle of Man, Gowan was selected as his successor. The choice gave much satisfaction, for he was generally liked both by Indians and his British colleagues. His dignified bearing and firmness of purpose were combined with a natural courtesy, and in times of stress and strain he was upheld by a serenity of mind which never deserted him. Now and again he gave eloquent expression to the clear-cut convictions on public matters by which he was guided. In Lady Gowan – Edna Brown, of Mere Oaks, Wigan—whom he married in 1905, he had a helpmeet who did specially valuable service in the cause of women's education.

A year ago Gowan was one of the Governors called upon to guide the Provinces from the old dyarchical to the new system of Ministerial responsibility. In the C.P. as in five other Provinces the leaders of the Congress Party, successful at the polls, made acceptance of office conditional on receiving certain assurances from the Governors which were held by higher authority to be inconsistent with obligations laid upon them by the Government of India Act, 1935. Gowan kept in step with his fellow Governors and in close touch with the Viceroy, and made his own contribution to the ending of the impasse last July by the Congress withdrawal, stage by stage, of the condition which had been laid down. Only a month ago Dr. Khare, the Premier, paid testimony to the happy relations between the Governor and his Ministers, and said that if on rare occasions there had been a conflict of opinion, the impressions left thereby were never of a rankling character.

These relations were of shorter duration than had been expected. In the ordinary course Sir Hyde would have been in charge until next September, but early in this year it was announced that as he had expressed a desire, for domestic reasons, to be relieved in the spring, the King had accepted his resignation as from May 27. Unhappily the Governor's illness took a sudden turn for the worse a month ago, and he relinquished charge and travelled to Bombay, where he was admitted to hospital. He was much cheered by a telegraphic message of good wishes from Lord Linlithgow, the Viceroy, referring to "outstanding service to his Province and India." and to "the most friendly and cordial relationships" existing between them. Indeed, the Viceroy's appreciation of his services so strong, that it is understood to have been the Viceroy's intention before Sir Hyde's breakdown in health, to offer him a two year extension of the governorship. Sir Hyde voyaged to this country and reached Tilbury on March 25th, only to be admitted at once to the Masonic Hospital in London. He was a keen Freemason, and was P.S.G.E of the Grand Lodge of England. He was made C.I.E. in 1928, C.S.I. in 1932, and K.C. on becoming Governor of the Central Provinces in 1933. He leaves three sons.

Cremation will take place privately Golders Green on Monday at 11a.m.

Telegram from The Viceroy.

000 LB NEW DELHIO 5 STE PTY 113 IMMEDIATE SIR HYDE GOWAN PASSENGER SS RAJPUTANA BOMBAY MY WIFE AND I SEND OR WARMEST GOOD WISHES TO YOU FOR YOUR JOURNEY HOME LET ME SAY HOW VERY DEEPLY I REGRET THE LOSS OF A COLLEAGUE WHO HAS RENDERED SUCH OUTSTANDING SERVICE TO HIS PROVINCE AND TO INDIA AND HOW MUCH I FEEL THIS PREMATURE SEVERANCE OF THE MOST CORDIAL AND FRIENDLY RELATIONSHIP WHICH HAS EXISTED BETWEEN US EVER SINCE I FIRST ASSUMED OFFICE. YOU CARRY WITH YOU IN YOUR RETIREMENT THE BEST WISHES AND THE SYMPATHY OF YOUR OWN PROVINCE AND ALL OF US WHO HAVE HAD THE PLEASURE OF WORKING WITH YOU.

And from The King

To Lady Gowan

The Queen and I have heard with great regret of the death of your husband whose distinguished services to India will be long remembered. We send our deepest sympathy to you and your family.

George R.I.

Acknowledgments by Timothy Gowan

The majority of the typing from the manuscript was done on a manual typewriter by James Gowan and transcribed into computer format by Timothy Gowan using Serif Pageplus software. Adobe .pdf was chosen as the most widely available final format.

It is intended to offer the original diaries to the British Library provided that they will make some contribution to defray the costs of the many hours work involved in the transcription.

ABBREVIATIONS used in the Diary

A.D. C.	Aide de Camp, (Military assistant)
A.G.	Advocate General
A.I.C.C.	All India Congress Committee, the ruling body of Congress.
A.J.C.	Assistant Justice Commissioner.
B.I.	British India.
B.R.'s	Business Rules.
B.N.	Zamindari Name of a big estate.
B.P.	Baden-Powell (Lord Baden-Powell)
Bo.	Bombay Presidency.
C.C.F.	Chief Controller of Forests.
c.d.	Civil Disobedience
Ch. S.	Chief Secretary
C.J.	Chief Justice
C.M.	Chief Minister
Cl.	Council
Commission	The whole of the Indian Civil Service, all branches.
C.P.	Central Provinces.
C/S	Civil Surgeon
C/w Management	Court of Wards Management, a form of receivership.
D.C.	Deputy Commissioner
D..F.O.	District Forest Officer.
D.G.I.M.S.	Director General, India, Medical Services
D.G.M.	Deputy Grand Master (Masonic term).
D.N.	Daily News, English language local (Nagpur) Newspaper
D.P.H.	Deputy Physician of Hospitals
D.P.I.	Director of Public Instruction;
D.S.P.	District Superintendent of Police.
Dt. Cl.	District Council.

E.	Mostly his wife 'Edna', but occasionally for 'Erskine', Gov. of Madras.
E.A.C.	Extra Assistant Commissioner.
E.G.S.A.	European Government Services Association.
F.C.	Financial Commissioner
F.D.	Finance Department, either Government of India in Delhi or locally in Nagpur.
F.&.P.	Finance and Political Department, ditto.
G.	Gandhi; or Gordon; or Grille
G.G.	Governor General, .i.e. the Viceroy.
G.A.	Advocate General
G.I. or G/I.	Government of India, Delhi.
G. in C.	Governor in Council.
G.I. Home	Home Dept., Govt. of India, Delhi.
G.H.	Government House.
G.S.C. Rule	Government Service Conduct Rule.
H.D.	Home Dept. Govt. of India, Delhi.
H.E.H.	His Exalted Highness, the Nizam of Hyderabad
H.E. or H.E. the V.	His Excellency the Viceroy of India.
	(Note: Sir Hyde was also 'H.E.' in the C.P.)
Hit.	The Hitavada, English language local (Nagpur) newspaper.
H.M.s	Honourable Ministers.
H.M.A.	Honourable Member for Agriculture
H.M.E.	Honourable Member for Education
H.M.H.	Honourable Member for Home Affairs.
H.M.I.	Honourable Member for Industry
H.M.R.	Honourable Member for Revenue.
Hon. Mags.	Honorary magistrates.
H.P.	Honourable President, President of the Council of Ministers.
H.S.	The Speaker, of the House.
I.D.	Indian Disobedience.
I.F.S.	Indian Forestry Service.

444

I.G.C.H	Inspector General of Civil Hospitals
I.G.Prison.	Inspector General of Prisons.
I.O.	India Office, Whitehall.
J.C.	Judicial Commissioner
J.S.C.'s Report.	Joint Services Commission Report, on the White Paper relating to the Government of India Act, 1935.
K.	Kedar
Kh.	Khaparde; or Khare
L.B.	Local Bodies.
L.R.	Legal Representative
l.r.	Land Revenue.
L.M.Banks	Land Mortgage Banks.
L.S.G.	Local Self Government.
M.	Morrison – Private Secretary in 1934; or Mangalmurti (who is sometimes also referred to as the Mangelwurzel); or Misra
M.B.	Maharashtra Brahmin (but sometimes used for Sir Montagu Butler, who is also referred to as Monty)
M.C	Municipal Council.
M.L.A.	Member of Legislative Assembly (equals our Parliament.)
M.L.C.	Member of Legislative Council (equals our Cabinet.)
M.S.	Military Secretary
N.	Nyogi, Vice Chancellor of the University; or Naidu; or Noel Roughton
N.I.T.	Nagpur Improvement Trust.
N.J.,	Noel, Noel James or Noel Jones. Noel James Roughton.
ODTAA	"One Damn Thing After Another". The title of a popular book of the era.
O.N.	Otto Niemeyer

P.C.C.	Provincial Congress Committee
P.S.	Private Secretary
P.S.C.	Provincial Services Committee
P.S.V.	Private Secretary to the Viceroy
P.V.	'The People's Voice'. Indian language local (Nagpur) newspaper.
P.W.D	Public Works Dept.
R-C-, or R.C.	Mr. Rajagopalachariar of Madras.
R.M.	Revenue Minister
R.S.	Revenue Secretary
R.S.D.S.	Rugby School Debating Society
R.T.C.	Round Table Conference.
Sectt.	Secretariat.
Sir S.H.	Sir Samuel Hoare, Secretary of State for India
S.J.	Silver Jubilee
S.R.	Service Rule.
S/S	Secretary of State for India, Whitehall.
T/I	Times of India
U.P.	United Provinces
U.S.	Under Secretary
V.L.	Viceregal Lodge
W.C.	Working Committee, of Congress. The high Command.
W/P.	Warrant of Precedence.

GLOSSARY

Amen Sebhas.	System of land tenure, with direct management of the village by Government which takes its revenue in kind. c.f. share cropping.
Ayah	Nursemaid, usually middle-aged, fat and devoted.
Bedmash	bad man, rogue or scallywag.
Badmashi	Trick
Banjar	Waste or fallow land.
Banya	Trader, shopkeeper or money-lender, but also used to mean "capitalist." From the Sanskrit word "vanij", a merchant, with a possible nasal termination. About 1600A.D. some banyans set up a trading post in Gombroon, now Banda Abbas in the Persian Gulf, under a "lul" tree, the Persian name for Ficus Indicus or Ficus Religiosus, and built a small pagoda. This gave rise to the tree being known as the "Banyan's Tree" or banyan and the name has spread (ref: Hobson-Jobson). It is now the name of the well-known tree of many roots widely spread throughout the East.
Basti.	Small circle of huts owned by one man; often the poorer part of the village.
Bearer	Personal Servant.
Bele, Belha, Beyla	Thug slang (Ramassi). Means either the person who selects the spot where the murder is to be committed, or the spot itself, usually in a mango grove.
Be-izzating	see Izzat.
Bhai Band	"Brothers in Arms."
Bidi	Local cigarette or cheroot, smoked between the two clenched hands without touching the lips, so that it can be passed from hand to men. One bidi does for half a dozen people.
Brahmin	The highest, the priestly caste of Hindus; more or less the only wholly literate caste in India.
Bhumiya	(Gondi, i.e. Telegu) Village headman
Chalak	Cunning, or rather, cheeky.
Chakra or charka	Spinning wheel, symbol of Gandhi's harijan movement; also with reference to the discus, the weapon of the god, Vishnu.
Chela	Pupil.
Chowkidar	Watchman or caretaker.
Chuprassi	Messenger.

447

Dak	Post or mail. Note: On all touring routes in India, every 15 miles, there was a "dak bungalow" with resident "chowkidar" for the use of visiting administrators.
Dacoity	Act of gang robbery, a dacoit being a member of the gang.
Dhobi.	Launderer. Laundry was always done by beating the clothes over a rock in a stream or pool. It got the clothes clean but was hell on the buttons!
Diwali	The Hindu festival of Lights, a very beautiful festival when all the doorsteps are decorated with intricate patterns and all houses outlined in tiny rushlights and candles.
Durbar, Durbaris	'Durbar' is the State Government, and a durbar is the Government holding a ceremony for the purpose of governing. In fact it means a ceremonial levee at which the (Nizam) accepts gifts, pronounces laws and hears petitions. The Durbaris are selected by Government according to the best Eastern principles, but in the C.P. have no overt function.
Gaoli	Name of a Hindu caste; very low; cowherds and milk sellers.
Garrow Hill.	Means an inferior type or cotton, probably with reference to the Garo Hills in Assam where much cotton is grown but in grade inferior to Amraoti and the cottons of BerarGitti.
Gonds	The Gonds were a large tribe of forest dwellers living in the eastern C.P.: small men, ethnically belong to the Andhra kingdom and speaking a dialect of telegu. They were excellent woodsmen.
Hakk, or hug.	Lien.
Hanuman Vayaganishala	
Hindu Akhara.	Both Vayaganishala and Akhara mean Hindu places of worship. Hanuman being one of the gods, usually portrayed as a monkey. One sees the religious tone in everything in India.
Harijan	Untouchable. The "Untouchables" were the lowest caste of all in the Hindu hierarchy and were much despised; they were not allowed into the temples and if the shadow of an Untouchable fell on a Brahmin's food, the food was declared unclean and the Brahmin threw it away, however hungry he might be. Only an Indian, (Hindu) could demand that a man, or woman, be rejected by a religion and yet forced to remain part of it. One of Ghandi's great aims was to raise the lot of the Untouchables, or Scheduled Castes as they became known.

448

Havildar	Sergeant.
Hindu Mahasabha	Grand Council of the Hindus, as much, if not more, political as religious.
Izzat.	Prestige or honour; equivalent to the Chinese use of the word "face". "Be-izzating" means "causing to lose prestige.".
Jihán	Yes
Jihán-wallah	Yes-man.
Khaddar	Coarse, home-spun, home-woven cloth; one of Gandhi's most treasured symbols.
Kharif	Season of autumn, after the rains, and the crops harvested, especially rice, cotton and jaraw.
Kho-kho	Chinese wrestling, mostly with the feet,
Kidmatgar	Butler.
Kishan Sabha	One of the political organizations.
Koi Hai.	Anglo-Indian, in the original sense, i.e. an Englishman who had lived all his working life in India. Literally it means: "Who is there?"; and was the call of every Sahib on returning to his bungalow to alert the staff of his presence. "An old koi-hai", meant someone versed in the customs of the country.
Koshtis	Name of a caste; spinners and weavers.
Lathi	A hefty bamboo pole, the chief weapon of the Indian police (pronounced lartee).
Lok Sabha	The Lower House of the Indian Parliament in Delhi.
Machán	A tree-top house from which to shoot tigers.
Mahakoshal	An area of the C.P., the Eastern states and districts, and the political party from there – Misra & Shukla.
Maharashtra.	Land of the Marathas, to the South and West, part of it being a province of the C.P. and part being in Bombay Presidency. Thence the name of the Dravidian Brahmins who occupied the region (M.B.s)
Mahasabha.	Grand Council
Mahatma	Sanscrit - High-souled. One skilled in mysteries or holy secrets; a wise and holy leader.
Mahseer	A fish.
Mahua	Bassia Latifolia or "Indian Butter Tree", used for food and distilling liquor.
Maidan	Field.

"Main bis dafe bola"	"I tell him twenty times."
Malguzar	Landlord: owner of the land of a village. The person who pays the revenue to the Government, whether as manager or owner.
Mali	Gardener
Marwari	Business man, same as banya; originally from Marwar.
Mehatar or sweeper	of thunderboxes. The lowest Caste of all.
Member	of the Executive Council.
Mohurram	Muslim religious festival.
Mowes.	Landless, casual labourers.
Mussulman	Muslim
Naqsha or Naksha	A picture, or plan, map or general description, an official report.
Nazar	A present or offering, especially one made by an inferior on presentation to a superior.
Nazarana	The ceremonial assembly for the above.
Pagri or Pagaree	(Hindi or Persian) Turban
Raj Gond	Local ruler of the Gonds. Ramassi. Thugees land (c.f. Romany)
Rashtrya Swangam Sewak Sangh	A Hindu society.
Rayat or ryot	Peasant or cultivator.
Rayatwari	Government owned village.
Risaldar	Indian officer commanding a troop of horse.
Roadstone.	All roads were either kunka, i.e. roughly metalled, or kacha, just mud. Tarmac was rare.
Sabha	Assembly or Council chamber.
Sahukari	"Take care". In this context using the money in commerce or trade, as opposed to industry.
Sadhu.	Hindu holy man. In view of Sir Hyde's remarks, it is interesting to note the dictionary entry under this title: "One who is perfect, a saint, a sage; also a merchant or money lender". The Jains apply the term to their djinns or deified saints. It is commonly used of all Hindu mendicants. Many Sadhus become such because they have keen turned out of their caste. See Mahatma! I think the dictionary is wrong in translating the word as: 'merchant or moneylender'; about the one thing a Sadhu isn't. Jains are a Hindu sect,
Sais or Syce	Groom.

Sanatanists	Militant, orthodox Hindus.
Satyagraha	Passive resistance.
Shamiana	Marquee.
Swami	Hindu religious teacher.
Swaraj	Self-government,
Tabula rasa	Latin! Tablet erased, or the slate is wiped clean.
Taecavi	A monetary transaction concerned with the land.
takoli	Levy due to Government.
Taluq	Subdivision of land; pargana.
Tahsil	a subdivision of land; a village.
Támásha	Show
Tiffin	A three-decker food container in which the Hindus carry their midday meal, hence the habit of a light midday meal. In Bombay nowadays there is a regular messenger service, entirely entrepreneurial, for carrying home-cooked midday meals from home to office, always in the tiffin. A more sophisticated version fits into a half-gallon thermos.
Ulta pulta desh	Upside down country - Arsi-tarsi-land.
Zamindar	Landholder, paving revenues direct to the Government.
Zamindari.	Office and rights of the Zamindar, also his land, his estate.
Zidd	Whim; unreasoning dislike; stubbornness; prejudice.

ND - #0435 - 270225 - C10 - 229/152/38 - PB - 9781909874862 - Matt Lamination